INSIGHT AND ILLUSION

INSIGHT AND ILLUSION

WITTGENSTEIN ON PHILOSOPHY
AND THE
METAPHYSICS OF EXPERIENCE

P. M. S. HACKER

OXFORD UNIVERSITY PRESS
London   Oxford   New York

OXFORD UNIVERSITY PRESS

London   Oxford   New York
Glasgow   Toronto   Melbourne   Wellington
Cape Town   Ibadan   Nairobi   Dar es Salaam   Lusaka   Addis Ababa
Delhi   Bombay   Calcutta   Madras   Karachi   Lahore   Dacca
Kuala Lumpur   Singapore   Hong Kong   Tokyo

FOR MY PARENTS

First published by the Clarendon Press, 1972
First issued as an Oxford University Press paperback, 1975
Printed in the United States of America

PREFACE

The structure of this book can best be captured by means of a theatrical metaphor. The book has, as it were, a central drama, a set, and a back-cloth. The subject with which I am primarily concerned, the drama which is enacted throughout the book, is Wittgenstein's metaphysics of experience. This Kantian term of art is chosen advisedly, for one of the *leitmotifs* consists in exploring the Kantian affinities of Wittgenstein's philosophy in general, both in the *Tractatus* and in the post-1929 works. Wittgenstein's metaphysics of experience can be seen as consisting of a triad of problems, two of which are examined comprehensively. These are: self-consciousness, our knowledge of other minds, and our knowledge of objects. The secondary concern of the book, the set upon which the main drama takes place, is Wittgenstein's general conception of philosophy. This theme is intended to illuminate, and be illuminated by, the examination of Wittgenstein's metaphysics of experience. For the latter, particularly in Wittgenstein's later work, is an exemplification of his conception of the task, process, and result of philosophical investigation. As my work progressed, it became increasingly clear that the back-cloth against which the two main subjects had to be seen could not be wholly neglected. The back-cloth consists of the development of his semantic theories from the strict realism of the *Tractatus* to the constructivist-inspired conventionalism of the *Philosophical Investigations*. I have explored this most difficult subject only so far as seemed to me necessary in order to grasp the nature of Wittgenstein's metaphysics of experience, his general contribution to epistemology, and his conception of philosophy. So the back-cloth is, as is customary in stage design, uneven. In parts it is filled in with colourful detail, at other points it is rough and ready.

Wittgenstein is almost unique among philosophers in having produced two complete philosophies, the later containing substantial criticism and repudiation of the earlier. The controversy over the degree of change and the degree of constancy will doubtless rage for many years to come. With respect to the subjects with which I am concerned in this book I have tried to plot both transformation and continuity. It is certainly impossible to understand Wittgenstein's later concern with and refutation of solipsism and idealism without seeing its roots in his fascination with Schopenhauer in the *Notebooks 1914–16* and the 'methodological solipsism' of the *Philosophische Bemerkungen*. Equally one can only obtain a proper grasp of his later conception of philosophy and metaphysics by comparing and contrasting it with his earlier views. And doubtless his later semantics must be seen against the background of his repudiation of his earlier realism. Accordingly the first four chapters of this book are concerned with Wittgenstein's first philosophy, tracing the development of his views upon the themes I have chosen, from the early 'Notes on Logic' through the high point of the *Tractatus* to the transitional period of the late nineteen-twenties and early -thirties. The last six chapters are concerned with much the same aspects of his later philosophy in which they loom so much larger.

I am grateful to Mr. Ray Frey, Dr. Kit Fine, and Dr. Joseph Raz for their criticisms of earlier drafts of parts of this book, for their encouragement and for the many illuminating discussions with them upon the topics on which I was working. My greatest debts are to Dr. Anthony Kenny and Dr. Gordon Baker. To Dr. Kenny I owe the original inspiration to pursue my interest in Wittgenstein seriously; what grasp I have of the private language argument I owe largely to the many conversations I have had with him. His detailed comments upon my first drafts of chapters IV, VII, VIII, IX were of very great help to me. To my colleague at St. John's, Dr. Baker, I owe the opportunity to sound out practically every idea I have had upon my subjects with a sympathetic and erudite listener. His criticisms, suggestions, and advice, as well as his comments upon my manuscripts, were of inestimable value to me. The privilege of reading his own unpublished work upon Wittgenstein's semantics gave me insights into the constructivist tenor of Wittgenstein's later philosophy which I would not have achieved unaided. I should also like to acknowledge my debt to Mrs. Pearl Hawtin and to my wife for their generous secretarial aid.

All quotations from *Ludwig Wittgenstein und der Wiener Kreis*, *Philosophische Bemerkungen*, and *Philosophische Grammatik*, have been translated. Where the translators of Wittgenstein's other works have seemed to me to err I have provided my own translation. I am grateful to Mr. T. J. Reed and to my mother Mrs. Thea Hacker for their assistance with the German. I am indebted to the publishers Basil Blackwell & Mott Ltd., Routledge & Kegan Paul Ltd. and The Humanities Press Inc., for kind permission to quote from works of Wittgenstein for which they own the copyright.

St. John's College, Oxford   P.M.S.H.
1971

CONTENTS

LIST OF ABBREVIATIONS   xiii

I. WITTGENSTEIN'S EARLY CONCEPTION OF PHILOSOPHY

  1. Introduction   1

  2. The 'Preliminary' on Philosophy   7

  3. Philosophy and Illusion   11

  4. Philosophy as Critique and as Analysis   25

II. 'EPISTEMOLOGY IS THE PHILOSOPHY OF PSYCHOLOGY'

  1. The Place of Epistemology in the *Tractatus*   33

  2. Psychological and Epistemological Presuppositions and Implications of the *Tractatus*   39

III. EMPIRICAL REALISM AND TRANSCENDENTAL SOLIPSISM

  1. Introduction   58

  2. The Self of Solipsism   59

  3. 'I am my World'   67

  4. 'The limits of language mean the limits of my world'   76

  5. Later Years   81

IV. DISINTEGRATION AND RECONSTRUCTION

  1. The Colour Exclusion Problem   86

  2. Dismantling   94

  3. A New Inspiration   98

  4. The Positivist Interlude   104

V. WITTGENSTEIN'S LATER CONCEPTION OF PHILOSOPHY

  1. A Cure for the Sickness of the Understanding   112

  2. The Phenomenology and Sources of Philosophical Illusion   126

3. 'A Method has been found . . .'   135
4. The Neglect of Architectonic Considerations   139

VI. METAPHYSICS AS THE SHADOW OF GRAMMAR
1. Forms of Representation   145
2. Grammar   150
3. The Autonomy of Grammar   156
4. Determinants of Grammar and Concept Formation   166
5. Grammar and Metaphysics   178

VII. THE REFUTATION OF SOLIPSISM
1. Introduction   185
2. From Transcendental Solipsism to Methodological Solipsism   188
3. The Solipsist's Predicament: A Restatement and Second
   Diagnosis   197
4. The Refutation   201

VIII. PRIVATE LINGUISTS AND PUBLIC SPEAKERS
1. Introduction   215
2. *Philosophical Investigations*, §243   218
3. The Private Language   224
4. The Epistemology of the Private Linguist   231
5. Wittgenstein's Criticism of the Private Language   233
6. Wittgenstein's Criticism of the Private Linguist's Epistemology   242
7. 'One Plays Patience by Oneself.'   248

IX. 'A CLOUD OF PHILOSOPHY CONDENSED
    INTO A DROP OF GRAMMAR'
1. Can One Know that One is in Pain?   251
2. The Non-Cognitive Thesis of Avowals   254
3. Rejection of the Truth-Valueless Thesis   265
4. Rejection of the Non-Cognitive Thesis   272
5. The Private Language Argument, Self-Conciousness, and the
   Foundations of Knowledge   277

X. THE PROBLEM OF CRITERIA
1. Introduction   283
2. Some Logical Features of the Criterial Relation   285

3. Further Ramifications 293

4. Applications: a recapitulation 303

BIBLIOGRAPHY 311

INDEX 319

LIST OF ABBREVIATIONS

Abbreviations used to refer to Wittgenstein's writings listed in chronological order:

NB   *Notebooks 1914–16*, ed. G. H. von Wright and G. E. M. Anscombe, trans. by G. E. M. Anscombe (Blackwell, Oxford, 1961).

PT   *ProtoTractatus—An Early Version of Tractatus Logico-Philosophicus*, ed. B. F. McGuinness, T. Nyberg, G. H. von Wright, trans. by D. F. Pears and B. F. McGuinness (Routledge and Kegan Paul, London, 1971).

TLP   *Tractatus Logico-Philosophicus*, trans. by D. F. Pears and B. F. McGuinness (Routledge and Kegan Paul, London, 1961).

LLW   *Letters from Ludwig Wittgenstein with a Memoir*, by Paul Engelmann, ed. B. F. McGuinness, trans. by L. Furtmüller (Blackwell, Oxford, 1967).

RLF   'Some Remarks on Logical Form', *Proceedings of the Aristotelian Society*, supp. vol. ix (1929).

WWK   *Ludwig Wittgenstein und der Wiener Kreis*, shorthand notes recorded by F. Waismann, ed. B. F. McGuinness (Blackwell, Oxford, 1967).

PB   *Philosophische Bemerkungen*, ed. R. Rhees (Blackwell, Oxford, 1964).

M   'Wittgenstein's Lectures in 1930–33', in G. E. Moore, *Philosophical Papers* (Allen and Unwin, London, 1959).

PG   *Philosophische Grammatik*, ed. R. Rhees (Blackwell, Oxford, 1969).

BB   *The Blue and Brown Books* (Blackwell, Oxford, 1958).

NFL   'Wittgenstein's Notes for Lectures on "Private Experience" and "Sense Data"', ed. R. Rhees, *Philosophical Review*, lxxvii (1968).

RFM   *Remarks on the Foundations of Mathematics*, ed. G. H. von Wright, R. Rhees, G. E. M. Anscombe, trans. by G. E. M. Anscombe (Blackwell, Oxford, 1964).

PI   *Philosophical Investigations*, ed. G. E. M. Anscombe, R. Rhees, trans. by G. E. M. Anscombe (Blackwell, Oxford, 1953).

Z   *Zettel*, ed. G. E. M. Anscombe and G. H. von Wright, trans. by G. E. M. Anscombe (Blackwell, Oxford, 1967).

OC   *On Certainty*, ed. G. E. M. Anscombe and G. H. von Wright, trans. by D. Paul and G. E. M. Anscombe (Blackwell, Oxford, 1969).

I

WITTGENSTEIN'S EARLY
CONCEPTION OF PHILOSOPHY

1. *Introduction*

Ludwig Wittgenstein came to Cambridge in 1912 in order to study under the supervision of Bertrand Russell. It was the beginning of seven years of intensive and single-minded research in logic and philosophy which resulted in the only book Wittgenstein published in his lifetime, the *Tractatus Logico-Philosophicus*. It is not to the present purpose to investigate the wide range of philosophical theories embodied in that work, but rather to examine the theory of philosophy propounded in it. In order to do so, some appreciation of Wittgenstein's intellectual background and the problem-setting context of his work is necessary. For a twenty-three-year-old research student in philosophy, Wittgenstein in 1912 was remarkably ill-read in the history of the subject. His intellectual milieu was that of a highly cultured and sophisticated member of the Viennese intelligentsia. His training was, however, scientific. In 1906 he had begun studying engineering in the Technische Hochschule in Berlin-Charlottenburg, and in 1908 he came to Manchester to pursue research in aeronautics. In the course of research into the design of a jet-reaction propeller he was led from dynamics to pure mathematics, and from there to logical and philosophical investigations into the foundations of mathematics. He read Russell's *Principles of Mathematics* and was greatly impressed by this imposing work which had, significantly, germinated in theoretical problems in dynamics.[1] It was probably the appendix to the *Principles of Mathematics* which led Wittgenstein first to read the works of Frege, and then to visit him. On Frege's advice he returned to England to study under Russell.

[1] For the origin of Russell's investigations into the foundations of mathematics, see *The Principles of Mathematics*, Preface, pp. xvi f. (2nd ed., Allen and Unwin, London, 1937).

Wittgenstein, like any well-educated Viennese at the turn of the century, had read Schopenhauer in his teens. He is reported to have been greatly impressed, and he told von Wright[1] that his first philosophy was a Schopenhauerian epistemological idealism. It was not, however, a Schopenhauerian interest which brought him to philosophical investigation. Although Schopenhauer's influence upon the later sections of the *Tractatus* is profound, it is clear from Wittgenstein's correspondence with Russell,[2] from the 1913 and 1914 'Notes on Logic'[3] and from the three remaining philosophical notebooks covering the periods from 22 August 1914 to 22 June 1915, and from 15 April 1916 to 10 January 1917, that the driving force behind his investigations was logic and its metaphysical implications. It was only in May 1915 that there emerged, amidst the logical speculations, a slight hint of the Schopenhauerian pre-occupation which dominates the third and final surviving notebook. This belated Schopenhauerian impact upon his logico-metaphysical researches did not influence his fundamental thoughts upon the nature of philosophy, although it moulded his conception of the metaphysics of experience and his notorious notion of the mystical.[4] To find the dominant influences upon the *Tractatus* in general, and its conception of philosophy in particular, one must look in a quite different direction from either classical or popular contemporary philosophy.

The end of the nineteenth century and first decade of the twentieth was a period of great philosophical ferment amongst some of the most distinguished physicists of the day. The problems of the nature of scientific explanation, of the structure of scientific theories, of the attainability of truth in science, were discussed in detail by such eminent figures as Duhem, Poincaré, and Mach. From the point of view of Wittgenstein's intellectual development, however, the most significant philosopher-scientists were Hertz, and to a lesser extent, Boltzmann.

Hertz's preoccupations in the philosophy of science were essentially Kantian. His salient problem was 'How is an *a priori* science

---

[1] G. H. von Wright, 'A Biographical Sketch' in N. Malcolm, *Ludwig Wittgenstein A Memoir* (O.U.P., London, 1966), p. 5.

[2] There are fifty-seven extant letters from Wittgenstein to Russell. I am grateful to Professor G. H. von Wright for access to them. A selection of them are printed in *NB*, Appendix III.

[3] Published in *NB*, Appendixes I and II.

[4] See below Ch. III.

of nature possible?' His answer, in his most famous work *The Principles of Mechanics*,[1] was given by means of undertaking a philosophical examination of the logical nature of scientific explanation. The point of science, Hertz argued, is the anticipation of nature. Its data are our knowledge of past events, its method is theory-construction, its mode of reasoning is deductive. The possibility of description of reality by an axiomatic mechanics is explained by reference to the nature of symbolization. We form pictures (*Scheinbilder*) to ourselves of external objects. These symbolic or pictorial conceptions of ours must satisfy one essential condition: they must be logically isomorphic with what they represent: 'the necessary consequents of the images in thought are always the images of the necessary consequents in nature of the things pictured.'[2] It is necessary to distinguish sharply in our pictures between what arises from necessity in thought, what from experience and what from arbitrary choice. Any acceptable scientific theory must satisfy three requirements. It must be logically permissible or consistent. This requirement arises from necessities of thought. It must be correct, i.e. the relations between elements of the picture must, when given an interpretation, mirror the relations between external things. Thus experience confirms the theory. Finally, it must be appropriate, i.e. the notation in which we chose to represent the theory must be as simple and economic as it can be, consistently with the other requirements. The bare structure of a theory thus conceived may be illuminated and supplemented by giving models or concrete representations of the various conceptions of the nature of the elements of the theory. This may aid our power of imagination but one must remember that the colourful clothing in which we dress the theory is heuristic and optional, and must not be allowed to obscure the underlying structure of the theory. Thus Hertz argued in *Electric Waves*[3] that three distinct models or interpretations of Maxwell's electromagnetic theory all have the same testable consequences, are all expressible by the same equations, and hence are the same theory.[4] With these considerations in

[1] H. Hertz, *The Principles of Mechanics*, trans. by D.E. Jones and J. T. Walley (Macmillan, London, 1899).

[2] H. Hertz, op. cit., Introduction p. 1.

[3] H. Hertz, *Electric Waves*, trans. by D. E. Jones (Macmillan, London, 1893).

[4] For a criticism of Hertz's dismissal of the theoretical significance of model-building in science, and his excessive deductivism, see M. B. Hesse, *Forces and Fields* (Nelson, London, 1961), p. 215.

mind, especially the requirement of appropriateness, Hertz undertook the rational reconstruction of Newtonian dynamics. The point of this endeavour was neither pedagogic nor practical. Hertz stressed that, from the point of view of the needs of mankind, the usual methods of representing mechanics cannot be bettered in as much as they were devised for these purposes. Hertz's aim was to display the logical structure of the theory. His representation stood to the normal one, so he claimed, as the systematic grammar of a language stands to a learner's grammar. Following the path laid out by Mach and Kirchhoff, Hertz intended to eliminate the concept of force from mechanics as anything other than an abbreviating convenience. The only primitive notions he employed were space, time, and mass. By displaying the logical structure of the theory, he dispelled the illusion that physicists had not yet been able to discover the true nature of force. In a brief passage Hertz outlined his conception of the analytic dissolution of conceptual confusion. This became for Wittgenstein a classical, concise, and beautiful statement of the philosophical elimination of pseudo-problems:

We have accumulated around the terms "force" and "electricity" more relations than can be completely reconciled amongst themselves. We have an obscure feeling of this and want to have things cleared up. Our confused wish finds expression in the confused question as to the nature of force and electricity. But the answer which we want is not really an answer to this question. It is not by finding out more and fresh relations and connections that it can be answered; but by removing the contradictions existing between those already known, and thus perhaps by reducing their number. When these painful contradictions are removed, the question as to the nature of force will not have been answered; but our minds, no longer vexed, will cease to ask illegitimate questions.[1]

These are the fundamental Hertzian themes which influenced the young Wittgenstein and which, as we shall see, continually reappear in his work. They were reinforced by reading the works of Ludwig Boltzmann, himself an admirer of Hertz, who further emphasized the hypothetico-deductive structure of scientific explanation,[2]

---

[1] Hertz, *Principles of Mechanics*, Introduction, pp. 7 f.

[2] See, for example, 'Theories as Representations' from Boltzmann's *Die Grundprinzipien und Grundgleichungen der Mechanik* I, trans. by R. Weingartner, and reprinted in *Philosophy of Science*, ed. A. Danto and S. Morgenbesser (World Publishing Co., Cleveland, 1960), pp. 245–52. S. Toulmin points out that phrases from the *Tractatus* such as 'logical space', 'ensembles of possibilities', etc. originate in Boltzmann's

and extended Hertz's account of representation to all branches of physics. Indeed, prior to studying at the Technische Hochschule, Wittgenstein had intended to study physics under Boltzmann in Vienna, a wish that was frustrated by Boltzmann's suicide in 1906, the same year that Wittgenstein finished school.

The other two great, specifically philosophical influences[1] upon Wittgenstein were Frege and Russell. Both had independently embarked upon the great logicist programme of reducing arithmetic to logic. In the course of so doing, they developed powerful artificial languages of symbolic logic, and highly sophisticated systems of philosophical logic. The invention of an ideal notation was not only justified by reference to the system and rigour required to fulfil the reductivist aims, but also as a quite general tool to solve logical and philosophical problems which hitherto had been intractable. Thought was enslaved, Frege remarked, by the tyranny of words.[2] Ordinary language is riddled with unavoidable confusions which can only be brought to light in an ideal notation. Frege's invention of the quantifier to bind variables, quite apart from the brilliant insight it afforded into the nature of generality, enabled a clear representation of other philosophical problems and a perspicuous revelation of classical fallacies. Russell went so far as to declare that 'Every philosophical problem, when it is subjected to the necessary analysis and purification, is found either to be not really philosophical at all, or else to be, in the sense in which we are using the word, logical.'[3] This ideal of logical analysis into constituents,

---

thermodynamics ('Ludwig Wittgenstein', *Encounter*, January 1969, p. 66). Boltzmann's view of the laws of thought, unlike Hertz's, was psychological and historical, and thus would certainly have been rejected by Wittgenstein after reading Frege's introduction to *The Basic Laws of Arithmetic*, if not before.

[1] There were of course minor philosophical influences at work. Wittgenstein mentions Mauthner in the *Tractatus* (*TLP*, 4.0031), and he apparently considered mentioning Paul Ernst; see B. F. McGuinness, 'Philosophy of Science in the *Tractatus*', in *Wittgenstein et le problème d'une philosophie de la science* (Colloques Internationaux du Centre National de la Recherche Scientifique (Paris, 1970)). These do not seem particularly important. No doubt the non-philosophical Viennese cultural context of Wittgenstein's thought, in particular the so-called 'Crisis of Language' epitomized in von Hofmannsthal's *Chandos Letter*, is extremely significant for the historian of ideas.

[2] Frege, *Begriffsschrift, eine der arithmetischen nachgebildete Formelsprache des reinen Denkens* (Halle, 1879), Preface, p. vi. Significantly, this was quoted by F. Waismann in *The Principles of Linguistic Philosophy*, ed. R. Harré (Macmillan, London, 1965), p. 4.

[3] Russell, *Our Knowledge of the External World* (Open Court, Chicago, 1914), p. 33. This was, one should stress, written in 1914 after almost two years co-operative work with Wittgenstein.

originating in its modern logical form in the work of W. E. Johnson,[1] was fervently espoused by Russell, and given considerable boost by his Theory of Descriptions. This theory, formally expressible with the iota operator in the language of *Principia Mathematica*, enabled a thinning out of the luxuriant Meinongian jungle,[2] although both Frege and Russell sided with Meinong's realist revolt against Hegelian and Bradleian idealism. Both logicians professed a thorough-going anti-psychologism in logic and semantics, although Frege's criticisms are more thoroughly, not to say more vehemently, elaborated than Russell's. Similarly, both adhered to realist theories of meaning, although again Frege's Platonist semantics, though fragmentary, is more sophisticated and better articulated than Russell's.

The setting of the stage at the time of Wittgenstein's entry upon the scene, first as Russell's pupil and very quickly as his equal, was far from final. The logicist reduction of mathematics stood, rather shakily propped up against the Russellian paradoxes by the Theory of Types. The Theory of Descriptions appeared as firm a philosophical achievement as ever attained. Not only had it solved important philosophical problems, it was, so one might hope, merely a foretaste of what might be achieved by the new methods of logical analysis. The conceptual notations of the *Begriffsschrift* and *Principia Mathematica*, whether completely satisfactory or not, seemed to hold out at last the promises of a true *characteristica universalis*. By means of such a language all the obscurities, ambiguities, and vagueness of natural language might be cleared up, leaving the structure of thought perspicuous to the philosophical vision. Equally, logic would at last be laid upon the true path of a science. Great steps forward had been taken by both Russell and Frege. But much remained obscure and much was contentious. The nature and status of the science of logic itself was unclear. To claim that it describes the immutable laws of thought tells us little, and supplies us only with a mystifying picture of a kind of super-physics. Equally unclear was the status of logical truths themselves.

---

[1] See J. Passmore, *A Hundred Years of Philosophy* (Penguin, Harmondsworth, 2nd ed. 1968), pp. 135 ff.

[2] It enabled one to dispose of entities such as the square circle, but needed support from the epistemology of knowledge by description, and knowledge by acquaintance, to yield any so-called 'new level analysis'. See J. O. Urmson, *Philosophical Analysis* (Clarendon Press, Oxford, 1956), pp. 39 f.

Numerous detailed problems demanded further elucidation. Wittgenstein's initial interests were focused, as it appears from his early correspondence with Russell, upon such logical issues. The specific problems with which he was first concerned were on the one hand the question of the nature of variables in propositions of a conceptual notation, and upon the other hand what Russell had called 'the chief part of philosophical logic',[1] namely the discussion of indefinables. It was to the 'abolition of the real variable' as Wittgenstein called it,[2] that he attributed all his progress to start with. Propositions contain only 'apparent variables' occurring within the scope of a quantifier. It was on the basis of this move that he had earlier conjectured that 'there are no logical constants',[3] a conjecture which was to develop into his analysis of the nature of logical connectives. Part of his contribution to the discussion of the 'indefinables of logic' was the contention that the logical connectives are not indefinables, nor are they symbols for objects, but fulfil a quite different function from names. Wittgenstein's investigations into the significance of logical constants led him rapidly to the problem of the internal structure of atomic propositions, and thence to an examination of Russell's Theory of Types. The movement of his thought was from relatively narrow logical considerations to general issues in semantics, which in turn led to the metaphysical speculations which set the tone of the *Tractatus*. It was, however, his repudiation of Russell's Theory of Types, which depended on his views on the nature and functions of variables, that determined the development of his conception of philosophy from the 'Notes on Logic' of 1913 to the *Tractatus*.

2. The 'Preliminary' on Philosophy

To understand Wittgenstein's brief remarks about philosophy in the *Tractatus* it is essential to realize that its practice and its theory are violently at odds with each other. The official *de jure* account of philosophy is wholly different from the *de facto* practice of philosophy in the book. The practice conforms to the account of philosophy which Wittgenstein had given in the brief 'Preliminary' of the 1913 'Notes on Logic'. The extent to which his conception of philosophy changed can be gauged by comparing the 'Notes on

---

[1] Russell, *The Principles of Mathematics*, Preface, p. xv.
[2] Letter No. 13 to Russell, 22 July 1913 (*NB*, p. 121).
[3] Letter No. 2 to Russell, 22 June 1912 (*NB*, p. 119).

Logic' with the *Tractatus*. The cause of the change can be attributed to the emergence of the doctrine of showing and saying.

The 'Preliminary' of the 'Notes on Logic' contains three theses jointly demarcating the domain of philosophy, and characterizing its nature. The first thesis claims that philosophy is purely descriptive and contains no deductions. Thus there are no privileged propositions in philosophy which enjoy logical or epistemological priority over other propositions deduced from them. Philosophy is 'flat'. This distinguishes philosophy from deductive *a priori* sciences such as geometry, and also, bearing in mind the Hertzian deductivist conception of scientific theories, from natural sciences thus conceived. Accordingly the second thesis states that philosophy is above or below, but not beside the natural sciences. Philosophy may be the queen of the sciences or their underlabourer; but either way the philosopher is not an ordinary enfranchized citizen of a republic of ideas.[1] The reason given for this line of demarcation is couched in Hertzian terms. The natural sciences give us *pictures* of reality, i.e. theoretical models. Philosophy does not; hence it is not in competition with the natural sciences, and can neither confirm nor confute scientific propositions. Together with thesis one, the second thesis yields the claim that philosophy is *sui generis*. The third thesis describes the domain of philosophy. It is the doctrine of the logical form of scientific propositions. Wittgenstein does not clarify what he means by 'scientific' here. But it is clear from other sources[2] that in one of his uses of the term 'scientific', a 'scientific proposition' is equivalent to an empirical proposition. Thus the

---

[1] This is a paraphrase of *Z*, §455, but is equally applicable here.

[2] e.g. in letter No. 23 to Russell, Nov. or Dec. 1913 he wrote: 'A proposition like $(\exists x)\ x = x$ is for example really a proposition of physics. The proposition "$(x): x = x . \supset . (\exists y).\ y = y$" is a proposition of logic: it is for physics to say *whether any thing exists*' (*NB*, p. 127). The domain of physics is the totality of the empirical. Similar uses of 'natural science' in the *Tractatus* occur at *TLP*, 4.11, 4.113, 6.53.

It is worth remarking here that the German '*Satz*' is ambiguous between 'sentence' and 'proposition'. Wittgenstein's use of the term is not consistent. Most frequently, but not always, he uses '*Satz*' to mean 'sentence'. However in the following discussions of Wittgenstein's early work and of his transitional verificationist phase I have conformed to his translators' practice of translating '*Satz*' by 'proposition'. This involves retaining a potentially misleading ambiguity which inevitably leads to a certain strain as e.g. in talk of the sense of propositions, or nonsensical propositions etc. For a discussion of Wittgenstein's practice see G. Pitcher, *The Philosophy of Wittgenstein* (Prentice Hall, New Jersey, 1964), pp. 27 ff. and M. Black, *A Companion to Wittgenstein's Tractatus* (C.U.P., Cambridge, 1964), pp. 98 ff. However in discussing Wittgenstein's later views I have found it preferable to talk of sentences as bearers of sense.

forms of proposition, and so of thought in general, provide philosophy with its subject-matter. On this issue, incidentally, there was agreement between Wittgenstein and Russell. In his Herbert Spencer lecture in 1914 'On Scientific Method in Philosophy',[1] and likewise in the Lowell Lectures of 1914, *Our Knowledge of the External World*, Russell emphasized that philosophy properly speaking is indistinguishable from logic, and is concerned above all with the study of logical forms. Russell, however, did not, in Wittgenstein's view, grasp the full methodological implications of this demarcation of subject-matter. For Russell argued in 'On Scientific Method in Philosophy', that it was by concentrating attention upon the investigation of logical form, that the new style analytic philosophy could avoid the holistic methods and consequent errors of past philosophy, and emulate the progressive methods of the sciences.

A scientific philosophy such as I wish to recommend will be piecemeal and tentative like other sciences; above all, it will be able to invent hypotheses which, even if they are not wholly true, will yet remain fruitful after the necessary corrections have been made. This possibility of successive approximations to the truth is, more than anything else, the source of the triumphs of science, and to transfer this possibility to philosophy is to ensure a progress in method whose importance it would be almost impossible to exaggerate.[2]

It is not surprising that in his philosophical notebook Wittgenstein remarked in 1915: 'Russell's method in his "Scientific Method in Philosophy" is simply a retrogression from the method of physics' (*NB*, p. 44). For, as Hertz had so convincingly shown, the method of physics is the construction of pictures of reality. These are indeed optional and tentative, enabling greater or lesser approximations in their hypothetico-deductive consequences to the facts. But logic, in so far as it is a condition of sense, can allow no hypotheses. If philosophy is a description of logical form, there can be nothing piecemeal or merely probably correct about it. For what would be a mere approximation in science would be nonsense in philosophy. It is inconceivable that philosophy should share in the methods of the natural sciences.

---

[1] Russell, 'On Scientific Method in Philosophy' in *Mysticism and Logic* (Penguin, Harmondsworth, 1953), ch. VI, pp. 95–119.

[2] Russell, *Mysticism and Logic*, ch. VI, p. 109.

The 'Preliminary' adds a programmatic demand: the correct explanation of logical propositions must give them a unique position as against all other propositions. This programme was faithfully fulfilled in the *Tractatus*, 6.1 ff., yet it is strangely inconsistent with the theses of the Preliminary. For if the correct explanation of logical propositions is part of philosophy, then either logical propositions are to be thought of, as Russell once did, as very general scientific propositions, or else the domain of the doctrines of philosophy is wider than stated. There is also a claim concerning the structure of philosophy itself—it consists of logic and metaphysics, the former its basis. It is, however, unclear how a purely descriptive account can have one part as a basis for another. Finally there is a methodological requirement in conformity with Fregean and Russellian doctrines: distrust of grammar is the first requisite for philosophizing. This receives further elaboration subsequently: ordinary language conceals the structure of the proposition, Wittgenstein remarks; in it, relations look like predicates and predicates like names (*NB*, p. 96).

The *Tractatus* conforms quite closely to the theses and requirements of the 'Preliminary' of the 'Notes on Logic'. It seems to be a purely descriptive, wholly *a priori* account of the logical forms of empirical propositions. According to the *Tractatus*, they are all truth-functional compounds of elementary propositions. Moreover, a comprehensive account of logical propositions as tautologies or contradictions is given. The structural claim is satisfied, and the methodological requirement fulfilled. But by the time he wrote the *Tractatus*, Wittgenstein had changed his mind upon some of the salient claims about the nature of philosophy which he had made earlier. The *de jure* status of philosophy had changed dramatically. The thesis that philosophy is the description of logical form, which both he and Russell had previously propounded, was now rejected. Logical form is indescribable, hence philosophy's concern with logical form cannot be aimed at its description. Everything, however, was not repudiated. The earlier demarcation of philosophy distinguished it sharply from the natural sciences. To this, at least, Wittgenstein continued to adhere.

In the *Tractatus*, 4.111, Wittgenstein declares 'Philosophy is not one of the natural sciences', and in parentheses adds a remark taken from the 'Preliminary' of the 'Notes on Logic': 'The word "philosophy" must mean something whose place is above or below the natural sciences not beside them.' He hammers this negative thesis home in 4.1121, in which he sides with Frege[1] against psychologism: 'Psychology is no more closely related to philosophy than any other science.' In the following remark he adds 'Darwin's theory has no more to do with philosophy than any other hypothesis in natural science' (*TLP*, 4.1122). This apparent *non sequitur* is, I conjecture, another barb aimed at the views expressed in Russell's Lowell Lectures. Russell[2] distinguished three kinds of philosophy —the classical tradition derived ultimately from the Greeks, Evolutionism derived from Darwin, and logical atomism which represents the same kind of advance in philosophy as Galileo introduced in physics. Although Russell rejected Evolutionism, as he did the classical philosophical tradition, because it was not a 'truly scientific philosophy', he conceived of it as a type of philosophy. Wittgenstein thought this involved a mis-classification based on an unclear grasp of the nature of philosophy.

Although the first and third theses of the 'Preliminary' were *de jure* rejected, the view that philosophy is *sui generis* was nevertheless adhered to. However, Wittgenstein ceased to believe that the uniqueness of philosophy is expressible in philosophical propositions describing a special *a priori* subject-matter. Its singularity lies in the activity of philosophy, not in its product. For reasons yet to be explained, Wittgenstein came to believe that there are no philosophical propositions. Hence philosophy is not a doctrine, neither of logical form, nor of anything else.

3. *Philosophy and Illusion*

In his preface to the *Tractatus*, Wittgenstein specifies the subject matter of the book as 'the problems of philosophy'. The outcome of the book, he continues, shows that 'the reason why these problems are posed is that the logic of our language is misunderstood'. A corollary of this, as we shall see, is that once the logic of our language is grasped, these problems will no longer be posed, for they are not genuine problems, but the product of illusion. As befits such a view of philosophy as *Scheinprobleme*, Wittgenstein provides a brief sketch of the sources of error and illusion. The doctrine that there exists a gulf between the ordinary grammar of

---

[1] See below ch. II.
[2] Russell, *Our Knowledge of the External World*, ch. 1; see also 'On Scientific Method in Philosophy', in *Mysticism and Logic*.

language and its logical form, implicit in the methodological requirement of the 'Preliminary', is reiterated in the *Tractatus* in a metaphor reminiscent of Hertz:[1]

Language disguises thought. So much so, that from the outward form of the clothing it is impossible to infer the form of the thought beneath it, because the outward form of the clothing is not designed to reveal the form of the body, but for entirely different purposes (*TLP*, 4.002).

Ordinary language does not show its logical structure, and it is not humanly possible to gather *immediately* from everyday language what its underlying logic is. Despite our ability to speak correctly, we may be blind to the logical structure of our language, and the outward aspect of ordinary language makes every kind of illusion and confusion possible (*PT*, 4.0015).

Wittgenstein gives a few illustrations of the way in which the conventional grammatical structure and the ordinary modes of speech conceal the logical structure. On the one hand, the same word has different modes of signification. The word 'is' does service for three logically distinct symbols, the copula, the sign of identity and the existential quantifier. This kind of homonymity is deceptive. Russell stressed, in *Our Knowledge of the External World*, how Hegelian logic came to grief through taking the 'is' of predication as the 'is' of identity.[2] On the other hand, two words that do have different modes of signifying are sometimes used in such a way that the formal similarity of their surface grammar deceptively suggests a similarity in their mode of signification. Thus the existential quantifier 'exist' and the predicate 'go' both appear in ordinary language as intransitive verbs. Similarly 'identical' appears as an adjective, erroneously suggesting that it is a predicate. We use one and the same word as a name variable ('There is something on the floor') and as a propositional variable ('Something happened yesterday'). In the *ProtoTractatus* Wittgenstein stresses the deceptive nature of homophones, e.g. '*Er ist*' and '*Er isst*', which thus conceal rather than manifest differences of syntactical categories (*PT*, 4.00151). In 'Green is green', where the first occurrence of 'green' is a proper name, the expressions not only have different meanings (*Bedeutungen*), they are different kinds of symbols. The apparent logical form of a proposition that is repre-

---

[1] Hertz, *Electric Waves*, p. 28.   [2] Russell, op. cit., p. 39.

sented in ordinary grammar, as Russell showed in his Theory of Descriptions, need not be its real form. Moreover ordinary language gives the appearance of being vague and imprecise. The complicated tacit conventions of language make this possible, but what is said, by itself, does not reveal the form of the underlying thought that is meant. We construct natural languages without knowing how each word has meaning or what its meaning is (*TLP*, 4.002). Thus, for example, man has used numerals for many millenia without knowing that they signify nothing (*NB*, p. 96). That they signify nothing cannot be seen from the signs.

One may summarize Wittgenstein's position on the relation of grammatical and logical form by an analogy. Wittgenstein's early conception of language is analogous to the Representational Idealist's conception of experience. Appearances, for Wittgenstein, are a poor kind of guide to reality—with respect to the logical form of language. The reality of language is buried deeply below its manifestations. The actual underlying structure is not revealed, the fact that certain combinations of symbols are illegitimate is not apparent, and the uniqueness and determinacy of meaning of each symbol is concealed by the signs.

It is this gulf between the appearance and the reality of language that produces fundamental confusions characteristic of philosophy (*TLP*, 3.324). The remedy for these philosophical confusions lies in the use of an adequate sign language or conceptual notation which is perspicuously governed by logical syntax (*TLP*, 3.325). The Fregean or Russellian notations, though not wholly adequate, are such sign languages. As is notorious, this passage in the *Tractatus* led to Russell's deep misinterpretation of the fundamental contentions of the book.[1] Russell took Wittgenstein to be concerned with the conditions which would have to be fulfilled by a logically perfect language,

not that any language is logically perfect, or that we believe ourselves capable, here and now, of constructing a logically perfect language, but that the whole function of language is to have meaning, and it only fulfils this function in proportion as it approaches to the ideal language which we postulate (*TLP*, Introd. p. x).

---

[1] Already pointed out by F. P. Ramsey in his review of the book in 1923 (reprinted in his *Foundations of Mathematics* (Routledge and Kegan Paul, London, 1931), pp. 270–86).

Wittgenstein, in Russell's opinion, was describing the conditions for accurate symbolism, since 'In practice, language is always more or less vague, so that what we assert is never quite precise.' In fact what Wittgenstein was doing was specifying the conditions which must be fulfilled by any language, for any language is and must be logically perfect. Russell overlooked Wittgenstein's comments on the adequacy of ordinary language. Natural languages which mankind constructs, Wittgenstein stressed (*TLP*, 4.002), are capable of expressing every sense. All the propositions of everyday language, he wrote, in direct opposition to Russell's interpretation, are in perfect logical order just as they are (*TLP*, 5.5563). Were this not so, language would not be capable of picturing, and so representing, reality. For, according to Wittgenstein's picture theory of meaning and representation, language can picture reality only in virtue of sharing a common logical structure with the world. Generalizing Hertz's conception of scientific representation, Wittgenstein argued that propositions are logical pictures of reality.[1] They are logical pictures, firstly, in so far as they are, as Frege had argued,[2] essentially complex or logically segmented (*TLP*, 4.032). Secondly, just as Hertz had required scientific models to be logically isomorphic with what they picture, so Wittgenstein claimed that propositions in general, if they are to be capable of picturing reality, must possess the same logical multiplicity as that which they depict (*TLP*, 4.04). This is a perfectly general condition of the possibility of language.[3] In his notebook Wittgenstein wrote on 17 June 1915:

But this surely is clear: the propositions which are the only ones that humanity uses will have a sense just as they are and do not wait upon a future analysis in order to acquire a sense (*NB*, p. 62).

It is not, as Russell thought, that we have a handmade but imperfect instrument which is to be replaced by a precision tool which is perfect. The very possibility of propositional signs, i.e. certain

---

[1] The fundamental idea is to be found in Leibniz; see W. and M. Kneale, *The Development of Logic* (Clarendon Press, Oxford, 1962), p. 327.

[2] Frege, *The Foundations of Arithmetic*, trans. by J. L. Austin (2nd ed. Blackwell, Oxford, 1953), p. x, §§60, 62; for a discussion and interpretation of Frege's principle see M. Dummett, 'Nominalism', in *The Philosophical Review*, lxv (1956), 491–505, and 'Frege, Gottlob', *The Encyclopedia of Philosophy*, ed. P. Edwards (Macmillan, New York, 1967), vol. 3, pp. 225–6.

[3] See 'Notes Dictated to G. E. Moore in Norway, April 1914' (*NB*, p. 107).

kinds of facts expressing propositions in virtue of a method of projection, requires that the 'logical pictures' thus expressed be logically in perfect order. Certainly we want a perfect conceptual notation *for philosophical purposes*, and the *Tractatus* is intended to provide the fundamental principles for such a notation. But again, analogously to Hertz's rational reconstruction of mechanics, this is not in order to put into language something which is not yet there, but to reveal the underlying logical structure of language.

Russell also misinterpreted Wittgenstein's views on vagueness and imprecision. For, like Frege, Wittgenstein thought that if any sense is expressed, it must be determinate. Frege's demand for determinacy of sense and completeness of definition is made in the course of his objections to piecemeal definitions to which mathematicians are addicted.[1] The definition of a concept must be complete, unambiguously determining with respect to any object whether it falls under it or not. A concept must have a sharp boundary if it is correctly to be termed a concept. If sense is not determinate, and if definition is piecemeal, the laws of logic will not apply to the putative concept thus introduced; propositions in which the concept is embodied will lack finality and definitiveness in so far as they may well not hold when the incomplete definition is extended; and the various piecemeal definitions may not be mutually consistent. The determinacy requirement for *all* expressions in any language, despite superficial appearances of vagueness and imprecision, became one of the corner-stones of the *Tractatus* semantics, and the fundamental source of its metaphysics.[2] 'The requirement that simple signs be possible', Wittgenstein wrote in exposition of the theory of common structure (*TLP*, 3.23), 'is the requirement that sense be determinate.' Interestingly enough, Wittgenstein, in the *ProtoTractatus*, elaborated upon this remark in two sections which most strikingly reveal the Fregean origin of his thought. Where Frege demanded completeness in definition of concepts, Wittgenstein demanded completeness in the introduction of the indefinable simples of language:[3]

[1] Frege, *The Basic Laws of Arithmetic*, vol. II, §56, trans. in *Translations from the Philosophical Writings of Gottlob Frege*, ed. P. Geach and M. Black (Blackwell, Oxford, 1960), p. 159.

[2] See below ch. II.

[3] See J. Griffin, *Wittgenstein's Logical Atomism* (O.U.P., Oxford, 1964), p. 11; had Frege been concerned with indefinables, he clearly would have extended his demand for completeness.

The analysis of signs must come to an end at some point because if signs are to express anything at all, meaning must belong to them in a way that is once and for all complete.

The requirement of determinateness could also be formulated in the following way: if a proposition is to have sense, the syntactical employment of each of its parts must have been established in advance. For example it cannot occur to one only subsequently that a certain proposition follows from it. Before a proposition can have a sense, it must be completely settled what propositions follow from it (*PT*, 3.20102–3).

Thus if language is properly analysed into its elements the complete sharpness which is a condition of the possibility of representation will be revealed. To be sure Russell is right if he means only that ordinary language is vague. But what we mean when we use these vague propositions[1] must be sharp (*NB*, p. 68), for 'There is enormously much added in thought to each proposition and not said' (*NB*, p. 70). This is implicit, at least in certain respects, in the complicated tacit conventions of our language which include a multitude of semantic and pragmatic norms of speech making possible the supplementation of what is said by reference to the speaker's intention and context of utterance. For if someone does not understand what I mean by a vague proposition, and demands that I state my meaning in more detail, I can often reply that the additional detail may be taken for granted. But it may be that I do not know what I mean by a certain term *in general*, as opposed to the specific occasion of its use. If I say 'The watch is lying on the table', and am asked whether, if the watch were in a peculiar position (e.g. balanced against a pencil on the table) I should still say that it is lying on the table, I might be uncertain. But this does not show that I did not know what I meant when I said 'The watch is lying on the table'. The sense of my thought is quite precise, and I could reply to any suggestion to the contrary by saying 'I *know* what I mean; I mean just THIS' (*NB*, p. 70), and I should point to the watch upon the table. Here the apparently vague sentence expresses a precise proposition in virtue of what is added to it in thought, namely my meaning THAT. What is referred to by ostention gives precise sense to what I say. This provides a *guarantee* that our proposition really is a picture of reality (*NB*, pp. 67 ff.),

---

[1] In the discussion of vagueness in *NB*, pp. 60–70, Wittgenstein talks of '*vagen Satz*' throughout.

for if reality is sharp, so too must be the propositions that represent it.[1] Wittgenstein's investigation is not, as Russell supposed, aimed at separating what is adequate in language from what is not, and then improving and refining it. It is aimed at revealing the structure of what already is, and must be, in perfect order.

We have seen in what ways everyday language and ordinary grammar can mislead, and we have noted that in a deeper sense all is well with everyday language. But it is still not clear what specific philosophical errors arise out of the misleading surface features of language and are to be eradicated by a proper conceptual notation. Almost all Wittgenstein's references to past philosophy are disparaging. Philosophy is full of fundamental confusion (*TLP*, 3.324). Most philosophers do not understand the distinction between internal and external relations and consequently produce nonsense (*TLP*, 4.122). In short, most of the questions asked in philosophy are nonsense, and the putative philosophical propositions purporting to answer them are nonsense too (*TLP*, 4.003). This is a result of failure to understand the logic of our language. These pseudo-questions are unobviously of the same class as 'Is the good more or less identical than the beautiful?' The task of philosophy is of course not to answer such nonsense, but to show that it is nonsense. 'For a long time now I have thought that philosophy will one day devour itself' —the words are Lichtenberg's,[2] but the sentiment is eminently Wittgensteinian.

The claim that all past philosophy is riddled with error is quite common in the philosophical world. But that it is all a subtle form of gibberish is not. To understand Wittgenstein's thought here we must look briefly at his notion of senselessness and nonsense. Genuine propositions that are contingent have sense. They picture facts and say, truly or falsely, that the world is thus or otherwise. The limiting case of propositions with sense are tautologies and

---

[1] The elimination of this Fregean corner-stone is one of the central themes of the *Philosophical Investigations*. Ramsey, who was influential in steering Wittgenstein away from the doctrines of the *Tractatus*, wrote: 'The chief danger to our philosophy . . . is *scholasticism*, the essence of which is treating what is vague as if it were precise and trying to fit it into an exact logical category. A typical piece of scholasticism is Wittgenstein's view that all our everyday propositions are completely in order and that it is impossible to think illogically' (op. cit., p. 269). It is amusing to recollect that in his notebooks Wittgenstein had written 'It has been what I should like to call my strong scholastic feeling that has occasioned my best discoveries' (*NB*, p. 28).

[2] Quoted in J. P. Stern, *Lichtenberg, A Doctrine of Scattered Occasions* (Thames and Hudson, London, 1963), p. 322.

contradictions. They do not violate any principles of logical syntax, but they are not pictures of reality. Being necessary truths or falsehoods they do not picture a possible state of affairs out of a range of possibilities. They do not *say* anything, and how things are in the world can neither confute nor confirm them. They are, in a technical sense, degenerate cases of propositions. Although they neither say, nor try to say anything, they show the logical structure of the world. They show the limits within which all possible worlds must be contained. Such logical propositions lack sense (for they say nothing), but they are not nonsense. They are *sinnlos* but not *unsinnig*. Nonsense, on the other hand is a feature, not of degenerate propositions, but of pseudo-propositions. Nonsensical pseudo-propositions violate the rules of logical syntax. Like senseless propositions they say nothing for they have no sense. But unlike senseless propositions they show nothing about the world, neither about its form nor about its content. Within the domain of nonsense we may distinguish overt from covert nonsense. Overt nonsense can be seen to be nonsense immediately. Thus, for example, Chomskian sentences such as 'Ideas furiously green sleep' are intuitively recognizable nonsense, and Wittgenstein's example of obvious philosophical nonsense—'Is the good more or less identical than the beautiful?'—falls into the same class of overt nonsense. But most of philosophy is not intuitively perceivable gibberish. It is covert nonsense for, in a way that is not obvious in ordinary language to the untutored mind, it violates the principles of the logical syntax of language. Philosophers try to say what can only be shown, and what they say, being nonsense, does not even show what they try to say. Nevertheless, even within the range of philosophical, covert nonsense we can distinguish, as we shall see, between what might (somewhat outrageously) be called illuminating nonsense, and misleading nonsense. Illuminating nonsense will guide the attentive hearer or reader to apprehend what is shown by other propositions which do not purport to be philosophical; moreover it will intimate, to those who grasp what is meant, its own illegitimacy. The task of philosophy in this respect then is twofold, to bring one to see what shows itself, and to prevent one from the futile endeavour to say it by teaching one 'to pass from a piece of disguised nonsense to something that is patent nonsense'.[1]

---

[1] *PI*, §464 and §524. This later comment is equally apt for *TLP*.

The source of the error of past philosophy lies in its failure to understand the principles of the logical syntax of language which are obscured by grammar. It is this that engenders the illusion that one can say things which can only be shown. This in turn leads to misleading nonsense. The cardinal problem of philosophy, and the main point of his own work, Wittgenstein wrote to Russell,[1] 'is the theory of what can be expressed [*gesagt*] by propositions and what cannot be expressed by propositions but only shown [*gezeigt*]'. How does misapprehension of this lead to philosophical nonsense? Wittgenstein delineates his view at *TLP*, 4.12–4.2. Philosophy, in one sense, is an endeavour to reveal the essence of the world (e.g. *TLP*, 3.3421, 5.4711), or, as Wittgenstein put it in the *Notebooks* (*NB*, p. 53), the *a priori* order of the world. The attempt to describe essence, or the structure of the world, has traditionally been done by describing formal, internal or structural properties and relations of objects or facts, i.e. necessary properties or relations that constitute the essence of things and without which they would be inconceivable (*TLP*, 4.123). Specification of such internal properties and relations is done by means of what Wittgenstein calls 'formal concepts'. Wittgenstein's examples in the sections in question are, significantly, concepts which, according to Russell's Theory of Types, are both type-ambiguous, and essential for the exposition of the theory, e.g. 'object', 'complex', 'fact', 'function', 'number'.

Past philosophers, in particular Frege and Russell, had employed such concepts in propositions which were either conclusions of arguments or essential links in a chain of a philosophical argument, e.g. 'There is only one Zero' (as in Frege's definition of One) or 'There is an infinite number of objects' (as in Russell's axiom of infinity). Frege laid it down[2] as a crucial requirement of adequate definitions of numbers that one's definitions should make it clear that e.g. Julius Caesar is not a number whereas, say, One is. Both Frege and Russell concluded their analyses of number with the claim that numbers are classes of classes. Finally, the *Tractatus* itself consists of similar propositions, such as 'objects are simple', 'the world is the totality of facts', 'a number is the exponent of an operation'. But all such philosophical propositions are nonsense. Some may be, in a sense, illuminating, and others merely misleading.

---

[1] Letter No. 37 to Russell, 19 Aug. 1919.
[2] Frege, *The Foundations of Arithmetic*, §56.

All, however, are pseudo-propositions. They try, illegitimately, to say what can only be shown.

Wittgenstein's notoriously obscure doctrine of showing and saying, in its application to pseudo-propositions of philosophy, is, in the first instance, his answer to Russell's Theory of Types.[1] It rests upon his views of the nature of variables and quantification on the one hand, and upon his insistence on determinacy of sense and completeness of introduction of indefinables on the other. It is also related to his metaphysics, which is itself an outgrowth of his semantic doctrines. A variable is introduced into a conceptual notation concurrently with the introduction of a constant naming an object of a given kind not yet represented in the symbolism. It has already been shown that on Wittgenstein's view, meaning must belong to signs in a way that is final and complete, and that the syntactical employment of each part of a proposition must be established in advance. Hence to stipulate values for a variable involves a complete determination of the range of significance of the values, i.e. giving the propositions whose common characteristic the variable is (*TLP*, 3.317). Thus the stipulation of values *is* the variable (*TLP*, 3.316). Hence in introducing an indefinable, we do not introduce two distinct primitive ideas—the concept of a function and specific functions. Similarly the concept of a number and specific numbers may not be separately introduced (*TLP*, 4.12721). For the one is the form of the other.

Some aspects of Wittgenstein's metaphysics, in particular his conception of simple objects, will be examined and criticized in subsequent chapters. For the moment only so much as is necessary to clarify the doctrine of showing and saying will be elaborated. The world, according to the *Tractatus*, is composed of facts that are concatenations of simple objects. These objects constitute the substance of the world: they are unanalysable and hence lexically indefinable. They have both form and content. In general space and time are forms of objects. Being coloured, however, is not a form of objects in general, but a particular form of visual objects (*PT*, 2.0252). Presumably pitch is a form of notes, degrees of hardness a form of tangibilia, and so on (*TLP*, 2.0131). The forms of an object are its internal or formal properties. A property is internal if it is unthinkable that its object should not possess it (*TLP*, 4.123). In

---

[1] See J. Griffin, *Wittgenstein's Logical Atomism*, ch. III.

addition to its formal properties an object has external or material properties. *The* form of an object is its ontological type, its possibility of occurring in states of affairs of various kinds (*TLP*, 2.0141). Its form is thus determined by the sum of its formal properties, for it is they in turn that determine the kinds of objects with which it can combine to constitute a fact. The contingent concatenations into which a specific object does as a matter of fact enter constitute the external properties of the object.

If I know an object I must know all its possible occurrences in states of affairs, i.e. its internal properties (*TLP*, 2.0123–2.01231). I may not know what colour a speck is, but I must know that it has a colour. The essence of a speck in the visual field is to have a colour. Corresponding to this strange notion of 'knowing an object' we find, in the linguistic domain, the claim that the logical syntax of a sign for an object must be established without mentioning the particular meaning (*Bedeutung*) of the sign. The syntax of a sign for a visual object must be established independently of the object being this or that colour. For names, the signs of objects, likewise have both form and content. Their content is their meaning. Their form is their logico-syntactical category. This is expressed in a notation by the variable for which the name is a value, which tacitly embodies the syntactical formation-rules for that name and for all names of objects of that ontological type. A formal concept therefore *is* the variable which *shows* the form of the objects over which it ranges. The form of the object is shown in that its sign is a substitution instance of a given kind of variable. Concepts are defined, in Fregean jargon, by their characteristic marks (*Merkmale*), i.e. the essential properties of the items falling under them. But formal properties, i.e. the combinatorial possibilities of objects, are not themselves objects, and cannot be named. They are shown in the notation by features of those symbols which have the identical range of possible syntactical combinations.

A theory of types is intended to tell us what the range of significance of a propositional function is, i.e. the combinatorial possibilities of a symbol. But, on Wittgenstein's view, if we understand the symbol we must already know this. It is shown by the symbolism. Moreover, it cannot be said. For a theory of types would only be expressible, according to Wittgenstein, by violating the rules of logical syntax, by employing formal concepts as values for variables, and allowing a function to be its own argument. It is easy to suppose,

Wittgenstein remarked in his first onslaught upon the Theory of Types (*NB*, p. 105), that 'individual', 'particular', 'complex', etc. are primitive ideas of logic (*Urzeichen*). But in so doing, we forget that these are not primitive ideas, but only schemes for them. The indefinables of symbols (*Urbilder von Zeichen*), namely variables, only occur under the generality sign, never outside it. Propositions contain only apparent variables, not real ones. If we further adhere to the eliminability of quantifiers by analysis into logical sums and products, it will be clear why Wittgenstein thought that formal concepts are pseudo-concepts. One can say nothing by means of them, and what one endeavours to say by using them is shown by the use of genuine concepts.

Wittgenstein's doctrine has been much discussed in recent exegetical literature. Here only a few brief criticisms will be mentioned. The doctrine of the inexpressibility of what is shown in a conceptual notation is of course not directed primarily at Russell's Theory of Types, but at the whole of metaphysics, and ultimately the whole of philosophy as traditionally conceived. The doctrine rests on a variety of premises which are assumed rather than properly argued for in the *Tractatus*, all of which were later repudiated by Wittgenstein. We are given no clue, in the *Tractatus*, how to determine which concepts are formal concepts and which are not. He merely remarks that to recognize a symbol by its sign we must observe how it is used with a sense (*TLP*, 3.326). If we are meant to go to ordinary language and its use to discover the ultimate syntactical categories that mirror the ontological categories of the world, it is far from clear that we shall discover what Wittgenstein expects. For it is false that, in ordinary language, words are interchangeable *salva significatione* either in all contexts or none.[1] If failure of interchangeability in *some* context suffices to show categorial difference, we may well find ourselves with as many types as words. If sense were perfectly determinate, if the range of significance of a concept were fixed once and for all with perfect precision, things might be otherwise. But that sense is and must be thus determinate is a dogma whose repudiation lies at the heart of the *Philosophical Investigations*. Equally, the assumption of a clear-cut line between what is contingently false because causally impossible, and what is nonsense, is founded on this dogma. The doctrine of showing and

---

[1] W. and M. Kneale, *The Development of Logic*, pp. 671 f.

saying rests upon the contention that the structure and formation-rules of a conceptual notation modelled on the language of *Principia Mathematica*, will be the logical syntax of natural language which is concealed by its conventional grammar. Hence what is illicit in the conceptual notation is held to be similarly ill-formed nonsense in natural language. This contention is not obviously correct. It depends, of course, upon a further set of claims, none of which stand firm. That ontological categories are objectively fixed, once and for all, independently of language, is an assumption of the doctrine. Since the picture theory requires syntax to mirror ontology, there are no options in language. We must, presumably, have as many styles of variables as there are types of objects. These claims may hang together. Lacking proper support, they certainly fall together. The first claim was to be totally rejected by Wittgenstein in his later theory of the autonomy of grammar.[1] What remained of the picture theory, liberalized and de-atomized, was to support as radically a conventionalist philosophy as the *Tractatus* was Platonist.

These doctrines then are the grounds upon which Wittgenstein abolishes all metaphysics, whether transcendent or descriptive, and outlaws all traditional philosophy. Metaphysics has traditionally been concerned with making categorial statements about the constituents of the world, and with describing the relations between different categories. In Wittgenstein's view, the inclusion of an item in a certain category would be clearly shown in a perspicuous notation (but is obscured in our everyday language) by the fact that the item is a value of a variable which can take any value within the range of that category. That A is an object is shown by the sign 'A' which is substitutable for a variable whose range is objects (as opposed, say, to numbers). The category itself, however, is represented in the symbolism not by a sign for a value of the variable, but by the variable itself. Formal concepts, by the use of which philosophers try to describe essences, i.e. the essential and invariable features which make a thing a member of its kind, are represented in the symbolism by the variable whose values possess the essence in question, and not by any predicate which is necessarily true of all values of the variable. That A is an object cannot be said because 'object' is a formal or pseudo-concept. It is not a function and the predicate 'is an object' can be given no subject so as to produce a well-formed proposition. 'Object' can no more signify the value of a predicate variable than an event can be fitted into a hole. The essence of a category will be reflected in the permissible ways in which elements of a language may be combined. In order for any symbolism in general, and of course natural languages in particular, to say anything, to picture facts, to specify external properties and relations, the *formal structure* of the symbolism must represent the internal properties and relations of that which the symbolism is capable of describing. The formal structure of the symbolism, however, cannot provide its own content; what it shows, in this sense, it cannot say.[1]

The remedy for the confusions characteristically engendered in philosophy is to be found in an adequate conceptual notation. Once this is devised (along lines indicated by the *Tractatus*), then we shall have a correct logical point of view (*TLP*, 4.1213). To be sure, the correct notation will be derived from the *actual* logical syntax of our language.[2] But what is obscured and concealed in ordinary language will be laid bare to sight. The form of the body will not be concealed by the clothing. Errors stemming from homonymity will be excluded, for the notation will be governed by the principle—one sign, one symbol. Errors arising out of deceptive grammatical form will be eliminated, for the notation will reflect different modes of signification in the ways it combines distinct kinds of signs. All sense will be explicit, for dependence upon tacit convention for determinacy of sense will be eschewed. There will be no gap between what is meant and what is said, and hence there will be no apparent imprecision which needs eradicating by ostention. Expressions for variables will not appear to be substitutable expressions for variables, and pseudo-concepts will not be confused with proper concepts. What Russell's axiom of infinity endeavours to say would be shown by the existence of infinitely many names with different meanings (*Bedeutungen*) (*TLP*, 5.535). Defining nought as the number belonging to the concept 'not identical with itself' is nonsense, for identity is not a relation between objects (*TLP*, 5.5301) and in a correct conceptual notation, propositions

---

[1] The ancestry of the doctrine is illuminatingly discussed in J. Griffin, *Wittgenstein's Logical Atomism*, ch. III, G. E. M. Anscombe, *An Introduction to Wittgenstein's Tractatus*, (2nd ed. Hutchinson, London, 1963), *passim*, and E. B. Allaire, 'The "Tractatus": Nominalistic or Realistic?', in *Essays on Wittgenstein's Tractatus*, ed. I. M. Copi and R. W. Beard (Routledge and Kegan Paul, London, 1966).

[2] See Griffin, op. cit., p. 138.

such as $(x) (x = x)$ cannot even be written down. Identity of object should be expressed by identity of sign and not by a sign of identity. The analysis of the essence of numbers by Frege or by Russell is not only nonsense, but also superfluous. A number is the exponent of an operation. The formal concept of a number is what is common to all numbers, the general form of a number, and this is unequivocally shown by the variable for numbers. In the correct, or ideally explicit notation, '*different kinds of things* are symbolized by different kinds of symbols which *cannot* possibly be substituted in one another's places'.[1] If the rules of logical syntax are understood and correctly followed, then in such a perspicuous notation it will be *impossible* to produce nonsensical philosophical propositions. However it will also be impossible to produce any philosophical propositions at all.

4. *Philosophy as Critique and as Analysis*

A critique is an investigation of the limits of a faculty. The aim of the *Tractatus* is to provide a critique, not of pure reason as in Kant, but of language. It is:

to set limits to thought, or rather—not to thought, but to the expression of thoughts: for in order to be able to set a limit to thought, we should have to find both sides of the limit thinkable (i.e. we should have to be able to think what cannot be thought) (*TLP*, p. 3).

The limits of the thinkable will be set in language, and what lies beyond the limits of intelligible language is unintelligible nonsense. The totality of genuine propositions constitutes the thinkable; the totality of true propositions constitutes the whole of what Wittgenstein calls 'natural science'. In specifying the limits of language, philosophy sets limits to the much disputed sphere of natural science, the sphere of possible knowledge. Can science thus broadly conceived tell us whether we possess an immortal soul or whether God exists? Only if the totality of propositions encompasses propositions about God and the soul. Is there any possible ethical or aesthetic knowledge? Only if there are ethical or aesthetic propositions. Kant's critique of speculative reason denied knowledge to make room for faith, for belief which is justified by practical reason. Wittgenstein's critique of language reaches far more radical conclusions. What we are not able, in principle, to know we cannot

[1] Letter No. 9 to Russell, Jan. 1913 (*NB*, p. 121).

think either. The traditional metaphysical subjects of God and the soul lie beyond the bounds of language. More radically, there can be no ethical or aesthetic propositions.[1] Knowledge is denied to make room for silence. Finally, and here the contrast with Kant goes very deep indeed, the critique itself, the description of the limits of language, lies beyond the realm of what can be said. Language can no more describe its own essence than it can describe the essence of the world.

Philosophy is not, as Wittgenstein had thought in 1913, the doctrine of the logical form of scientific propositions. There can be no such doctrine. A doctrine consists of a body of propositions, but there are no philosophical propositions (*TLP*, 4.112). Philosophy is an activity of logical clarification. It is the analysis of propositions of natural science, i.e. of genuine, putatively true propositions which, barring their opacity, have nothing to do with philosophy. It will consist of producing clear presentations of empirical propositions by analysing them into their constituents, ultimately, if need be, into atomic propositions, and presenting this analysis in a per-spicuous notation. In his first post-*Tractatus* paper,[2] written in 1929 just before the deep change in his philosophy, Wittgenstein sketched a conception of analysis which is some guide to his thought in the *Tractatus*. The subject-matter of all propositions is contained in the totality of atomic propositions. The way in which this material is developed in non-atomic propositions and expressed in ordinary language is to be made clear by analysis:

The idea is to express in an appropriate symbolism what in ordinary language leads to endless misunderstandings. That is to say, where ordinary language disguises logical structure, where it allows the forma-tion of pseudo-propositions, where it uses one term in an infinity of different meanings, we must replace it by a symbolism which gives a clear picture of the logical structure, excludes pseudo-propositions, and uses its terms unambiguously.[3]

---

[1] Although they may apparently be contained, in some sense, in poetry or music; see letter to Engelmann, 9 Apr. 1917, in *LLW*, p. 7.

[2] 'Some Remarks on Logical Form', *Proceedings of the Aristotelian Society*, supp. vol. ix (1929), pp. 162–71. Wittgenstein repudiated this paper, correctly characterizing it as 'weak'. Nevertheless it does indicate his conception of analysis hinted at in the *Tractatus*. Indeed this is one of the reasons for his vehement repudiation of it.

[3] ibid., p. 163.

The need for such an analysis will arise according to the unclarity one feels regarding the meaning of a given empirical proposition. Whether such analyses will need to be pursued to the level of atomic propositions or not will depend upon whether the difficulties which need to be resolved are eliminated at a higher level than the ultimate atomic structure.

In addition to its role as clarifier of good sense, philosophy has a more negative, dialectical task. Whenever someone wants to state metaphysical truths, the philosopher must show him that he has given no meaning to certain signs in his propositions. If someone, trying to describe essences, endeavours to use 'is a number' or 'is an object' as predicate expressions, one must point out that *as* substitutable expressions for predicate variables, these signs have been given no sense. They are signs for variables, not for values of variables. This clarificatory and dialectical method may seem unsatisfactory to the person whose puzzlement we are resolving and whose metaphysical pronouncements we are demolishing, for in doing this sort of philosophy we shall say nothing metaphysical about the essence of the world, nor present any doctrine of logical form about the essence of language. But this method is the only *strictly correct* one. It sets limits to what can and cannot be thought by working outwards through what can be thought. It signifies what cannot be said by presenting clearly what can be said (*TLP*, 4.114–5). Traditional philosophical problems are nonsense, and cannot be answered, but only, dialectically, shown to be nonsense. The metaphysician's hankering after the essence of the world cannot be satisfied in philosophical propositions, but can be satisfied by looking at the form of non-philosophical propositions. Every genuine proposition, in addition to saying what it says, shows some logical property of the universe.[1] When the form of language is laid bare in a proper conceptual notation, then the essence of the world, which philosophy has always striven to describe, though still unutterable, will be lying upon the surface in full view.

It follows from these views that the method of the *Tractatus* is not strictly the correct one. The *Tractatus* does not set a limit to thought by a clear presentation of what can be said. The propositions of the *Tractatus* are not clarifications of propositions of

[1] 'Notes Dictated to G. E. Moore', *NB*, p. 107.

'natural science'.[1] On the contrary, they are, like the propositions of traditional philosophy, pseudo-propositions, and must be recognized to be nonsensical. A critique of language, such as that constituted by the *Tractatus*, would have to stand on both sides of the limit of the thinkable. Such a critique could not possibly make sense. What then is its rationale? What point can such nonsense have?

Wittgenstein's penultimate remark in the *Tractatus* that whoever understands him will recognize that the propositions of the *Tractatus* are nonsense was of course greeted by philosophers with incredulous indignation. In his preface Russell remarks that 'after all Mr. Wittgenstein manages to say a good deal about what cannot be said'.[2] Black, like Russell, cannot doubt that we understand the book and learn much from it. There must therefore be some way out of this paradox. Black suggests[3] that we may concede to Wittgenstein that if communication is equated exclusively with 'saying' then the *Tractatus* communicates nothing. But even if this is conceded, there is, on Wittgenstein's own theory, much that can be shown though not said. Hence we may say that there is much that the *Tractatus* shows, and this is salvageable. Black proceeds to erect what he calls a 'line of defence'. According to this, all cases in which Wittgenstein is seeking the essence of something, which result in *a priori* statements belonging to logical syntax or philosophical grammar (Black gives as an example 'A proposition is not a complex name'), consist of formal statements 'showing' something that can be shown. These, Black says, are no worse than logical statements which involve no violation of the rules of logical syntax.

This is, I think, completely misguided. Logical propositions are senseless but not nonsense. They say nothing but they show the scaffolding of the world. So-called 'formal statements', however, neither say nor show anything (barring perhaps their own nonsensi-

---

[1] Thus I take issue with K. T. Fann who claims that 'Philosophy *in* the *Tractatus* is an activity of clarification and elucidations. It shows the logic of our language by presenting clearly what can be said;' *Wittgenstein's Conception of Philosophy* (Blackwell, Oxford, 1969), p. 30.

[2] *TLP*, p. xxi. With apologies to F. P. Ramsey, *Foundations of Mathematics*, p. 268, the *Tractatus* clearly gives a strong impression of similarity to the child's remarks in the following dialogue: 'Say "breakfast".' 'Can't.' 'What can't you say?' 'Can't say "breakfast".'

[3] M. Black, *A Companion to Wittgenstein's Tractatus*, pp. 378 ff.

cality). They do violate the rules of logical syntax for they wrongly try to employ formal concepts as if they were proper concepts. Thus, in Black's example, 'proposition', 'name', and 'complex' are all formal concepts. Consequently they are, on Wittgenstein's theory, illegitimately employed as values for variables. Wittgenstein is quite correct and consistent; on his own theory the *Tractatus* consists largely of pseudo-propositions. To be sure, what Wittgenstein means or intends by these remarks (just as what, in Wittgenstein's view, the solipsist means (*TLP*, 5.62)) is, he thinks, quite correct, only it cannot be said. What someone means or intends by a remark can be grasped even though the remark itself is strictly speaking nonsense (thus Wittgenstein claims to understand what the solipsist means). So whoever understands Wittgenstein, as opposed to understanding what he has said, will recognize that his propositions are nonsensical.

Earlier I distinguished between illuminating nonsense and misleading nonsense. This unhappy distinction has frequently been attacked in Wittgensteinian exegesis. Ramsey[1] pointed out that either philosophy must be of some use, or else it is a disposition which we have to check. If philosophy is nonsense, then it is useless and we should not pretend as Wittgenstein does that it is important nonsense. Later commentators[2] have followed Ramsey in finding the notion of important nonsense absurd, and it has been objected in defence[3] that Wittgenstein neither said nor intended any such absurdity. To be sure, Wittgenstein does not use the phrase 'illuminating nonsense'. What he says is that the propositions of the *Tractatus* elucidate, by bringing whoever understands their author to recognize them as nonsensical.[4] They are not elucidations in the sense of analyses of 'scientific' propositions into their constituents. These pseudo-propositions are the means by which one can climb beyond them. They lead one to see the world aright, to a correct logical point of view. From this point of view one will realise that the *Tractatus* itself is nonsense, and one will thus throw away the ladder upon which one has climbed.

[1] F. P. Ramsey, 'Philosophy', in *Foundations of Mathematics*, p. 263.
[2] e.g. R. Carnap, *The Logical Syntax of Language* (Routledge and Kegan Paul, London, 1937), pp. 282 ff., G. Pitcher, *The Philosophy of Wittgenstein*, (Prentice Hall, New Jersey, 1964), p. 155.
[3] K. T. Fann, op. cit., p. 34.
[4] 'Meine Sätze erläutern dadurch, dass sie der, welcher mich versteht, am Ende als unsinnig erkennt.'

If this interpretation is correct, then there are, as Ramsey thought, grounds for attributing to Wittgenstein the view that the kind of philosophy embodied in the *Tractatus* is important nonsense, and that it is important because it is illuminating. The *Tractatus* violates the rules of logical syntax in order to bring one to see how the different elements of language are articulated. It differs from past philosophy in that past philosophy, according to Wittgenstein, rested on a deep misunderstanding of the depth structure of language. The correctness of the *Tractatus* inheres in the fact that whoever understands its author will become aware of what he has always implicitly known—the logical structure of language. When he sees that, he will also see the illegitimacy of the pseudo-propositions of the *Tractatus*. If one wishes to object to this, as so many sympathizers with the general tenor of the *Tractatus* have, if one wants to deny that literal nonsense can illuminate the essence of the world, then one must modify some of the central theses of the *Tractatus*, for the conclusion follows from them.

Ramsey claimed that if philosophy is nonsense, it must be a disposition that ought to be checked. Does this consequent follow? In one sense it does. Philosophy of the *Tractatus* kind should no longer be written. If anyone tries to say anything metaphysical we should, dialectically, bring him to see his errors. His metaphysical questions will not have been answered, but his mind, 'no longer vexed, will cease to ask illegitimate questions'. To this extent philosophy in the post-*Tractatus* period must be therapeutic. The *Tractatus* itself, though a manifestation of this natural disposition to metaphysics, is a justifiable undertaking which has been fully and finally discharged. It is, as it were, the swan song of metaphysics.

A comparison with Kant's view of the *Critique of Pure Reason*[1] is instructive here. The true purpose of philosophy, Kant claimed (A 735, B 763) is to expose the illusions of reason by reminding us of its limits. It does not extend knowledge, but rather prevents error, thus securing the well-being, general order and harmony of the non-philosophical, scientific commonwealth (A 851, B 879). Its task is to expose that transcendental illusion which stems from misunderstanding the subjective status of the fundamental rules

---

[1] Kant, *Critique of Pure Reason*, trans. by N. Kemp Smith (Macmillan, London, 1933). Subsequent references in the text of this chapter are, as is customary, to the pagination of the first (A) and second (B) German edition.

for the use of our reason (A 297, B 353). Its method is the critique of pure reason. Such a critique can be conceived of as metaphysics, or, more strictly, as a propaedeutic to it. So conceived, metaphysics is unique among the sciences, for it alone, if laid upon the right path, is capable of attaining exhaustive knowledge of its entire field, leaving nothing to posterity but its didactic adaptation (A xx, B xxii). The reason for this is that its subject-matter is wholly *a priori*, and no experience can enlarge it. The principles of pure reason which it investigates are so closely interrelated that proper specification of each involves the complete investigation of all.

Metaphysics has to deal only with principles and with the limits of their employment as determined by these principles themselves, and it can therefore finish its work and bequeath it to posterity as a capital to which no addition can be made. Since it is a fundamental science it is under an obligation to achieve this completeness (B xxiv).

Kant's work has undertaken this task, specifying the problems exhaustively, according to principles. To be sure, he has not filled in all the details. The *Critique* is a treatise on method, not a system of science itself. But it delineates the complete plan of the science, both its limits and its internal structure (B xxii). Others will have to fill in the details of derivative concepts and their analysis (A xxi), such as the predicables (A 82, B 108); their service in explaining the doctrines of the *Critique* with Humean elegance, of which Kant professed himself incapable, is sorely needed. However, Kant proclaims, 'I venture to assert that there is not a single metaphysical problem which has not been solved, or for the solution of which the key at least has not been supplied' (A xiii). There will always be metaphysical illusion in the world, for man can as little give up metaphysics as he can give up breathing in order to prevent himself from breathing impure air. It is a natural disposition of reason, but as such it is deceptive.[1] The only task which is left to critical philosophy and which has been completed in outline by Kant is to fill in the details of the system and thereafter to employ it didactically in restraining our over-adventurous reason in its natural urge to overreach itself.

The *Tractatus* is a critique of language. It brings us to see the limits of language, and also to see that such a critique of language,

---

[1] Kant, *Prolegomena to Any Future Metaphysics*, trans. P. G. Lucas (Manchester University Press, Manchester, 1953), pp. 134, 136.

unlike the projected logical analyses of philosophy, lies itself beyond the bounds of language. Yet, like Kant's critique of pure reason, the task needs to be undertaken if past confusion, error, and illusion are to be eradicated and future phantasmagoria prevented. As in Kant's case, the task can be completed. The structure of language is such that a correct determination of any one part requires a proper grasp of the whole. The method of this critique is the investigation of the nature of a proposition. Although a single proposition determines, as it were, only one place in logical space, only one fact amongst all possible facts, 'the whole of logical space must already be given by it' (*TLP*, 3.42). The 'logical scaffolding' of each proposition is the logical scaffolding of all. To understand the nature of a proposition requires a complete understanding of all its articulations, of its potentialities, together with other propositions of forming all possible structures describing the facts of which the world is constituted. Explaining the nature of the proposition is explaining the nature of all being (*NB*, p. 39). This is the task that is undertaken and completed in the *Tractatus*; 'the truth of the thoughts that are here set forth', Wittgenstein writes in the Preface,[1] unconsciously echoing Kant, 'seems to me unassailable and definitive. I therefore believe myself to have found, on all essential points, the final solution of the problems.' All that remains for philosophy is to fill in inessential points and matters of minor detail, and to express Wittgenstein's thoughts more clearly than he was able. This apart, the future of philosophy lies in giving logical analyses and in the didactic elimination of the illusions embodied in purported metaphysical assertions. Had Kant not pre-empted the title, the *Tractatus* might well have been called 'Prolegomena to Any Future Metaphysics'.

[1] Fann (op. cit., pp. 33 f.) makes much of Wittgenstein's speaking about the truth of what he ultimately claims to be nonsense. I think that this is strictly inconsistent, but the reader of the Preface would hardly have understood the claim that the *Tractatus* is the ladder by which to climb to the correct logical point of view.

II

'EPISTEMOLOGY IS THE PHILOSOPHY OF PSYCHOLOGY'

1. *The place of Epistemology in the* Tractatus

What, according to the author of the *Tractatus*, is the place of epistemology in philosophy in general and philosophical logic in particular? In the account given of Wittgenstein's early conception of philosophy no mention was made of epistemology. It is clear from his early writings—the 'Notes on Logic', the 'Notes Dictated to G. E. Moore', and the pre-*Tractatus* notebooks, as well as from the *Tractatus* itself, that Wittgenstein had little genuine interest in the theory of knowledge. From the beginning of his philosophical career to its end, Wittgenstein's central concern was the nature of language. How is it possible to describe the world by means of a system of representation? How can symbols capture the manifold of phenomena and say both how the world is, and even more remarkably, how it is not? What must the world be like, and how must language be structured if these apparently simple yet mystifying actualities are to be possible? The *Tractatus* is an attempt to supply a complete answer to these questions by developing a rigorously realist theory of meaning.[1] The *Philosophical Investigations* is an attempt to answer the same questions along radical constructivist lines. In neither case was Wittgenstein's endeavour to develop a proper theory of knowledge. But his development of a constructivist semantics from the *Philosophische Bemerkungen* through to *On Certainty* at the end of his life necessitated an important change in his conception of the relations between philosophical logic on the one hand and epistemology and philosophy of mind on the other. The contribution of his later work to

[1] See M. Dummett, 'The Reality of the Past', *Proceedings of the Aristotelian Society*, lxix (1968–9), 239–58, for a discussion of the contrast between 'realist' and 'anti-realist' conceptions of meaning; also 'Truth', by the same author, ibid., lix (1958–9), 141–62.

epistemology, with which subsequent parts of this study will be concerned, is a by-product of his later doctrines of meaning. Epistemology looms large in his post-1929 writings not as a result of a sudden change of interest, nor as a result of his realization that philosophical semantics can incidentally contribute to epistemology, but because the analysis of meaning cannot be wholly separated from the epistemological notions of evidence and justifiable cognitive claims. In the following discussion, the views of the *Tractatus* on epistemology will be examined.

The seventeenth-century revolution in philosophy heralded by Bacon and Descartes professed a deep distrust of classical Aristotelian logic and its scholastic offshoots. Both Bacon and Descartes had an obsessive concern with a method for the discovery of truth, and were more involved in developing a system of heuristics than in examining principles of inference and formal validity. Traditional logic was rejected precisely because it was not a 'logic of discovery'. The New Way of Ideas, introduced by Descartes and developed by Locke, infected both British Empiricism and continental Rationalism with a psychologism in logic and philosophical analysis which, with some notable exceptions, was to taint philosophy and hinder the development of logic for the next three centuries. The subordination of logic to psychology, the adherence to genetic accounts of putative concept-acquisition as a means of conceptual analysis, the commitment to introspection as the source of philosophical knowledge and the analysis of knowledge in terms of 'mental vision' and the perception of agreement and disagreement of ideas culminated in the nineteenth century with the Psychologistic School in Germany and with J. S. Mill in England. Although Frege was not the first to attack psychologism, his onslaught was decisive.

Frege rightly associates psychologistic logic with epistemological idealism. The roots of the errors which he exposes lie in a misguided conception of truth and its relation to knowledge, and a radically incoherent notion of what a concept is. A proposition is true independently of whether it is taken to be true or thought to be true by all or any persons. The conditions under which people are able to think of a proposition as true are irrelevant to the proof of the proposition. Hence a genetic account of how men came to think that a proposition is true is irrelevant to the proof of that proposition. The history of discovery is distinct from the logic of justification. Concepts, according to Frege's Platonistic theory, have no history. They do not sprout in the mind like leaves on a tree. To be sure they are not perceptible or actual, but it is only the confusion of psychologism which leads one to equate the non-actual with the subjective or mental contents of a person's mind. Concepts are objective, awaiting discovery. The pursuit of knowledge of concepts is not a process of creation but of exploration. Knowledge does not create its object. Frequently it requires centuries of effort to achieve knowledge of a concept in its pure form by 'stripping off the irrelevant accretions which veil it from the eyes of the mind'.[1] Hence the description of the origin of an idea is not a definition of a concept any more than a description of Colombus's first chart of the American seaboard is a description of the geography of the continent. What masquerades as the history of concepts is merely the history of our knowledge of concepts and our use of words. Psychologistic definitions of concepts lead to logical incoherence and epistemological absurdity. By using the ambivalent notion of an idea to define concepts, the distinction between what is perceptible and what is objective is lost at an early stage and ultimately the actual or perceptible is treated as constituted of ideas.[2] If all thinking consists of creating, connecting, and altering of ideas, if subjects and predicates alike are ideas, then the notion of objectivity and with it truth disappear. Thus misapprehensions in logic lead to epistemological idealism and hence, with perfect consistency, to solipsism. But the idea of the moon is not the moon, and the number one is not the idea I have of it. The examination of ideas is part of psychology, but the examination of concepts or of numbers or of anything else which belongs to the domain of the objective, be it Platonistic or perceptible, is not. Introspective psychology has no more bearing on logic than it has upon astronomy or geology. Ideas may be sensations or mental images, but concepts are not. Idealists and psychological logicians, because they blur the logical and the psychological, also violate a fundamental methodological principle in philosophical logic, which is never to ask for the meaning of a word except in the context of a sentence. The consequence of equating concepts with ideas is to make communication impossible, and so conflict of opinion resting on mutual understanding becomes

[1] Frege, *The Foundations of Arithmetic*, p. vii.
[2] Frege, *The Basic Laws of Arithmetic*, trans. M. Furth (University of California Press, Berkeley, 1964), p. 17.

equally impossible. Hence logic as an arbiter in conflicts of opinion is made dispensable. Logic may be conceived as consisting of the laws of truth, but the laws of truth thus conceived are, unlike laws of grammar, ahistorical, and unlike laws of nature, normative. If truth were identical with what is thought to be true, then the laws of truth would be psychological laws, and logic part of psychology. But psychological laws are inductive generalizations, not norms. Psychology is a new, uncertain, and imprecise science. Its objects are fluctuating and indefinite. Logic and mathematics are certain and precise and their objects are definite and fixed. Psychological considerations have no place in logic; on the contrary psychology itself requires its own logical first principles.

The upshot of this onslaught is Frege's principle of purity: 'always to separate sharply the psychological from the logical, the subjective from the objective.' The result was as far reaching as the Cartesian revolution which it was overturning. For Frege's endeavour was to displace epistemology from the centre of philosophy.[1] Other elements of philosophy, even including metaphysics, require a logical underpinning. Logic is prior to all other parts of philosophy, but epistemology has no special privileges.

This commitment to a pure theory of logic undoubtedly influenced Wittgenstein very substantially. We have already noted his claim that the basis of philosophy is logic. In the *Tractatus*, 4.1121 he points out that past philosophers considered the study of thought-processes essential to the philosophy of logic. But in most cases they got entangled in unessential psychological investigations. Psychology, he declares, is no more closely related to philosophy than any other science. Epistemology, apparently a relatively insignificant part of philosophy, is relegated to the status of the philosophy of psychology. What do these oracular remarks amount to?

Wittgenstein certainly draws his boundary-lines in unusual ways. Epistemology, as we conceive it, is concerned with the legitimate ways of justifying cognitive claims. Thus conceived, it is both broader and narrower than the philosophy of psychology. We are concerned in epistemology with rendering an adequate account of psychological concepts pertinent to the description of cognitive powers, such as knowledge and belief, remembering and imagining, thinking and understanding. This is a narrower concern with the array of

[1] See M. Dummett, 'Frege, Gottlob', in *The Encyclopedia of Philosophy*, vol. 3, pp. 225–6.

central concepts which describe the powers of the mind, than that of philosophical psychology. For philosophical psychology is not restricted to the intellectual powers of man but extends to the active powers too. On the other hand epistemology's distinctive concern is with the principles of evidence which justify rational belief, knowledge, and certainty within any domain of possible knowledge. It is not obvious in what sense this latter kind of investigation can be thought of as part of the philosophy of psychology, even if one thinks as Wittgenstein did, that all inference is logical, deductive inference.

If we turn to look at Wittgenstein's practice in the *Tractatus*, we find that among the offhanded remarks which he makes in the course of the exposition of his theory of meaning, there are some which fall into each kind. He tries to show that logic can contribute to the analysis of propositions describing propositional attitudes, but his interest in the matter is determined by the fact that propositions like '*A* believes *p*' look as if they are compound propositions without being truth-functions of the apparent component *p*, and so appear as counter-examples to the thesis of extensionality to which Wittgenstein is committed.[1] The answer to the 'epistemological questions concerning the nature of judgement and belief' lies in a correct grasp of the form of the proposition (*NB*, p. 97), and it is the latter which is his fundamental concern. Similarly he pronounces judgement on induction and our knowledge of the future. We could know the future only if we could infer from the existence of one situation the existence of another entirely logically distinct situation (*TLP*, 5.135–5.1361). This we could do only if causal relations provided a genuinely necessary nexus. But they do not. Belief in a causal nexus is, as Hume had claimed, a superstition. It is only an hypothesis that the sun will rise tomorrow, so though we may believe it, we cannot know it (*TLP*, 6.36311). There are no grounds for our beliefs in future events. Our beliefs are determined by our acceptance of inductive procedures which involve choosing the simplest law reconcilable with past experience. But this procedure has no logical justification, and our choices cannot force nature into simple channels if she has, as it were,

---

[1] Moreover, once this has been shown to be illusory, Wittgenstein shows no further interest in the nature of belief. The 'psychological' part of belief which correlates the constituents of '*p*' with the objects of the fact *p* is a matter for psychology (see below ch. III, §2).

chosen complex ones. The sole justification for inductive procedures is in fact psychological. Again, the reasons for the epistemological digression are primarily due to considerations in logic, i.e. it is made in order to emphasize the depth of commitment to, and the unavoidable consequences of, the claims that all necessary truth is logical truth and that all inferences are in accordance with the principles of tautology. Not only are general problems in epistemology such as the justification of induction brushed aside and relegated to the domain of psychology, but apparently logical issues which had preoccupied Frege and Russell are similarly dismissed. Assertion, judgement, command, and question are all matters for psychology not philosophy (*NB*, Appendix I, p. 96).

In his introduction to the *Tractatus*, Russell wrote:

There are various problems as regards language. First, there is the problem what actually occurs in our minds when we use language with the intention of meaning something by it; this problem belongs to psychology (*TLP*, ix).

This was certainly Wittgenstein's attitude. To be sure he thought that understanding something, meaning something by an utterance, endowing a sign with meaning, and thinking, all involve mental states or processes. What these are, however, is of no philosophical relevance, but is a matter for the empirical sciences. Moreover, Russell continues, there is a second problem, namely:

what is the relation subsisting between thoughts, words, or sentences, and that which they refer to or mean (ibid.).

Russell consigns this problem to epistemology. Yet ten pages later he appears to re-allocate the very same problem to psychology:

a symbol does not mean what it symbolizes in virtue of a logical relation alone, but in virtue also of a psychological relation of intention, or association, or what-not. The psychological part of meaning, however, does not concern the logician (*TLP*, xix).

This latter division of labour is, I think, more in tune with Wittgenstein's views at the time. Persuasive though it might be, however, quoting Russell does not prove Wittgenstein's views; nor does it explain why Wittgenstein was committed to relegating to empirical psychology matters which, since the *Philosophical Investigations*, have been quite central to philosophical logic, theory of meaning and philosophy of mind. We must explain precisely how the *Tractatus*'s theory of meaning rests upon unacceptable psychological and epistemological assumptions, how the Pure Theory of Logic which Wittgenstein developed out of Frege's semantics rested upon psychological quicksands.

2. *Psychological and Epistemological Presuppositions and Implications of the* Tractatus

If the fundamental question of the *Tractatus* is 'how is language as a means of representation possible?' then the fundamental answer lies in the theory of common structure. This in turn determines the basic doctrine or sense of the whole book, 'what can be said at all can be said clearly, and what we cannot talk about we must pass over in silence'. This rests on the central Fregean demand for absolute determinacy of sense. The theory of meaning which Wittgenstein elaborates enables epistemological issues to be forced into the background, but the requirement of a metaphysical theory to back up the conjunction of the theory of common structure with the demand for determinacy of sense reveals severe lines of stress. It is at that point of the theory where a semantic interpretation has to be added to the pure logical syntax in order to give content to the abstract propositional forms and to correlate it with the substance of the world, that deep psychological and epistemological myths lie hidden.

'My *whole* task', Wittgenstein wrote in his notebook on 22 January 1915 (*NB*, p. 39), 'consists in explaining the nature of the proposition', a claim which crystallizes into the *Tractatus* pronouncement: 'To give the essence of a proposition means to give the essence of all description, and thus the essence of the world' (*TLP*, 5.4711). The general outline of his reply can be sketched thus: All genuine propositions are either compound or elementary (atomic). Though many propositions of ordinary language appear non-compound, Russell's technique of analysing propositions containing definite descriptions shows how deceptive such appearances are. Compound propositions are truth-functions of their constituent atomic propositions. The sense of a compound proposition is the set of truth conditions determined by the sense of its constituents and can be perspicuously represented by the method of truth-tables. Given that the sense of the constituent propositions is perfectly determinate, then the truth conditions, i.e. the sense, of the compound proposition too is perfectly determinate. What the truth conditions of an elementary proposition are, i.e. its sense, is a function of its constituents. It is essential that the proposition be articulated or complex for, among other things, it is by reference to the syntactical rules determining its articulations and the 'method of projection' determining or fixing the meaning or *Bedeutung* of its constituent elements, that justice can be done to the most fundamental features of language. These are, firstly, that we can use propositions to communicate a new sense, i.e. the creative feature of methods of representation; and secondly, that a proposition is either true or false, thereby determining a possible state of affairs in the world, i.e. the depicting feature of language. The requirement for elementary propositions is the requirement that not all propositions should be dependent for their sense upon the truth of other propositions, for if they were, it would not be possible to depict states of affairs (*TLP*, 2.0211–2.0212). Though the sense of elementary propositions is independent of their actual truth-value, they stand in a direct relation to the world via their constituents. Thus the possibility of logical analysis, as a programme for future philosophy, is *a priori* possible.[1] Elementary propositions are logically independent, for one proposition will imply another only if the sense of the one is contained in the sense of the other, which will be the case only if the one is a constituent of the other.

The theory of the elementary proposition must now bear the weight of the dual account of the essence of language and the essence of the world. As we shall see, it is only capable of doing so by concealing its foundations in psychological myth and epistemological fantasy. The elementary proposition is composed of expressions. An expression is any part of a proposition that contributes to its sense (*TLP*, 3.31). An expression has both form and content. Its form is determined by the syntactical rules that determine all possible meaningful combinations with other expressions. For the meaning of a word is no more independent of the range of meaningful propositions in which it can appear than is the sense of a proposition independent of the words that constitute it. The form of an expression thus presupposes the forms of all the propositions in which it can occur. The elementary expressions or constituents of elementary propositions are names. These are, of course, not names as ordinarily conceived, which do not stand for bearers but rather for describable complexes. Names in the *Tractatus* are the primitive unanalysable signs that combine according to rules of

[1] Suggested by *NB*, pp. 46, 60, 61.

logical syntax to form propositions which are capable of describing any state of affairs. The logical syntax of a sign is completely independent of its meaning or *Bedeutung* (*TLP*, 3.33).

In addition to the rules for the use of elementary signs there must be a method of projection or mode of signification which will provide the forms of names with content. The formal system must be correlated with elements in the world in order that language be capable of representing. Names have a meaning or *Bedeutung* only in propositions, i.e. only in so far as the sign is used according to the logico-syntactical rules by virtue of which it is a symbol. The way in which this semantic requirement is satisfied in Wittgenstein's theory is determined by his commitment to the doctrine of determinacy of sense as a *sine qua non* of the possibility of language. As we have already seen, the sense of a compound proposition is a function of the sense of its constituent elementary propositions and hence will be determinate only in so far as their sense is. The sense of an elementary proposition is a function of its constituents. Hence the sense of an elementary proposition will be determinate only in so far as names have a uniquely determinate meaning. Wittgenstein's metaphysics is an outgrowth of his semantics. For names to have a determinate meaning they must be uniquely and unambiguously correlated with simple constituents of the world. 'The demand for simple things', he noted on 18 June 1915, '*is* the demand for definiteness of sense' (*NB*, p. 63), and again:

It seems that the idea of the SIMPLE is already to be found contained in that of the complex and in the idea of analysis, and in such a way that we come to this idea quite apart from any examples of simple objects, or of propositions which mention them and we realise the existence of the simple object—*a priori*—as a logical necessity (*NB*, p. 60).

The meaning of a logically proper name is a simple object, the object *is* the meaning. The essential point is that there must be unanalysable non-composite objects if language is to be related to the world. These simple objects must be indestructible; they are the substance of the world. For only thus can the need for a completely firm anchor for language be met. A simple object is no more than that which can be referred to without having to fear that maybe it does not exist.[1] Simple objects must exist in order that it be possible for us to say something false yet meaningful, in order

---

[1] See *PB*, §36.

that we be able to imagine[1] how things are not. It is they which give language a foundation, and it is by their means that names provide the connection between language and reality.

Notoriously, the nature of the simple objects of the *Tractatus* ontology remains shrouded in obscurity throughout the book. Although the matter cannot be explored in detail here, the issue is sufficiently controversial that a brief digression may be permitted to indicate the general grounds for the realist interpretation adopted here, which was hinted at in the previous chapter. Wittgenstein's concept of simple objects as the subsistent indestructible substance of the world is, I believe, the heir to Russell's notion of a term, which was itself a development of Moore's notion of a concept.[2] A term, according to Russell,[3] is 'whatever may be an object of thought, or may occur in any true or false proposition, or can be counted as *one*'. Synonyms of 'term' are 'unit', 'individual', and 'entity'. Examples of terms are: a man, a moment, a number, a class, a relation, a chimaera. Terms have being even if they do not exist. They are immutable and indestructible. Russell distinguished among terms between things and concepts, the former including points and instants, as well as much else, the latter including attributes. A certain affinity with Wittgenstein's objects is evident. The programme of analysis suggested a diminution of the excessively rich domain of subsistence. Did it pare objects down to bare particulars or did it encompass universals too? The favoured nominalist interpretation[4] of Wittgenstein's doctrine explains the absence of any explicit ontological distinction in the *Tractatus* between particulars and universals, by attributing to Wittgenstein the view that universals are nothing but concatenations of bare particulars. But the absence of the distinction in fact reflects Wittgenstein's repudiation of the idea that they are as unlike as traditionally conceived. This is paralleled by his repudiation of Frege's distinction between names and functions in terms of saturatedness. In the final analysis all objects are dependent, incomplete entities that exist only concatenated in states of affairs.

---

[1] See *BB*, p. 31. For a similar principle see Descartes, *Meditations*, Meditation I.

[2] G. E. Moore, 'The Nature of Judgment', *Mind*, viii (1899), 176–93.

[3] Russell, *The Principles of Mathematics*, p. 43.

[4] e.g. G. E. M. Anscombe, *An Introduction to Wittgenstein's Tractatus*, ch. 7; J. Griffin, *Wittgenstein's Logical Atomism*, chs. VI.4, VII.3, XI.2 and 4; I. M. Copi, 'Objects, Properties and Relations in the *Tractatus*', repr. in *Essays on Wittgenstein's Tractatus*, ed. I. M. Copi and R. W. Beard, pp. 167–86.

Pari passu it is impossible for words to occur in two different ways, alone and in propositions (*TLP*, 2.0122). The pre-*Tractatus* writings contain passages suggesting that prior to the *Tractatus*, Wittgenstein included universals amongst objects (e.g. *NB*, pp. 53, 61, 65). The nominalist interpretation of the *Tractatus* suffers from serious defects,[1] and makes the book less intelligible than necessary. The theory of categories implicit in the doctrine of showing and saying and in the distinction between formal and material properties of objects strongly suggests, as we have seen, a realist interpretation of the book. All the post-*Tractatus* writings, from 'Some Remarks on Logical Form' onwards, which discuss the problems and illusions of logical analysis into simple subsistent entities, intimate that the target of later criticism is realistic rather than nominalistic.[2] This will be substantiated in the examination of these criticisms in subsequent chapters. I shall thus take it that the objects of the *Tractatus* include not only particulars, i.e. specifically: spatio-temporal points, but also objects such as the ultimate unanalysable determinates of perceptual determinables.

The function of objects, in the *Tractatus*, is to enable language to be unambiguously connected with the world. The method of projection uniquely correlates a name with such simple constituents of facts:

if the general description of the world is like a stencil of the world, the names pin it to the world so that the world is wholly covered by it (*NB*, p. 53).

Thus language can represent possible states of affairs because it shares a common structure with the world. Names only have meaning in propositions, objects can only exist concatenated in facts. The form of a name, shown by the variable for it, determines its logico-syntactical category and hence the ways it can legitimately be combined with other names to constitute a well-formed proposition. The form of an object is its ontological category. The

---

[1] See E. B. Allaire, 'The "Tractatus": Nominalistic or Realistic?', repr. in *Essays on Wittgenstein's Tractatus*, pp. 325–41. It is significant that Ramsey does not conceive of the book as propounding an extreme nominalism, but as denying the validity of the traditional ontological distinction between particulars and universals in terms of incompleteness (see especially his 'Universals', and the subsequent 'Note on the preceding Paper', in *The Foundations of Mathematics*, pp. 112–37).

[2] It is interesting to note that, quite apart from the later criticisms, Wittgenstein takes it that 'individuals' in Russell's sense include colours; see M, p. 297.

concatenation of names in a proposition depicts a possible combination of objects in a state of affairs. All possible combinations of objects fix the limits of all possible worlds. The totality of elementary propositions describes all possible worlds. If the objects named in an elementary proposition are arranged in a fact as the proposition represents them as being, then the proposition is true; otherwise it is false. The totality of true elementary propositions is a complete world-description. The world is the totality of facts thus described.

The starkly realist features of the *Tractatus* semantics, inherited from Frege, help to explain its indifference to epistemology. The sense of a proposition consists in its truth conditions. It is wholly independent of the ways in which we come to know whether it is true. We know what a proposition means when we know what has to be the case if it is true. If we know that, then we simultaneously know what has to be the case if it is false.[1] Whether we are able in principle or in practice to find out whether it is true is irrelevant to its sense. The truth conditions may be such that we lack a procedure to determine their occurrence. For every true proposition there is some determinate state of affairs independent of our cognition that makes it true. If the truth conditions are not satisfied the proposition is thereby made false. Every proposition is either true or false. The commitment to the Excluded Middle is merely another form of the requirement of determinate sense. But again, whether a proposition is true or false is independent of whether it is possible to tell which it is. All necessary truth is a matter of logical necessity, and logical necessity is independent of how things happen to be in the world. *A fortiori* it is independent of our knowings and ways of knowing, and indeed independent of natural languages.

There are three points of intolerable tension at the limits of the theory. The first is located at the point where the doctrine of the ideal notation connects with the view that ordinary language is in perfect logical order just as it is. The conjunction of the demand for absolute determinacy of sense together with the doctrines of logical atomism i.e. the thesis of extensionality and the programme of analysis into simples, drive the essence of language, as it were,

---

[1] See *WWK*, p. 86, for clarification of *TLP*, 4.024. It has nothing to do with the Principle of Verification. See also P. T. Geach, 'Frege', in *Three Philosophers*, by G. E. M. Anscombe and P. T. Geach (Blackwell, Oxford, 1961), p. 141.

deep beneath the surface until it becomes quite unrecognizable.[1] Secondly, the doctrine of categories pulls in the opposite direction from the radical empiricism of the book. The doctrine that all necessity is logical conceals important incompatibilities. These two issues will be examined in subsequent chapters. The third point of maximum stress concerns the epistemological and psychological assumptions underlying the theory of the elementary proposition and the logically proper name. It is to these that we shall now turn. The consequences of the theory for that part of epistemology known as the metaphysics of experience will be deferred until the next chapter.

In the *Tractatus*, only the tips of the icebergs of psychological and epistemological commitments are visible on the surface. This is readily explicable by reference to the Fregean anti-psychologism and the commitment to the Pure Theory of Logic. Our task is to probe beneath the surface.

In the 'Notes on Logic', at the initial stages of development of the theory of common structure, Wittgenstein already remarked that the correlation of name and its meaning (the object which is its meaning) is psychological (*NB*, p. 99). In the *Notebooks 1914–16*, the general impression is given that such correlation must be the result of some mental act of meaning or intending a certain word to signify an object one has in mind. It is an act of will which correlates a word with an object. A brief survey of some important passages will substantiate this. It is by means of my correlating the components of the picture with objects, it is by *these means*[2] that it comes to represent a situation and to be right or wrong (*NB*, p. 33). Wittgenstein speaks of a 'feeling of a simple relation' when we think of the relation between name and thing named. He goes so far as to suggest that it is the main ground for assuming the existence of 'simple objects', and rightly worries over having the same feeling when thinking of the relation of an ordinary name (e.g. '*A*' as the name of a book) and the complex object it names. It is clear that the phenomenology of the thought of naming fascinated him:

What is the source of the feeling "I can correlate a name with all that I see, with this landscape, with the dance of motes in the air, with all this; indeed what should we call a name if not this" ? (*NB*, p. 53).

---

[1] As Wittgenstein himself stresses in *PI*, §92.

[2] '*Dadurch*'; the double use of the term, and the second emphasis is lost in the translation.

His main (though, of course, not sole) examples of simple objects and of complexes are points or *minima sensibilia* in the visual field,[1] and parts or areas of the visual field. These provide paradigms of items to which the name-sign can *occurrently* be attached. It is perhaps with reference to this that he remarked in the *Investigations'* gloss on the perversities of the *Tractatus* that 'we rack our brains over the nature of the *real* sign—It is perhaps the *idea* of the sign? or the idea at the present moment?' (*PI*, §105). Names are necessary, he remarked, 'for an assertion that *this* thing possesses *that* property' (*NB*, p. 53). In the discussion of determinacy of sense and of my knowing exactly what I mean[2] he emphasizes that I can show exactly what I mean by 'lying on' and thus fix the special *Bedeutung* of the expression on *this occasion* of its use (*NB*, p. 68) by pointing with my finger at the complex or fact, e.g. the book (or watch) lying on the table, and saying emphatically 'I mean just THIS' (*NB*, p. 70). It is interesting and significant that the underlying theory of meaning appears static, not dynamic— tailored to deal with the language of a particular person (me) at an instantaneous point in time (now). It is, as it were, a momentary language-system. That the analysis of a proper, non-momentary language-system out of a conjunction of momentary ones might prove philosophically problematic clearly did not occur to Wittgenstein, and in all probability would have seemed a matter for psychological science rather than philosophy.

Towards the end of the last of the three extant notebooks (*NB*, p. 84) Wittgenstein enters the following three remarks:

It is true: Man *is* the microcosm
15.10.16   What cannot be imagined cannot even be talked about.
(Was man sich nicht denken kann, darüber kann man auch nicht reden)
Things acquire "significance" only through their relation to my will.
("Bedeutung" bekommen die Dinge erst durch ihr Verhältnis zu meinem Willen.)
For "Everything is what it is and not another thing".

This section is significant for our purposes, for it is echoed by an important cue in the final work. The corresponding passage in the *Tractatus* (5.61) reads, 'We cannot think (*denken*) what we cannot think; so what we cannot think we cannot *say* either.' It is of this remark in the *Tractatus* that Wittgenstein says that it

---

[1] See e.g. *NB*, pp. 3, 45, 50-1, 64-5.   [2] See above ch. I, p. 16.

provides the key to the problem of how much truth there is in solipsism. This is indeed closely related[1] to the thought that things acquire '*Bedeutung*' only in relation to my will. '*Bedeutung*' is in scare-quotes, I conjecture, because two distinct points are being linked. The world or life only acquires ethical meaning or sense or significance (Wittgenstein's term is always '*Sinn*' (e.g. *NB*, pp. 73, 74)) through its relation to my will, and equally the signs that are elements of signifying facts only acquire *Bedeutung* through their relation to my will. The will is thus central to ethics, and to semantics. But, as he remarks in the *Tractatus*, 6.423, the will, in so far as it is the bearer of value, cannot be spoken of, and as phenomenon is of interest only to psychology.

Further confirmation of this interpretation of Wittgenstein's general direction of thought at the time of writing the notebooks can perhaps be extracted from his later writings. In the *Blue Book* he wrote the following revealing, ironical passage:

It seems that there are *certain definite* mental processes bound up with the working of language, processes through which alone language can function. I mean the processes of understanding and meaning. The signs of our language seem dead without these mental processes; and it might seem that the only function of the signs is to induce such processes, and that these are the things we ought really to be interested in. Thus, if you are asked what is the relation between a name and the thing it names, you will be inclined to answer that the relation is a psychological one, and perhaps when you say this you think in particular of the mechanism of association.—We are tempted to think that the action of language consists of two parts; an inorganic part, the handling of signs, and an organic part which we may call understanding these signs, meaning them, interpreting them, thinking. These latter activities seem to take place in a queer medium, the mind; and the mechanism of the mind the nature of which, it seems, we don't quite understand, can bring about effects which no material mechanism could (*BB*, p. 3).

The view that the skeleton of language only takes on flesh and blood through occult mental mechanisms—that the logical syntax, which is *a priori* determined, is given a semantic dimension by means of a hypothetical psychological process which the natural science of psychology must investigate—is implicit in the *Notebooks*. Only in thought do signs become symbols, for it is only in thought that a method of projection is supplied. Thinking and language are the

---

[1] See below ch. III, p. 77.

same, Wittgenstein remarks (*NB*, p. 82); 'For thinking is a kind of language. For a thought too is, of course, a logical picture of the proposition, and therefore it just is a kind of proposition.' This view was held throughout the period of writing the *Tractatus*, for in his letter to Russell from Cassino in 1919 he emphasizes that a thought is a fact. It does not consist of words, but of psychical constituents which correspond to words and have the same sort of relation to reality as words. What these constituents are, he says, he does not know. What relation these constituents have to the fact they picture by means of their configuration is irrelevant. It is a matter for psychology to discover this (*NB*, pp. 129–30).

'Proposition, language, thought, world, stand in line one behind the other, each equivalent to each' (*PI*, §96), Wittgenstein said in commenting on the *Tractatus* system. It is now clear why Wittgenstein thought that his study of sign-language corresponds to the study of thought processes by philosophers writing on the philosophy of logic (*TLP*, 4.1121). These philosophers got entangled in unessential psychological investigations and there is an analogous risk in his method. The objects of both studies have the same essential structure. But mental mechanisms involved in thought processes and language use are no concern of philosophy. It was with this principle of purity in mind that Wittgenstein eradicated[1] so many traces of 'psychological' conjectures about language from the final version of the *Tractatus*. But some minor points show through.

Knowledge of the syntactical rules for the use of a sign is knowledge of how a sign signifies. *What* it signifies is, however, independent of syntax. All expressions can be analysed until one reaches propositions containing only simple expressions, i.e. names. A name is a primitive sign and therefore lexically indefinable. Its meaning must be explained if we are to understand it (*TLP*, 4.026). This is done by means of elucidations (*TLP*, 3.263). Elucidations are propositions containing primitive signs. Hence, Wittgenstein concludes with deliberate paradox, they can only be understood if the meaning of signs is already known. No other passage in the

[1] See Engelmann, *LLW*, pp. 99–100. In the original typescript of the *Tractatus*, 'Die Tatsachen begreifen wir in Bildern' was replaced by 'Wir machen uns Bilder der Tatsachen' (*TLP*, 2.1). Engelmann may be wrong about this particular example. I should guess that the alteration is in order to bring the formulation into line with Hertz's Introduction to *The Principles of Mechanics*: 'Wir machen uns innere Scheinbilder oder Symbole der äusseren Gegenstände.'

Tractatus explains this wilful obscurity. The received interpretation[1] is that an elucidation is a proposition, or an elementary proposition the use of which serves, in some way or other which psychology will perhaps explain, to generate an understanding of the proposition which is expressed by the arrangement of these signs. But if this is all Wittgenstein had in mind, it is unclear in what sense such elucidatory propositions are able to *explain* what the meanings of their constituent signs are. It is customary to assume that Wittgenstein eschewed the notion of ostensive definition or explanation,[2] and that the logical positivists' employment of the notion, though perhaps partly inspired by the *Tractatus*, was not legitimized by it. The arguments to demonstrate the absence of some kind of doctrine of ostensive explanation in the book are meagre. It is true that according to the *Tractatus*, all definitions are intra-linguistic. It is true that the term 'ostensive definition' (coined by Johnson)[3] is not used, and it is true that Wittgenstein does not say that 'This' is a name. Nevertheless I think that sufficient evidence can be amassed to make it very plausible to suppose that 3.263 is alluding to ostensive explanation, understood in a peculiar fashion yet to be explained.

The frequent reference in the pre-*Tractatus* writings to the psychological nature of the establishing of the meaning of a simple name has already been discussed. This, together with the recurrent emphasis upon indexical expressions, e.g. 'Names are necessary for an assertion that *this* thing possesses *that* property' (*NB*, p. 53), 'What seems to be given us *a priori* is the concept: *This*—Identical with the concept of the *object*' (*NB*, p. 61), 'I mean [by 'lying on'] just THIS' (*NB*, p. 70), strongly intimates that it is ostension that binds language to the world. Further support for this contention comes from the *Tractatus*, 2.1511: 'Das Bild ist *so* mit der Wirklichkeit verknupft; es reicht bis zu ihr.' The italicization of '*so*' is a natural way of indicating an ostensive gesture, whether physical or 'mental'. Two further pieces of evidence favour taking elucidations to be, in some sense, ostensive explanations. In the *Philosophische Bemerkungen*, §6, the following significant passage occurs

---

[1] e.g. M. Black, *A Companion to Wittgenstein's Tractatus*, pp. 114 f.

[2] e.g. S. Toulmin, 'From Logical Analysis to Conceptual History' in *The Legacy of Logical Positivism*, ed. P. Achinstein and S. F. Barker (Johns Hopkins, Baltimore, 1969), p. 39, or H. Ishiguro, 'Use and Reference of Names' in *Studies in the Philosophy of Wittgenstein*, ed. P. Winch (Routledge and Kegan Paul, London, 1969), pp. 29 ff.

[3] W. E. Johnson, *Logic* (C.U.P., Cambridge, 1921), Part I, ch. VI, §7.

in the course of a criticism of the idea that ostensive definition provides a means of 'extricating oneself from language'.

When I explain to someone the meaning of a word *A* by saying 'This is *A*' and pointing at something, this expression can be meant in two different ways. Either it is itself a proposition and then can only be understood if the meaning of *A* is already known, i.e. I have to leave it to fate whether the hearer will grasp the proposition as I meant it or not. Or the proposition is a definition.

It is important to note here that the second sentence, in the original, runs thus: 'Entweder ist er selber schon ein Satz und kann dann erst verstanden werden, wenn die Bedeutung von *A* bereits bekannt ist' (*PB*, p. 54). The sentence to which this corresponds in the *Tractatus* is in 3.263: 'Sie Können also nur verstanden werden, wenn die Bedeutung dieser Zeichen bereits bekannt sind.' Finally, in his conversations with Waismann in July 1932, Wittgenstein remarked 'Logical analysis and ostensive explanation [hinweisende Erklärung] were unclear to me in the *Tractatus*. I thought at the time that there is a "connection between language and reality" [Verbindung der Sprache mit der Wirklichkeit]' (*WWK*, pp. 209 f.).

It is therefore plausible to suggest that the explanatory elucidations of the *Tractatus*, 3.263 were indeed intended as the means in language of leading beyond language. For if we take an elucidation to be expressed by a sentence such as 'This is *A*' then it appears to satisfy the stipulated conditions. It serves as an explanation of the primitive signs it contains. It is not a definition, for definitions are intra-linguistic, and simple signs are of course, in this sense of definition, indefinable. It is a proposition which serves as an ostensive explanation, but which will not be understood unless the hearer grasps that '*A*' means *A*. Of course doubts arise because it is unclear in the *Tractatus* whether indexical expressions such as 'this' can logically be proper names. On the other hand ostensive explanation is the most obvious, although most misguided, mechanism with which to provide the substructure of the psychological processes involved in understanding a method of projection. Moreover, this interpretation would explain one of the more obscure features of Wittgenstein's later tirades concerning inadequate understanding of the nature of ostensive explanation. He frequently remarks[1] that ostensive explanations of simple concepts

---

[1] e.g. NFL, p. 320; *BB*, pp. 174–5; *PI*, p. 18 n., and §§49–51.

by means of utterances such as 'This is *A*' (his usual examples in his later writings are colour-concepts or sensation-concepts) involve a confusion of sample and description. Precisely this error would be present here if 'elucidation' is interpreted along these lines.[1]

Understanding a proposition requires knowledge of the syntactical rules which ensure its formal correspondence with what it depicts, and knowledge of the correlation between its constituent names and the objects they name. This will be the case either if I have endowed the name-signs with a *Bedeutung* by correlating them through a mental act with elements in my experience, or alternatively if they have been explained to me by means of elucidations so that the right correlation between the public name and its object is set up in my mind. Either way a mechanism of a psychological nature is generated to project lines of projection onto the world.

In the *Blue Book* Wittgenstein remarks that 'without a sense, or without the thought, a proposition would be an utterly dead and trivial thing' a mere sign. Its life, it seems, is spirit, something immaterial added to the bare sign. In the *Tractatus* he stresses that a propositional sign has to be applied and thought out (*gedachte Satzzeichen*) (*TLP*, 3.5). Applying and thinking a sign, it is plausible to assume, is to use the sign together with a method of projection. When a propositional sign is thus thought out, it is a thought, a proposition with a sense (*TLP*, 3.5–4). The method of projection is to think of the sense of the proposition (*TLP*, 3.11). This makes it appear as if clothing the propositional sign in its mental accoutrements which determine the projective relation of the proposition to the world (*TLP*, 3.12) generates a mental shadow of possible states of affairs. Certainly Wittgenstein was greatly concerned with such misconceived generation of ghostly intermediaries in his later criticisms. The following remark may perhaps be directed at the *Tractatus*:

The next step we are inclined to take is to think that as the object of our thought is not the fact it is a shadow of the fact. There are different names for this shadow, e.g. 'proposition', 'sense of a sentence' (*BB*, p. 32).

However illegitimate this spirit-raising is, it was of some importance to the *Tractatus* doctrines, and nowhere more so than in the explanation of knowledge. A proposition can be true or false only in

[1] See below ch. VI, §3.

virtue of being a 'picture', of having a sense which determines a 'logical space'. Its sense is independent of the facts, independent of its actual truth or falsity. It is the agreement or disagreement of its sense with reality that constitutes its truth or falsity (*TLP*, 2.222). Notoriously the origin of the primary metaphor to capture the doctrine of common structure lay in the notion of a *tableau vivant*[1] which is explicitly referred to in the *Tractatus* (*TLP*, 3.1431 and 4.0311). A *tableau vivant* is true if it agrees with reality. In order to tell whether a *tableau vivant*, a logical picture, a proposition is true we must compare it with reality (*TLP*, 2.223 and 4.05). Knowledge has its foundation in recognition of agreement and disagreement.

Wittgenstein, when writing the *Tractatus*, had no concern with epistemological issues of how we come to know what we know or what patterns of justification legitimize our cognitive claims. It may well be that his brief remarks on telling whether a proposition is true by comparing it with reality is nothing more than a way of emphasizing the difference between propositions with a sense, and senseless propositions. Empirical propositions say something about the world, and it is to the world that we must look to see if they say truly. But even if that was all he intended by his remarks, it is difficult to see how he could cope with serious epistemological issues arising over the verification of propositions. For non-elementary propositions can only be known to be true if the truth-values of their constituent elementary propositions are known. So there must be some way of coming to know that a given elementary proposition is true. There must be some kind of 'comparison' of proposition with reality.

It is clear that the paradigm from which the theory was derived involves a literal sense of 'compare' such as is involved in comparing a portrait with the person whom it portrays, or a three-dimensional model with what it is a model of. The notion of comparison is stretched, as is the notion of picture, when we speak of comparing a musical score with the music which it 'depicts'. Such comparisons have three important features. The items, if they are literally to be compared and not simply 'compared from memory', must be co-present, they must be perceptible, and there must be some criterion of fit. We can judge that a *tableau vivant* is a correct or 'true' model by perceiving what it models, perceiving the model,

[1] *NB*, p. 7.

and perceiving that the elements of the model 'agree' in the relevant respects with what it models. But this in turn requires that I be able to bring both model and what it models under the appropriate concepts in order to be able to say in what respect the model 'agrees' with reality. Agreement of picture and pictured, as a paradigm of cognition, presupposes what it is meant to explain. In order that I be able to judge that the model is accurate (neither models nor pictures are strictly speaking 'true'), I must already be able to judge how the facts which it models are. I can 'compare' a musical score with a tune only if I can both pick out the notes I hear and bring them under concepts, and if I am able to read and understand the score. Perception of agreement or disagreement, a relic of Cartesianism, cannot explain true judgement since it presupposes it.

If we try to apply this kind of paradigm to the analysis of a proposition in ordinary language and not in an ideal notation we shall rapidly encounter difficulties. Take Schlick's example[1] of verifying that the cathedral has two spires. The cathedral is a perceptual object, so is a propositional sign. A literal comparison of propositional sign with the cathedral, as Hempel pointed out,[2] may yield uninteresting propositions such as—'there are more words in the sentence than spires on the cathedral'. This will in no way verify the proposition expressed by the sentence. If we wish to verify the proposition, we must observe the cathedral, look at its spires, and judge that it has two. Our judgement, itself justifiable by reference to a perceptual proposition, could then be 'compared' with the proposition we were meant to verify. But here one proposition, i.e. the proposition recognized as true in our judgement, is being 'compared' with another proposition, rather than a fact with a proposition. And what need do we have of comparing the judgement with the proposition? Our judgement *is* that the cathedral has two spires. The idea that there are some propositions which stand in an 'immediate' relation to reality and are verified by acts of comparing requires that we be able to conceive of facts without bringing them under concepts, and that we be able to 'sense' the sense of a proposition.

[1] M. Schlick, 'Facts and Propositions', *Analysis*, vol. ii, no. 5, April 1935, p. 66.
[2] C. G. Hempel, 'Some Remarks on "Facts" and Propositions', *Analysis*, vol. ii, no. 6, June 1935, pp. 93-4.

If we try to apply the paradigm to an elementary proposition we are no better off. The atomic fact is a concatenation of objects. In order to be able to compare the facts with the sense of a proposition the objects must be perceptually distinguishable; simples must be 'given' in experience. Moreover we require principles of individuation for facts in order that we know which particular chunk of reality is to be compared with the proposition, since the subsistence of objects corresponding to the names is guaranteed and only their concatenation is at issue. But here again we are required to explain our judgement, e.g. that aRb by a comparison of an unconceptualized sensing of the fact aRb with the thought that aRb. Such a comparison is impossible. Picture may be compared with pictured for similarity, accuracy and insight. Sense may be 'compared' with sense for consistency, contradiction or inclusion. But a proposition cannot be compared with a fact. What makes a proposition true cannot be what justifies asserting it.

Even if one allows the paradigm a certain initial plausibility with respect to observations of atomic facts, conceiving perhaps of the sense of a proposition as a shadow of what it depicts, a mental *tableau vivant* of the state of affairs pictured, and thus iconically comparable, one runs into further insuperable difficulties. One undesirable consequence of the theory is that only I can know whether I know. Knowledge becomes a unique introspectible state of mind. But now further complications arise in any attempt to explain knowledge of knowledge, or, for that matter, of any other propositional attitudes. For me to know that p I must perceive the fact that p and compare it with the sense of the proposition. This seems to make it impossible to judge truly that p if 'p' depicts the fact that I perceive r. The difficulty here is not over the principle of extensionality but over the epistemological point that I cannot perceive my own perceptions. We have already noted that future tense propositions are unknowable because induction has only psychological, not logical, justification. Past tense propositions will presumably have to be analysable into truth-functional constituents which are to be compared directly with reality. In some sense, it seems, only the present is real. Propositions about other minds are going to force a reductive analysis, and it would appear that universal generalizations are unverifiable. It is true that when Wittgenstein wrote the *Tractatus* he was not a logical positivist, but it is clear that the positivists' epistemological theories were a natural outgrowth of his ideas in the *Tractatus*.

We may try to sum up the psychological and epistemological assumptions and implications of the *Tractatus* under three headings. The first may be called the Doctrine of the Linguistic Soul. This is the view that essential symbolic phenomena occur in the soul by means of special psychological processes. These constitute an essential, but non-logical contribution to language. What is perceptible, what we hear and see in spoken and written speech is only the appearance of language, the reality is in the soul. What is objectionable here is not the contention that the use of symbols is always accompanied by mental processes. Wittgenstein was right to think that what causal, psychological or neurological processes accompany linguistic acts is of no concern to philosophy. Indeed he adhered to this view throughout his life. What is objectionable is the claim that there *must* be such processes in order for a system of signs to constitute a language at all, and that it is of the essence of such processes that they occur in the mind. The underlying thought is that the psyche 'can do much more in this matter'[1] than bare signs. The miracle of language can, as it were, only occur in the medium of the mind. Mental acts can, in some miraculous way, do things that no overt physical acts of manipulating dead signs on paper or in speech could do. What such hypothetical mechanisms are, on the *Tractatus* view, is a matter for psychological research. It does not lie open to view. It is not a matter for description but for theory, not a matter for logic but for science.

Related to the doctrine of the linguistic soul was a tacit assumption concerning the nature of the psychological states of thinking, knowing, understanding and meaning. It was assumed that these essential accompaniments of meaningful use of language were conscious or unconscious mental states which are logically independent of any behavioural manifestation. Whether a person understands what he says or hears, whether a person means anything by what he says is known only to him. All we can observe are overt actions whose essential psychic background is accessible only to the speaker. The *Tractatus* theory of meaning can make no room for the notion of a criterial connection between inner states and outward manifestations. That another person under-

[1] Wittgenstein, *PG*, §59.

stands what I say must be an hypothesis that transcends all possible experience.

A second salient element in the *Tractatus* was the relegation of philosophical semantics to psychology. I have suggested above that the standard way of explaining the meaning of a simple sign for Wittgenstein at the time of the *Tractatus* was ostensive explanation. Even if that conjecture is wrong, it is clear that the ways in which the meaning of a name is explained or conveyed to a person has no bearing upon the meaning of the name, but only upon the psychological processes necessary to generate understanding. Whatever correlates a name with an object, be it mental act, some other mechanism or even the 'rule' embodied in ostensive definition, it must bring it about that the name is used in the future for the same object. How identity is established, however, is, from the *Tractatus* viewpoint, a matter of psychology. As Wittgenstein remarked in the *Investigations*:

> Perhaps a logician will think: The same is the same—how identity is established is a psychological question. (High is high—it is a matter of psychology that one sometimes *sees* sometimes *hears* it.) (*PI*, §377.)

On Wittgenstein's later view, of course, stipulating a criterion of identity for a name constitutes an essential element in explaining the meaning or sense of the name, for indeed the criterion of identity is part of the sense of the name. Philosophical semantics cannot be thus dismissed with the brief remark that a method of projection must, in some way—no matter what, no matter how— correlate a name with an object. But, of course, given the logical simplicity of the *Tractatus* names, given the fact that they have no sense but only *Bedeutung*, the criterion of identity could not be logically related to the name, but only psychologically.

The final salient feature of considerable epistemological import in the *Tractatus* is the correspondence theory of knowledge. This makes all knowledge rest on recognition of agreement or disagreement between elementary propositions and atomic states of affairs. This in turn would seem to require that I can 'step outside' language, and compare it with what it depicts.[1] Or, if there is any possibility of knowing the truth of propositions about my own psychological states, it requires that I be able to 'step outside'

---

[1] M. Black, *A Companion to Wittgenstein's Tractatus*, pp. 93–5.

myself, and compare my observed inner state with a proposition. We have seen that such a correspondence theory of knowledge makes it impossible for us to know most of the kinds of things which we take ourselves to know. If these are the implications of a theory of meaning for epistemology, we would be well advised to look again at the theory of meaning.

III

EMPIRICAL REALISM AND
TRANSCENDENTAL SOLIPSISM

1. *Introduction*

It has been argued thus far that the epistemology and psychology of the *Tractatus* is largely concealed in the form of tacit presuppositions. There is, however, one area of epistemology which comes explicitly, if enigmatically, to the surface. These are the oracular remarks in the 5.6's on solipsism and the self which belong, roughly speaking, to that part of epistemology commonly known as the metaphysics of experience. The fundamental contention of the section is that there is a sense in which solipsism is true, 'what the solipsist *means* is quite correct; only it cannot be *said*, but makes itself manifest [*es zeigt sich*]' (*TLP*, 5.62). In the sense in which solipsism is true, however, the expression of it coincides with pure realism (*TLP*, 5.64). The obscure argument supporting these claims rests upon two struts. Firstly, it rests upon considerations of the relationship of language, the world, and the self. Secondly, it rests upon the analysis of the relations between the concepts of the knowing self, the empirical self, and the metaphysical self. Our aim is to explore these relationships.

Firstly, it is necessary to discover whether Wittgenstein was, in any sense, a solipsist. If he was, then we must explain in what way he was a solipsist and how a strictly thought out solipsism coincides with realism. Secondly, the connections between any solipsistic views in the 5.6's and the rest of the *Tractatus* must be examined to see whether the putative solipsism follows from the semantic doctrines of the book. These are our immediate purposes. One of the primary means to attain them will consist of a detailed comparison of some of Wittgenstein's doctrines with those of Schopenhauer from whom they are derived.[1] This will not only throw light upon

---

[1] Schopenhauer's influence upon Wittgenstein is illuminatingly, if briefly, discussed in P. Gardiner, *Schopenhauer* (Penguin, Harmondsworth, 1963), pp. 275–82.

the *Tractatus* but will also serve a more long-term objective which is of greater significance from the point of view of the topics discussed in later parts of this book. This is to show that the detailed refutation of solipsism and hence of idealism, which Wittgenstein produced in the 1930s and incorporated, in low key, in the *Investigations*, is directed against views which he himself held as a young man. The Schopenhauerian influence upon Wittgenstein is most prominent in the *Notebooks 1914–16*, where his idealist and solipsist bent is most readily demonstrable. Thus even if the explanations I shall suggest of the *Tractatus*' solipsism are incorrect, the latter purpose will be satisfactorily fulfilled if the explanations of the Schopenhauerian sections of the *Notebooks* are correct.

2. *The Self of Solipsism*[1]

I shall begin the examination of the topic not at section 5.6 where the discussion begins, but at 5.631 where the analysis of the self commences. Once some light is thrown upon Wittgenstein's doctrines of the soul in the *Tractatus* some leeway can be made against the intractable remarks on solipsism.

Wittgenstein's first point is that there is no such thing as the thinking, representing subject (*denkende, vorstellende, Subjekt*). The argument supporting this contention is the standard Humean argument[2] of the non-encounterability of the self in experience. If I wrote a book entitled *The World as I found it* I should mention my body, but the subject, my self, would not be mentioned in the book for I do not find it in the world. Similar points are made in the *Notebooks*. On 4 August 1916 we find him querying 'Isn't the representing subject in the last resort mere superstition?' (*NB*, p. 80). A week later he remarks 'The I is not an object. I objectively confront every object. But not the I. So there really is a way in which there can and must be mention of the I in a *non-psychological sense* in philosophy' (*NB*, p. 80). Two months later he repeats the same points in a slightly altered terminology. The illusory non-existent subject is called the 'knowing subject' (*erkennendes Subjekt*). It is important to bear in mind that the Humean argument of non-encounterability was directed against the Cartesian conception of the self as a *res cogitans*.

[1] This section is a rewritten version of my paper 'Wittgenstein's Doctrines of the Soul in the *Tractatus*', published in *Kantstudien*, 62 (1971), 162–71.

[2] Hume, *A Treatise of Human Nature*, I.iv.6.

The similarity of Wittgenstein's argument to that of Hume goes beyond the repudiation of the thinking, knowing subject as an object of experience located within the world. Section 5.641 points out *en passant* that the subject-matter of psychology is the human soul. Wittgenstein's suggestions for the proper analysis of the human soul bear strong affinities to Hume's constructive analysis of the self. The clues to Wittgenstein's proposal lie in the earlier discussion of propositions about belief as potential counter-examples to the thesis of extensionality (*TLP*, 5.541). The superficial view of the meaning of propositions such as '*A* believes *p*', which Wittgenstein attributes to Russell and Moore, is that the proposition *p* stands in some relation to an object *A*, i.e. that a certain fact configured of objects is correlated with a self or judging mind. Moore[1] had claimed that judgement consists of a relation between a thinker and the constituent concepts of a proposition. Russell's theory of judgement had played an important role in his philosophical work in general, but it was against the views expressed in 'On the Nature of Truth and Falsehood'[2] in particular that Wittgenstein was arguing.[3] The essentials of the theory are expressed in the following paragraph:

judgment is not a dual relation of the mind to a single objective, but a multiple relation of the mind to the various other terms with which the judgment is concerned. Thus if I judge that *A* loves *B*, that is not a relation of me to "*A*'s love for *B*", but a relation between me and *A* and love and *B*. If it were a relation of me to "*A*'s love for *B*" it would be impossible unless there were such a thing as "*A*'s love for *B*", i.e. unless *A* loved *B* i.e. unless the judgment were true; but in fact false judgments are possible. When the judgment is taken as a relation between me and *A* and love and *B*, the mere fact that the judgment occurs does not involve any relation between its objects *A* and love and *B*; thus the possibility of false judgments is fully allowed for.[4]

Wittgenstein's central (but not only) objection was that Russell had purchased the possibility of false judgement at the price of allowing nonsensical judgements. Nothing in Russell's theory ensured the preservation of logical form between the elements of

---

[1] G. E. Moore, 'The Nature of Judgment,' *Mind*, viii (1899), 179.

[2] B. Russell, 'On the Nature of Truth and Falsehood,' in *Philosophical Essays* (Longmans, London, 1910), pp. 170 ff.

[3] The issue is discussed in detail in D. F. Pears, *Bertrand Russell and the British Tradition in Philosophy* (Fontana, London and Glasgow, 1967), chs. XII-XIII.

[4] Russell, ibid., p. 180.

the judgement. But a correct theory of judgement must make it impossible for one to judge that 'this table penholders the book' (*NB*, p. 96).[1] This objection, Russell said, paralysed him, leading to the recantation in 'The Philosophy of Logical Atomism',[2] although it was not until even later that Russell was prepared to dispense with the self as an element in the final analysis of '*A* judges that *p*'.

The appearance that '*A* judges that *p*' involves a relation between an object *A* and a fact is, in Wittgenstein's view, deceptive. The form of such apparently intentional propositions is '"*p*" says *p*', which does not correlate a fact with an object, but correlates two facts by correlating their objects. This analysis is subsequently said to show that the so-called 'soul' is composite and hence not really a soul. This gives a clue to the interpretation. Facts, it must be remembered, are always composites of objects, and only composite things can 'say' something, for the possibility of saying depends upon the existence of an articulated structure whose elements can be correlated with what is said by means of projection rules. '*A* believes *p*' involves the correlation of two facts in the same way as the proposition '*p*' says that *p* in virtue of the correlation of the elements of the proposition-constituting fact with the objects configured in the fact that *p* (if it is a fact). The obscure relation between the mind and the unco-ordinated terms of the judgement in Russell's theory is here replaced with the (hardly less obscure) method of projection correlating elements of thought or utterance with objects. It should now be clear why the analysis was thought to show the complexity of the 'soul'. The apparent unitary subject *A* which seemed related to a fact is a multiplicity of objects some of which are structured into a fact that pictures the fact or possible fact that *p*.

We have already mentioned Wittgenstein's remark in the *Notebooks* that thinking, even though non-verbal, is a kind of language (*NB*, p. 82). In a letter to Russell dated 19 August 1919 Wittgenstein writes as follows:

'. . . But a *Gedanke* is a *Tatsache*: what are its constituents and components, and what is their relation to those of the pictured *Tatsache*?' I don't

---

[1] Wittgenstein's first objection to Russell's theory of judgement is in his letter of June 1913 (*NB*, p. 121). It is developed in 'Notes on Logic' (*NB*, p. 96), but does not reach final formulation until the 'Notes Dictated to Moore' (*NB*, p. 118), where the subject is eliminated from the analysans.

[2] B. Russell, 'The Philosophy of Logical Atomism,' repr. in *Logic and Knowledge*, ed. R. C. Marsh (Allen and Unwin, London, 1956), p. 226.

know *what* the constituents of a thought are but I know *that* it must have
such constituents which correspond to the words of Language. Again
the kind of relation of the constituents of the thought and of the pictured
fact is irrelevant. It would be a matter of psychology to find out. . . . [A
Gedanke consists] of psychical constituents that have the same sort of
relation to reality as words. What those constituents are I don't know
(*NB*, pp. 129–30).

The person *A* is not an object, but a complex array of psychical
objects. '*A* believes *p*' is allegedly analysable into a series of elementary propositions such that the existence of the psychical
constituents which correspond to the constituents of the possible
fact that *p* is specified. These psychical constituents are related in
some contingent way to whatever other facts or configurations of
objects constitute the person *A*. *A*'s belief consists of these psychical
elements of a manifold being correlated with objects constituting
a fact, together perhaps with some kind of colouring. For, to be
sure, the differences between distinct propositional attitudes are
not captured by the suggested analysis. These differences are, in
Wittgenstein's view, a matter for psychology not logic.[1] From the
logical point of view the only important points to establish are that
'*A* believes *p*' is—appearance not withstanding—extensional and
that it has the same logical multiplicity as *p*. It thus emerges that
Wittgenstein was willing to adopt a neo-Humean analysis of the
empirical self. There is no empirical soul-substance thinking
thoughts, there are only thoughts. The self of psychology is a
manifold, a series of experiences, a bundle of perceptions in per-
petual flux. However, the claim in 5.5421 that this analysis of
propositions about belief shows that 'there is no such thing as the
soul—the subject, etc.—as it is conceived in the superficial psychology of the present day' is, when juxtaposed with 5.641, misleading.
For 5.641 refers to the human soul as the legitimate subject-matter
for empirical psychology. Yet 5.5421 says that 'a composite
soul would no longer be a soul', and the analysis does show the soul
to be composite. The claim should be interpreted thus: the soul
conceived of as a unitary simple subject does not exist. But conceived
of as a manifold, it is the legitimate subject-matter of psychology.

---

[1] See above ch. II, p. 38, for Russell's views on the matter. A remarkable illustration
of Russell's conception, which may well have been tacitly shared by Wittgenstein is to
be found in Russell's 'On Propositions', section III (repr. in *Logic and Knowledge*,
pp. 285–320), in which he discusses the problems of 'adapting language to psychology'
for the purpose of an analysis of belief.

All that empirical psychology needs to say about the psyche can be said. Philosophy has no concern with this. But nevertheless philosophy must discuss the I in a non-psychological sense. The reason given for this in the *Notebooks* is that the I is not an object I confront. In the *Tractatus* the reason given is that 'the world is my world'—a contention whose meaning will only become clear later on.

The philosophy which is concerned with the self is not the philosophy of analysis of the post-*Tractatus* era but the nonsensical philosophy of the *Tractatus* itself. The self with which philosophy is concerned is not the human being, nor the human body, nor the soul which is the concern of psychology. It is rather the metaphysical self (*TLP*, 5.641). We are introduced to this concept immediately after the thinking self has been dismissed as illusory. In 5.632 Wittgenstein writes 'The subject does not belong to the world: rather, it is a limit of the world.' The subject here referred to is not, of course, the thinking, representing subject, but the metaphysical subject. This is clear from the following section 5.633, and confirmed by the source of the remark in the *Notebooks* (*NB*, p. 79). The metaphysical subject is the bearer of good and evil. Why is it not part of the world? Wittgenstein merely hints at an argument by way of analogy. The metaphysical subject is related to the world as the eye is related to the visual field. Nothing in the visual field entitles one to infer that it is seen by an eye. The eye of the visual field (not of course the physical eye, but what Wittgenstein later called 'the geometrical eye' (*NFL*, pp. 297, 299)) is the source of the visual field, not a constituent of it.

The point is not that I always notice the position from which I see what I see, but that 'I also always find myself at a particular point of my visual space, so my visual space has as it were a shape' (*NB*, p. 86). Section 5.634 hints at the shreds of an argument. No part of our experience is *a priori*. Whatever we see could be otherwise. But, by implication, that our experience belongs to us and could not belong to another is *a priori*. It could not happen that we should need to employ some principle of differentiation to distinguish within the flow of experience those experiences that belong to us from those that belong to others. The owner of experience in general, the possessor of all the experience I can ever encounter, is the metaphysical subject.

How is this to be interpreted? The received interpretation is that Wittgenstein is in effect dismissing the notion of a metaphysical self. Black[1] claims that Wittgenstein entertains the idea of a transcendental ego and eventually rejects it. The Cartesian ego, he claims, is not part of experience but the limits of experience. But since this way of speaking is nonsense, there is no sense in talking of a metaphysical subject. Hence consistent solipsism leads to realism, and he who intends to be a solipsist can be brought to see that there is nothing he really intends to say. Considerable light can be thrown upon the issue by a brief comparison of Wittgenstein and Schopenhauer. Schopenhauer[2] accepted Kant's masterly refutation of the Cartesian doctrine of the soul as a unitary thinking substance. Kant's diagnosis was that Descartes confused the unity of apperception with the perception of a unitary subject. This rejection of the thinking, knowing, representing self as a constituent of the world did not, however, prevent Schopenhauer reifying the transcendental ego to constitute the foundation of his particular version of idealism. The transcendental self, he claims, is 'as an indivisible point' (*WWR*, ii.278). Though it is simple, like the *res cogitans*, it is not a substance (ibid.). The metaphysical subject and its object, i.e. the world as representation, 'limit each other immediately' (*WWR*, i.5). The transcendental ego is a presupposition of the existence of the world (ibid.): the knowing subject thus conceived lies outside space and time which are merely the forms of its sensible intuition. As the source of the forms and categories of experience, it is 'a presupposition of all experience' (*WWR*, ii.15). It is the 'supporter of the world, the universal condition of all that appears' (*WWR*, i.5). The self is 'the eye (which) sees everything except itself' (*WWR*, ii.491), the ego is the 'centre of all existence' (*WWR*, ii.486).

Wittgenstein's metaphors are identical with Schopenhauer's. There can be little doubt that the last of the three extant notebooks was written while Wittgenstein was re-reading Schopenhauer. To be sure, he is only mentioned once by name: 'It would be possible to say (à la Schopenhauer): It is not the world of Idea that is either good or evil; but the willing subject' (*NB*, p. 79). Immediately following this remark another Schopenhauerian thought is entered:

---

[1] M. Black, *A Companion to Wittgenstein's Tractatus*, pp. 308 f. See for similar views G. Pitcher, *The Philosophy of Wittgenstein*, pp. 144 ff.

[2] Schopenhauer, *The World as Will and Representation*, ii.198 f. trans. by E. F. J. Payne (Dover, New York, 1966); subsequent references in the text—abbreviated as *WWR*—will be to this two-volume translation.

'the subject is not part of the world but a presupposition of its existence'. Schopenhauer's transcendental subject limits the world as idea. Wittgenstein's metaphysical subject is a 'limit of the world'. Schopenhauer compared the I to the 'dark point in consciousness, just as on the retina the precise point of entry of the optic nerve is blind ... the eye sees everything except itself'. This metaphor first appears in Wittgenstein's 'Notes on Logic' of September 1913, without any overt reference to the self and without any Schopenhauerian overtones:

> The comparison of language and reality is like that of a retinal image and visual image: to the blind spot nothing in the visual image seems to correspond, and thereby the boundaries of the blind spot determine the visual image—just as true negations of atomic propositions determine reality (*NB*, p. 95).

As we shall see below, this original employment of the metaphor to illuminate the relation of language and reality, seen in the light of its subsequent use, is important. In the 1916 notebook the eye metaphor is used to illustrate the relation between subject and experience. On 11 June 1916 Wittgenstein wrote 'I am placed in it [the world] like my eye in its visual field' (*NB*, p. 73). The metaphor recurs repeatedly in subsequent remarks (e.g. on 4 August 1916, 12 August 1916, 20 October 1916,—*NB*, pp. 80, 86) in obvious idealist, Schopenhauerian contexts. It reappears, as we have seen, in the *Tractatus*, 5.633–5.634. Finally, even Schopenhauer's reference to the self as the centre of all existence reappears in the *Notebooks* 'If the will did not exist, neither would there be that centre of the world, which we call the I ...' (*NB*, p. 80).

These Schopenhauerian influences provide us with important evidence for interpreting Wittgenstein's remarks on the self. Firstly, the Humean argument of non-encounterability of a Cartesian self appears in both Kant and Schopenhauer as part of the refutation of the rationalist doctrine of the soul. Given the Schopenhauerian influence upon Wittgenstein it is plausible to take its reappearance in the *Tractatus*, 5.631 to be directed at the same target, as we have already conjectured. Secondly, the common view that the metaphysical self is identical with the illusory thinking self and hence is not countenanced by Wittgenstein can be conclusively rejected. In the first place, the non-encounterability argument is effective in demolishing a naïve[1] conception of a thinking soul-substance but is wholly ineffective in dismissing the conception of a metaphysical self, since the latter is not alleged to be part of the world, but its limit, not a constituent of the world, but a presupposition of its existence as idea. In the second place, the parallels with Schopenhauer run sufficiently deep to make it a plausible conjecture, in the absence of countervailing evidence, that Schopenhauer's distinction between the illusory Cartesian self and the transcendental self was adopted by Wittgenstein. In the third place, the enigmatic claims that the self is a presupposition of the existence of the world and that it is the centre of the world do not suggest its illusoriness. Finally, the existence of the metaphysical self as a non-empirical object is required by Wittgenstein's doctrines of the will and of good and evil.

Wittgenstein has little to say about ethics in the *Tractatus*. Ethics, in his view, is transcendental. It belongs to those things that cannot be put into words, the mystical. The will is the bearer of value, but as such, not being a phenomenon in the world, cannot be spoken of. Value does not lie in the world, for all that is within the world is contingent. Hence the good or bad exercise of the will cannot alter what is in the world but can alter only the limits of the world by making it, as it were, wax or wane as a whole. Since Wittgenstein did not believe that good and evil are illusory, he could hardly have believed that the ethical will which is the bearer of good and evil is illusory. The ethical will, like the metaphysical self, lies 'at the limits of the world' indeed it is identical with the metaphysical subject. This is evident from the *Notebooks*. The entry for 2 August 1916 reads as follows:

Good and evil only enter through the *subject*. And the subject is not part of the world, but a boundary of the world. . .

As the subject is not part of the world but a presupposition of its existence, so good and evil are predicates of the subject, not properties in the world (*NB*, p. 79).

Three days later he repeats that the thinking subject is illusory, but continues, 'the willing subject exists. If the will did not exist, neither would there be that centre of the world, which we call the I, and which is the bearer of ethics' (*NB*, p. 80).

---

[1] It is worth pointing out that Descartes' conception of a *res cogitans* is not as naïve as the non-encounterability argument implies.

The discussion thus far sets some preliminary order into the remarks about the self. Most importantly, it implies that we should take the notion of the metaphysical self seriously. For the moment our main interpretative key is the Schopenhauerian discussion of the *Notebooks*. It should be borne in mind that the concept of a metaphysical self is introduced in the sections 5.631–5.634 as comment upon 5.63 'I am my world. (The microcosm.)' This remark follows the claim in 5.621 that 'The world and life are one', which was a gloss upon the explanation of how much truth there is in solipsism. This suggests that the notion of the metaphysical self may provide the key to understanding Wittgenstein's remarks about solipsism, and that the transcendental idealist context from which the notion is derived may be pertinent to our investigation. Bearing these conclusions in mind one can now return to Wittgenstein's discussion of solipsism.

3. '*I am my World*'

The sense in which philosophy can (*TLP*, 5.641) and must (*NB*, p. 80) talk about the self is with reference to the metaphysical self. What brings the metaphysical self into philosophy is the fact that 'The world is my world' (*TLP*, 5.641). That the world is my world is, according to the *Tractatus*, what the solipsist means, but it cannot be said, it can only show itself. The only explanation of the obscure remark identifying my world and the world, in the *Tractatus*, is the identification of the world and life, and of the self and its world. Neither remarks are, as they stand, perspicuous.

In the *Tractatus* Wittgenstein tells us that the key to the problem how much truth there is in solipsism is to be found in the contention that 'We cannot think what we cannot think; so what we cannot think we cannot *say* either.' It is important to note that this apparent truism of the inexpressibility of the unthinkable appears in the *Notebooks* in a Schopenhauerian context. The entry for 12 October 1916 (*NB*, p. 84) claims that a stone, the body of a beast, the body of a man, and my body all stand on the same level. This contention can only be grasped if one realises that Wittgenstein is arguing against Schopenhauer's view that my body stands on a different level from other objects in as much as my direct knowledge of my intentional actions gives me an awareness of my body not merely as idea or representation but also as will. My awareness of my will constitutes, according to Schopenhauer, an awareness of noumenal reality, the underlying thing-in-itself, behind the phenomenal idea. The idea that one part of the world be closer to me than another as Schopenhauer suggests is, Wittgenstein later remarks, intolerable (*NB*, p. 88).[1] The discussion on 12 October 1916 in the notebook concludes with the remark 'It is true: Man *is* the microcosm: I am my world.' The next entry three days later is 'What one cannot think, thereof one can also not speak.' This makes it plausible to conjecture that this is the key to solipsism precisely because the solipsist's doctrines, though in some sense true, are inexpressible. Those doctrines are the identification of the world with life, of life with the self, of the self with its world, and thus of the world with the world of the self.

Further confirmation of this conjecture comes from the *Notebooks*. For there the key to how much truth there is in solipsism is not held to be the inexpressibility of the unthinkable, but the fact that 'There really is only one world soul, which I for preference call *my* soul and as which alone I conceive what I call the soul of others.' This key to the truth of solipsism (which is remarked upon in the second notebook on 23 May 1915 (*NB*, p. 49)) follows the claim that, '*The limits of my language* stand for the limits of my world.' This remark suggests a semantic rather than a metaphysical route to solipsism. We shall explore this possibility below. The entry following the 'key to solipsism' is that it is possible for me to write a book 'The world I found', which, like the key statement itself, intimates the epistemological and metaphysical route to solipsism which is the concern of the third notebook. This array of evidence gives support to the suggestion already mooted that the clue to Wittgenstein's solipsism lies in the notion of the metaphysical self as derived from Schopenhauer's transcendental idealism. It is to this that we shall now turn.

Section 5.621 of the *Tractatus*—'The world and life are one'—originally appeared in the third notebook on 11 June 1916 as one of the items Wittgenstein claims to know about God and the purpose of life:

> I know that this world exists.
> That I am placed in it like my eye in its visual field.
> That something about it is problematic, which we call its meaning.
> That this meaning does not lie in it but outside it.
> That life is the world (*NB*, pp. 72–3).

[1] See also *NB*, p. 82.

The thought gets its final formulation 'The World and Life are one' on 24 July 1916, together with the beginning of an explanation. Physiological life, Wittgenstein explains, is of course not 'life' in the sense in which the world and life are identical. Nor, for that matter is psychological life. Life, he repeats, is the world. On 1 August 1916 Wittgenstein remarks 'Only from the consciousness of the *uniqueness of my life* arises religion—science—and art' (*NB*, p. 79). On the following day he adds 'And this consciousness is life itself.' Thus the world is identified with life, life is identified with consciousness and consciousness in general with the solitary self of solipsism. It is not surprising that the subsequent comment in the notebook is 'Can there be any ethics if there is no living being but myself?', and even less surprising that he remarks 'I am conscious of the complete unclarity of all these sentences.'

Confirmation for the solipsistic interpretation of these passages can be found in Wittgenstein's 'Notes for Lectures on "Private Experience" and "Sense Data"', written between 1934 and 1936. These lecture notes were written long after Wittgenstein's repudiation of solipsism. Indeed much of the discussion in them is concerned with uncovering the deep errors of the solipsist. On p. 296 Wittgenstein's 'younger self', if one may so refer to the antagonist of the internal dialogue, objects to his critic:

But aren't you neglecting something—the experience or whatever you might call it—? Almost *the world* behind the mere words?

In the course of the lengthy reply of Wittgenstein's 'wiser self' to the solipsist's case he says:

It seems that I neglect life. But not life physiologically understood but life as consciousness. And consciousness not physiologically understood, or understood from the outside, but consciousness as the very essence of experience, the appearance of the world, the world (NFL, p. 297).

It is, I think, not coincidental that the mature Wittgenstein should phrase his solipsist objector's contentions in words highly reminiscent of his own notes of 1916.

The extent of Wittgenstein's preoccupation with solipsism is further revealed by a series of remarks on 2 September 1916. For the moment the significant ones are as follows:

What has history to do with me? Mine is the first and only world! I want to report how *I* found the world.

What others in the world have told me about the world is a very small and incidental part of my experience of the world.
I have to judge the world, to measure things (*NB*, p. 82).

The I that thus confronts the world is, he clarifies in the following entry, the metaphysical self, not the human being, nor the body, nor the empirical self, all of which belong to the world and are on one level. A month later we find Wittgenstein entering a remark couched in pure Schopenhauerian jargon—'As my idea is the world, in the same way my will is the world-will' (*NB*, p. 85).

The remark at 5.63 in the *Tractatus*—'I am my world. (The microcosm.)'—originates in the *Notebooks*' entry for 12 October 1916—'It is true: Man *is* the microcosm.' The identification of the individual consciousness with the microcosm, and the microcosm with the macrocosm, is a central Schopenhauerian thesis. The salient doctrine in Schopenhauer's metaphysics is that of the dual nature of the world as will and idea or representation (*Vorstellung*). As representation the world is relative to the transcendental knowing subject who imposes upon it its forms of representation, space and time, and the principle of sufficient reason. Independently of these forms of representation, the world is pure will, which is the noumenal reality with which we are acquainted through our knowledge of our own actions. Thus man himself mirrors the duality of the world:

Everyone finds himself to be this will, in which the inner nature of the world consists, and he also finds himself to be the knowing subject, whose representation is the whole world; and this world has existence only in reference to the knowing subject's consciousness as its necessary supporter. Thus everyone in this twofold regard is the whole world itself, the microcosm; he finds its two sides whole and complete within himself. And what he thus recognises as his own inner being also exhausts the inner being of the whole world, of the macrocosm (*WWR*, i.162).

Schopenhauer admitted that the limitation of one's insight into noumenal reality to one's knowledge of one's own literally embodied will may well incline one to solipsism, or, as he called it, 'theoretical egoism'. Although this theoretical egoism can never be refuted, nevertheless, he claimed, it is really no more than a sceptical sophism which need not be taken seriously. Despite this repudiation there are very many passages in Schopenhauer that make it difficult to grasp how solipsism can be avoided. Thus, for example:

the whole of nature outside the knowing subject, and so all remaining individuals, exist only in his representation; that he is conscious of them always only as his representation, and so merely indirectly, and as something dependent on his own inner being and existence ...

... every individual, completely vanishing and reduced to nothing in a boundless world, nevertheless makes himself the centre of the world ... (*WWR*, i.332).

Such passages[1] evidently struck a deeply responsive chord in Wittgenstein. Equally, one would not expect a purist such as Wittgenstein to rest content with Schopenhauer's glib dismissal of solipsism.

Schopenhauer's doctrines of man as microcosm bulk large in his discussions of death. 'An understanding of the indestructibility of our true nature', he claims, 'coincides with that of the identity of macrocosm and microcosm' (*WWR*, ii.486). Wittgenstein, like Schopenhauer, has interesting comments on death both in the *Tractatus* and in the *Notebooks 1914–16*. They are, as so much else, darkly mysterious. These remarks will be examined first, and subsequently compared with Schopenhauer's writings, in order to illuminate them and to further our investigation into Wittgenstein's attitude to solipsism.

The remarks on death in the *Tractatus* occur at 6.431–6.4312:

6.431   So too at death the world does not alter, but comes to an end.

6.4311 Death is not an event in life: we do not live to experience death. If we take eternity to mean not infinite temporal duration but timelessness, then eternal life belongs to those who live in the present.
Our life has no end in just the way in which our visual field has no limits.

6.4312 Not only is there no guarantee of the temporal immortality of the human soul, that is to say of its eternal survival after death; but, in any case, this assumption completely fails to accomplish the purpose for which it has always been intended. Or is some riddle solved by my surviving for ever? Is not this eternal life itself as much of a riddle as our present life? The solution of the riddle of life in space and time lies *outside* space and time.

(It is certainly not the solution of any problems of natural science that is required.)

---

[1] See also *WWR*, ii.443. There are many similar remarks throughout the book.

This apocalyptic passage follows the section which we have already examined in which Wittgenstein claims that the good or bad exercise of the will can only alter the limits of the world not its content; it makes the world as a whole wax and wane. So too at death the contents of the world do not change, one object among the many does not alter. Rather the world as a whole comes to an end. The solution to the riddle lies outside space and time. These are mysterious claims, and are usually dismissed as poetic licence or mystical metaphor. It is, however, worth probing deeper than that.

The claim that death is not an object or mode of experience is readily intelligible even to a hard-headed empiricist. But the suggestion that at death the world ends is puzzling. Considerable illumination is shed by Schopenhauer's doctrines about death and eternal life. Indeed it is only by reference to these that Wittgenstein's remarks can be taken to have a limited degree of intelligibility. We have already seen Schopenhauer's claim that the identity of the microcosm and the macrocosm are essential to understanding the indestructibility of our nature. Part of Schopenhauer's explanation of our indestructibility involves an essential reference to transcendental idealism. The riddles of life, of the existence of the world before our birth and of the continuance of the world after our death, can only be solved with the aid of Kant's doctrine of the transcendental ideality of time (*WWR*, ii.467). For Kant, as Schopenhauer explains, showed that time is the form of all phenomena, but noumena, things as they are in themselves, are 'outside' time. Not only is time the form of empirical appearances, but it is part of the structure of the human mind; time is in us, prior to experience; it lies, in Schopenhauer's words, 'preformed in our apprehension'. The knowing subject 'is not in time, for time is only the more direct form of all its representing' (*WWR*, ii.15). Death, Schopenhauer claims, is the cessation of a temporal phenomenon. But as soon as we abstract time, which is a feature of the constitution of our mind, the notion of an *end* becomes meaningless. If time is transcendentally ideal then from the metaphysical viewpoint it is senseless to speak of life ending with death, or of the world continuing after life has ceased. The conception of eternal life, as commonly understood, is vacuous: it has no experience as its foundation. It does, however, have a negative content, interpreted as a 'timeless existence' (*WWR*, ii.484). It is the present that is truly timeless. Empirically apprehended it is wholly transitory, but it 'manifests itself to the metaphysical glance that sees beyond the forms of empirical perception as that which alone endures, as the *nunc stans* of the scholastics' (*WWR*, i.279).

Wittgenstein's remarks about death are now recognizably derived from Schopenhauer. Most important of all is the fact that little sense can be made of his thinking these thoughts without presuming that he saw some deep truth in the Schopenhauerian metaphysical vision and the transcendental ideality of time. Nothing thus far said, however, suggests that it is possible to make sense of *what* he thought. This should not be surprising.

One final piece of evidence may serve to clinch the interpretation. That what Wittgenstein called 'the mystical' was of supreme importance to him is indubitable. But what he meant thereby is opaque. In the *Tractatus*, 6.45 he wrote:

To view the world *sub specie aeterni* is to view it as a whole—a limited whole.
Feeling the world as a limited whole—it is this that is mystical.

It would be rash to try to explain or justify a man's intensely serious and passionate views about the mystical. But one can, with much less audacity, try to trace the development of his thought. In the *Notebooks* on 7 October 1916, Wittgenstein entered one of his few comments on aesthetics:

The work of art is the object seen *sub specie aeternitatis*; and the good life is the world seen *sub specie aeternitatis*. This is the connection between art and ethics (*NB*, p. 83).

The alleged connection between aesthetics and ethics is baldly stated in the *Tractatus*, 6.421, in parentheses: 'Ethics and aesthetics are one and the same.' Neither can be spoken of; both are transcendental. There is, however, a further connecting-thread between what Wittgenstein jotted down on aesthetics in the *Notebooks* and the doctrines of the *Tractatus*. Immediately prior to the passage under consideration, at 6.44, he wrote 'It is not *how* things are in the world that is mystical, but *that* it exists.' This thought, in the *Notebooks*, is related to the aesthetic point of view, rather than to the mystical. On 20 October 1916, he remarked: 'Aesthetically, the miracle is that the world exists. That what exists does exist.' Indeed the term 'the mystical' (*das Mystische*) only appears once in the *Notebooks* (p. 51). But we now have two pieces of evidence to associate the

aesthetic viewpoint and the mystical one. Further important clues
can be discovered in Schopenhauer's aesthetic theory.

Only in the artistic vision, Schopenhauer claims, can one be
released from one's bondage to the will. Only aesthetic experience
can free the intellect from its servitude to desire and appetite, and
emancipate it from the restrictive categories of thought under which
we are constrained to view phenomenal experience. Through this
emancipation we can come to contemplate, in a will-less freedom,
the Platonic Forms or Ideas, and thus achieve a deep comprehension
of the inner nature of reality. The artistic temperament and the
philosophical one are closely connected in Schopenhauer's view:
'the high calling of these two has its root in the reflectiveness which
springs primarily from the distinctness with which they are conscious
of the world and of themselves' (*WWR*, ii.382). The phenomenology
of aesthetic contemplation is described in some detail by Schopenhauer, and it appears to involve a mysterious transformation of the
self. One must rid oneself of the normal categories of thought,
cease considering 'the where, the why and the whither of things'
and contemplate the 'what'. One must free oneself from the will,
from any guidance given by the categorial forms of the principle
of sufficient reason, and sink oneself in perceptual experience. One
must fill one's whole consciousness with the object of contemplation and lose one's individuality in so doing. One then continues to
exist only as pure subject, as unblemished mirror of the object;
one stands outside space and time; one becomes a '*pure* will-less,
painless, timeless subject of knowledge'. It was this, Schopenhauer
claims,

that was in Spinoza's mind when he wrote:
Mens aeterna est, quatenus res sub aeternitatis specie concipit (*WWR*,
i.179).[1]

The reappearance of this striking application of Spinoza's[2] third
form of knowledge to the aesthetic vision in Wittgenstein can hardly
be coincidental. What is, however, most significant is the correlation
of the aesthetic experience thus interpreted with the solipsistic

---

[1] Schopenhauer's reference is to Spinoza's *Ethics*: 'The mind is eternal in so far as it
conceives things under the form of eternity.' (Book V, Prop. XXXI Note.)

[2] This, incidentally, gives some historical justification for Moore's Spinozistic title
of the English translation of *Logisch—Philosophische Abhandlung*. See Ogden's letter
to Russell, of 5 November 1921, in Russell, *The Autobiography of Bertrand Russell 1914–
1944* (Allen and Unwin, London, 1968), ii.121.

viewpoint. Just as Schopenhauer associated the philosophic and artistic spirit with self-consciousness, so too Wittgenstein, as we have seen, located the springs of religion, science, and art in the consciousness of the uniqueness of one's life. This consciousness was said to be identical with life. The switch from the aesthetic point of view to the solipsistic one occurs in the course of the continuation of the same entry in the *Notebooks* for 7 October 1916 which we have examined. Having drawn the connection between ethics and aesthetics by reference to a vision of things *sub specie aeternitatis*, Wittgenstein goes on to suggest that the difference between the ordinary way of looking at things and the view *sub specie aeternitatis* is that the former sees things from the midst of them and the latter views them from outside with the whole world as their background. When seen thus, he says, 'the object is seen *together with* space and time instead of *in* space and time', it is seen 'together with the whole logical space'. On the following day, 8 October 1916, the metaphysical, solipsistic application of the fragmentary Schopenhauerian aesthetic doctrines previously discussed is even more striking:

If I have been contemplating the stove, and then am told: but now all you know is the stove, my result does indeed seem trivial. For this represents the matter as if I had studied the stove as one among the many things in the world. But if I was contemplating the stove *it* was my world, and everything else colourless by contrast with it . . .

For it is equally possible to take the bare present image as the worthless momentary picture in the whole temporal world, and as the true world among shadows (*NB*, p. 83).

With this the large part of the evidence supporting the claim that Wittgenstein adhered to some form of solipsism between 1915 and 1919 which is prominent in the *Notebooks* and *Tractatus* is concluded. The argument has traced a genetic route to this conclusion. Wittgenstein's solipsism was inspired by Schopenhauer's doctrines of transcendental idealism. These he adapted to his own peculiar form of 'theoretical egoism' which Schopenhauer had brushed aside. What the solipsist means, and is correct in thinking, is that the world and life are one, that man is the microcosm, that I am my world. These equations have nothing to do with traditional mysticism and are not descriptions of mystical experiences. Nor are they connected with ethical Stoicism, involving a refusal to identify oneself with part of the world.[1] They express a doctrine which I shall call Transcendental Solipsism. They involve a belief in the transcendental ideality of time[2] (and presumably space), a rather perverse interpretation of the Kantian doctrine of the unity of apperception together with the acceptance of Schopenhauer's reification of the unity of consciousness, and other related and undigested theories about ethics, the will, aesthetics and religion. The originality of the doctrines in Wittgenstein is negligible, their ancestry is of dubious legitimacy, and their validity more than a little questionable. Wittgenstein's originality in the matter lies in his attempt to dovetail these doctrines into the sophisticated theory of meaning with which most of the *Tractatus* is concerned. Unlike Kant and Schopenhauer, Wittgenstein thought that his transcendental idealist doctrines, though profoundly important, are literally inexpressible. Although what the solipsist means is correct, it cannot be said; it shows itself. It is to this aspect of the doctrine that we must now turn, and try to trace the faint semantic route to solipsism which converges with the idealist route.

4. '*The limits of language mean the limits of my world*'

We have seen in the previous chapter that the theory of meaning which Wittgenstein propounds in the *Tractatus* is strongly egocentric on the one hand, and concerned with a 'momentary' language on the other. Anything which I can understand as language must, as

---

[1] This is the interpretation given by B. F. McGuinness, 'The Mysticism of the *Tractatus*', *The Philosophical Review*, lxxv (1966), 305–28. McGuinness suggests that realization that the world is my world is an essential part of happiness, that 'I am my world' is a refusal to identify oneself with one part of the world rather than another, and equally with a refusal to identify oneself with the physiological or psychological peculiarities and life of a particular individual. He supports this interpretation primarily by reference to *NB*, p. 82 paragraph 7, *NB*, p. 82 paragraphs 8 and 9, and *NB*, p. 84 paragraph 2, and associates it with traditional mysticism. The last two passages are concerned with combatting Schopenhauer's doctrine of our knowledge of noumenal reality via our knowledge of our intentional actions. The first is concerned with identifying the philosophical self with the transcendental subject. These doctrines have nothing to do with the attribution of importance to parts of the world, or with the happiness of the Stoic attitude.

[2] There is, rather surprisingly, very little about the nature of time in the early writings. That some interpretation can be given to the doctrine that space and time are forms of intuition is intimated in Wittgenstein's 'Notes Dictated to Moore', of Apr. 1914 (*NB*, p. 117). That space and time are relative is suggested in letter No. 25 to Russell, Jan. 1914 (*NB*, p.129). The views already examined on death, the significance of life and the solution of its riddle, as well as the conception of the aesthetic or mystical vision, commit Wittgenstein to some form of the doctrine of the ideality of time.

it were, have a substance as well as an appearance. The appearance is the propositional sign, spoken or written. The substance is the mental accompaniment. The substance of language must be supplied by me. 'Things acquire "*Bedeutung*" only in relation to my will' is not only an ethical principle, but a semantic one 'Everything is what it is' Wittgenstein adds mysteriously, 'and not another thing.'[1] Propositional signs are merely 'inscriptions'; only in relation to *my will* do they constitute symbols. The metaphysical route to solipsism involves trying to grasp consciousness 'from the inside'. The semantic route tries to grasp language from the inside. From this point of view language is *my* language. In order for propositional signs to have sense I have to think the method of projection. What I cannot project is not language. Without the accompaniment of my consciousness language is nothing but a husk. '*I* have to judge the world, to measure things' (*NB*, p. 82), and the measure of the world is the proposition whose sense *I* think.

This thin semantic route to linguistic solipsism, i.e. the identification of language with my language, is paralleled by a semantic route to the metalinguistic soul as the analogue of the metaphysical self. For the self which thinks the method of projection cannot, so it might seem, be captured by the language it creates. The metalinguistic soul is, as it were, the blind spot upon the retinal image to which nothing in the visual image corresponds. The boundaries of the blind spot determine the visual image (*NB*, p. 95; see above p. 65). Without it the comparison of language and reality is impossible. A similar suggestion is to be found in a paper by Wiggins.[2] One might argue (fallaciously, Wiggins suggests) that a mind M which is aware of a fact $\langle x.y.z. \rangle$ and knows the truth of the proposition describing it, must in some way assume a structure which mirrors $\langle x.y.z. \rangle$ by means of an array of psychical elements $\langle t.u.v. \rangle$ with a matching multiplicity of elements analogously concatenated by a given method of projection. A mind M, so runs the argument Wiggins demolishes, could not within itself both represent a state-description S, and represent itself M within such a state-description, knowing both the state-description and its own state. For there, it seems, lies an infinite regress—just as a map of a city

---

[1] See also *PB*, §163 for a similar oracular pronouncement of Butler's dictum.

[2] D. Wiggins, 'Freedom, Knowledge, Belief and Causality,' in *Knowledge and Necessity*, Royal Institute of Philosophy Lectures, 3 (1968-9), ed. G. N. A. Vesey (Macmillan, 1970), pp. 150-1.

cannot include a depiction of the map of the city which stands in the High Street.

The evidence for this semantic route is slim to say the least. It is, however, the only way of linking the discussion of the philosophical self, and of death and immortality with the rest of the book. It is common to view the *Tractatus* as a complete and wholly integrated work, and hence to think that the so-called 'mystical' parts of the book are 'a culmination of the work reflecting back on everything that went before'.[1] This is, I think, at best misleading, at worst erroneous. It is true that these sections of the *Tractatus* are connected with what went before, although the connection is tenuous. It is also true that they were of great importance to Wittgenstein. It is, however, false that they follow from the earlier sections of the book, that one cannot accept the semantics without embracing solipsism, ethical non-cognitivism and aesthetic ineffabilism. The connections can be seen to be a little tighter by reference to two further considerations. The first concerns the doctrine of the manifestation of the inexpressible but correct solipsism.

Section 5.5561 expresses a point already mentioned—that empirical reality is limited by the totality of objects. Since objects neither come into being nor pass away, all possible worlds are determined by the totality of objects and their possible concatenations. This limit of empirical reality, this set of all possible worlds, makes itself manifest in the totality of elementary propositions. That there are, indeed must be, elementary propositions we know on *a priori* grounds (see above ch. II, p. 40). However, logic cannot produce an example of an elementary proposition; to do so would be to anticipate both experience and the application of logic. Logic is prior to every experience (*TLP*, 5.552). It requires only that something exists. It is, he remarks with a possible Schopenhauerian allusion,[2] prior to the question 'How?', not prior to the question 'What?'. How the substance of the world is arranged is an *a posteriori* matter. That the world has a substance is not. The limits of logic are the form of the world, and what belongs to its content is a matter for the application of logic, i.e. experience and its analysis.

It is on the background of these remarks that Wittgenstein moves to the exposition of his views on solipsism. The conclusions thus far

---

[1] E. Zemach, 'Wittgenstein's Philosophy of the Mystical,' in *Essays on Wittgenstein's Tractatus*, ed. I. M. Copi and R. W. Beard, p. 359.

[2] *WWR*, i.121.

arrived at can now be brought to bear upon the discussion. The 5.6's open with the equation of the limits of *my* language with the limits of my world. The following remark equates the limits of *the* world with the limits of logic. This is explained by reference to the foregoing claims that logic cannot anticipate the contents of the world. This explanation concludes with the thesis of the inexpressibility of the unthinkable which, section 5.62 claims, gives the key to the problem of how far solipsism is true. The answer is that what the solipsist means is correct only it cannot be said; it shows itself. What the solipsist means is that *the* world is *my* world. This inexpressible truth shows itself in the fact that 'the limits of *language* (of that language which alone I understand) mean the limits of *my* world'. ('die Grenzen der Sprache (der Sprache, die allein ich verstehe) die Grenzen meiner Welt bedeuten') (*TLP*, 5.62).[1]

That the limits of my language are identical with the limits of my world is readily intelligible by reference to the foregoing. The limits of language, and hence of my language, are formed by the non-contingent. Language can only express contingent truths, it can only say that things are thus and so if they could be otherwise. Only propositions with sense say anything. Tautologies and contradictions say nothing—they are senseless. They show the structure, and so the limits of the world. For tautologies and contradictions, being respectively true and false in all possible worlds, show the limit of empirical reality which is constituted by the totality of elementary propositions, which are in turn determined by the totality of objects. That the limits of logic are the limits of the world is equally obvious. Logic is limited to the non-contingent, to the necessarily true or necessarily false. It cannot anticipate experience. It cannot overstep its limits to tell us which of all possible worlds this is, just as experience—the world—cannot tell us what must be thus or otherwise. That the world is my world, that the world and life are one, that I am my world, are all expressions of the doctrines of transcendental solipsism already examined. These doctrines are inexpressible. For the fact that the world is my world is not a contingent truth that could be otherwise. The self whose representation the world is, is not one among others. That experience in general, the only experience that I encounter, is mine—is not

---

[1] The heated controversy over the correct translation of this passage has now been settled by reference to Wittgenstein's corrections to Ramsey's copy of the first edition of the *Tractatus*. 'Allein', it is now clear, refers to 'Sprache' and not to 'Ich'. See C. Lewy, 'A Note on the Text of the *Tractatus*', *Mind*, lxxvi (1967), 419.

something which could be otherwise. 'Whatever we can describe at all could be other than it is' (*TLP*, 5.634), hence this non-contingent ownership is indescribable. Moreover the solipsistic doctrines involve an essential reference to the metaphysical self. But the metaphysical self is neither an object that constitutes the reference of a name in fully analysed language nor is it a composite structure consisting of such objects. Hence 'the self of solipsism shrinks to a point without extension' about which nothing can meaningfully be said. But language mirrors the necessities which limit reality in its structure. That the world is my world manifests itself in the identity of the limits of language—which is my language—and the limits of the world—which is my world.

This leads us to the final solipsistic doctrine of the *Tractatus*. 'Solipsism, when its implications are followed out strictly, coincides with pure realism. The self of solipsism shrinks to a point without extension and there remains the reality coordinated with it' (*TLP*, 5.64). Wittgenstein's doctrines have of course followed out the implications of solipsism. How do they show that solipsism, paradoxically, coincides with pure realism? The analysis of propositions about other minds will not mention the metaphysical self, nor a Cartesian *res cogitans*. It is plausible to think that they will be analysed in some way or other in terms of names referring to elements of my experience.[1] Hence if epistemological realism is, roughly speaking, the commonsense view of the world expressed in propositions such as '*A* has toothache', 'the tree is shedding its leaves', then transcendental solipsism does not deny that such propositions are sometimes true. Nor indeed does it claim that 'I am the only person who exists' is true. What it claims is that the analysis of such propositions into elementary propositions is to be carried out in a certain way. The truth of solipsism will manifest itself in the fact that the analysis of 'I have toothache' will differ in important ways from the analysis of '*A* has toothache' (where *A* is not myself). The former will involve reference to the experience

---

[1] This is suggested by much of the material already analysed. Further support is to be found in Wittgenstein's 1929 paper 'Some Remarks on Logical Form'. An interesting debate on Wittgenstein's solipsism arose out of S. Stebbing's lecture 'Logical Positivism and Analysis', *Proceedings of the British Academy*, xix (1933), 53–88, and was pursued by R. B. Braithwaite, J. O. Wisdom, M. Cornforth, and S. Stebbing in *Analysis*, i (1933). Of course by that time Wittgenstein had changed his position radically, hence his irate letter to *Mind* in response to Braithwaite's paper in *University Studies, Cambridge 1933* (see *Mind*, xlii (1933), 415 f.).

of toothache. The latter will refer only to the behaviour which others manifest when they are said to have toothache. But even in the analysis of 'I have toothache' the metaphysical self, the self of solipsism, will not appear. It will be the constant form of all experience, represented in the ideal notation by the variable or variables taking names of unanalysable elements of experience or perhaps names of objects in general as values.

Thus everything the realist wishes to say can be said; and nothing the Wittgensteinian solipsist wishes to say can be spoken of. There will be no practical disagreement between them, nor will they quarrel over the truth-values of propositions of ordinary language. But the analysis of such propositions will manifest the transcendental truths that cannot be said. Wittgenstein's doctrine in the *Tractatus* is best described as Empirical Realism and Transcendental Solipsism.

5. *Later Years*

If we turn to Wittgenstein's writings from 1929 onwards we do, of course, find great changes. Certainly he 'cut out the transcendental twaddle' (*transcendentales Geschwätz*).[1] But there is much evidence in what he wrote that there remained interesting continuities through the change. Both differences and similarities will concern us in the following chapters. For the moment, there are two points which are worthy of attention. The first concerns mention of further *ex post facto* evidence for the transcendental solipsist interpretation which has thus far been propounded. The second is an ethical digression.

G. E. Moore, in his notes taken at Wittgenstein's lectures in 1930–3, relates that in the lectures of 1932–3, Wittgenstein said that he himself had often been tempted to say that all that is real and certain is the experience of the present moment. Anyone who is at all tempted to believe that idealism or solipsism are true, he continued, knows the temptation to say that the only reality is my present experience. Given our previous discussion it is now plausible to suppose that Wittgenstein himself was not only tempted, but succumbed. The thought that *this* moment alone has true reality is recognizably connected with the *Notebooks* contention that it is possible to conceive of the 'bare present image' as the 'true world

[1] The phrase is Wittgenstein's, though used in a different context in which it is unclear to what he is referring. It was written in a letter to Englemann in 1918. See *LLW*, pp. 10 f.

among the shadows'. It is also related to Schopenhauer's claim that 'the *present* alone is the form of all life' (*WWR*, i.278). It is therefore not coincidental that in his many later arguments against solipsism and idealism he should formulate his adversary's case in terms, metaphors, and similes highly reminiscent of his own youthful thoughts. We have already seen an element of this correlation in the 'Notes for Lectures'. It is not a solitary one. Wittgenstein repeatedly associated the phenomenology of the solipsistic frame of mind with staring (see e.g. *BB*, p. 66; NFL, p. 309; *PI*, §398). Similarly the Schopenhauerian reference to the self as 'the centre of the world', which Wittgenstein used to state his case in the *Notebooks*, reappears in the extensive criticism of the solipsist in the 'Notes for Lectures', p. 299. 'But I am in a favoured position', remarks Wittgenstein's adversary, 'I am the centre of the world.' As we shall see in the following chapters, many of his most famous discussions in his later work are directed against his earlier beliefs and some of their consequences which he only subsequently discerned.

I have suggested that the primary inspiration of the so-called 'mystical' sections of the *Tractatus* lies outside the book. To be sure, some aspects of the transcendental theses dovetail into the theory of meaning with the added advantage of emerging from this union as inexpressible. This does not, of course, imply any belittling of the significance of these doctrines for Wittgenstein. On the contrary, the fact that the two strands of thought could be interwoven thus may well have struck Wittgenstein as partial confirmation of each. For there is no doubt that when he compiled the *Tractatus*, it was the very fact that the philosophy of logic which he propounded drew the limits of language at the boundary of all that is 'higher'— ethics, aesthetics, and religion, as well as philosophy itself and the attendant doctrines of transcendental solipsism—which seemed the main achievement of the book. In a letter to Ludwig von Ficker written apparently in October 1919, Wittgenstein wrote:

The book's point is an ethical one. I once meant to include in the preface a sentence which is not in fact there now but which I will write out for you here, because it will perhaps be a key to the work for you. What I meant to write then, was this: My work consists of two parts: the one presented here plus all that I have *not* written. And it is precisely this second part that is the important one. My book draws limits to the sphere of the ethical from the inside as it were, and I am convinced that this is the ONLY *rigorous* way of drawing those limits. In short, I believe that where *many* others today are just *gassing*, I have managed in my book to put everything firmly into place by being silent about it ... I would recommend you to read the *preface* and the *conclusion*, because they contain the most direct expression of the point of the book.[1]

It is of course the preface and conclusion that emphasize the importance of setting limits to thought. Moreover the passages just prior to the concluding comment emphasize the inexpressibility of the 'higher'. Despite this avowal it must be remembered that the argument in support of the ineffability of ethics is tenuous to say the least. It hangs on nothing more than the non-contingency of the ethical, a point asserted rather than argued. But logically necessary truths are expressible by the senseless propositions of logic. Categorial necessities are reflected in the formation-rules of language, but cannot be expressed in language. Any attempt to express them involves the use of formal concepts and hence the violation of rules of logical syntax. But ethical pseudo-propositions are not tautologies or contradictions, and certainly it is not obvious that ethical predicates are formal concepts. If they were, then it would be clear why putative ethical propositions are pseudo-propositions. But equally, if they were, they would represent variables taking a range of objects of a given category as their values. Yet no clue is given us as to what these might be. In short, Wittgenstein's letter to von Ficker is either self-deluding, or disingenuous.

In 1929 Wittgenstein overthrew his earlier semantic theory and embarked upon the dual task of refuting the semantics of the *Tractatus* and revealing its erroneous presuppositions, and constructing a new theory of meaning with quite different implications. With the collapse of the logical independence of elementary propositions, the bulk of the doctrines of meaning in the *Tractatus* went down like a row of dominoes. With them went the peculiar form of solipsism and the implicit transcendentalism that accompanied and supported it. It is, however, of interest that, in 1929–30 at any rate, the ethical theories were retained. In the *Tractatus* the ethical views received slender support from the semantics and metaphysics. In the transitional period the same doctrines appear to be completely free-floating. The evidence for this is to be found in Waismann's notes of conversations with Wittgenstein, and in Wittgenstein's lecture

---

[1] Quoted in the Editor's Appendix to *LLW*, pp. 143–4.

on ethics[1] given at Cambridge within the period covered by Waismann's notes.

The identity of ethics and aesthetics is reaffirmed (p. 4); that ethics is transcendental is not restated in the same words. It is, Wittgenstein now says, supernatural. The doctrine that the world consists only of facts, and that value does not exist within the world, is quite explicitly stated. If an omniscient man were to write all he knew in a book, Wittgenstein suggests, that book would contain a complete description of the world. But it would contain no judgement about ethics. A corollary of this view is, as previously, radical non-naturalism. Nothing in a world-description would even imply an ethical judgement, for no statement of fact can ever be or imply a judgement of value (p. 6). The ineffability thesis of the *Tractatus* is likewise affirmed. Our words can only express facts, not the supernatural. If the essence of the ethical could be explained by means of a theory, then the ethical would be valueless (*WWK*, pp. 116 f.). The attempt to express ethical judgements cannot but yield literal nonsense. It is of their essence that they should do so. For the attempt to state the ethical is to try to 'go beyond the world' and hence beyond significant language. The thought or experience of ethical value, Wittgenstein stresses, can, paradoxically, be conveyed by similes, although even the similes are literal nonsense. Wittgenstein picks upon three experiences which enable him, he says, to fix his mind upon what he means by ethical or absolute value. The first is wonder and amazement at the existence of the world.[2] The second is the experience of feeling absolutely safe, and the last is the experience of guilt. The first is, of course, identical with what in the *Notebooks* he called 'the aesthetic miracle', and in the *Tractatus* 'the mystical'. The second phenomenon, of feeling absolutely safe, is probably related to the meditations in the *Notebooks* upon making oneself 'independent of the world' (*NB*, p. 73; 11 June 1916 etc.). The descriptions of the first two experiences (he does not dwell upon the third) are nonsensical because it does not make sense to wonder at the existence of the world for, he claims, it is unimaginable that it should not

---

[1] Published in *The Philosophical Review*, lxxiv (1965), 3–12; page references in the text are to this volume.

[2] This experience seems much the same as that described by Schopenhauer as the origin of philosophy in general—namely 'a wonder or astonishment about the world and our own existence',—a view derived ultimately from Plato (see *WWR*, ii.170 f.).

exist. One can wonder at so-and-so being the case only if so-and-so could not be the case. Similarly it is nonsense to speak of being 'safe whatever happens'. These are only more or less futile attempts to express the inexpressible. They are manifestations of the deep tendency of the human mind to run up against the limits of language:

... all those conclusions of ours which profess to lead us beyond the field of possible experience are deceptive and without foundation; it likewise teaches us this further lesson, that human reason has a natural tendency to transgress these limits, and that transcendental ideas are just as natural to it as the categories are to [the] understanding ...[1]

The Kantian idea echoes in Wittgenstein, but what in eighteenth-century Königsberg led to an *a priori* critical rationalist ethics, produced in the twentieth century a romantic existentialist ethics of the unspeakable.

[1] Kant, *Critique of Pure Reason*, A 642, B 670.

IV

DISINTEGRATION AND RECONSTRUCTION

1. *The Colour-Exclusion Problem*

The philosophy expounded in the *Tractatus* seemed to Wittgenstein to contain at least the blue-print for the solution or dissolution of all the problems of philosophy. Between the completion of the work in 1918 and 1929, Wittgenstein abandoned philosophical research. His task subsequent to his return to philosophy in 1929 involved the pursuit of two general aims. The critical and destructive task concerned the dismantling of most of the *Tractatus* philosophy, and a detailed probing into the deep faults inherent in the *Tractatus* picture of language. The positive and constructive objective was to rebuild an equally comprehensive set of answers to much the same array of philosophical problems set by the *Tractatus*. The conception of philosophy remained relatively constant;[1] the conception of language altered profoundly. This chapter is concerned primarily with the disintegration of the *Tractatus* philosophy, and secondarily with a brief outline of the inspiration for and general direction of the reconstruction in the 1930s.

With the qualifications implicit or explicit in the last two chapters, the *Tractatus* is a well-integrated philosophy. It is thus plausible to suppose that one could begin dismantling the structure from more than one point. For Wittgenstein himself, however, the weakness became exposed at what might appear a matter of detail. Just as a great scientific theory may *in special circumstances* be confirmed or falsified by one single crucial kind of observation (e.g. relativity theory and the precession of the perihelion of Mercury) so Wittgenstein's first philosophy collapsed over its inability to solve one problem—colour exclusion. Once the intractability of this problem became clear, the main struts of the whole system collapsed.

[1] See below ch. V.

Our first task is to examine the insolubility of colour incompatibility.

The initial set of relevant doctrines of the *Tractatus* which should be borne in mind in this context are the following. Elementary propositions are constituted by a well-formed arrangement of names which refer to eternal, elementary, non-composite objects. Objects concatenated in an atomic fact are described by an isomorphic elementary proposition whose logical independence of other elementary propositions mirrors the logical independence of atomic facts. The specific forms of elementary propositions are a matter to be discovered later. Truth is determined by laying each elementary proposition alongside reality like a measuring rod; the proposition is bipolar thus leaving reality room only for a yes or no answer. Non-elementary propositions are truth-functional compounds connected by topic-neutral logical connectives whose meaning is given by the truth-tables. All inferences result from the principle of tautology.

The colour-exclusion problem is introduced in the *Tractatus*, 6.3751 to exemplify the contention that all necessity is logical necessity. Appearances notwithstanding, the impossibility of the simultaneous presence of two colours at the same place is not a *synthetic a priori* truth, but a logical truth. The claim that '*A* is red and *A* is blue' is contradictory (where '*A*' refers to a point in the visual field at a given time) implies, in the *Tractatus* system, that the two conjuncts are not elementary propositions and that 'red' and 'blue' are not names of simples. For elementary propositions are logically independent, hence their conjunction cannot be contradictory. The programme implicit in 6.3751 is to show that when '*A* is red' is fully analysed into its constituents, its truth will entail that *A* is not blue. 'If statements of degree were analysable— as I used to think', Wittgenstein explained later,[1] 'we could explain this contradiction by saying that the colour *R* contains all degrees of *R* and none of *B* and that the colour *B* contains all degrees of *B* and none of *R*.'

Wittgenstein's first post-*Tractatus* piece of philosophical writing, 'Some Remarks on Logical Form', returned to this problem. In it he states clearly the inadequacy of the solution suggested in the *Tractatus*. For the suggested solution merely pushes the problem

---

[1] This remark is taken from RLF, pp. 168 f., and refers to the *Tractatus* programme.

back one stage. The original idea was to analyse degrees of a quality into a logical product of single statements of quantity together with a supplementary clause—'and nothing else'. While this will show that '*A* is red' entails '*A* is not blue', it re-introduces the same problem. For either the degrees of brightness into which '*A* is red' is analysable are identical, in which case the logical product will not yield anything other than the specific degree, just as the logical product '*A* is 20°C. & *A* is 20°C.' does not yield '*A* is 40°C.', or they are not identical. But if they are not identical then one degree again excludes the other—which was our original problem at the colour level. Two obvious solutions remain:[1] either one modifies the syntax and semantics of the *Tractatus*, or else one abandons the notion of simples as the correlates of logically proper names and as the foundations of language. In 'Remarks on Logical Form', Wittgenstein opts for the first alternative, thus adhering to the notion of analysis and the conception of an ideal notation. The option involves two independent moves. The first is the suggestion that numbers must enter into elementary propositions in order that the irreducible propositions attributing degrees of quality (whether colour, pitch, length, temperature or whatever) have the same logical multiplicity as the quality they attribute. The second and crucial move involves modifying the TF notation-rules for logical connectives. Mutual exclusion of statements of degree of a quality could not be shown to be a consequence of the logical product of logically independent constituents of the analysans, so it might seem plausible to try to show that the conjunction of incompatible determinates is, in a certain respect, ill-formed. Wittgenstein's suggestion amounts to claiming that logical connectives are not topic-neutral, and that the semantic rules for the connectives given in the *Tractatus* were incomplete. The meaning of the connectives will be accounted for by truth-tables specific to kinds of propositions. Thus for the conjunction of two propositions expressing possession of degrees of one quality, FF, TF and FT are well-formed, but TT must be ruled out as ill-formed; it is a nonsensical construction which must be excluded from a perfect notation. Thus '*A* is red' does not *contradict* '*A* is blue', for elementary propositions cannot contradict each other; they *exclude* each other (RLF, p. 168). What is the extra-linguistic status of this exclusion? That which

---

[1] See E. B. Allaire, '"Tractatus" 6.3751', repr. in *Essays on Wittgenstein's Tractatus*, ed. I. M. Copi and R. W. Beard, p. 192.

corresponds in reality to a function containing spatio-temporal co-ordinates and taking names of colours as its arguments, *leaves room* for only one entity, e.g. red, at a given place and time, not two, e.g. red and blue. There is no room for two, in the same sense, Wittgenstein stresses, in which we say that there is room for only one person in a chair (RLF, p. 169).[1] The mutual exclusion of incompatible determinates will be represented in a proper notation by the modification of the rules for the logical connectives in the context of connecting two such propositions. The syntactical rules of a perfect notation will prohibit combinations such as '*A* is red and *A* is blue' (RLF, p. 171). But the final formulation of such rules must await the ultimate *a posteriori* analysis of the phenomena in question.

Wittgenstein was, understandably, wholly dissatisfied with this attempted patching-up. The thought that the structure of elementary propositions is, in some sense, an *a posteriori* matter yet to be discovered by logical analysis was indeed part of the *Tractatus* vision, although Wittgenstein was subsequently to condemn it vehemently as dogmatism (*WWK*, p. 182). But the idea that the TF notation-rules giving the meaning of the logical connectives must await *a posteriori* researches makes nonsense of the *Tractatus* spirit. Moreover the strategy to maintain the logical independence of elementary propositions and thus to save the notions of analysis and ideal notation and hence the metaphysics of simple objects and atomic facts did not give an adequate comprehensive account of the relations between determinates of a determinable. The fragmentary account given in fact creates more problems than it solves.

In the *Tractatus* all necessity is boldly said to be logical necessity. Logical necessity is elegantly and simply accounted for in terms of truth or falsehood in all possible worlds, heavy reliance being placed upon the truth-table decision-procedure for the propositional calculus, and upon the alleged reducibility of quantified propositions. Logical necessity is shown by tautologies and contradictions, i.e. senseless but well-formed propositions. But beneath the bold façade serious difficulties lie concealed. Categorial relations and features, like logical truths, are shown and cannot be said. But

---

[1] Russell too had argued that colours, like matter, 'possess impenetrability, so that no two colours can be in the same place at the same time', although they are distinguished from matter in virtue of the same colour being capable of being in many places at once (*Principles of Mathematics*, §440, p. 467).

unlike logical truths, they are not only shown by the senseless propositions of logic, but also by well-formed propositions with sense whose constituents are values of the variables which express the relevant formal concept. Indeed, strictly speaking, they are not shown by propositions as such, as are logical truths, but by features of the symbolism by means of which propositions are expressed. The grammatical categories of the logical syntax of language show categorial features. Showing that objects are simple, that they exist concatenated in facts, that visual objects are coloured, etc. is made possible by the syntactical rules determining the use of a variable and so the range of possible values for it. The attempt to express what is thus shown is futile and results in literal nonsense, for it must illegitimately employ formal pseudo-concepts as if they were genuine ones. As already mentioned, the notion of a grammatical category that is at work here is an over-simple one. Two names belong to a given category if and only if they are inter-substitutable *salva significatione*, i.e. are different values of the same variable. But we are offered no criterion for preservation of sense through substitution.

From the metaphysical point of view, however, the most serious puzzle lies in the absence of any account of the nature of the constraints upon the combinatorial possibilities of objects which are reflected in the syntax of language. Putting the colour-exclusion problem aside for a moment, it is evident that, according to the *Tractatus*, combinatorial possibilities and impossibilities of simple objects are necessary (*TLP*, 2.0121). Each object is in a 'space of possible states of affairs', and every possible combination is necessarily possible. Visual objects are thus surrounded by a colour space, notes by a pitch space etc. A spatial object cannot be outside space, a note cannot have a colour and a smell cannot have a taste. The substance of the world determines a form (*TLP*, 2.0231), i.e. a range of combinatorial possibilities. But what is the nature of this determination? What necessity prevents a colour concatenating with a note? Why cannot a note be hard as well as high? The answer must of course be that these questions are nonsensical. They violate the bounds of language. The only necessary *truths* are logical truths. Logical necessities can be explicitly captured by language. They are shown by special, logical propositions. To be sure, these are senseless, but they are not nonsense. Their whole point, in so far as they have any, is to show logical necessities that limit the world.

Nevertheless it is misleading to say that all necessity is logical necessity. Categorial or metaphysical necessities can find no unique propositional counterpart whose prime function is to express them. There are no metaphysical truths describing the combinatorial constraints upon objects, because there can be no propositions describing these necessities to which truth values can be assigned. The only way in which these constraints can be captured in language is in formation-rules and variables. Nevertheless these inexpressible categorial necessities do have a certain reality, they are the logical properties of the universe (*NB*, p. 107). The super-physics of objects, as it were, determines the form of the world. The tacit admission of metaphysical necessities was brushed under the carpet due to the doctrine of formal concepts and formal properties. But this could not be done readily with the colour-incompatibility problem.

The *Tractatus* suggested that colour incompatibility was to be dealt with by showing the conjunction '*A* is red and *A* is blue' to be logically contradictory and thus senseless. The 'Remarks on Logical Form', realizing the failure of the *Tractatus* solution, tries to cope with the apparent necessity by dismissing it not as a senseless logical truth, but as nonsense and so on a par with other metaphysical necessities. But while the categorial nonsense of past philosophers always involved the use of formal concepts, the nonsense sentence '*A* is red and *A* is blue' involves no formal concept. Nor is the general categorial truth that two properties from one dimension exclude each other shown by features of the relevant grammatical categories. Moreover 'red' and 'blue' belong to the same grammatical category. Modifying the TF notation-rules for the logical connectives destroys the simple account of being of the same grammatical category, for 'if this is scarlet, then it is red' becomes nonsensical if we substitute 'blue' for 'red'. Finally, we can explain that '*A* is red' logically implies '*A* is not blue' if '*A* is red and *A* is blue' is logically contradictory. But if '*A* is red and *A* is blue' is nonsense one cannot show why *A*'s being red implies that it is not blue.

In the *Philosophische Bemerkungen*, ch. VIII, Wittgenstein returned to the subject in an unusually long piece of sustained argument. A proposition *p* attributing a degree of a quality to an object, e.g. '*A* is 5*R*', is either elementary or compound. If *p* is compound then it must be a conjunction of elementary propositions each attributing a 'quantity' of *R* to *A*, conjunctively implying *A*'s possession of $5R$. But this is not possible. For, as we have seen, the conjunction of five identical elementary propositions 'A is $1R$' will not imply p, but only 'A is $1R$'. On the other hand, if p is analysable into 'A is $1R$ & A is $2R$ & ... & A is $5R$', then firstly, what is meant by the co-presence of these degrees—how are they to be distinguished? Will we not be led to claim that white is present in every instance of black? Secondly, 'A is $5R$' is the very proposition we were called upon to analyse. Thirdly, these various degrees again mutually exclude each other, they cannot be co-present. Finally, the suggested analysis of p is in terms of a conjunction of five alleged constituent degrees of R. It also requires, as Wittgenstein suggested in 'Remarks on Logical Form', a supplementary clause specifying that this is all the R present. But this, Wittgenstein now says, is nonsense. For the logical 'and' is a sign of conjunction not of addition. One cannot analyse 'A is 3 metres long' into 'A is 2 metres long and A is also one metre long'. If it makes no sense to speak of adding further degrees of R by conjunction, it makes no sense to lay down that no further R can be added.

If p is an elementary proposition then the sum of constituent degrees of R is internal to p. One might conceive of them in terms of the *Tractatus* metaphysics as 'objects which in some way line up together like links in a chain' (*PB*, §80). Even so, 'A is $5R$' and 'A is $6R$' must be logically related to each other even though they are elementary. 'A is nR' may mean 'only n' or 'also n'. It makes no difference from the point of view of saving the independence doctrine. If it means 'only n' then any other degree or quantity is logically excluded. If it means 'also n' then every degree or quantity less than n is logically implied.

Wittgenstein's conclusions are accordingly that elementary propositions are not logically independent. There seem to be non-truth-functional logical relations (*PB*, §76). Elementary propositions belong to systems of propositions such that although two elementary propositions from different systems or dimensions are logically independent, two such propositions from one and the same dimension are not. Wittgenstein still thinks, as he did in 'Remarks on Logical Form', that the rules in the TF notation are incomplete and must be adapted for different combinations of kinds of elementary propositions, but we do not wait for 'the logical analysis of the phenomena themselves' to complete them. The proper simile for a proposition is not a picture or ruler with a mere yes or no answer; but a ruler with multiple gradations is analogous to a system of propositions which are syntactically interrelated. We compare the whole ruler, i.e. the whole propositional system, with reality, and determining one single point upon it—e.g. 'this is scarlet'—simultaneously determines all other points upon it, e.g. 'this is red, this is not green, not blue, not yellow, etc.' In the *Tractatus* conception of the elementary proposition there had been no determination of the value of a 'co-ordinate', i.e. a determinate of a determinable, but, Wittgenstein rightly says, his remark that a coloured body lies in a colour space (*TLP*, 2.0131) should have brought him to see this.

It may well be that some kind of reconstruction of the *Tractatus* philosophy is possible which will deal with elementary propositions by means of a theory of multiple dimensions to cope with the problem of the determinate-determinable relation. Stenius sketches the fragment of such a theory in his book on the *Tractatus*.[1] There is no doubt that Wittgenstein did not think that the *Tractatus* system was worth refurbishing. For a short time he seems to have thought that an account of a proposition in terms of a propositional system would be possible. In his discussions with Waismann he allotted to philosophy no more than the task of tabulating the linguistic rules which we unknowingly use (*WWK*, p. 184). The correct formulation of such a rule is never a surprise. If I know what 'long' means, then I know that if a man is 1.6 metres tall, he is not 2 metres tall. In the *Bemerkungen* Wittgenstein stresses that the task of philosophy is to describe the grammatical conventions which govern the determinate-determinable relations for different determinables. The chapter-headings of our philosophical grammar, he says (*PB*, §3), will be 'Colour', 'Tone', 'Number', but these terms, like the formal concepts of the *Tractatus*, will not appear in the text. That red is a colour is shown by the fact that 'red' is a value of the variable 'colour'. He appears to have thought both that one could reduce all empirical predicates to determinates, and that the *Tractatus* distinction between showing and saying could be preserved more or less intact. But he became increasingly convinced that the discovery of the insolubility of the colour-exclusion problem and the corresponding non-independence of elementary propositions necessitated the dismantling of most of the *Tractatus* doctrines. Indeed

[1] E. Stenius, *Wittgenstein's 'Tractatus'* (Blackwell, Oxford, 1960), ch. IV.

he did not adhere for long to the view that one should bend one's efforts to the elucidation of propositional systems conceived on the above pattern. By the time he wrote the *Philosophische Grammatik*, the notion had almost disappeared, and in the *Blue Book* it has quite sunk from sight. It was, of course, ultimately replaced by the notion of a language-game, involving very different kinds of considerations and conceptual relations from that of determinate-determinable. For the moment, however, our concern is not with the anticipation of Wittgenstein's later theory of meaning, but with the implications involved in the colour-exclusion problem.

2. *Dismantling*

The rejection of the *Tractatus* conception of elementary propositions as propositions which are not only compared directly with reality for their truth, but also logically independent of one another, had far reaching consequences. The irreducibility of propositions ascribing degrees of a quality to propositions containing mention of nothing but logically independent quantities, required that either the doctrine that all necessity is logical necessity be sacrificed, or that the concept of objects as the substance of the world, the constituents of logically independent atomic facts, and the meanings of logically proper names be discarded. Had Wittgenstein been willing to admit an expressible non-logical form of necessity, whether attributable to the world[1] or to the constitution of the mind, it might have been possible to retain much of the *Tractatus* structure. One might then accommodate the logical relations between propositions belonging to one and the same propositional system by attributing them to relations of exclusion and inclusion between the simples belonging to the same category.[2] That A is both R and B, where 'R' and 'B' name simples of the same category, is contradictory, and that A's being R implies A's not being B would then be attributable to necessary relations between simples of one and the same category. But to save the *Tractatus* at the price of admitting expressible metaphysical necessities or *synthetic a priori* truths into its austere structure would have been tantamount to stabbing it in the back in order to prevent its being stabbed in the front. That all

[1] Kneale argues, as I have above, that Wittgenstein unwittingly admitted a form of non-logical necessity in the *Tractatus*, although he locates it elsewhere; see W. and M. Kneale, *The Development of Logic*, p. 633.

[2] See for example the discussion by R. Chisholm, *Theory of Knowledge* (Prentice Hall, New Jersey, 1966), ch. 5.

necessary truths are logical truths is one of the few doctrines to which Wittgenstein remained committed throughout his life, although to be sure its retention after 1930 was only possible through a deep modification of his conception of logic and its proper domain. Why then did the notion of a *Tractatus* object have to be discarded, and what else is dragged in its wake?

The role of simple objects in the *Tractatus* is large and it is large because the role of logically proper names is large. From the point of view of metaphysics, the totality of objects determines the limits of all possible worlds. A possible world is constituted by a determinate concatenation of all objects. From the semantic point of view, objects secure the required determinacy of sense for language in virtue of being the *Bedeutungen* of names in the ideal notation. They also provide an essential element of the picture theory, their concatenation in a fact being isomorphic with the arrangement of names in a proposition, and the contingency of their concatenation constituting part of the explanation of the bipolarity of elementary propositions. If, in one's endeavour to account for degrees of qualities and their relations, one refuses to introduce non-logical necessity (other than the tacit necessities inexpressibly mirrored in formal concepts, i.e. the variables of the ideal notation) then not only must the assumption of independence of elementary propositions belonging to the same dimension be renounced, but the idea of an elementary proposition as a well-formed array of names which have a *Bedeutung* but no *Sinn* cannot be retained either. For this precludes an account of exclusion and inclusion of degrees of quality. In order to understand the name of a degree of a quality it no longer suffices to be acquainted with its bearer. Nor can an explanation of its syntax, i.e. its grammatical category, together with ostensive definition (i.e. a *Tractatus* elucidation (*TLP*, 3.263)), suffice to explain it. Syntax can no longer be a stencil of the world, nor can logically proper names pin it to the world. A proposition ascribing a degree of a quality cannot be understood unless one understands its position within a system of similar propositions. One must understand that instantiation of a degree of a quality excludes all other degrees of a quality. Accordingly, to know that A is nR requires one to know that A is not $1R \ldots (n-1)R$. The meaning of nR depends not on the misguided idea of a predetermined number of objects of the given category which the world happens to contain, but on the richness and logical multiplicity of the language laying down determinates of R. Every language is complete, although one may have a greater multiplicity and so lend itself to the expression of greater discrimination. A number-system '1, 2, 3, many' is not less complete than our number-system although it is relatively impoverished. Whether a man who has spent his life in a red room knows that it is red, Wittgenstein told Schlick (*WWK*, pp. 65 ff. and pp. 88 ff.), depends upon whether his language contains a vocabulary of colour in which 'red' and hence 'green', 'yellow', 'blue', etc. appear; there can be no gaps in a colour language, only greater or lesser potentialities for the expression of colour discrimination. If this is correct then ostensive definition, though by no means illegitimate, cannot play the central role which the *Tractatus* tacitly allocated to it. Its role will not be to provide a link between language and reality and so to sink the foundations of language. It will be *inter alia* to introduce samples into language.[1] Nor could the atomistic picture theory of the proposition survive the demise of the simple object and the logically independent elementary proposition.[2] The isomorphism inherent in the picture theory could not account for the colour-exclusion problem without allowing for explicit non-logical necessities, and the idea of comparing the picture of the individual elementary proposition with reality for agreement or disagreement is not readily adaptable to the idea of comparing a propositional system with reality. It is not easy to see, on the picture theory of the *Tractatus*, why Schlick's man in a red room should not make himself a picture of the fact that the room is red. Finally, the conception of a determinate, language-independent totality of possible worlds, as conceived in the *Tractatus*, must be jettisoned. For the notion of the limits of the world is, in the *Tractatus*, dependent upon the notion of the eternal substance of the world, i.e. the totality of simples. Dispensing with the concept of simples precludes giving this neat account of possible worlds, and the colour-exclusion issue, once it has led one to the Wittgensteinian answer to the problem of the man in the red room, strongly suggests an account of necessity that will be thoroughly language-relative.

As these central elements of the *Tractatus* structure collapsed, it is not surprising to find Wittgenstein turning a critical eye towards

[1] See below ch. VI, §3.

[2] In January 1930 Wittgenstein was still arguing that the essence of a proposition is that it is a picture (*WWK*, p. 90), but his concern by this point was only to argue that a proposition is essentially articulated, composed of function and argument. This Fregean point is detachable from the semantics and metaphysics of the atomistic picture theory.

the very conception of a *Tractatus* object. His general line of criticism in the appendix to the *Bemerkungen* (June 1931) and in the appendix to part 1 of the *Grammatik* is to claim, and demonstrate, that his use of 'object' had been confused, misleading, and the root cause of far reaching error. His related notions of complex and fact, he claimed, had been equally misguided. A complex is not identical with a fact. A complex can move from one place to another. Facts are not mobile. Although a complex such as a house is made up of parts such as bricks, a fact, e.g. that this circle is red, or that I am tired, is not a complex constructed out of parts, e.g. circularity and redness or a circle and redness, or I and tiredness. More generally, a fact is neither a complex constituted out of a concatenation of properties, nor a complex constituted out of a particular, or substance, and its attributes. The relations (e.g. spatial arrangements) of the parts of a complex, which are crucial to the description of the complex, are not themselves parts of the complex. The fact that the parts are thus arranged to form such a complex is not 'composed' out of anything. The part is smaller than the whole, but it is nonsense to think of a 'constituent of a fact' as smaller than the fact. We shall not follow Wittgenstein's early criticisms of the abuses of language in the *Tractatus* any further. By the time he wrote the *Philosophical Investigations* his criticisms of the notion of object and complex had been worked into a comprehensive and devastating censure of the notions as employed in the *Tractatus*, and an equally careful criticism of the correlative conception of names. Some features of these charges will be examined later.

Since the need for simple objects was, as Wittgenstein declared, to satisfy the requirement for determinacy of sense and security of reference, the rejection of that conception of a simple object found in the *Tractatus* necessitated either finding an alternative support for determinacy of sense, or dispensing with the requirement altogether. The requirement for determinacy of sense was nothing else than a total commitment to the Law of the Excluded Middle. This was a commitment to the fundamental 'laws of thought' of classical logic. To relinquish it requires a deep revolution of philosophy—and it was precisely this which Wittgenstein undertook. Already by the end of 1929 we find Wittgenstein expressing his disillusion with symbolic logic as a perfect notation which lays bare the substructure of all possible languages. The symbolism of formal logic 'is greatly handicapped in comparison with our actual language' he remarked to Waismann on 22 December 1929. Frege, Peano, and Russell developed their artificial languages with mathematics in mind; in the last resort, they thought, if this invented symbolism does not apply to reality, at least it will apply to mathematics (*WWK*, p. 46). This too, however, was an illusion, Wittgenstein stresses, for today we can see that the system does not even apply to mathematics. It is plausible to suppose that this complete disillusion with the ideal *Begriffsschrift* to which the *Tractatus* was committed, as well as the rejection of formal logic as the embodiment of the structure of all possible forms of representation, was brought about in part by Wittgenstein's encounter with Brouwer's ideas which we shall examine below.

Discarding the concept of simple objects and atomic facts, together with the parallel notions of logically proper names and elementary propositions, involved rejecting the notion of logical analysis as intimated by the *Tractatus* and described in the 'Remarks on Logical Form'. The point of the clarifications of logical analysis was to reveal the logical structure concealed by ordinary language, to show the illegitimacy of pseudo-propositions—particularly those of philosophers—to eliminate ambiguities and apparent vagueness, and prevent misunderstandings arising out of those and other grounds. But if ordinary language is all right as it is, and if ideal conceptual notations have no privileged status, however useful they may be for limited purposes (*WWK*, p. 46), if they are defective in relation to ordinary language, then the clarification of ordinary language, out of which confusion and misapprehension arise, cannot be by means of an analysis into an ideal notation. If the primary functions of philosophy are what the *Tractatus* alleged them to be, then we must find a different way to fulfil them.

3. *A New Inspiration*

Contrary to received opinion a theory, whether scientific or—in a different sense of 'theory'—philosophical, is not *normally* rejected merely because it is falsified.[1] Other things being equal, falsification and discovery of counter-examples and exceptions merely spur one on to greater ingenuity either in modifying the theory to accommodate the nuisance or in showing that the apparent counter-example can be explained away. If the worst comes to the worst it can be

---

[1] See T. S. Kuhn, *The Structure of Scientific Revolutions* (2nd ed., University of Chicago Press, Chicago, 1970), ch. VIII.

entered in the ledger as a debt to be repaid in the future, and then conveniently shelved. Those who thirst for knowledge will not discard their only cup just because it is cracked. A comprehensive theory is discarded only if there is an intimation of a better one to replace it.

Although Wittgenstein was not wholly bereft of philosophical contacts during his dormant period in the 1920s (e.g. Russell, Ramsey, Waismann, Feigl, Carnap, Schlick) his colleagues were doing little more than developing, or tinkering with the superstructure, of the type of philosophical system which Wittgenstein had sketched in the *Tractatus*. No doubt some of the development and tinkering was extremely important in the evolution of philosophy in general, and in its influence on Wittgenstein in particular. This is especially true of the verificationism of the members of the Vienna Circle with whom Wittgenstein came into contact. But whereas the verificationism of Carnap, Feigl, and Schlick, was quite self-consciously an application and development of the realist semantics of Frege, Russell, and Wittgenstein, the verificationism with which Wittgenstein briefly experimented from 1929–32 was a stepping-stone to a new kind of semantics. The inspiration for this must be found elsewhere. In 1928 a wholly novel and totally revolutionary approach to the problems of the critique of language which were Wittgenstein's main philosophical concern came to his attention. On 10 March 1928, L. E. J. Brouwer, the main proponent of the intuitionist philosophy of mathematics, came to Vienna to give a lecture entitled 'Mathematics, Science and Language'.[1] Wittgenstein attended this lecture together with Feigl and Waismann. Feigl reports that Wittgenstein came away from it in a state of great excitement and intellectual ferment. In his view, 'that evening marked the return of Wittgenstein to strong philosophical interests and activities'.[2] Until more biographical material comes to light it will be difficult to evaluate the extent of the immediate impact of Brouwer's lecture. What can be done is to outline Brouwer's ideas in order to show three things. Firstly, the fundamental spirit of Brouwer's approach is wholly revolutionary from the point of view of the type of critique in the *Tractatus*. Secondly, there are elements in Brouwer's general approach that would be likely to

[1] L. E. J. Brouwer, 'Mathematik, Wissenschaft und Sprache', *Monatshefte für Mathematik und Physik*, xxxvi (1929), 153–64.
[2] See G. Pitcher, *The Philosophy of Wittgenstein*, p. 8n., in which Feigl is quoted.

appeal to Wittgenstein, despite its being diametrically opposed to the system of classical logic of the *Tractatus*. Thirdly, there are many points of convergence between some of Brouwer's general views and Wittgenstein's later philosophy.

Unlike most of his other writings, Brouwer's lecture is not confined to the philosophy of mathematics. It is a thumb-nail sketch, couched in a dense obscure Germanic style, of a comprehensive intuitionistic philosophy aimed at exploring the nature and limits of thought. Mathematics, science, and language are the main functions of human activity by which order and intelligibility are imposed upon nature. The will to live manifests itself in three ways: (a) in 'mathematical reflection' (*die mathematische Betrachtung*); (b) in mathematical abstraction; (c) in the imposition of the will by means of sounds. The two fundamental modes of apprehension which the will imposes upon the world are time and causation. It is interesting from the point of view of Wittgensteinian thought that the categorial forms Brouwer specifies—temporality and the principle of sufficient reason—place him firmly in the Schopenhauerian tradition.[1] However, Brouwer stresses there is no extraneous justification for these 'phases of mathematical reflection' other than their usefulness (*Zweckmässigkeit*) in enabling us to master nature. There is no objective causal nexus, causation is merely our means of ordering phenomena, enabling us to distinguish subjective experience from the phenomenal world. The supposition of the hypothetical objective spatio-temporal and phenomenal world is the primary result of mankind's collective reflection. Mathematical abstraction involves abstracting from temporal succession and causal correlation to the bare notion of difference or 'two-oneness' from which the whole series of natural numbers, and ultimately all of pure mathematics can be constructed. It has no foundation in eternal verities, but is a construction which enables man to extend his dominion over nature by making possible theoretical science with its concomitant practical benefits. The essence of natural language lies in its being

---

[1] It is curious to note Brouwer's strange remarks upon the voluntary character of the imposition of the categories upon phenomenal experience whereby the latter is ordered and 'stabilized'. 'Everyone can satisfy himself', Brouwer wrote, 'that it is possible at will either to sink into a reverie, taking no stand in time and making no separation between self and the external world, or else to affect such a separation by one's own effort, and to evoke the condensation of individual objects in the apprehended world' (*op. cit.*, p. 154). Compare this with Schopenhauer's views on the ideality of time, and with Wittgenstein's comments on the reality of the bare present image (*NB*, p. 83).

a means of expression or transference of the will (*Willensübertragung*). Its origin in primitive society lies in gestures and cries. In a developed society, more complex systems of communication involving complex grammatical rules of organized language are necessary. Language is through and through a function of the social activity of man. Non-communicative uses of language (e.g. recording of memories in solitude) are parasitic upon its social uses.

Certainty and exactness, Brouwer claims, are not to be found in language or in mathematics. Misunderstandings in discourse and mistakes in recollection (e.g. of confusing one mathematical entity with another) can never in principle be altogether eliminated. The formalist endeavour to construct a meta-language in which certainty and clarity are completely ensured is futile. It is an illusion resting upon thoughtless faith in classical logic. The laws of classical logic are the specific forms of inference resulting from a language constructed by mathematical reflection upon finite groups. The application of these logical principles, the Excluded Middle, Non-Contradiction, Identity, etc., in ordinary language proved sound— normally, linguistically competent speakers agree in their use of these principles. But this agreement was not the result of the autonomous power of the principles but of two quite different factors: firstly, in the event of apparently false results in reasoning about the world, an explanation was given by re-formulating the facts in question or attributing the error to fallaciously construed natural laws, and not by modifying the principles of logic. Secondly, the phenomenal world happens to display sufficient constancy to allow the useful application of these principles to it. But this, by implication, is a mere contingency.

Classical thinkers (and formalists), Brouwer explains, are unaware of the exclusive character of the word as a means of expression or 'transference' of the will. Instead they took words to express concepts—abstract entities independent of causal law—and they took logical principles to be descriptions of the *a priori* connections of these concepts. Just as the application of logic to reality was never *allowed* to falsify logical principles, so too any apparent inconsistencies in logic itself was never *allowed* to throw doubt on the reliability of the logical principles, but was taken to necessitate modification of the axioms which led to inconsistencies. That logical principles had this status of apparent privilege on sufferance and by the grace of human will only became clear, and the errors of the formalists correspondingly highlighted, when mathematicians developed set theory. The principles of classical logic which had been abstracted from reflection upon sub-sets of a definite finite set, and then accorded independent *a priori* status, were unthinkingly and unjustifiably applied to the mathematics of infinite sets. But here contradictions arose that could not be swept under the carpet. The remedy to these deep-rooted confusions lies in a wholesale reconstruction of mathematics on intuitionist principles. Those parts of mathematics that can be justified thereby are sanctioned, those that are not must be relinquished. Logical principles which allow for preservation of significance in constructivist mathematical inference are retained, those which do not must be discarded. Brouwer did not, of course, pursue this daunting programme in his 1928 lecture in Vienna. He exemplified his approach by showing that not all the logical principles that hold good for mathematics of a definite finite set hold good for the mathematics of infinite sets. In particular the Law of the Excluded Middle must be rejected.

Brouwer's whole approach clashes with the main intellectualist tradition of European thought. His anti-rationalist voluntarism is a repudiation of the mainstream of mathematical and philosophical thinking. To someone like Wittgenstein who found in Schopenhauer both inspiration and insight,[1] there is a *prima facie* likelihood that Brouwer's emphasis on the primacy of the will would have an intrinsic appeal. The fundamental idea that neither language, nor mathematics, nor logic are anything but free creations of the human will imposing an order on reality may well have appeared a deeply liberating conception. The idea that mathematics and logic are not justified by anything, that they are not reflections of the *a priori* structure of reality but rather that the appearance of such an *a priori* structure is nothing but a shadow cast upon the world by our voluntarily created forms of representation or 'mathematical reflections' is a philosophical conjecture pregnant with possibilities of development.

Brouwer's outline of his attitude to language, logic, and mathematics conflicted with some of the most fundamental tenets of the *Tractatus* and the realist semantics which it had developed out of Frege. Two of the deepest *Tractatus* doctrines are assailed by the

---

[1] Wittgenstein's continued high regard for Schopenhauer is attested to by Carnap, 'Intellectual Autobiography', in *The Philosophy of Rudolf Carnap*, ed. P. Schilpp (Open Court, Illinois, 1963), p. 27.

contention that neither natural language nor an artificial language or meta-language can ensure certainty, perfect clarity and unambiguousness, and by the claim that purely hypothetical truth-values independent of constructive reasoning are senseless and hence that the Law of the Excluded Middle is not universally valid. Moreover, the demand for determinacy of sense—a corner-stone of Fregean as well as *Tractatus* theory—is implied to be futile. Equally threatened by this line of thought is another facet of the central core of the *Tractatus*, namely its realism and epistemological indifference. The fundamental doctrine that for every proposition there must be some state of affairs in reality independent of our cognition which makes it either true or false can no longer be adhered to with quite the customary élan.

Brouwer's schematic outline of his views not only challenged the key doctrines of the tradition of thought in which the *Tractatus* was firmly embedded, it pointed the way to a diametrically opposed theory not just of mathematics but of general critical philosophy. The forms of representation created, in Brouwer's jargon, by 'mathematical reflection' are without foundation either in the constitution of the mind or in an *a priori* structure of the world. They are not forced upon us but are created by us in our endeavour to master the world, and their only justification lies in their expediency. Language is through and through social, its essence lies in its constituting a means of expressing or transmitting the will. It is fundamentally a means of communication and its non-social exercise is parasitic. Logic and its subject matter are in no way privileged relative to the rest of language. The 'hardness of the logical must' as Wittgenstein calls it, is taken by Brouwer to be only so hard as we permit it. Logic and language alike are moulded by our needs and conditioned by the relatively high degree of constancy we find in the world.

Just how much of the potentialities of Brouwer's embryonic ideas occurred to Wittgenstein in 1928 is impossible to know without biographical evidence. That hearing the lecture stimulated him to return to philosophy is of some biographical interest and, given the content of the lecture, readily comprehensible. However, the writing in 1929 of 'Remarks on Logical Form', which is very much in the *Tractatus* vein, suggests that it took some time before the new ideas bore fruit. To be sure, the later semantics, founded on the idea of criteria as determinants of sense, did not spring fully fledged from

Wittgenstein's mind. Likewise the later epistemology, founded upon the idea of criteria as non-inductive evidence, developed only after other routes had been tried and rejected. Wittgenstein toyed with verificationism and flirted with phenomenalism before the new conceptions began emerging, around 1933, with a recognizable resemblance to their ultimate form. What is, however, of greater importance than either biographical speculation or genetic exegesis is the obvious deep affinity between Wittgenstein's later philosophy and Brouwer's outline of the constructivist *Weltanschauung*. The general convergence of ideas between Brouwer's sketch and Wittgenstein's later work, whether causally explicable or not, is crucially important from the point of view of interpreting Wittgenstein's notoriously controversial later philosophy of language. For it suggests that we should look at the transformation of Wittgenstein, the theorist of formal semantics, into Wittgenstein, the theorist of communication-intention,[1] as being merely one aspect of a deeper and more general transformation. The convergence and affinities suggest that we view Wittgenstein's later philosophy as a generalized intuitionist theory, and that we view his transformation as being from realism in semantics to constructivism. Such an interpretation of Wittgenstein has been pioneered by M. Dummett[2] in a series of papers, and substantially furthered and given preliminary systemization by G. P. Baker.[3] There are no more fruitful tasks in Wittgensteinian exegesis than the elaboration of this interpretation, and few more important undertakings in philosophical logic than the examination of the nature and implications of a constructivist semantics.

4. *The Positivist Interlude*

It has already been noted that the new philosophy did not emerge immediately. Not *all* the *Tractatus* views were repudiated and, moreover, not all the doctrines that were ultimately rejected were

[1] See P. F. Strawson, 'Meaning and Truth', *Inaugural Lecture* (Oxford, 1970), pp. 4–5.

[2] M. Dummett, 'Truth', in *Proceedings of the Aristotelian Society*, lix (1958–9), 141–62; 'Wittgenstein's Philosophy of Mathematics', *The Philosophical Review*, lxviii (1959), 324–48; 'The Philosophical Significance of Gödel's Theorem', *Ratio*, 5 (1963), 140–55; 'The Reality of the Past', *Proceedings of the Aristotelian Society*, lxix (1968–9), 239–58. It must be stressed however that Dummett's constructivism is different from Wittgenstein's.

[3] G. P. Baker, an unpublished D.Phil. thesis entitled 'The Logic of Vagueness', submitted at the University of Oxford, in 1970.

rejected in 1929–30. A thorough study of the transitional period would have to disentangle the old from the new, the threads of continuity from the decaying remnants of the *Tractatus* philosophy, and the beginnings of the new philosophy from the temporary improvisations of the transition. Here only those themes will be touched upon that are necessary to clarify the topics which are the central concern of this study. A brief examination of Wittgenstein's conception of meaning during his verificationist phase will illuminate his views upon solipsism in the same period,[1] and hence his later refutation of solipsism and idealism. It will also provide a partial explanation of the emergence of Wittgenstein's later conception of criteria as determinants of sense which is crucial to the understanding of his later philosophy in general and his metaphysics of experience in particular.

In later years Wittgenstein denied that he had ever adhered to the Principle of Verification.[2] Although it is true that even during the period of close contact with members of the Vienna Circle, Wittgenstein's views upon meaning differed from those of the logical positivists upon some quite crucial matters, the denial is disingenuous. Even a cursory examination of Waismann's conversation notes, Moore's lecture notes, and Wittgenstein's *Philosophische Bemerkungen* shows that between 1929 and 1932 Wittgenstein adopted an extreme verificationism.

Wittgenstein was, it seems, impressed by Weyl's remark[3] that the formalists conceive of the axioms of mathematics as analogous to rules of chess. To be sure one cannot apply chess, whereas it is a distinctive feature of mathematics that it is applied. One of the salient difficulties of the formalists is to give a convincing account of the possibility of applied mathematics. Nevertheless the analogy between mathematics and chess, or even more generally, between language and chess, is a fruitful one. For the 'essence' of chess is not to be found in the pieces of wood upon the chess board, nor in ideal, abstract objects which might be thought to be represented by them, but rather in the rules of chess which determine the meaning of the pieces (*WWK*, p. 134). One understands chess when one can move the pieces correctly; the game is a form of calculus, a

---

[1] See below ch. VII, pp. 191 ff.

[2] See 'Wittgenstein as Teacher', by D. A. T. Gasking and A. C. Jackson, repr. in *Ludwig Wittgenstein: The Man and his Philosophy*, ed. K. T. Fann (Dell Publishing Co., New York, 1967), p. 54.

[3] *WWK*, pp. 103 f., and note 54.

geometry. The analogy with language is a strong one, despite accompanying disanalogies. To ask 'what is a word?' is like asking 'what is a chess piece?' (*PB*, §18). Our grasp of chess is seen by the correctness of our manipulation of chess pieces in accordance with the rules of chess. Our grasp of a proposition (*Satz*) is seen in our application (*Anwendung*) of it (*WWK*, p. 167). Understanding is not a mental state or process, but the ability to use a proposition. Understanding is 'operating' with propositions, the point of a proposition is that we 'operate' with it. What makes a piece of wood a chess king are the rules which determine its possible movements. What makes strings of noises into language is their use or application, in the same sense in which it is the application of a stick with notches on it which makes it into a measuring rod, namely the way in which it is laid alongside reality (*PB*, §54). It is striking that Wittgenstein re-employs this *Tractatus* metaphor in exposition of his verificationism, for the way in which language is 'laid alongside reality' is the method of verification that constitutes the sense of propositions.

Moore relates that early in his lecture-course in 1930 Wittgenstein remarked that the sense of a proposition is the way in which it is verified (M, p. 266).[1] This positivist dictum is reiterated again and again in the conversations with Waismann.[2] In the *Philosophische Bemerkungen* Wittgenstein states his position quite clearly: 'How a proposition is verified is what it says. . . . Verification is not *a* mark of truth, but *the* sense of propositions. (Einstein: How a magnitude is measured is what it is.)' (*PB*, §166.) The point is frequently repeated and extended: 'The sense of a question is the method of answering it . . . Tell me *how* you look and I will tell you *what* you seek' (*PB*, §27), and again:

I want to say: a question always corresponds to a method of finding out. Or one could say: a question designates a method of seeking. . . . To understand the sense of a proposition means knowing how to produce the

---

[1] One must bear in mind that in his English lectures and notes Wittgenstein tends to use the term 'proposition' as indiscriminately as he used '*Satz*', a fact remarked upon by Moore (M, p. 263). In the following translations from the works of the intermediate period I have translated '*Satz*' by 'proposition' in order to keep the remarks from *PB* and *WWK* in line with Wittgenstein's own words from the 1930–3 lectures (see note 2 on page 8 above). When talking of his later criterial semantics, however, I shall take sentences as bearers of sense.

[2] e.g. *WWK*, pp. 47–8, 53, 79, 97–8, 159, etc.

decision whether it is true or false. . . . One cannot compare a picture with reality if one cannot lay it alongside as a measuring rod. One must be able to lay the proposition alongside reality (*PB*, §43).

One cannot believe that which one cannot conceive of as verified in some way (*PB*, §59), and there cannot be an error which is not in principle discoverable (*PB*, §75). A proposition that is not verifiable is one without sense (*PB*, §34). Identity of verification implies identity of sense, difference of verification implies difference of sense (e.g. *WWK*, pp. 53, 70), for there is only one verification for a genuine proposition (*WWK*, p. 159), and verification must be complete and conclusive (*WWK*, pp. 47 f., M, p. 261, *PB*, §228 (by implication)).

It is interesting that Wittgenstein continues to employ the metaphors of a picture and measuring rod to illuminate the nature of the genuine proposition. The metaphors can no longer bear the weighty load for which they were originally designed. For, as we have seen, the atomistic picture theory has not survived. The proposition is not conceived as composed of names with *Bedeutung* but no sense, its constituents are not correlated with simple subsistent objects, and therefore the strict mathematical isomorphism of the atomistic picture theory cannot hold. Similarly the measuring rod which is laid alongside reality is now, strictly speaking, representative of a 'system' of propositions, for the idea of *logically independent* propositions that are compared directly with reality has been rejected too. The metaphors now serve only to capture the remaining features of the original conception. The genuine proposition is essentially articulated (and hence too the thought that *p*, the expectation, wish or command that *p* (*PB*, §32)). It determines a place in a logic space, and is essentially bipolar. Finally, it is compared directly with reality for truth or falsity (*WWK*, pp. 73 ff.).

The combination of the strict verificationism, the repudiation of the eliminability of quantified propositions by reduction to logical sums and products and the above remaining *Tractatus* doctrines led to a distinction between propositions and hypotheses. Wittgenstein distinguished three kinds of proposition (M, p. 261) falling into two classes. Experiential propositions were composed of two sub-classes: genuine propositions and hypotheses. Apart from experiential propositions he distinguished mathematical propositions. Genuine propositions satisfy the above requirements of verificationism and pictoriality. Such propositions are verified by phenomena, or primary experience. Experiential propositions which are not thus directly and conclusively verifiable by reference to phenomenal experience are hypotheses. Propositions about 'objective particulars', about the past, about laws of nature, etc. are hypotheses. Hypotheses are not conclusively verifiable, and they are not true or false in the same sense in which genuine propositions are, they are probable. Hypotheses should be conceived of as forms of representation of reality, unifying genuine propositions. If genuine propositions can be conceived as points, hypotheses are the graphs which connect the points. The governing principle in forming hypotheses is inductive, namely always to form the simplest connecting graph compatible with experience. Hypotheses can thus be conceived as rules for constructing statements (*WWK*, p. 99), or for forming expectations (*PB*, §228). Two hypotheses are identical in sense if all possible experience which supports or confirms the one also supports or confirms the other (*PB*, §65, §225). Genuine propositions are thus 'slices' through hypotheses (*WWK*, p. 100; *PB*, §§227–8). Phenomena are different 'facets' unified by an hypothesis. A proposition which supports an hypothesis is a 'symptom' for the hypothesis (*WWK*, p. 159). The relationship is hypothetico-deductive, an hypothesis entails the truth of its symptoms, and a symptom confirms or makes probable a given hypothesis.

Thus far Wittgenstein's views were, in general,[1] in harmony with those of his positivist Viennese colleagues. When it came to the interpretation of mathematical propositions, however, matters were very different. Unlike his associates, Wittgenstein drew the inspiration for his verificationism from the same source as the insights of his new philosophy of mathematics. The principles which he applied to the analysis of mathematical propositions were akin to the principles which he applied to the two groups of experiential propositions. The meaning of a proposition is in general to be identified with the conditions which legitimate its use. Just as the verification of a genuine proposition is not merely a mark of the truth, a route to something beyond itself, but the veritable sense of the proposition, so too, by parity of reasoning, the proof of a mathematical proposition is not a vehicle to arrive at some further independent matter, but is the thing itself (*WWK*, p. 109). A mathematical proposition says what its proof proves, and no more (*PB*, §154). The meaning of a mathe-

---

[1] There were of course considerable differences in detail, e.g. over the role of ostensive definition, the connection between language and reality, etc.

matical equation must issue from its proof, the meaning of the proposition is what the proof proves (*PB*, §122n.).[1] This constructivist approach to the problems of the meaning of mathematical propositions renders Wittgenstein's verificationism a much more general theory of meaning than that of the logical positivists. The contrast is most striking in the comparison of Hahn's views of the status of mathematics with Wittgenstein's. Hahn, writing in 1933, accepts the logicist programme of the reduction of arithmetic to logic as being in principle indisputably correct. Mathematical propositions are, he claims, tautologies. To Poincaré's objections that mathematics must contain some unique *a priori* principle, Hahn retorts by saying that this overlooks our intellectual frailty,

An omniscient being, indeed, would at once know everything that is implicitly contained in the assertion of a few propositions. It would know immediately that on the basis of the conventions concerning the use of numerals and the multiplication sign, '24 × 31' is synonymous with '744'. An omniscient being has no need for logic and mathematics. We ourselves, however, first have to make ourselves conscious of this by successive tautological transformations, and hence it may prove quite surprising to us that in asserting a few propositions we have implicitly also asserted a proposition which seemingly is entirely different from them . . .[2]

This logicist stance which takes mathematical truths as existing independently of our cognition or possible cognition, and independently of our ability to construct a proof stands in dramatic contrast with Wittgenstein's posture:

It would have been a good question for the scholastics: 'Can God know all the places of π?' The answer in all such cases is: The question is senseless (*PB*, §128).

Although highly schematic, this brief survey is, I think, a fair representation of Wittgenstein's point of departure at the beginning of the 1930s. Thenceforth his views undergo rapid change and development. From Moore's lecture notes it would seem that the decisive discovery with respect to the abandonment of logical positivism concerned the status of the two kinds of experiential propositions which he had earlier distinguished. So-called 'genuine propositions' constituted the kingpin of Wittgenstein's verificationism, being conclusively verifiable by collation with reality. However,

[1] It is important to note that Wittgenstein's new views on the nature of mathematics, just as his verificationist theories, undergo profound change later on.

[2] H. Hahn, 'Logic, Mathematics and Knowledge of Nature', in *Logical Positivism*, ed. A. J. Ayer (Allen and Unwin, London, 1959), p. 159.

in the academic year of 1932–3, it occurred to Wittgenstein that the idea of comparing a proposition such as 'I see red' with the naked unconceptualized experience that verifies it is absurd. 'Genuine propositions' have no verification, it makes no sense to ask 'How do you know that you have toothache?' (M, p. 266). There is no *way* of knowing, and no *method* of verifying. The problem looms large in 'Notes for Lectures on "Private Experience" and "Sense Data"'. 'If I say what it is I see,' Wittgenstein queries, 'how do I compare what I say with what I see in order to know whether I say the truth?' (NFL, p. 280). Is there always a collating? The issue is debated at length, and Wittgenstein concludes that with respect to the kind of sentence in question 'Wir haben hier keinen Vergleich des Satzes mit der Wirklichkeit! (Kollationieren)' (NFL, p. 294). This difficult and controversial issue lies at the root of Wittgenstein's notorious non-cognitive doctrine of avowals. It will be examined in detail in chapter IX of this study. The change in his conception of 'genuine propositions' brought with it a corresponding change in his conception of the second group of experiential propositions which he had called 'hypotheses'. Not everything that confirms a so-called 'hypothesis' is part of its meaning. A newspaper report of the result of the boat-race confirms the fact that so-and-so won, but it is not part of the meaning of 'so-and-so won the boat-race' that a given report occurs in *The Times*. Verification, the ground for asserting a proposition, contributes to its meaning only insofar as the verifying proposition is grammatically, i.e. not inductively but *a priori*, related to the verified proposition. Inductive evidence is something we discover not something we enact. Non-inductive evidence on the other hand is fixed by us. While it does not entail that for which it is good evidence, nevertheless the fact that it is good evidence is an *a priori* matter.

During his positivist phase the sense of 'genuine propositions' is determined by verification and the sense of hypotheses by their symptoms. By the time Wittgenstein wrote the *Blue Book*[1] his views

---

[1] In the *Blue Book*'s discussion of criteria (e.g. pp. 51 ff.) Wittgenstein continues to use the term 'proposition' as previously. When quoting him I shall abide by his usage. In quotations from his later, translated works I shall abide by his translators' version of '*Satz*'. But when paraphrasing his remarks and discussing his criterial semantics I shall ascribe sense to sentences and so speak of criteria as determining the sense of sentences. When discussing his views in the *Tractatus* and in his transitional phase and comparing them with his later conception of language I shall conform to the previous convention (see note 2, p. 8 and note 1, p. 106 above) for the early and intermediate works.

had changed considerably. The idea of the use of a sentence bulks even larger than before, and the sense of a sentence is held to be determined by those conditions which non-inductively justify the use or application of the sentence. These conditions are the grounds for asserting a sentence; they are conventionally fixed as such. The grounds for a sentence are part of what Wittgenstein calls its 'grammar'. The non-inductive evidence for an assertion is called 'a criterion', and the sense of the sentence asserted is determined by its criteria. As in the case of inductive justification, the truth of the non-inductive evidence is compatible with the falsity of the sentence the assertion of which it justifies. Unlike inductive justification criterial relations are fixed by grammatical convention, not discovered by empirical research. The concept of a criterion and of the criterial nexus is obscure, complex and controversial. Wittgenstein's comments upon criteria and his use of the term are opaque and apparently inconsistent. Yet the notion lies at the heart of his later philosophy and plays a crucial role in his refutation of solipsism and idealism and in his own constructive account of the structure of our thought concerning the world and our experience of it. In the following chapters, in particular chapters VII–IX the concept will be encountered frequently. I shall, however, postpone a detailed examination of Wittgenstein's views upon the criterial nexus until the final chapter, preferring to show the use to which the concept is put and the results which its application yields in the field of critical metaphysics of experience. Then, and only then, will a preliminary attempt be made to provide an exegesis of Wittgenstein's concept of a criterion, to elaborate its general implications for epistemology, and to indicate the lines along which further advance may be made in resolving the great problems surrounding this difficult logical tool.

V

WITTGENSTEIN'S LATER CONCEPTION OF PHILOSOPHY

1. *A Cure for the Sickness of the Understanding*

The two conceptions of philosophy in the *Tractatus* bear, over quite a wide range of issues, considerable affinities to Wittgenstein's later conception of philosophy which evolved from 1929 onwards and found its final and polished expression in the *Philosophical Investigations*. There are also, however, deep differences which lie concealed in Wittgenstein's semi-ironical use of similar slogans in both works. His oracular epigrammatical style lends itself to ambiguity. His liking for such masters of irony, paradox, and pun, as Lichtenberg, Kierkegaard, Kraus, not to mention Frege, should be a warning to the superficial reader. His repetition of *Tractatus* slogans frequently constitutes the re-employment of old bottles to hold new wine. It is more misleading than revealing to claim that he frequently only later came to see the truth in earlier remarks. The author of the *Tractatus* had, in the opinion of the author of the *Investigations*, succumbed to most kinds of deep philosophical illusion. On the flyleaf of Schlick's copy of the *Tractatus*, Wittgenstein is reported to have written: 'Jeder dieser Sätze ist der Ausdruck einer Krankheit.' (Each of these sentences is the expression of a disease.)[1] The general conception of philosophy was accordingly distorted on many matters, necessitating reinterpretation and correction. Any attempt to trace out continuity and contrast between the earlier and later work with respect to the conception of philosophy must bear in mind the fact that the axis of reference of the whole investigation has been rotated upon a fixed point (*PI*, §108). The need to grasp conceptual structures remains, but they are now conceived *sub specie humanitatis*.

In the course of the lectures in 1931–3 Wittgenstein claimed that

---

[1] See A. Maslow, *A Study in Wittgenstein's Tractatus* (University of California Press, California, 1961), p. x.

philosophy as he was now practising it was not merely a stage in the continuous development of the subject, but a new subject (M, p. 322). Using a simile reminiscent of Russell's extravagant claims about logical atomism, Wittgenstein declared that with the emergence of his new style of philosophizing there was a 'kink' in the evolution of philosophy comparable to that which occurred when Galileo invented dynamics. He repeats the point, somewhat more modestly, in the *Blue Book* (*BB*, p. 28). His work, he says, is one of the heirs of the subject that used to be called philosophy. The important thing, he claimed in his lectures, was not whether his results were true or false, but that a new method has been found,[1] as had happened when chemistry was developed out of alchemy. As a result of the discovery of this method it is now possible to have not only great philosophers but also skilled ones. The new method has reduced philosophy to a skill. The justifiability of these far reaching claims will be evaluated in the course of exploring the new philosophy, its aims and methods, its status *vis à vis* other sciences and other conceptions of the subject and its relation to its *Tractatus* ancestor.

The aims of philosophy are variously stated by Wittgenstein, sometimes in a mildly positive fashion, but more often in a negative vein. Positively, philosophy aims at putting in order our ideas as to what can be said about the world (M, p. 323), it is essentially a rearrangement of something we already know, like arranging books in a library (*BB*, p. 44). The aim of philosophy is to establish an order (not THE order) in our knowledge of the use of language (*PI*, §132). It strives after the notions of a sound human understanding (*RFM*, p. 157). The most general and recurrent positive formulation of the task of philosophy is the claim that its purpose is to give us an *Übersicht*,[2] a surview or synoptic view.[3] In the *Investigations* Wittgenstein states unambiguously:

---

[1] The remark requires some minor modification. If there are no 'philosophical propositions' then some obvious strain is generated by talking of the results of philosophical investigation as true or false. A similar problem arose, it will be remembered, with regard to the preface to the *Tractatus* (see above chapter I, p. 32). A further modification is necessitated to make the claim that *a* method has been found consistent with *PI*, §133 (see below pp. 137 f.).

[2] The expression is significantly used by Frege in *The Foundations of Arithmetic*, §5: '. . . one of the requirements of reason . . . [is] . . . to embrace all first principles in a survey' ('dem Bedürfnisse der Vernunft nach Uebersichtlichkeit der ersten Grundlagen').

[3] The terms '*Übersicht*', '*Übersichtlichkeit*' and the related verb '*Übersehen*' have given Wittgenstein's translators much trouble. They have chosen to translate it

The concept of a surveyable representation (*Übersichtlichen Darstellung*) is of fundamental significance for us. It designates our form of representation, the way we look at things. (Is this a '*Weltanschauung*'?) (*PI*, §122; my translation.)[1]

A surview enables us to grasp the structure of our mode of representation, or whichever segment of it is relevant to a given philosophical problem. The concept of a surview is central to Wittgenstein's later philosophy. It is the heir to the 'correct logical point of view' of the *Tractatus* (*TLP*, 4.1213). But while the *Tractatus* had sought to achieve a correct logical point of view by 'geological' means, by delving beneath the appearances of language to uncover its latent structure, Wittgenstein's later philosophy seeks a correct logical point of view by 'topographical' means.

Consider the geography of a country for which we have no map, or else a map in tiny bits. The difficulty about this is the difficulty with philosophy; there is no synoptic view. Here the country we talk about is language and the geography grammar. We can walk about a country quite well but when forced to make a map we go wrong (Lectures, Michaelmas 1933).[2]

The main source of misunderstandings characteristic of philosophy is the difficulty of surveying our use of language (*PI*, §122). Language is the means of representation. Its inner structure, constituted by the rules which determine the use, and thereby the meaning, of sentences and their constituents is the form of representation, the tangle of conceptual connections by means of which we conceive of the world. We obtain a proper surview of our form of representa-

---

non-systematically in conformity with the demands of English style, thereby partially obscuring the significance and pervasiveness of the concept in Wittgenstein's work, e.g. 'command a clear view' (*Übersehen PI*, §122); 'perspicious representation' (*Übersichtlichen Darstellung PI*, §122); 'synoptic account' (*Übersichtliche Darstellung Z*, §273); 'Survey' (*Übersicht Z*, §273); 'synoptic view' (*Übersichtlichkeit Z*, §464); 'perspicuity' (*Übersichtlichkeit RFM*, p. 45); 'capable of being taken in' (*Übersehbar RFM*, p. 81). I shall try to avoid this multiplicity of approximate synonyms by employing the archaic term 'surview' and related terms ' to survey', 'surveyable', etc. When quoting Wittgenstein I shall use the translator's version (unless it is misleading for other reasons) together with the relevant German term in parentheses.

[1] Anscombe's translation of the last sentence is misleading. The original runs thus: 'Er bezeichnet unsere Darstellungsform, die Art, wie wir die Dinge sehen. (Ist dies eine "Weltanschauung"?)'

[2] Reported by A. Ambrose, 'Wittgenstein on Universals', in *Ludwig Wittgenstein, The Man and his Philosophy*, ed. K. T. Fann, p. 336.

tion when we grasp the grammar[1] of language. To understand a mathematical proof, for example, is to grasp the grammar of the proven sentence, for the acceptance of a theorem in mathematics is the acceptance of a new grammatical rule. The repeated insistence that proof in mathematics must be surveyable (*RFM*, pp. 65–71) is tantamount to the claim that grammar must be surveyable. A non-surveyable putative proof, e.g. proof of a multiplication in the Russellian notation, involving thousands of signs, could not be accepted as a proof. Although grammar in general, in Wittgenstein's sense of the term, will not be allowed to rise above a certain level of complexity, it rarely if ever falls to a level of straightforward unambiguous and obvious surveyability. An ideally simple surview of a segment of grammar would be constituted by the concretization of the rules, by, e.g. a spatial representation of the normative modalities governing the use of linguistic signs. An example of this which Wittgenstein repeatedly referred to in the early thirties is the colour octahedron as a concrete representation of part of the grammar of colour words. However, this is not in general possible. Our grammar is above all lacking in surveyability (*PB*, §1; *PI*, §122). Moreover, some segments of our language, e.g. psychological terms, present greater barriers to the achievement of a proper surview than others, e.g. terms in mechanics (*Z*, §113). Grammar is not embodied in a static instantly surveyable medium, but is the structure of our dynamic linguistic practices. We can, in general, obtain a surview only by patient examination of how sentences and expressions are supposed to be applied (*Z*, §272), of their rule-governed relations to other sentences and expressions. The complete surview of all sources of unclarity by means of an account of all the applications, illustrations, conceptions of a segment of language (e.g. the transition from mathematics of the finite to mathematics of the infinite (*Z*, §273)) will produce an understanding of logical connections which will dissolve confusion.

As will be seen from the latter remark, even the formulation of the surview-giving task of philosophy is given a negative slant. For the point of producing a surview is to dispel philosophical illusion. The apparently positive formulations of the aims of philosophy are almost always coloured with a negative tinge.

[1] For a detailed examination of Wittgenstein's conception of grammar see chapter VI below.

Although we wish to arrive at the notions of a sound human understanding, philosophers need to be cured of many diseases of the
understanding before they can do so (*RFM*, p. 157). The order we
seek to establish is an order which is necessary to banish philosophical worries. The dominant view of the purpose of philosophy is
negative—the elimination of confusion, the disappearance of philosophical problems (*PI*, §133). Philosophy aims to dissolve philosophical problems which arise out of language (*PI*, §90); it is a fight
against the fascination exercised by forms of language (*BB*, p. 27;
PI, §109). It destroys those houses of cards, which always seem
interesting, great, and important in philosophy, namely putative
insights into the real, the metaphysical, structure of the universe,
the essence of the world. The importance of philosophizing in the
new way lies in disillusionment, in curing philosophical thought of
the madness which besets it.

The conception of philosophy is predominantly therapeutic. It is
true that once illusion is dispelled by a correct surview we will have
a correct logical point of view. But we sought it, according to Wittgenstein, not for its own sake, but for the sake of a cure. Accordingly,
the aim of philosophy is not completeness or comprehensiveness
(*PI*, II.xi, p. 206; *Z*, §465); where classifications are given they are
merely meant to enable us to disentangle the knots in our own
thought. Nor is the aim exactness (*Z*, §464). Wittgenstein's philosophy does not aim at a systematic account of our form of representation, but only at a surview of those parts that generate illusions.
It may be that once a proper surview is achieved a comprehensive
account will be possible, but the point of giving a surview is to dispel
illusion.

It will be remembered that in his earliest *credo* about philosophy,
in the first paragraph of 'Notes on Logic', Wittgenstein declared
that philosophy was purely descriptive; unlike the natural sciences
to which Russell had compared it, it contained no deductions. It was
conceived to be the description of logical form. According to the
Tractatus, philosophy, as practised in the book, had the *de facto*
status of a description of logical form but a *de jure* status of nonsense. The future philosophy, the ground-work of which is laid
by the *Tractatus*, is purely elucidatory. The only strictly correct
method in philosophy is to say nothing except what can be said,
i.e. empirical, non-philosophical propositions, and, whenever someone tries to say something metaphysical, to demonstrate to him,

by means of analysis, that he has failed to give a meaning to certain signs in his propositions (*TLP*, 6.53). The contention that philosophy is purely descriptive pervades Wittgenstein's later work (e.g. *PG*, §30; *BB*, pp. 18, 125; *PI*, §124, etc.). Philosophy is a description of the workings of language (*PI*, §109). It solves certain non-empirical problems by a quiet weighing of linguistic facts (*Z*, §447). Philosophy is a conceptual investigation (*Z*, §458), it describes our conceptual structures from within. It shows how in philosophy, or in psychology or mathematics, we go wrong by taking our concepts wrong—it does so by turning our attention towards the employment of words (*Z*, §463).

The descriptive status of philosophy was thus in a sense adhered to, but given a twist away from the now rejected notion of logical form, in the direction of the substituted notion of the uses of language, and the so-called 'grammatical rules' governing the use of language. Similarly, the 'correct method in philosophy', so apparently unsatisfactory and unphilosophical (*TLP*, 6.53) is adhered to, but again modified in the direction of rules of use determining sense and away from logical analysis. In a discussion with Waismann in December 1931, Wittgenstein remarked:

I once wrote: The only correct method in philosophy would be to say nothing and to leave it to others to make claims. I now adhere to this. What the other cannot do is to separate out, gradually and in the right order, the rules of grammar, so that all questions solve themselves (*WWK*, pp. 183 f.).

This modified programme for philosophical clarification determines the dialectical nature, the dialogue form and the interrogative method of Wittgenstein's later philosophy. The task of the philosopher is not to lay down rules of language (*PI*, §124; *WWK*, p. 184), but to elicit the rules from the minds of the bewildered: 'I make the other person aware of what he is doing, and refrain from giving any instructions' (*WWK*, p. 186). If one discovers through questioning that someone is using different and conflicting rules for one and the same word, then one brings him to see a source of confusion, and the necessity for a decision. But the decision should be his, not the therapist's (*PI*, §125).

The descriptive status of philosophy was originally contrasted by Wittgenstein with the theoretical status of the sciences. Despite the shift in what was meant by 'philosophy is purely descriptive' the contrast remained firm and the antagonism to the Russellian comparison of philosophy to science was maintained. Scientific investigations are irrelevant to philosophy. The discovery of new facts, the invention of new theories, can contribute nothing to the solution or dissolution of the non-empirical problems of philosophy. 'It was true to say', Wittgenstein remarks, referring to the *Tractatus*, 4.111 'that our considerations could not be scientific ones. It was not of any possible interest to us to find out empirically "that, contrary to our preconceived ideas, it is possible to think such-and-such"—whatever that may mean' (*PI*, §109). Likewise no discoveries in mathematics can advance philosophical solutions in the philosophy of mathematics (*PI*, §124). That Gödel's theorem can appear as a solution and final answer to the logicist programme for mathematics is merely a measure of the confusion of the logicists about the status of mathematics and mathematical proof, just as, for example, the view that relativity theory provides a decisive *empirical* answer to the controversy between Leibnizians and Newtonians over the substantiality of space and time merely reveals the depth of the misunderstandings involved in an essentially philosophical, conceptual dispute. Such momentous discoveries nevertheless have a great impact upon philosophy, not for the solution of old philosophical problems, but rather as alterations in our form of representation, presenting novel problems calling out for a proper surview. Natural science may indeed investigate the causes of the formation of concepts, but the conceptual investigations of the philosopher are not scientific (*PI*, II.xii). The concept of seeing aspects is of paramount importance in investigating the relation of thought and experience, but the problems presented by this concept cannot be resolved by the experimental psychologist. What philosophers are concerned with are conceptual connections. It is the task of the psychologist, not the philosopher, to study causal connections (*PI*, p. 193). Problems in the philosophy of mind concerning, e.g. thought, are not scientific. The oddity about thought which, as we have seen, led Wittgenstein in the *Tractatus* tacitly to attribute to it so many miraculous hidden operations, does not stem from lack of causal knowledge. The apparent strangeness of mentality stems from lack of a proper surview of mental concepts. The construction of models of the mind, or 'black boxes' in psychological theory can contribute nothing to the solution of philosophical problems (*BB*, pp. 5 f.). Philosophy is not on a level with natural science, the philosopher is not a citizen of any community of ideas (*Z*, §455). Natural science is characterized by theory-construction which frequently involves idealizing reality (e.g. Newtonian mechanics). It characteristically constructs hypotheses which are confirmable or falsifiable, sometimes by reference to new facts the existence of which, hitherto unsuspected, is suggested by the theory. Science explains phenomena by deduction from general laws embodied in its theories; in short, science is stratified.

By contrast, Wittgenstein continued to think, philosophy is flat. It is, of course, no part of this claim that there are no deductive consequences within philosophical therapeutics; it may well be claimed that the truth of the argument against the possibility of a private language implies the falsity of all forms of dogmatic idealism. There is no theory, in the scientific sense, in philosophy, nor is there any idealization analogous to that which occurs in physics (*PG*, §36). Philosophy, Wittgenstein stresses recurrently, explains nothing (*PG*, §30; *BB*, p. 125; *PI*, §109); it only describes. The notion of explanation at work here is, I conjecture, that of deductive-nomological explanation characteristic of the advanced sciences. In a somewhat different way, however, it could be said that philosophy explains, for it is part of Wittgenstein's prognosis for philosophical illusion that we be brought to our senses by examining intermediate cases in order that we grasp connections. Revealing conceptual connections, which were not hitherto explicit or articulated even though they are an integral part of our linguistic practice, seems as legitimate a sense of 'explain' as any. Moreover, not only does Wittgenstein explain, in this loose sense, in order to rid us of illusion. He also explains, in great detail and profundity, the multifarious sources and processes which generate philosophical illusion. Since there are no hypotheses to be confirmed or falsified, no new information is needed. We are concerned with examining the concepts we have, not those we do not have, and our having the concepts consists in our unarticulated knowledge of the use of words.

The two aspects of the claim that philosophy is purely descriptive, namely its concern with describing linguistic use, and its lack of a stratified structure of a theory, meet in the claim that everything relevant to a philosophical problem lies open to view (*BB*, p. 6). That there is something new to find out is the hallmark of a misguided theory-perverted philosophy. In the above-mentioned discussion with Waismann, Wittgenstein castigates himself for his mistake in the *Tractatus* of thinking that there could be new discoveries in philosophy. He had thought that it was the task of logical analysis to discover elementary propositions, and while he was right to think that one could not assume, or hypothesize, or predict on *a priori* grounds what the form of elementary propositions would be, he was deeply misguided in thinking that one would later discover it. There is nothing new to find in philosophy (*WWK*, pp. 182–3). New, hitherto unknown information is pertinent for science and its methods, but not for philosophy. What is needed in philosophy is simply a rearrangement yielding a surview of what we already know (*PI*, §109; M, p. 323). If anything is hidden, e.g. psychological facts about thought and perception, it is of concern to the scientist, but irrelevant to us, for it can, by token of its concealment, play no part in our rule-governed employment of concepts (*PI*, §153). The psychological mechanisms of belief cannot solve any of the philosophical problems concerning belief[1] (*PG*, §63), for these unknown mechanisms cannot be part of the conditions which conventionally justify the claim that A believes p and hence constitute part of the sense of the psychological sentence. The nature of our concepts lies open to view in our linguistic practice. What cannot be seen there cannot be an aspect of the concepts. Meanings are not assigned to words by anything but human will and convention, a word has the meaning we have given it (*BB*, p. 28), and we cannot milk more out of the word than we put into it. Thus a second juncture-point of the dual aspects of the descriptive status of philosophy is Wittgenstein's trenchant opposition to logical analysts, whether atomistic like Russell (and the *Tractatus* programme for future philosophy), or non-atomistic, like Moore. There can be no 'scientific investigation' into what a word *really* means, independently of the meaning given it by the practice of a normal speaker (*BB*, p. 28). The idea, which Moore was inclined to adopt, that logical analysis explains to people what they mean when they say something, and whether, indeed, they mean anything at all, is an infernal notion (*WWK*, pp. 129 f.). We do not wait

---

[1] The *Tractatus* had not suggested otherwise, for it, like all of the later work insisted upon the independence of philosophy from psychology. What it did, however, was to claim that certain problems which in fact belong to philosophy, e.g. the differences between the concepts of belief and imagination or desire, are matters for psychology.

upon philosophy to discover whether our ordinary sentences have any meaning. Such confusion rests upon a misguided analogy between philosophical analysis and chemical or physical analysis, and a deep-rooted misunderstanding of the nature of meaning. Meanings are erroneously conceived as the cash-value of words, like money and the cow one can buy with it, instead of conceiving the relation as analogous to that of money and its use (*PI*, §120).

Considerable problems still remain. If one aspect of the doctrine that philosophy is purely descriptive is that philosophy describes our use of language, that it simply tabulates and expresses clearly the rules we have unknowingly been using (*WWK*, p. 184), then does this not make philosophy an empirical science, and truth in philosophy a matter requiring the final arbitration of brute fact? Does it not require philosophers to emerge from their armchairs and indulge in lexicography? May not philosophy be riddled with incorrectly tabulated rules of linguistic use? The questions rest on a misunderstanding. Philosophical problems are conceptual, not empirical. Their answers do not lie in the production of empirical assertions about linguistic use, nor in the production of special 'philosophical propositions'. Or, in so far as they do, the 'philosophical propositions' are indisputable and undisguised grammatical truisms. Philosophy is an activity whose primary product is the disappearance of philosophical problems. An essential part of the activity is indeed the eliciting and arrangement of obvious rules of use. But the linguistic investigation receives its purpose from conceptual problems of philosophy, not from empirical problems in linguistics (*PI*, §109). To be sure the descriptions are empirical— but their correctness is guaranteed by the fact that they are elicited from the person whose bewilderment is in question. The typical form of a philosophical question is modal—How is it possible that things be thus or so? Things must be thus, and yet they cannot? It is inconceivable that things be otherwise! Such questions and assertions are conceptual. They arise, as we shall see, out of confusions concerning aspects of our form of representation. They can be dissolved by a surview which the philosopher endeavours to attain by arranging the grammatical rules which he elicits from the person who suffers from the bafflement. The touchstone of the correctness of the rules he thus elicits is the language user, not the independent judgement of the philosopher (*WWK*, p. 186). The conceptual entanglement stemmed from the former's intuitive command of concepts, and any intuitive evaluation he makes of correctness or incorrectness must be relevant to the survey of his concept. Like the psycho-analyst, all the philosopher does is make the patient aware of what he is doing (*WWK*, p. 186). Of course, the philosophical interest of the problem is in general going to depend upon common linguistic practices reflecting a shared form of representation. If someone claims that a combination of words has perfectly good sense for him, while we can discern none, we can only assume that he uses language differently from us, or else that he is talking thoughtlessly (*PB*, §7). If the former is the case then if we wish to carry on we must proceed to elicit his novel use.[1] This process requires skill which needs to be exercised in dialogue, skill in asking the right questions at the right time in order to illuminate the conceptual connections embodied in our linguistic practices. But the end-product of the skilful philosophical debate is, according to Wittgenstein, merely the disappearance of a philosophical problem.

In the *Tractatus* Wittgenstein had argued that ordinary language 'is in order as it is'. In the *Investigations*, §98 he quotes the *Tractatus* with approval, and then proceeds to criticize the conception in the *Tractatus* of the perfect logical order that is to be found underlying ordinary language. The agreement between the two books over the propriety of ordinary language is in a sense superficial. For the perfect logical order which the *Tractatus* found in ordinary language it found not in the appearances of language but despite them. The perfect order was the hidden essence of language which is only revealed by analysis. The preconceptions of the *Tractatus*, in particular the demand for determinacy of sense, forced an ideal upon language. Labouring under the illusion that this ideal must be found in language, the *Tractatus* had sublimed logic, twisted its central concepts of sentence, word, and meaning out of all recognition in order to meet the requirements of a prejudice.

To be sure, ordinary language is in good order. But the goodness of its order lies open to view. We are not striving after an ideal language which a philosophical mythology persuades us lies within ordinary language. We seek a surview over ordinary language. For

---

[1] Some confirmation for this interpretation can be found in F. Waismann, *The Principles of Linguistic Philosophy*, ed. R. Harré (Macmillan, London, 1965), pp. 34 f. This book, if judiciously used, is an important aid to Wittgensteinian exegesis.

what should such an ideal language express? The same as that which we express in ordinary language? Then logic must investigate ordinary language and not something else (*PB*, §3; *PI*, §120). For were there something else how should we come to know what it is? Logical analysis is analysis of something we have, not of something we lack; it is analysis of sentences as they are. To be sure some philosophical misunderstandings can be removed by substituting one form of an expression for another (*PI*, §90). Russell's technique of eliminating definite descriptions is effective in dispelling Meinongian worries. Such a process has the appearance of taking things apart and hence was, with some justice, thought of as analysis. But this led to the illusion that there is a form of language consisting of completely analysed expressions, and thus an ideal of analysed language. Since the process of analysis appeared to be a process of eliminating misunderstandings by making expressions more exact, the success of Russellian techniques led to a further illusion of an ideally exact language. And these ideals were sought not in something we all know which is surveyable by a rearrangement, but in unknown and hidden recesses.

The philosophy of logic talks of sentences and words in a perfectly ordinary sense. One must take the viewpoint of a healthy human understanding, Wittgenstein remarks in the *Bemerkungen* (*PB*, §18), and it is precisely here that the change of conception lies. 'Language', 'word', 'sentence', are not, as the *Tractatus* intimated, super-concepts between which a super-order holds, containing the quintessence of language. They are ordinary words having mundane uses like any other words (*PI*, §108). We are talking in logic of a spatio-temporal phenomenon of language, not of a non-spatial atemporal *Unding*. Our talk of language and its elements is analogous to talking of chess pieces when explaining the rules of chess, and we must avoid the temptation to sublime language into ideal essences. We would not treat the king in chess as an abstract essence, and we should not think of propositions as ideal essences, classes of sentences with equivalent meanings (*PG*, §77; *PI*, §108). The scruples of the author of the *Tractatus*, Wittgenstein claimed, are themselves misunderstandings. Just as analysis of the Russellian type is not illegitimate as long as it does not bewitch us, so too, constructing ideal languages is not illegitimate. For certain purposes it may serve well (*WWK*, pp. 45 ff.). But two points must be borne in mind: firstly, we *construct* them, and secondly, such languages are not *improvements* over ordinary language designed to replace it, but are relatively handicapped.

Philosophical problems arise out of ordinary language and are, in general, to be resolved by looking into its workings by considering the diverse uses of expressions. The *Tractatus* had pursued the real logical form of the proposition. The new method in philosophy demands a clarification of linguistic use, but not in order to achieve an understanding for the first time, but to eliminate misunderstanding. We use words without first giving or even being able to give the rules for their use (*PG*, §72) just as we use money as a means of exchange and store of value, without being able to describe the underlying conventions, rules and laws which enable it to fulfil these functions (*Z*, §525). One can find one's way around a city although one may be unable to draw a map of it (*Z*, §121). Being able to use words correctly, as well as recognize correct and incorrect uses of them, is to understand them, to know their meaning. But in pursuit of our need to press against the limits of language, in trying to gratify our natural inclination for metaphysics, we engender illusion. In the sciences, concepts are frequently and fruitfully extended for theoretical purposes, yet this process often drags confusion in its wake through failure to grasp that such extensions amount to alterations of the grammar of the concepts in question, and hence that not all the previously accepted logical connections need hold good under the same interpretations for the extended concepts. It is in both such contexts that we need to clarify use to attain a surview, not to achieve an understanding of words which we previously used without understanding, but to eradicate misconceptions, or to achieve an understanding of our understanding (*Z*, §454).

Philosophy, Wittgenstein stresses (*PI*, §124), leaves everything as it is. It does not give mathematics a foundation, as the logicists had tried to do (*RFM*, p. 171). It does not give language a foundation, as the *Tractatus* had misguidedly tried to do in constructing its metaphysics and ontology. Nor does it interfere with the actual use of language, it does not lay down new linguistic rules (*PI*, §133) but merely describes existing rules for its own purposes. This does not mean, as some philosophers have suggested, that Wittgenstein was committed to denying the propriety of recommending or bringing about linguistic change. His view of language is organic and dynamic. As we shall see, his view of forms of representation was through and through historical. Indeed so convinced was he of the alterability of *any* element in our forms of representation that his later work, like Brouwer's, for all its retained Kantian flavour, runs deeply counter to the Kantian belief in the necessary constancy of our categorial framework. Wittgenstein does not object to suggestions for reform of language for practical purposes; 'an improvement in our terminology designed to prevent misunderstandings in practice, is perfectly possible' (*PI*, §132). Nothing in Wittgenstein's philosophy precludes giving explications for the purpose of furthering clarity and scientific fruitfulness. For his own philosophical, therapeutical purposes it is on the whole not necessary to introduce new technical terminology nor to tamper with existing use. This is partly due to his distaste for discourse in the formal mode, partly due to his restrictive concerns. But he does, to be sure, introduce some semi-technical terms such as 'family-resemblance concepts', 'language-games', and perhaps most important of all 'criterion'.

Though these defences of Wittgenstein's dictum 'philosophy leaves everything as it is' do rebutt some of the stock-in-trade criticisms, yet for all that, the dictum is highly misleading. To be sure language is, by and large, left as it is. Nor does philosophy uncover new facts about the world. But those regions of our thought previously obscure to us and now perspicuously surveyed do not remain the same. Or, if one wishes, the fact that we now see them differently will lead to our treating them differently. For a mathematician like Hilbert who believed that Cantor had opened the gates to paradise the world will not remain the same after Wittgenstein has shown him that what he saw was nothing but a mirage in waterless desert.[1] If something was thought to be good sense, and is revealed by a surview to be nonsense, it is at best misleading to claim that since it was nonsense before and is nonsense still therefore philosophy leaves everything as it is. Nor does psychology emerge unscathed, neither old-style psychology of William James[2] nor experimental psychology.[3] In a science which consists of

---

[1] See R. Rhees, *Discussions of Wittgenstein* (Routledge and Kegan Paul, London, 1970), p. 46.

[2] For comparative references see *A Wittgenstein Workbook*, ed. C. Coope, P. Geach, T. Potts and R. White (Blackwell, Oxford, 1970), Appendix II.

[3] e.g. see A. J. P. Kenny's criticisms of Woodworth, Hebb, Flugel, Watson, and others in *Action Emotion and the Will* (Routledge and Kegan Paul, London, 1963), ch. II.

experimental methods and conceptual confusion (*PI*, II.xiv) not everything will remain the same after it has been subjected to philosophical investigation. To insist upon the autonomy of philosophy does not require one to believe that philosophy, be she under-labourer or queen of the sciences, leaves *everything* as it is.

2. *The Phenomenology and Sources of Philosophical Illusion*

No philosopher has paid greater attention or displayed greater sensitivity to the phenomenology of language than Wittgenstein. The way in which we 'feel at home' in a language, the aura and 'soul' of words is not merely of great intrinsic interest, but of considerable philosophical relevance in as much as it presents great pitfalls to the understanding bereft of the correct logical point of view. Wittgenstein was equally fascinated in the phenomenology of philosophical illusion itself which is in part a product of the phenomenology of language use. To some extent the reason for this is autobiographical, but it is no less important and profound for that. 'To get clear about philosophical problems', he wrote (*BB*, p. 66), 'it is useful to become conscious of the apparently unimportant details of the particular situation in which we are inclined to make a certain metaphysical assertion.' This injunction holds more broadly than for metaphysical errors alone. Wittgenstein gives an array of examples, most of which are culled from his own youthful philosophical explorations. The solipsist's doctrine that 'Only *this* is really seen' will be examined in detail in chapter VII. The temptation to make the remark embodying what Russell called 'solipsism of the moment' arises, Wittgenstein suggests, when we stare at unchanging surroundings. We are considerably less tempted by it when we look around while walking (*BB*, p. 66). It is no coincidence that Wittgenstein's suggestion in the 1916 notebook that it is possible to take the bare present image as the true world among shadows follows a discussion of the visual contemplation of a stove as a world (*NB*, p. 83). A similar phenomenon accompanies the illusion, to which Frege among others succumbed,[1] that there is some sense in which colours are essentially private to each perceiver. To the representative idealist, what initially appears (and in fact is)

---

[1] Frege, *Foundations of Arithmetic*, pp. 36–7; and his review of Husserl's *Philosophie der Arithmetik* repr. in *Translations from the Philosophical Writings of Gottlob Frege*, ed. P. Geach and M. Black, p. 79.

a commonly accessible element in a public world becomes by some strange trick of the understanding a subjective impression which we detach from the world like a membrane (*PI*, §276). When one assures oneself that one knows how green looks to oneself then one turns one's attention upon something that appears to belong to oneself alone. One, as it were, immerses oneself in a colour impression; and it is easier to produce this aberrant state of mind when one is looking at a bright colour or impressive colour scheme. Related to this is a further deep and pervasive mistake especially pertinent to the private language argument which will be examined in chapter VIII. In the case of one's own sensations, for example, one brings items under concepts without using a criterion of identity. It is an easy and natural illusion to take one's confrontation with the object itself to provide a criterion of identity for the object. When one contemplates one's own subjective experience the experience itself seems to play a part in one's thought. But what is needed here is a concept and a surview of its use, not an object. In these three kinds of delusion, staring or attending play a prominent role as they do in the confusion of sample and description.[1] It is of course no part of Wittgenstein's claim that all idealists, phenomenalists, or solipsists adopted their doctrines because of such experiences. Nevertheless the experiences are revealing, if only because they show how language can 'go on holiday'.

Wittgenstein gives many examples of the frame of mind of the philosopher transfixed by his own forms of representation. Dissatisfaction with grammar, or, more probably, exasperation at one's inability to achieve a surview of it, often expresses itself in a feeling of the inadequacy of language. One is strongly inclined to feel, as William James did, that one knows, experiences, grasps the inner complexity and multiplicity of the world and the stream of experience, but that it is inexpressible in ordinary language. The language we have is too crude to describe the richness and subtlety of experience (*PI*, §436 and §610). One may then hanker after an ideal language, ideally precise and rich. One's longings, however, are a displacement of a desire for an absurdity. The richness one thinks one finds in experience and which one believes cannot be discursively conveyed to another is due merely to the non-transferability of experience, not to the impotence of thought. What appears

---

[1] See below ch. VI, § 3

to be the poverty of language is attributable to the fact that concepts are not intuitions; both are necessary for discursive knowledge. The disquietude of philosophical obsession is described by Wittgenstein in connection with the *Tractatus*. Held captive by a picture, a preconception of form, a philosopher thinks that he has grasped an essence. Faced with contradictions he feels both that 'this isn't how it is' and also 'this is how it has to be' (*PI*, §112). So indeed had Wittgenstein himself responded as he struggled to force language and thought into the Procrustean bed he had made for it (*NB*, p. 17). The conflict and dilemma are symptoms of an inadequate understanding of conceptual relations.

The *Tractatus* had produced a mythology of symbolism and psychology. Its errors, however, were neither trivial nor unimportant, but deep and significant. They stem from multiple sources of which we can only become aware by careful philosophizing in the new vein (*RFM*, p. 57). Though the metaphysical errors contained in the previous philosophy must be eradicated by the new style of investigation, it must be borne in mind that they contained much truth, even though seen through a glass darkly. Once the illusory impressiveness and uniqueness of language as a mirror of the structure of reality is dispelled, the impressiveness retreats to the illusions themselves (*PI*, §110). The author of the *Tractatus* laboured to reveal that the structure of the world cannot be said but only shown. The author of the *Investigations* bent his efforts to reveal how what seemed to show itself was an optical illusion. The dominant tone of the later philosophy is critical rather than constructive. Its exposure of error is more comprehensive and systematic than its positive contribution to our understanding of our form of representation. The latter must be laboriously pieced together from many hundreds of fragmentary deliverances, the former is overwhelming in its richness and thoroughness.

Wittgenstein gives us no principles of classification for sources of error in philosophy. Perhaps it is not possible to do so with any fruitfulness; certainly the spirit of Kant's transcendental dialectic and doctrine of method were quite alien to Wittgenstein. Hence the five-fold classification which follows is merely meant to bring together a representative sample of Wittgenstein's diagnoses, and has no pretensions to completeness or exclusiveness. Wittgenstein locates the roots of illusion in (1) superficial analogies in the surface grammar of language, (2) the phenomenology of the use of language,

(3) pictures or archetypes embedded in language, (4) the model of presentation and solution of problems in the natural sciences, (5) natural cravings and dispositions of reason.

(1) Wittgenstein distinguishes between the surface grammar and the depth grammar of the use of expressions (*PI*, §664). Although the metaphor is more apt to the *Tractatus* account of language, it is readily applicable to the later conception of language too. The surface grammar of a word is the superficial impression of its syntactical category given by the way it is used in the construction of the sentence, that part of its use, Wittgenstein says, that can be taken in by the ear. The surface grammar frequently leads us to misunderstand the use of words. When we see an analogy between forms of words in surface grammar we misguidedly assume an analogy in depth grammar. But this need not be so. Concepts with very different forms, possessing fundamentally dissimilar conceptual relations to other concepts, may display a surface similarity. The clothing of our language, Wittgenstein remarks in a phrase reminiscent of the *Tractatus* (*TLP*, 4.002), makes everything look alike. Consequently we are unconscious of the great diversity of language (*PI*, p. 224). The thought is indeed a similar one, but the therapy lies not in analysis but in careful plotting of use and circumstances justifying the use of expressions in order to distinguish what at first glance looked similar. Superficially 'thinking', 'writing' and 'speaking', 'thought', 'script' and 'speech' appear grammatically similar. This, Wittgenstein suggests, is one of the many reasons why we tend to ascribe to thought some of the features of speech and script, e.g. a locality (*BB*, p. 7). Writing and speaking are activities performed by means of hand and larynx; we therefore conceive of thinking as an activity of the mind, forgetting that the agency of the mind, as its substantiality, is wholly different from that of the hand. Since writing produces inscriptions and speaking produces phonemes, we readily conclude that thoughts are analogous products of thinking, only in an ethereal medium. A similar pervasive source of confusion lies in our hankering for substances. Our concept of a substantive expression is, as its name suggests, constructed on the paradigm of a name of a substance. Consequently it is a natural inclination in us to look for a substance for every substantive. We exacerbate this inclination when we couch our philosophical, conceptual questions in the form of questions about entities, e.g. 'What is length? What is meaning? What is number?' instead of

'What is an explanation of meaning? How are lengths measured? How are numerical expressions used?' Consequently we assume Platonistically the existence of special objects to correspond to substantival expressions for which we can find no ordinary objects. We talk of numbers as ideal objects, obscuring the fact that all that can coherently be meant thereby is that the use of numerical expressions is in certain respects similar to that of signs that have objects even though numerals do not (*RFM*, p. 136). Subsequently we construct a metaphysics out of our fairytale.

(2) The perennial temptation to explain the notion of meaning something by an expression in terms of mental acts and processes accompanying overt utterances has its roots, in part at least, in certain phenomenological features of speaking, reading, writing and hearing. Thus, for example, we feel at home with our native language. Its 'atmosphere' is familiar to us, the sound of a word in speech, its appearance in writing are 'comfortable'. When confronted by gross spelling mistakes, mispronunciations, or nonsense writings such as '&8§≠ $≠?+%', the powerful feeling of abnormality and alienation leads us to assume that a positive feeling of familiarity makes a special contribution to an hypostatized inner process allegedly necessary to reading or hearing with understanding. Similarly we tend to project grammatical differences onto the hypothetical mechanisms of the mind, and to try to account for them in terms of mental acts. In the sentence 'Mr. Scot is not a Scot' (*PI*, p. 176; see for comparison *TLP*, 3.323) the first occurrence of 'Scot' is a proper name, the second is a common name. We can readily induce a feeling that the difference between the identical tokens is attributable to a special mental contribution. For try, Wittgenstein says, to mean the first occurrence as a common name, and the second as a proper name. One blinks with effort as one tries to parade the meanings before one's mind thus, and the sense seems to disintegrate. Hence one assumes that the sentence ordinarily means what it does because one parades the meanings readily in the familiar order. This is misguided. None of this charade affects the sense of what one says, the feeling of comfortable familiarity is not a parade of meanings in the mind. It may be true that words, or some words, carry with them a special psychological 'corona'. Philosophers have indeed tried to account for the meanings of logical connectives in terms of feelings, e.g. of hesitation (for disjunction) or denial (for negation), or if-feelings (for implication). But the identity of the

concept is independent of the feelings associated with its employment, the feeling of hesitation is quite independent of disjunction (what feelings accompany 'not both not p and not q'?) and the so-called if-feeling is not a feeling that accompanies the word 'if' and that could be identified as the if-feeling independently of the word (*PI*, pp. 181–3). Wittgenstein is not trying to disparage the experiences we associate with language. In the first place, the 'soul' of language which we experience is intimately connected with our cultural history and essential to the power of language in metaphor and poetry, evocation and association. In the second place, our expressiveness in our use of language is closely related to our different experiences of meaning, although the differences of meaning are not a function of either experience or expressiveness (*PI*, pp. 175, 214). Most important of all, our obscure conception of experiencing the meaning of a word is a reflection of an absolutely crucial capacity of language-users, namely sensitivity to aspects of the meaning of words (*PI*, p. 214). For without the ability to see one word as holding within it its range of linguistic potentialities, to see it unthinkingly in one context as obviously fulfilling one function, and in another context as obviously fulfilling another, we could not operate with our language. This applies not merely to a word such as 'is' which can function in different contexts as a sign of identity, copula and existential quantifier, but to ambiguities such as 'bank', 'March', 'till', and the like.

(3) The term 'picture' is used by Wittgenstein with great laxity. One of the many different senses given to the expression is analogous to Bentham's conception of an archetype[1] embedded in language. Bentham argued that our concepts of fictitious entities have associated with them archetypal images drawn from operations of objects in the physical world and applied analogically in the context of the fictitious entity. He suggested that archetypes can be a source both of confusion and illumination. They confuse when they are taken literally,[2] illuminate when the analogy betweeen the archetypal image and the sense of the expression of which it is an archetype is

---

[1] Bentham, *Works*, ed. J. Bowring (Tait, Edinburgh, 1843), viii.246, 'Essay on Logic', ch. VII, section 7.

[2] An example of such confusion can be found in the writings of the Scandinavian legal realists, e.g. A. Hagerstrom or K. Olivecrona, who took the archetype of obligation literally instead of examining its use, and thought that by pointing out that obligations are not occult chains or weights they were dispelling metaphysical illusions rather than knocking down straw men.

revealed. Wittgenstein argued similarly that our language contains vivid pictures which continually mislead us in philosophy. Certain forms of expression, metaphors and similes absorbed into our language beguile us, forcing us to think that the facts must conform to the pictures thus embedded in language. The correctness of such pictures qua pictures, is not in dispute; it is rather their application which is. For normally the application is given with the picture (*PI*, §§423–5). But in the philosophically most interesting and baffling cases this is not so. A picture forces itself upon one, but the sense of the relevant expression is obscured. The application, and thus the nature of the conceptual connections determining the sense of the expression, is not given by the picture, and is not easy to survey. Both mathematics and the natural sciences abound in such pictures, for clearly the notion of a *ring* of carbon atoms (*PI*, §422), and the Law of the Excluded Middle in set theory (*PI*, §352, §426) give us pictures whose application is extremely unclear. Wittgenstein's favourite examples, however, are drawn from philosophy of mind and psychological language. We hanker to know what is going on in someone's head, we reveal to others what is going on inside us. We believe that men have souls. Such expressions present pictures to us, Wittgenstein contends. These pictures seem to point to a particular use, and thus they take us in. The false appearance must be resisted, for although the picture may embody fruitful or essential analogies, may show how our imagination presents a given concept (*OC*, §90), it will mislead us unless we grasp the use of the expression by a surview of its grammar. When we want to know what is going on in someone's head we are effectively asking to know what he is thinking. But the picture of the 'inner' and 'outer' which is embedded in our language obscures the use of psychological language and provides a rich source of illusion. We readily come to think that true knowledge of another's mind could only come about by looking into his head, or better, seeing with his eyes. To avoid this, the picture of 'inner' and 'outer' and the metaphor of revealing what is 'inside' must be clarified. Otherwise, Wittgenstein warns, 'we shall be tempted to look for an inside behind that which in our metaphor is the inside', we shall hypostatize an inner process from which we *read off* the inner (NFL, p. 280). So indeed we succumb when we allow the picture of thought as a process in our head to dominate our conception of the mental. We generate an illusion of an occult process in an enclosed space, we conceive of thinking as an activity of the mind as writing is an activity of the body, and we think of expressing an idea which is before our mind as a process of translation from one medium (of ideas) into another (of words). We thus succumb to pictures of the mental in a way in which we would not dream of doing for physical ones. We do not ask a person who 'has a word on the tip of his tongue' to open his mouth to let us see. But faced with the 'problem of other minds' philosophers have often thought that our claims about the mental states of others were uncertain because the minds of others are *stricto sensu* inaccessible to us. We are deluded by a picture because we do not understand the grammar of expressions associated with 'mind' and 'thinking'.

The aethereal and the occult are the analogues, in the natural dialectic of psychological concepts, of the abstract object hypostatized in the dialectic of logic and mathematics. No less typical is the craving to ground potentialities in existing states (*BB*, p. 117). We are strongly inclined to conceive of the ability of an object or machine to act in certain ways as being a peculiar state of the object or machine. Equally human abilities, e.g. to solve a mathematical problem, to enjoy music, etc., are readily conceived as states of mind, hypothetical mental mechanisms which will explain conscious mental or physical phenomena. Thus we speak of unconscious and subconscious mental states as parts of such an explanatory mind model, and find it difficult to resist the Lockean temptation to conceive of memory as a storehouse of ideas, or the Central State Materialist's lure to conceive of all mental phenomena as strange properties of the neural (*BB*, pp. 117 f.; *Z*, §§605-15). Although science may succeed in explaining all potentialities in terms of states and their structures, we are far from that goal at present. In particular our concepts of mental abilities and dispositions are not thus explicable at the moment. Thus our temptation to conceive of an ability as a state, and so to misconstrue our *concept* of an ability must be resisted.

(4) Russell's misconception of philosophy as sharing with natural science a general method was, as we have seen, a natural one. The scientist's method of asking questions, not to mention his methods of solving them, have proved so fruitful in the past four centuries that it is altogether intelligible that we should entertain similar ambitions for philosophy and wish to set it upon the sure and certain path of a science. Science characteristically explains phenomena

nomologically, and hence is stratified. It strives to reduce to a minimum the number of natural laws by reference to which it explains nature, and in order to do so it does not hesitate to idealize reality, disregarding subordinate influences in order to generate precise and fruitful laws. To succumb to the scientific method in philosophy is one of the sources of metaphysics. It is easy to think of logic as a 'kind of ultra-physics, the description of the "logical structure" of the world' (*RFM*, p. 6); easy but misguided. The assumption of a shared method of reduction led to the myths of logical atomism; the method of idealization merely serves to avert our attention from our task of achieving a surview of language as it is. The confusion of methods results in the obfuscation of the conceptual nature of philosophical problems, leading to that blurring of boundaries between empirical and grammatical issues character- istic of metaphysics (*BB*, p. 18).

(5) The final source of error which will be classified here lies in the nature of the human mind itself. We have certain kinds of natural cravings of reason and intellectual drives which, if uncontrolled by criticism, lead us into illusion. These have already been remarked upon in some detail. Our metaphysical urge leads us to fruitless philosophical searches for the essence of things. We display a strange kind of displacement behaviour within the domain of the understanding, projecting, as we do, our forms of representation upon the world. And we generate further illusions by conferring a spurious legitimacy upon our use of words in metaphysics. Like Kant, Wittgenstein saw the illusions of metaphysics as the product of a deep-rooted need to thrust against the limits of language. Related to these tendencies is a craving for generality on the one hand and for clear-cut distinctions upon the other. Frege's determin- ation of concepts by *Merkmale* is intellectually more satisfying than the imprecision and untidiness of family-resemblance relations, and the psychological logicians' account of concept possession in terms of general abstract ideas gratifies our preference for states over potentialities in explanation. Finally, again analogously to Kant, Wittgenstein draws attention to what can be thought of both as a regulative principle of science, if not as an engrained feature of the understanding, namely to search always for the prior con- dition of every conditioning element we discover in our explana- tions of phenomena. But this principle distorts our judgement in philosophy. For one of the main difficulties in philosophy is knowing

when to stop, recognizing as a solution what looks as if it is only a preliminary to one (*Z*, §314). We account for our true judgement by reference to the applications of rules. But rules are not unambiguous, so we proceed to look for a rule to guide us in applying a rule, and do not rest satisfied until we think we have reached an unconditioned rule which cannot be misapplied, e.g. a mental ostensive definition. We confuse the fact that one *can* go on indefinitely supplying rules of interpretation and translation with the contention that one *must*. And then we search for a necessary terminus. Yet, in fact, explanation of concepts needs to go only so far as is necessary for mastery of the concept. It ends in good judgement, not in an unambiguous rule. Concept-acquisition is a matter of learning a technique of using words, and educators should bear in mind that 'any explanation has its foundation in training' (*Z*, §419).[1]

3. '*A Method has been found* . . .'

So much then for the general pathology of the understanding. The prognoses of specific sicknesses of the understanding will be described in some detail in subsequent chapters. The general nature of Wittgenstein's grammatical therapies should, however, be clear from the foregoing discussion. In this section, therefore, only a brief summary of the general method and a short survey of specific techniques will be given.

What was the 'new method' which Wittgenstein proclaimed so triumphantly in the 1930 lectures? A possible interpretation of an obscure metaphor in *Zettel* may illuminate his direction of thought:

Disquiet in philosophy might be said to arise from looking at philosophy wrongly, seeing it wrong, namely as if it were divided into (infinite) longitudinal strips instead of into (finite) cross strips. This inversion in our conception produces the *greatest* difficulty. So we try as it were to grasp the unlimited strips and complain that it cannot be done piecemeal.

---

[1] An interesting comparison can be made here with Kant: 'If [logic] sought to give general instructions how we are to subsume under these rules, that is, to distinguish whether something does or does not come under them, that could only be by means of another rule. This in turn, for the very reason that it is a rule, again demands guidance from judgment. And thus it appears that, though understanding is capable of being instructed, and of being equipped with rules, judgment is a peculiar talent which can be practised only, and cannot be taught . . . [an error in subsumption under rules] may be due to . . . not having received through examples and actual practice, adequate training for this particular act of judgment . . . Examples are thus the go-cart of judgment.' *Critique of Pure Reason*, A 133–4, B 172–3.

To be sure it cannot, if by a piece one means an infinite logitudinal strip. But it may well be done, if one means a cross strip.—But in that case we never get to the end of our work!—Of course not, for it has no end.

(We want to replace wild conjectures and explanations by quiet weighing of linguistic facts.) (*Z*, §447.)

Looking at philosophy as if it were divided into infinite longitudinal strips is the Fregean and *Tractatus* conception. Philosophy is conceived as a search for *the* ultimate order in language, for the *a priori* structure of the world. This order and structure reveal the eternal forms of thought, predetermined and immutable. Thought *must* move along fixed lines, otherwise we would have a 'hitherto unknown type of madness'.[1] Here piecemeal methods of science are inapplicable, the structure must be grasped in its entirety, and any error will affect everything else. However difficult philosophy is, it is essentially completable. By contrast the Brouwerian and *Investigations* approach to philosophy looks at the forms of thought as composed of finite cross strips. Each strip can be completely described, although its permanence is not ensured. Novel forms of thought are not predictable; there is no end to conceptual innovation, and the task of philosophy never ceases. Philosophy patiently describes each strip of the fabric of thought, replacing wild conjectures and explanations about the ultimate forms of the proposition and the necessary laws of thought with descriptions of linguistic facts. The unknown types of madness against which Frege expostulated, are, in Wittgenstein's view, simply different forms of thought founded upon different forms of life. The need for a warp upon which to weave the weft is here, as elsewhere in Wittgenstein, obscured.[2]

The new method then is the new style of philosophical clarification, not by analysis, but by description of grammar, not aimed at revealing the structure of the world, but the structure of our thought, not directed at eternal metaphysical verities, but at those facts of the natural history of the mind which will dispel confusion. Our aim is to achieve a surview, but its point and correctness can only be appreciated if we grasp the extent of our lack of explicit knowledge of the grammar of the language of which we possess perfect tacit knowledge. Descartes, for similar reasons, recommended his readers

---

[1] Frege, *The Basic Laws of Arithmetic*, p. xvi, commented on by Wittgenstein in *RFM*, pp. 41, 44, and again *OC*, §494.

[2] See below ch. VI, pp. 171 ff.

to dwell upon the dilemmas and paradoxes of the First Meditation for months or at least weeks, before proceeding further.[1] In similar vein Wittgenstein stressed the importance of a slow cure, of letting a disease of thought run its full course (*Z*, §382). His practice in the refutation of large-scale philosophical theses such as solipsism and idealism, or the semantics of the private linguist which underpin such metaphysics, is never to rest satisfied with the revelation of one or two defects, but to return again and again from different angles to the same error, uncovering more and more fallacious presuppositions. It is the concealed roots of our thought which hold us immobile and inflexible, hence Wittgenstein's preference, occasionally pushed to the point of tedium, for answering questions with questions (*RFM*, p. 68). For while further questions may reveal the grounds and assumptions upon which the original question rested, an intelligible answer would be unfair to the original question in as much as it would not rest upon common agreed ground. The new philosophy is adamantly opposed to the holistic style of the *Tractatus*. Although objecting to 'scientific method in philosophy' it is eminently piecemeal and tentative. Philosophy is an endeavour to find a specific kind of arrangement, a surveyable one, of things we already know, comparable to arranging books in a library. Achievement in philosophy is not to be equated with finality, but with uncovering affinities and differences which are important. It is comparable to putting two hitherto separated books together, or putting two hitherto juxtaposed books upon separate shelves. Nothing need be final about the positions except that what belongs together is conjoined, and what should be put apart is separated.

The new style of clarification in philosophy involves many specific methods. There is no one unique way in philosophy of solving problems and bringing one to a correct surview (*PI*, §133). Rather there are many different ways of combatting the diverse sources of bewitchment which prevent us from arriving at the notions of the sound human understanding. Where analogies in language mislead us, we should counteract their effects by describing the grammar of the expressions in question, and by inventing new uses, sometimes absurd ones, to help loosen the grip of customary forms of language (*BB*, p. 28). Where our form of representation seems inevitable, and wholly correct, we should imagine such changes of natural

---

[1] Descartes, 'Reply to the Second Set of Objections', in *Philosophical Works of Descartes*, trans. by E. S. Haldane and G. R. T. Ross, ii. 31.

history as would vitiate the conditions under which our normal concepts have use and point. When pictures embedded in our language give us a misleading bias towards a given form of expression, we should scrutinize the use of the expression in diverse circumstances, examine particular cases, set up artificial language-games as objects for comparison in order to see that we are dealing with conventions not with natural laws or metaphysical necessities. Against our natural temptation to search for essences, Wittgenstein pits a careful examination of numerous concrete cases which may reveal no more unity to a concept than there is a single fibre to a rope. The mythology of the mental which we invent can be revealed as fictitious not only by the already mentioned techniques, but by other powerful methods. Our attempts to explain mental phenomena in terms of the aethereal and the ineffable, which stem from diverse sources already described, can be counteracted by concretization of the mental. Where we hypostatize mental mechanisms to resolve certain philosophical problems, Wittgenstein recommends that we replace them by physical mechanisms (*BB*, p. 4). For then we shall see clearly how empty is the putative explanation. Against our inclination to explain meaning in terms of mental accompaniments of speech, we should imagine detaching the allegedly correlated pair of phenomena, for then we will realise that one member is a sleeping partner (*BB*, p. 42). Such techniques are used with striking force in Wittgenstein's later philosophy. Their exemplification will be described in the following chapters.

Wittgenstein's claims for his new method in philosophy were extremely ambitious. His method, he said, was an heir to the subject as practised by past philosophers such as Plato or Berkeley, and was certainly very different from their undertakings. He claimed that now for the first time it was possible to have not only great philosophers but also skilful ones. I do not wish to belittle Wittgenstein's achievement. His work dominates twentieth-century philosophy as Descartes' philosophy dominated that of the seventeenth century. But his claims are over-inflated, his sense of originality, of a total break with all previous tradition, though as fervent as that of Descartes', was as exaggerated. For while both were great innovators, they were inevitably arguing within a certain kind of philosophical tradition, if only in a negative fashion. Nor did they repudiate everything in the tradition against which they argued. Wittgenstein's anti-metaphysical fervour was not novel, although its extent and ferocity were as thorough-going as any before. His extreme voluntarism is not without precedent, even though it is a muted theme in the history of western thought. His claims that philosophical error stems from unclarity about language are certainly not new. They can, to be sure, be found both in Plato and Berkeley with whom he contrasts his work. That philosophical confusions can be removed by scrutiny of the use of words is a claim which, if held with slightly more modesty than Wittgenstein did, would command the assent of many past philosophers, although few, if any, would have considered this the only tool in the philosophical work-box. Although his careful unravelling of errors by grammatical therapy certainly makes room for skill, his is not the first kind of philosophy to do so. Skill is employable in philosophy, as in any other creative endeavour, when the subject enters what might be called a 'scholastic' phase, in which the fundamental presuppositions of the inquiry are, for a time, uncontentious. Of the five main philosophical influences upon Wittgenstein, Hertz, Frege, Russell, Schopenhauer, and perhaps Brouwer, at least three were deeply indebted to Kant. It is therefore not surprising that Wittgenstein's philosophy bears deepest affinities to Kant's, despite the fact that he never studied Kant, and despite the substitution of an austere Bauhaus style for the effusions of the Kantian baroque.

4. *The Neglect of Architectonic Considerations*

The survey of Wittgenstein's later conception of philosophy in this chapter is intended to provide the setting upon which his critical metaphysics of experience may be fruitfully paraded. But before turning to this task it is worth pausing for a brief critical evaluation of his views about the nature of philosophy. The main criticism of Wittgenstein's general conception of philosophy in the post-1930 years derives from a Kantian source. In the preface to the second Critique Kant wrote:

There is another thing to be attended to which is of a more philosophical and *architectonic* character, namely, to grasp correctly the *idea of the whole*, and from thence to get a view of all those parts as mutually related ...[1]

---

[1] Kant, *Critique of Practical Reason*, Preface, trans. by T. K. Abbott in *Kant's Critique of Practical Reason and Other Works* (6th ed., Longmans, London, 1909), p. 95.

The surface of Wittgenstein's later work is littered with hints and suggestions of the absurdity of systematic philosophy. But no good arguments are anywhere adduced to show that it is either absurd or impossible, nor indeed is much indication given of the grounds of the undesirability or pointlessness of such an endeavour. Indeed at one point Wittgenstein declares that his object is still to understand the essence of language—its function and structure (*PI*, §92). The *Tractatus* was imbued with the architectonic spirit, contemptuous of the particular case and at home only in the most abstract and general pronouncements upon thought and reality. Wittgenstein's later work over-reacted, I suggest, to the defects of his first book. For it is by no means obvious that one cannot both do justice to the indeterminacy of sense, the openness of concepts and the flexibility of language, and also be systematic and comprehensive. Philosophers who take Wittgenstein's failure to produce more than an album of sketches of a landscape (*PI*, p. ix) to be an indication of the impossibility or senselessness of trying to produce a definitive painting, commonly point to a number of related themes in Wittgenstein. It is stressed that his claim that philosophy is neither a theory nor a doctrine precludes systematic philosophy.[1] It is sometimes claimed that Wittgenstein's denial that philosophy should or can search for essences rules out a comprehensive account of any element of our conceptual scheme. It has been suggested that since, in his view, the purpose of a particular description of grammar is to remove a particular puzzle, and since there is no limit to what can confuse and puzzle us about the use of an expression, therefore there cannot be a complete description of its grammar.[2]

Such contentions are misguided. The claim that philosophy is not a theory dates back to Wittgenstein's earliest writings upon the subject. The intended contrast is not between systematic and unsystematic philosophizing (e.g. a contrast between Kant and Nietzsche) but between science and philosophy. The descriptive non-stratified status of philosophy did not preclude the systematic enterprise of the *Tractatus*. The denial that there are any theses or doctrines in philosophy does not, it seems, amount to more than

---

[1] e.g. J. J. Thomson, 'Private Languages', in *American Philosophical Quarterly*, i (1964), 31.

[2] e.g. N. Malcolm, 'Wittgenstein on the Nature of Mind', in *American Philosophical Quarterly Monograph, No. 4: Studies in the Theory of Knowledge* (1970), p. 29.

claiming that clarification of grammar must always be obvious (*WWK*, p. 183), must not contain surprises, nor be a matter for hesitation nor dispute. Surprises, hesitation or dispute are, in Wittgenstein's view, a sign of lack of skill in revealing conceptual structures, of having jumped a number of steps or not having expressed them clearly. Whether this is correct or not, it in no way precludes comprehensive surviews of segments of grammar; it is not only what is incomplete that is indisputable and obvious. Wittgenstein's anti-Fregean remarks concerning the indefinability of concepts in terms of their characteristics in no way imply that a complete account of admittedly vague and imprecise concepts is not possible. The fact that Wittgenstein found the primary point of achieving a surview in dispelling a metaphysical illusion in no way debars others from seeking a comprehensive surview of a segment of grammar which goes far and beyond what is necessary for purely therapeutic purposes. It should further be born in mind that Wittgenstein was certainly not satisfied with the 'album of sketches' he produced. Waismann's attempted systematization of Wittgenstein's work in *The Principles of Linguistic Philosophy* may ultimately be a failure, both in its representation of Wittgenstein's thought, and in its integration of the diverse elements it contains. But it is certainly a step in the right direction and shows that the *Bemerkungen* style of writing, and the snippet-box method of composition are not inevitable corollaries of Wittgenstein's philosophy. Indeed as will be seen below, many aspects of Wittgenstein's critical philosophy can be systematically presented and readily reveal the thoroughness and comprehensiveness of his work. More importantly, it is far from obvious that his later views on semantics cannot be coherently represented and indeed formalized so as to yield what most philosophers would call a comprehensive theory of meaning.[1]

Nothing but superficial interpretation of Wittgenstein's philosophy shows the impossibility of architectonic endeavour. One may find it uninteresting in comparison with the pathology of the understanding which so preoccupied Wittgenstein. But the pathologist of the understanding has no monopoly of interest over the anatomist. Completeness and comprehensiveness are perfectly intelligible goals for a philosopher, and it should be emphasized that even though Wittgenstein stressed that, in his investigation of psychological

---

[1] As has been attempted by G. P. Baker, 'The Logic of Vagueness'.

concepts, *his* aim was neither exactness nor completeness (*Z*, §§464–5), nevertheless the plan for the treatment of psychological concepts which he outlined in *Zettel*, §472, and began to fulfil in the following sections, gives some indication of the comprehensive possibilities left open. It might, however, be argued that the imposing Kantian architectonic presupposes a tidy unity and coherence to our conceptual scheme which in all probability is missing. It is a fact of life, which Wittgenstein laboured to bring to our awareness, that we manage to live with contradictions. Our conceptual scheme as a whole is more likely to be akin to a motley ramshackled structure produced by many hands over many generations, crumbling here and there, propped up and reinforced by arbitrary improvisations, than a great, unified, and well-balanced edifice. But this, far from being an argument against attempting to achieve a thorough and systematic surview of our forms of thought, seems to me to be a powerful argument for it. For not only would contradictions and incoherences be precisely and thoroughly revealed by such a 'descriptive metaphysics'[1] which would certainly be of some intrinsic interest, but the door would be opened for potentially fruitful speculative metaphysics. Disagreement with Wittgenstein's contention that philosophy leaves everything as it is has already been expressed above. It should, in this context, be noted that historically, at any rate, the owl of Minerva has often taken wing at high noon. Furthermore, as an eminent philosopher of science has recently remarked, 'A society which is uninterested in metaphysics will have no theoretical science.'[2]

If systematic philosophizing of a constructive kind is thus possible, then it is no longer at all clear that, in the course of displaying the structure of our concepts, the philosopher will not claim many unobvious things about that structure. It may be true that philosophy will neither increase nor decrease our knowledge of the world but in so far as it makes claims about conceptual relations it is not clear that all such claims are uncontentious, unsurprising once understood, and fundamentally trivial. Nor is it obvious that the expression of such insights has doubtful claim to cognitive status and makes only questionable sense. The contention that there is no such thing

[1] P. F. Strawson, *Individuals—An Essay in Descriptive Metaphysics* (Methuen, London, 1959), pp. 9 ff.

[2] M. B. Hesse, *Forces and Fields* (Nelson, London, 1961), p. 303.

as something being red and green all over or as enumerating all cardinal numbers may seem trivial and indisputable once understood. But the explanation of these claims need be neither obvious nor trivial. And in so far as the explanation is non-trivial it may well be claimed that the appearance of the philosophical conclusion is in this respect deceptive. Moreover the general claims about conceptual structures which Wittgenstein makes, e.g. that inner states stand in need of outer criteria, are far from being uncontentious. The contention that the Law of the Excluded Middle has no application in certain domains of thought can only very misleadingly be said to be something we all knew anyway. Finally, what have traditionally been thought of as large-scale philosophical theories, e.g. empiricism and rationalism, phenomenalism and realism, are, directly or by implication, defended or refuted by Wittgenstein. His Kantian contention that there can be no knowledge of objects which transcends all possible experience (because it makes no sense to talk of such objects) can hardly be a truism and a triviality in as much as it rules out of court, or forces a drastic reinterpretation of common cognitive claims.

Finally, Wittgenstein's intense preoccupation with the critique of language, and with the central philosophical subjects which bear upon it, e.g. philosophical logic and philosophy of mind, lead him to overlook branches of philosophy in which the stipulative and explicative task of philosophy is larger than it is in the areas which were of greater interest to him. Thus while it can plausibly be claimed that a purified metaphysics of experience is essentially descriptive, this cannot be said of the philosophy of law, for example. Structural analysis of law[1] involves the search for illuminating and fruitful canonical forms for normative statements of law which will represent the logical relations between different legal norms or parts of legal norms. It is no part of structural analysis to think that this can only be done in one uniquely correct way. Moreover the various envisaged possibilities are comparable and can be evaluated relative to the purposes of a legal theory. Similarly, explication of important legal concepts, e.g. rights, duties, powers, etc., is a central element in an adequate philosophy of law. Here the legal philosopher does not merely extract a surview of the use of users of legal language, but fixes a concept, explicating a novel

---

[1] J. Raz, *The Concept of a Legal System* (Clarendon Press, Oxford, 1970), *passim*.

concept which will be fruitful for legal and meta-juristic purposes.[1] Although Wittgenstein allows such conceptual legislation, his own restrictive concerns led him to underestimate its importance for branches of philosophy with which he was unfamiliar or unsympathetic.

---

[1] e.g. the explication of the concept of a legal right, from the work of Bentham through that of Salmond and Hohfeld, culminating in the work of Hart and Raz.

VI

METAPHYSICS AS THE SHADOW OF GRAMMAR

1. *Forms of Representation*

By contrast with the philosophical ideals of the youthful Wittgenstein, the viewpoint of the mature Wittgenstein may well seem tarnished and disillusioned. The dramatic change in his point of view led to a re-allocation of the metaphysical from the domain of ineffability, in which it lay protected by a penumbra of necessary silence, to the domain of philosophical illusion, a fit subject for the pathology of the intellect. This seems a picture of philosophy fallen from grace, no longer queen of the sciences with a title to investigate and an authority to pontificate upon the ultimate structure of the world, but at best a mere handmaiden. A deeper explanation of this transformation can be provided by exploring Wittgenstein's later conception of grammar and its relation to reality. This will also render further clarification of the therapeutic view of philosophy. Although the change runs deep, it is instructive to conceive of it as a transformation rather than a substitution, a matter of rotating the axis of the investigation one hundred and eighty degrees about the fixed point of our real need (*PI*, §108). In the *Tractatus* the structure of language or thought provided the insight into the structure of reality. In the *Investigations* the structure of language is still the subject of investigation. Moreover it is still isomorphic with the structure of reality, not because language must mirror the logical form of the universe, but because the apparent 'structure of reality' is merely the shadow of grammar.

Towards the end of the *Tractatus* Wittgenstein has a brief Hertzian discussion of the status of scientific theories. The most general propositions of a scientific theory, Wittgenstein contends, are all '*a priori* insights about the forms in which the propositions of science can be cast' (*TLP*, 6.34). Newtonian mechanics imposes a unified form on the description of the world (*Form der Weltbeschreibung*).

Wittgenstein likens it to a network with a chosen pattern and fineness of mesh. The choice of one kind of scientific theory, one kind of network rather than another, is not a matter of one being true and the other false. It is partly determined by simplicity, partly by the degree of recalcitrance which the world displays in being fitted under the network. The most general laws of Newtonian mechanics, e.g. the Law of Inertia, the Law of Equal Reaction, etc., are not to be conceived of as empirical propositions about the world, but 'are about the net and not about what the net describes' (*TLP*, 6.35).[1] They are forms of representation by means of which genuine empirical propositions may be expressed within the framework set up by the theory.[2] They are not refutable or falsifiable by experience, but are replaceable by different forms of representation. Thus, for example, Einsteinian physics does not simply replace falsified Newtonian laws by other more precise laws. Nor are Newtonian laws special cases of Einsteinian ones and so derived from them by restricting the parameters of the variables. Einsteinian physics replaces the concepts of the Newtonian network by novel and more satisfactory concepts. The concepts of space, time, mass, etc. do not remain identical throughout a change of theory.

It is in many ways illuminating to consider Wittgenstein's later work as a generalizing of the concept of a 'form of world-description' from the domain of scientific theory to that of language in general. The atomistic picture theory is rejected, the Platonist conception of petrified, necessarily isomorphic structures of thought, language, and reality is transmuted. The notion of pictorial form (*Form der Abbildung*) is greatly relaxed, becoming radically conventionalist. The conceptions of strict isomorphism and composition out of

---

[1] It is far from clear how Wittgenstein's contentions fit in with the logical atomism of the book. It is unclear what the status of such general scientific propositions is; are they reducible to atomic propositions or to logical truths? Black argues that the discussion of scientific theories is poorly integrated into the book (op. cit., ch. LXXXI). For a different view see J. Griffin, op. cit., ch. VIII sections 4–6, and B. F. McGuinness, 'Philosophy of Science in the *Tractatus*', in *Wittgenstein et la problème d'une philosophie de la science* (Colloques Internationaux du Centre National de la Recherche Scientifique, Paris, 1970).

[2] Wittgenstein gives no examples of the processes of transformation. But a useful example of the initial stages of such transformations is given by T. S. Kuhn, *The Structure of Scientific Revolutions* 'Postscript'. Newton's Second Law of Motion $f = ma$ is, he suggests, a law-schema. In order for it to be used in various contexts, e.g. free fall, simple pendular motion, pair of interacting harmonic oscillators, etc., it requires more or less complex transformations.

simples are dropped, and the theory of the structure of language as the mirror of the structure of reality is turned on its head. In this way the theory of pictoriality is loosened until it has the flexibility and optional character of the net of a form of world-description. If Brouwer's ideas did indeed have a causal influence upon the development of Wittgenstein's thought, then they no doubt provided an impetus for a move in just this direction.

The task of philosophy is to eradicate misconceptions by giving us a perspicuous representation of our grammar, to designate the way we look at things—our form of representation (*PI*, §122). As we shall see, a form of representation is as arbitrary as the pattern and fineness of mesh in the network of a scientific theory as conceived in the *Tractatus*. Just as the most general laws of a scientific theory are not falsifiable by experience, so, too, certain general assertions in non-scientific parlance appear to be about the world, but are in fact merely 'about the net and not about what the net describes'. They are *a priori*, yet they only reflect our form of representation, the conceptual connections which give sense to the sentences by means of which we describe the world. The unalterability and uniqueness of the pictorial form indicated in the *Tractatus* does not apply to the later conception of form of representation. Our form of representation, the way we look at reality, is part of our history. It changes as we change, and it can be altered; but not by arguments lying within the network of concepts concerned, nor by arguments whose legitimacy is guaranteed by an alternative structure of concepts. One cannot *prove* one form of representation to be more 'correct' than another. 'A reason can only be given *within* a game', Wittgenstein remarks, 'The chain of reasons comes to an end at the limits of the game' (*PG*, §55). There is a strong analogy here with the forms of world-description provided by a scientific theory. To revert to the example previously used, the replacement of Newtonian mechanics by Einsteinian theory was a switch from one conceptual system of physical science to another. The choice between two such paradigms, Kuhn has argued,[1] cannot be determined by normal standards of scientific procedure, for the determination of those standards is a function of a scientific paradigm and the arguments between the proponents of the two paradigms will frequently pass each other by. The

[1] T. S. Kuhn, op. cit., ch. IX.

nature of the persuasion to adopt the novel framework must be different. Similar considerations apply to Wittgenstein's later conception of a form of representation.

The notion of a form of representation in Wittgenstein's later writings is never elucidated nor given a precise meaning. It bears some obvious affinities to the Kantian idea of a categorial framework, variously exploited by contemporary philosophers,[1] although it need not be limited to the very general character of this conception. It is similar to the equally imprecise notion of a conceptual system or conceptual scheme, frequently employed in current philosophical jargon. Wittgenstein uses a range of closely related concepts to convey the direction of his thought. The ambiguous notion of a language-game is, in one of its senses, explicitly equated with 'our method of representation' (*Darstellungsweise*) (*PI*, §50). The notion of a world-picture, prominent in the last notes published as *On Certainty*, includes the idea of a form of representation but encompasses more than just the salient concepts and their logical relations which constitute 'the way we look at things'. Like the notion of a language-game, a world-picture is said to be the background against which truth and falsity are distinguished. A language-game such as inductive reasoning is not, Wittgenstein contends, based on grounds. It is not reasonable or unreasonable, he says, it is just there—like our life (*OC*, §559). It sets the standards of rationality and determines the limits of the logical space within which truth and falsity may be distinguished. Similarly, one does not acquire a world-picture by satisfying oneself that it is correct (*OC*, §94). It is the inherited framework within which one learns to reason, the substratum of all enquiry and assertion (*OC*, §162).

Concept formation is part of the constitution of a world-picture. The formation of a concept guides our experience into particular channels, determining the ways in which we see things (*RFM*, p. 123). Hence it constitutes the limits of the empirical (*RFM*, p. 121). Thus, for example, a mathematical proof constitutes the *formation* of a concept or concepts. According to Wittgenstein's constructivist philosophy it is something we accept or reject, it is never forced upon us. In as much as we accept it, it guides our experience into particular channels. For the acceptance of a proof and the consequent sacrosanctity of the resultant theorem—its allocation to the 'arch-

[1] See especially S. Körner, *What is Philosophy?* (Allen Lane, London, 1969), Part 4, and *Categorial Frameworks* (Blackwell, Oxford, 1970).

ives' (*RFM*, p. 78)—is simply a determination to treat the theorem, as Brouwer had suggested we treat the laws of logic, as unassailable by experience. Moreover the unassailability is normative not factual. Acceptance of a proof is thus a determination to view experience through the framework of the theorem. For apparent recalcitrance will be dealt with not by relinquishing the theorem, but by blaming our observations or our instruments, by conceiving the recalcitrance as a novel phenomenon constituting a challenge to science, perhaps even by forcing a modification of scientific theory, or by attributing it to illusion or hallucination. These limits of empiricism are neither unguaranteed assumptions, nor intuited truths, but the ways in which we make comparisons and in which we act (*RFM*, p. 176).

But it is not only the network of our concepts which constitutes our world-picture, guiding our experience into channels. We must include within it a wide range of unassailable or entrenched empirical sentences. These, Wittgenstein suggests, could be thought of as a kind of mythology. The role of these sentences is analogous to that of rules of a game which can be learned practically, rather than by explicit enunciation of rules. Such sentences constitute as it were the river-bed of thoughts:

. . . the river-bed of thoughts may shift. But I distinguish between the movement of the waters on the river-bed and the shift of the bed itself; though there is not a sharp division of the one from the other . . .

. . . And the bank of the river consists partly of hard rock, subject to no alteration or only to an imperceptible one, partly of sand which now in one place now in another gets washed away, or deposited (*OC*, §§97, 99).

The metaphor bears obvious affinities (as well as differences) to Quine's notorious metaphor of the field of force.[1] The waters of the river are our empirical sentences. Some apparently empirical sentences such as 'The world is many years old', 'Human beings have two parents', etc. fall into a special category. They might be likened to ice through which the waters of the river must make their way. Thus, Wittgenstein suggests:

It might be imagined that some propositions of the form of empirical propositions, were hardened and functioned as channels for such

---

[1] W. O. Quine, 'Two Dogmas of Empiricism', repr. in *From a Logical Point of View* (Harper and Row, New York, 1963), pp. 42 ff.

empirical propositions as were not hardened but fluid; and that this relation altered with time, in that fluid propositions hardened and hard ones became fluid (*OC*, §96).

Such sentences, i.e. most of the sentences of the kind the truth of which Moore[1] had claimed to know with certainty and which constitute the main subject of *On Certainty*, are embedded in the structure of our knowledge. Such claims are part of the core of judgements which are interwoven with all the other judgements which we learn. Their truth belongs to our frame of reference (*OC*, §83). To relinquish the claim that the world has existed for many years would drag most of our empirical knowledge with it to perdition. A serious doubt as to whether I have a body is a serious ground for doubting my sanity or my understanding of what I say. Some beliefs of the category do, however, alter as our world-picture alters. The flatness of the earth, animatism, the anthropocentricity of the universe, the Great Chain of Being—these are beliefs or systems of beliefs which have 'joined the waters of the river'. The implications which the existence of such embedded sentences has for philosophical logic and epistemology were never fully worked out by Wittgenstein.

The banks of the river, in Wittgenstein's metaphor, may be taken as our form of representation. Here too there is no uniformity, there is both rock and sand. Some concepts and conceptual links are by and large stable throughout human history. Others change in response to a multitude of factors. Although attempting to grasp and survey our form of representation for the clarificatory purposes of philosophy is not an exercise in natural history, our form of representation, its transformations, alterations, and disorderly growth is part of our natural history. This fact is of great importance to philosophy. For only by appreciating it can we avoid one of the deepest and most pervasive errors in philosophy, namely predicating of the world what lies in our method of representation (*Darstellungsweise*) (*PI*, §104). We shall return to this point later.

2. *Grammar*

Although the concept of a form of representation receives relatively little elucidation in Wittgenstein's writing, the concept of

---

[1] G. E. Moore, 'Proof of an External World', and 'A Defence of Common Sense', repr. in *Philosophical Papers* (Allen and Unwin, London, 1959).

grammar is extensively discussed. It is, in one of its senses, closely allied with the idea of a form of representation. Our grasp of the latter notion can therefore be improved by an examination of Wittgenstein's concept of grammar. He employs this term equivocally.[1]

Like 'logic' which we use both to mean the science of logical structures and the structures studied by that science, so too 'grammar' is used by Wittgenstein to mean the study and description of the rules of language (primarily semantic) and also to mean the network of rules themselves. Employing the term in the former sense, he says of philosophy that it is a grammatical investigation (*PI*, §90); remarks concerning conceptual relations are referred to as grammatical notes (*PI*, §232), or remarks (*PI*, §574); logical problems are contrasted with experiential ones, and said to be in effect grammatical (*Z*, §590). Grammar thus conceived, Wittgenstein says, is the accounting book of language (*PG*, §44), it contains the rules of language and describes the use of words (*PG*, §23). It is the accounting book of language in the sense that the eliciting of the rules of language will determine which combinations of words are legitimate. By describing rules of language, in particular the rules determining the sense of sentences, it will become clear that certain kinds of expressions and sentences are nonsensical and thus withdrawn from circulation and excluded from language (*PI*, §§498–500). Grammar, understood not as the description of the structure of our language, but as the structure thereby described is, I suggest, identical with the notion of a form of representation. For everything said thus far about forms of representations, their arbitrariness, mutability, etc. holds too for grammar conceived as the network of concepts and conceptual connections formed by the rules determining the use of language, as well as those rules themselves.

Wittgenstein speaks of the grammar of words (*BB*, p. 24; *PI*, p. 18n.; *PI*, §§187, 257), of expressions (*BB*, pp. 20, 109; *PI*, §660), of phrases (*BB*, p. 70), and of propositions or sentences (*BB*, pp. 51, 53; *PI*, §353). He also occasionally speaks of the grammar of states (*PI*, §572) and processes (*PG*, §41). I shall regard the latter uses as lax (like 'the logic of states and processes') and treat only linguistic entities as subject to grammar. The sense of words,

---

[1] See E. K. Specht, *The Foundations of Wittgenstein's Late Philosophy* (German edition, Köln, Kölner Universitätsverlag, 1963; English edition, Manchester University Press, Manchester, 1969) for an illuminating discussion of 'grammar' in Wittgenstein's later works.

expressions, phrases, and sentences is determined by the rules for their use. Every change of rules implies a change of sense, just as a change of characteristics (*Merkmale*) for Frege is a change of concept (*PB*, §154; *PI*, p. 147n.). What is a rule of grammar, and what kinds of rule are there? In accord with his prejudice against comprehensiveness Wittgenstein never attempts to classify grammatical rules nor even to give us a canonical form of corresponding rule-specifying sentences.[1] In conformity with his distaste for generality and abstraction he very rarely makes any explicit statements about grammatical structures in general. This greatly hampers comprehension. The two kinds of rules in which he is most interested (barring mathematics) concern ostensive definition conceived as a rule introducing a sample into language, and rules determining criterial relations between sentences. Whether a word can or cannot be ostensively defined is itself an important grammatical feature of the word.[2] However, the correlation of a word with a sample by means of ostensive definition involves only one among many rules which determine the sense of the word. The reason for Wittgenstein's deep interest here is determined by pathological considerations, for the role of ostensive definition was a source of error in the *Tractatus*, and is revealed in the *Investigations* to be a central feature in the confusions surrounding the private language problem. The deep concern with the rules determining criterial relations is Wittgenstein's main constructive contribution to contemporary philosophy. The account of sense in terms of truth conditions which dominated the *Tractatus* is replaced in Wittgenstein's later work (from the *Blue Book* onwards) by an account in terms of criteria: 'to explain my criterion for another person's having toothache', Wittgenstein wrote (*BB*, p. 24), 'is to give a grammatical explanation about the word "toothache" and, in this sense, an explanation concerning the meaning of the word "toothache"'. Kinds of sentences, Wittgenstein suggests, can be characterized by the nature of the criterial evidence which supports their assertion. Thus the grammar of material-object sentences is characterized by having multiple criterial evidence provided by sentences

---

[1] Cf. G. H. von Wright, *Norm and Action* (Routledge and Kegan Paul, London, 1963), ch. 6, for the concepts of normative statement, norm-proposition, and deontic sentence.

[2] See the report by A. Ambrose on Wittgenstein's lectures in the early 1930s, in A. Ambrose, 'Wittgenstein on Universals', repr. in *Ludwig Wittgenstein: The Man and his Philosophy*, ed. K. T. Fann, p. 343.

describing subjective experience (*BB*, p. 51).[1] The grammar of sentences concerning mental states is characterized by the fact that sentences describing behaviour in certain circumstances are fixed as criteria for such sentences. The rules in question are non-inductive, non-deductive inference-rules which allow us to move from an assertion of criterial evidence to a justified though not necessarily true assertion of that which it supports. These rules are fixed by us, they are grammatical conventions (*PI*, §§354–5). Both these kinds of rules will concern us later in our investigations into Wittgenstein's refutation of idealism.

Some of Wittgenstein's remarks have a genuine meta-linguistic nature, and it should not be surprising to dub them 'grammatical'. Thus he points out that if there were a verb meaning 'to believe falsely' it would have no first person present indicative (*PI*, p. 190). But sentences which Wittgenstein himself calls 'grammatical sentences' are very different from this. They are exemplified by a mixed bag of sentences: 'Every rod has a length', 'This body has extension' (*PI*, §§251–2), 'The class of lions is not a lion but the class of classes is a class' (*RFM*, p. 182). 'White is lighter than black' (*RFM*, p. 30). Another kind is formed by mathematical sentences. These are, despite the misleading form of the verbal expressions of mathematical proofs, grammatical sentences. They show us what it makes sense to say (*RFM*, p. 77). Of the assertion 'Three by eighteen inches won't go into three feet' Wittgenstein says that it is a grammatical rule and states a logical impossibility (*BB*, p. 56). The form of this sentence brings one to the class of grammatical sentences which most fascinated Wittgenstein. These are grammatical sentences dressed in metaphysical guise. They are of at least two kinds. The first are grammatical sentences couched in modal form, characteristically employed for stating that something can or cannot, must or must not, be thus or otherwise. These typically occur in philosophy, e.g. 'One cannot ennumerate all the cardinal numbers', 'I cannot exhibit my own sensations' (*Z*, §134), 'Green and blue cannot be in the same place simultaneously' (*BB*, p. 56). Finally there is a range of completely disguised grammatical sentences. 'Of course I know what I wish', Wittgenstein says, *can be interpreted* to be a grammatical statement (*BB*, p. 30). Both these

---

[1] Wittgenstein did, I suspect, change his view on this matter later. See below ch. X, pp. 306 ff.

kinds of sentences are 'metaphysical' sentences which 'hide grammatical rules' (*BB*, p. 55).

None of these sentences have a recognizable canonical form of a rule-sentence. However, their truth does not depend upon facts in the world, but upon linguistic conventions. A trivial analytic sentence such as 'All bachelors are unmarried males' can be shown to be logically true by a substitution which is sanctioned by a definition. In this sense it depends for its truth upon a convention which lays down inter-substitutable expressions.[1] Analogous considerations apply to all Wittgenstein's so-called 'grammatical sentences', although the dependence upon linguistic rules is often more complex and less obvious than in the trivial analytic case. Like the analytic sentence, the grammatical sentences Wittgenstein cites are misguidedly called 'rules', but appropriately thought of as 'concealing rules' or depending for their truth upon linguistic conventions rather than upon facts in the world which they apparently describe.

The first class of cases lies on a par with sentences in the *Tractatus* which Wittgenstein originally dismissed as nonsensical and as constituting a violation of the rules of syntax. They all concern internal relations and properties. His later view was less dogmatic, for he no longer wished to take such sentences as nonsense, but as proper sentences, at least if one takes them right, i.e. not as in the *Tractatus* (*RFM*, p. 182). To be sure, he still occasionally refers to such sentences as nonsense (*PI*, §252), but not with the same fervent condemnation. For we take such sentences as we should if we realize that they depend for their truth not upon the essence of the world, but upon rules of language. And taken thus such sentences too have a use. 'All rods have a length' is a grammatical sentence the truth of which follows from the conventions determining the sense of the expressions 'rod' and 'length'. 'Being a rod' entails 'having a length' since the criteria justifying us in claiming something to be a rod are also criteria justifying us in saying of the same thing that it has a length. That one colour stands to another in the 'internal relation' of lighter to darker (*TLP*, 4.123) is a consequence of the fact that the rules assigning sense to the colour expressions allow us to introduce one and the same pair of samples to serve as paradigms as do the rules assigning sense to the expressions 'lighter'

---

[1] See Specht, op. cit., ch. VI, section 11.

and 'darker'. The connection of paradigms and expressions is set up in our language (*RFM*, pp. 30–1).[1]

The alleged normative status of mathematical sentences involves highly complex and controversial issues. It will not be examined here. But the claim that 'Three by eighteen inches won't go into three feet' specifies a grammatical rule can be briefly explained. It is misleading to call it a rule. Yet, like the previous sentences, its truth is a consequence of rules rather than facts. For it rests upon the definition of 1 foot as 12 inches, together with equations of elementary arithmetic which can be conceived of as substitution-rules. Its apodeictic status secures it against falsification by experience, although it does not of course ensure that we may not find three eighteen-inch segments of a given material which, when put together end to end, measure only three feet. But if this does occur we shall search for a cause in the world rather than for a mistake in the laws of arithmetic.

The truth of the grammatical sentences dressed in metaphysical guise is likewise shown to depend upon linguistic conventions in more or less complex ways. A brief sketch must suffice for the moment, other more detailed exemplifications of the method will be discussed in a later chapter. The grammatical interpretation of 'Of course I know what I wish' (when I am in pain, what I believe, etc.), must first transform the sentence into a modal one, e.g. 'I cannot doubt what I wish'. This form may then be reinterpreted as 'There is no such thing as . . .'. Thus instead of 'One cannot enumerate all cardinal numbers', one should say 'There is no such thing as enumerating all cardinal numbers'. Instead of 'Green and blue cannot be in the same place simultaneously' one should point out that there is no such thing as something being green and blue all over. For this will help shift our gaze from hypostatized limits in the world to counterfeit currency in language. The impossibility resides not in any barrier but in an expression's being excluded from circulation. To say that there is no such thing as . . . is tantamount in such cases to claiming that the expression in question lacks sense. 'Being green and blue all over' or 'enumerating all the cardinal numbers' are nonsensical expressions. That they are nonsensical now has to be shown. This can be done by exhibiting the rules determining the use of the relevant expressions. Thus the colour-exclusion case does not show a metaphysical limit preventing green

[1] See Specht, op. cit., pp. 161–3, for a more detailed discussion of this point.

and blue residing in the same place, but conventions governing the use of the colour names. These conventions involve the use of samples as paradigms, and the existence of these conventions within a linguistic community involves a uniformity of response to such paradigms. We *do not* take a paradigm for 'green' to be also a paradigm for 'blue'. To be sure we *could*,[1] but then the expressions would no longer mean the same. Our paradigms for 'blue' include both what we call 'light blue' and what we call 'dark blue'. They have in common the fact that they are both blue. But *goluboj* and *sinij* for a Russian[2] only have the fact that they are colours in common. In the English colour grammar a surface is blue all over even if it is part light blue and part dark blue, for a paradigmatic sample for 'blue' may be either light blue or dark blue. It is thus that metaphysical sentences hide grammatical rules:

The only correlate in language to an intrinsic necessity is an arbitrary rule. It is the only thing which one can milk out of this intrinsic necessity into a proposition (*PI*, §372).

The arbitrariness of grammar is the arbitrariness of autonomy, and the necessary truths which the metaphysician seeks in his investigations into the essence of the world are mere reflections of grammar.

3. *The Autonomy of Grammar*

Two distinct doctrines can be entitled 'Wittgenstein's Doctrine of Linguistic Autonomy'. They are related to one another, yet one is of considerably greater importance than the other. I shall call the first and less significant thesis 'The Doctrine of the Autonomy of Language' in order to avoid confusing it with the second thesis, which I shall call 'The Doctrine of the Autonomy of Grammar'.

The doctrine of the autonomy of language is simply the repudiation of the attempt made by the *Tractatus* to reveal the foundations of language. The *Tractatus* had presented a conception of language according to which language has an *a priori* structure which is then matched on to a given reality like a stencil which is pinned onto the world (*NB*, p. 53) by means of simple names which 'constitute a connection between language and reality'. These unanalysable, logically irreducible names are the materials out of which ele-

---

[1] See F. Waismann, *The Principles of Linguistic Philosophy*, ch. III, section 3.
[2] See J. Lyons, *Introduction to Theoretical Linguistics* (C.U.P. Cambridge, 1968), pp. 56 ff.

mentary propositions are constructed. Such propositions constitute the foundations of language in so far as all other propositions are allegedly analysable into truth-functional compounds of such propositions; yet the elementary propositions themselves are not analysable into more primitive ones, but stand in a direct and immediate relationship to reality. We come to understand such elementary propositions by means of elucidations (*TLP*, 3.263) which, as conjectured above in chapter II, are ostensive explanations of the form 'This is *A*'. If '*A*' is taken to name a simple, then it may readily seem to one that one is in possession of a form of language which both expresses a true proposition (for to be sure this is *A*!) and also explains the meaning of '*A*' by establishing a direct connection with reality. While nominal definitions remain closed within language, elucidations reach out to reality. Of course I will not understand this true proposition until I grasp what '*A*' means. But my learning the meaning of the word and my understanding the proposition appear to constitute one and the same mental act.

Whether this is a correct interpretation of a *Tractatus* elucidation of primitive signs or not is of no great importance for present purposes. What is important is that this error fascinated Wittgenstein in the 1930s, and was thought of as being one of the roots of the belief that language has foundations, a belief which is beyond doubt one of the corner-stones of the *Tractatus*. Indeed, as we have seen, he attributed his belief in a connection between language and reality in the *Tractatus* to his confusions concerning logical analysis on the one hand, and ostensive definition on the other (*WWK*, pp. 209–10). The errors involved here are numerous, but only two aspects of the confusion Wittgenstein diagnoses will be discussed at present. Firstly, 'This is *A*' can be either a proposition or an ostensive definition but not both simultaneously. If it is a proposition then it is essential to bear in mind that it could be false. It would retain its sense even if uttered while gesturing at an 'object' *B*. Like a *Tractatus* elucidation, it could not be understood unless the meaning of '*A*' were already known. By the same token it does not explain the meaning of '*A*'. If it is an ostensive explanation or definition, however, it is no longer a proposition saying something about the world and capable of being either true or false. Moreover qua definition it is not unambiguous. The same ostension can explain a host of different words belonging to different categories, e.g. shape, colour, number, etc., and in each case the ostensive explanation plays a different role in the grammar of the word explained (*PG*, §25). Moreover, in each case the ostension only gives one element of the complex grammar of the word. In order to grasp the equivocal ostension a great deal of the grammar must already be understood, e.g. the grammatical category of the expression and so the categorial status of the object picked out by the gesture.

Secondly, if '*A*' is, e.g. the name of a primitive shade of colour, then if one stares at an expanse of such a shade and says to oneself 'this is *A*' one may well seem to oneself to be saying something true, while simultaneously explaining to oneself, and thereby convincing oneself, that one knows the meaning of '*A*'. It is here that one confuses sample and description. This error stems partly from failure to appreciate the first distinction, partly from too narrow a view of language which fails to include samples as part of language, and partly from an obsession with the phenomenological pecularities of a situation in which language is idling (*BB*, pp. 174–5), being employed in a context in which it can fulfil no genuine function. Such an ostensive definition of a shade does not provide a connection between language and reality. It introduces, as it were, a fragment of reality into language. The expanse of the shade at which one points is not described by 'this is *A*'. It is incorporated into language as a sample to serve as a paradigm. A sample which is connected with a word by ostensive definition is as much a part of language, Wittgenstein claims provocatively, although a very different kind of part, as is a word which is connected with another word or words by a nominal definition. It is not something that is represented, but is a means of representation (*PI*, §50), although to be sure a given patch of colour (unlike the standard metre in Paris) is often used now as a sample and later as an item for description. The possibility of the 'language-game with colour', as Wittgenstein puts it, depends upon two kinds of pervasive regularity. Firstly, that colour properties of objects should be reasonably constant over time (*NFL*, p. 306), secondly, that the reactions of members of the linguistic community to coloured objects in general and samples in particular, should, in respect of colour, be in general agreement, and that the application of samples should likewise agree. Acquiring a colour vocabulary is acquiring a discriminatory and linguistic capacity. To learn the meaning of a simple predicate is not, as it were, to acquire a drawing-pin by means of which, through the grace of God, one pins an element of the structure of one's own language to the same point in reality to which the same elements of other people's languages are pinned. One acquires a technique of using a word the correctness of which is determined by reference to a public paradigm and agreed samples. The explanation has its foundation, not in the ultimate constituents of reality, but in training (*Z*, §419).

Thus ostensive explanations do not provide one with a connection between language and reality via the nexus between names and objects. Nor could elementary propositions provide one with a foundation for language, for their sense cannot be grasped by reference to a putative direct connection between their constituent elements and reality. Language can never provide one with a means of extricating oneself from language. Every way of explaining language already presupposes a language, and the use of language, *in a certain sense*, cannot be taught, i.e. it cannot be taught through language in the way in which piano playing can be learnt through language (*PB*, §6). The eternal substance of the world, the indestructible objects of the *Tractatus* with which language was connected by means of names are, as we shall see below, nothing but metaphysical illusion. These unalterable simples, lying beyond existence and inexistence, are merely samples incorporated into language. 'The connection between "language and reality" is made by means of the clarification of words, which belongs to the learning of language, so that language remains closed in within itself, and autonomous' (*PG*, §55).

The doctrine of the autonomy of grammar is closely related to the doctrine of the autonomy of language. If language had foundations in metaphysical simples, grammar could not be autonomous. The doctrine of the autonomy of language is a repudiation of the *Tractatus* conception of the connection between language and reality. The consequent doctrine of the autonomy of grammar is a dramatic transformation of earlier views. For it is the heir of the doctrines of the indescribability of the limits of thought, of the inexpressibility of essences and of the distinction between showing and saying. The whole of the *Tractatus*, it will be remembered, is condemned as nonsense because it tried to say what can only be shown. It tries to describe the limits of thought from the outside, an endeavour which cannot but be futile, for it violates the bounds of sense. The formal isomorphism between language and reality, the fact that language is the great mirror of the essence of the world, can only be shown in language but not expressed by means of it.

The doctrine of autonomy is as central to Wittgenstein's later philosophy as was the doctrine of showing and saying to his earlier.

The problem to which this doctrine is a negative answer may be expressed thus: if our grammar constitutes our form of representation, the way we see the world, is it not facts in the world which justify us in adopting the grammatical rules we have, in wearing the particular kind of conceptual spectacles we wear? Is it not the fact that the world has the structure which it has, independently of our cognition or possibility of cognition, that justifies us having the concepts and principles which we do have? We have a colour system, as we have a number system. Do these systems reside in the nature of numbers and colours or in *our* nature? (*Z*, §357). *Not* in the nature of numbers or colours, is Wittgenstein's emphatic reply. We are continually tempted to take our grammar as a projection of reality, instead of taking our conception of the structure of reality to be a projection of our grammar. For we are driven to justify our grammar by reference to putative facts about the world, e.g. 'But there really are four primary colours'. So we think of our concepts of colour justified, for they characterize the world as it is. For I *would* look in vain for a fifth primary colour; we put the four primary colours together because they are similar, and we contrast colour with shapes and notes because they are different (*Z*, §331). It is against the conception of this sort of justification, which is analogous to the idea of justifying a sentence by pointing to what verifies it, that the claim that grammar is arbitrary is directed (ibid.). The relevant sense in which grammar is arbitrary is the doctrine of the autonomy of grammar.

The central thought of the doctrine is a difficult one, and Wittgenstein wrestled with it as persistently as with its ancestral doctrine of showing and saying. It recurs in virtually all his later works,[1] with occasional remarks concerning the difficulty of expression. The task of attempting to throw light upon this doctrine can conveniently begin by examining the above-mentioned analogy with verification, even though this necessitates mentioning prematurely doctrines in Wittgenstein's later views on meaning and justified judgement which will only be explained in subsequent chapters.

If I assert of an item in a collection that it is red, it is not the fact that it is red that is a criterion of its being red and hence that justifies

---

[1] e.g. M, p. 277; *PB*, §§4, 7; *PG*, §55; *PI*, §§496-500; *Z*, §320 ff.

my assertion, although it is this fact that makes it true. For the fact that it is red is only available to me as a piece of evidence, and hence as a ground for my claim, if I already know that it is red. Thus the contention that what verifies a sentence can also be what justifies its assertion presupposes what it is meant to explain. How then do I know that this, which I see, is red? The question in contexts other than abnormal perceptual conditions, is misleading—but the correct answer would be simply to say 'I have learnt English' (*PI*, §381).[1] I have a right to assert without justification, i.e. in the absence of further grounds, in virtue of a capacity, or mastery of a technique (*PI*, §289 and §386). Moreover I can show this by giving the rule for the use of 'red', i.e. by showing a sample of red (NFL, p. 301), provided that I do not choose the item I am describing to function simultaneously as sample. Hence the indispensability of agreement in reaction to coloured objects and samples mentioned above. The criterion that two people mean the same by 'red' is that they give the same names to the colours of objects and use samples in the same ways.

This point can be expressed more generally in terms of Wittgenstein's semantics. The paradigm of a genuine proposition for verificationist theories of meaning, and for Wittgenstein in 1930–1 during his brief flirtation with verificationism, was an experiential proposition conceived of as conclusively verifiable by its subject by reference to the experience it describes. The separation of the justification or ground of a proposition from what verifies it has far reaching consequences. For what was thought of as a paradigm of a verifiable proposition becomes a paradigm of a proposition concerning which it makes no sense to speak of verifying it. The underlying thought is the insistence that what makes a proposition true cannot be identical with what gives it sense.[2] Wittgenstein embraced this principle in his earliest writings and adhered (*PB*, §23) to it, though with a special qualification, throughout his life. For only, it seems, by adopting this principle, is the possibility of expressing false yet meaningful propositions adequately secured. In the 'Notes on Logic' the principle was expressed by the bipolarity thesis. The same principle is evident in the

---

[1] There is the further possibility of regression to 'I see that it is red'. This makes no difference to the present argument (see below ch. IX, pp. 280 f, and ch. X, pp. 306 ff.)

[2] See A. J. P. Kenny, 'The Verification Principle and the Private Language Argument', in *The Private Language Argument*, ed. O. R. Jones (Macmillan, London, 1971), pp. 219–22.

emphasis in the *Tractatus* (2.22–2.225) upon the independence of sense from truth-value. However, the price paid for securing the semantic flank was, as it were, the opening of a large gap in the epistemological one. For, as has been seen in chapter II, the correspondence theory of knowledge presupposes what it is meant to explain. Because of the minor role of epistemology in the *Tractatus* this weakness did not come to light. But in the 1930s it became crucial. For Wittgenstein's later conception of meaning shifts from accounting for the sense of sentences in terms of their truth conditions to accounting for their sense in terms of their criteria, i.e. the grounds which are fixed or conventionally determined as justifying one in claiming them to be true. For now epistemological considerations, far from being peripheral, *are built into the account of meaning*. If the sense of a sentence is to be given by specifying the criteria for its truth, then the verificationist conception that what justifies 'I am in pain' or 'I see red' is the experience which verifies it implies that what gives the sentence sense is also what makes it true. Thus sense and truth collapse into each other. To be sure the verificationist may not see this as a weakness, for he may conceive of this as identical with the claim that sense and truth stand or fall together, and hence as a support for the incorrigibility of protocol sentences. The argument against a private language is designed to reveal the weakness as fatal.[1]

Returning from this digression to the problem of the justifiability of grammar by reference to facts, it will be seen that the analogy with the verificationist error is a close one. For the salient feature of any attempt to justify the grammar of, e.g. colour words by reference to, e.g. the alleged fact that there really are only four primary colours, is that such justifications presuppose what they are trying to justify. Just as I cannot use the fact that *A* is red as a ground for believing *A* to be red without employing the very sentence the assertion of which it is meant to support, so too I cannot adduce facts as justifications of the correctness of grammar without employing the very grammar I am trying to justify. Sentences formulated in existing 'justified' grammar are either true or false. They presuppose the existing grammatical conventions and therefore cannot justify them (*PB*, §7). For any attempt at justification would have to state reasons, using language in com-

---

[1] See below ch. VIII.

pliance with grammar. The reasons given would have to be a description of reality, that is, of those features of reality in terms of which grammar is justified as correct. But any description of reality must be capable of being false (unless one allows some form of natural necessity, which Wittgenstein did not). Yet if the justifying sentence is stated in the grammar of the justified sentence, then its falsity would imply the unjustifiability of the grammar. Hence its truth is a condition of its having sense. In which case it is no longer capable of being false, and therefore no longer qualifies as a description of reality (M, pp. 277–80). The similarity we think we see between the four primary colours is determined by nothing more than the fact that we define the concept of primary colour by a four-termed disjunction. One is inclined to rebel against the arbitrariness suggested by this. Could one take red, green and circular together as falling under a single concept? (Z, §331). Why not, Wittgenstein retorts: of course concepts other than those akin to ours seem weird (Z, §373), hence the importance in philosophy of the invention of fictitious natural histories (PI, II. xii). For the only way to combat our natural inclination to take our conceptual structures to be the absolutely correct ones is to make intelligible the formation of concepts very different from ours. One way of so doing is by narrating fictitious natural histories and inventing alternative forms of representation.

Grammar may be compared to a method of measurement. A method of measurement is antecedent to statements of lengths. The absurdity of trying to justify grammar by reference to features of reality which are described by means of that grammar is exemplified in trying to justify our employment of the metric scale by reference to the fact that a kilometre really does contain 1,000 metres. Of course it does not follow that the grammar of the metric system cannot be explained in the grammar of the British Imperial system, nor that its justification by reference to its relative simplicity cannot be said. As far as I can see, nothing in the doctrine of autonomy expounded by Wittgenstein requires that it be impossible to justify one grammatical structure from the point of view of another, not, to be sure, as *correct* in virtue of a correspondence with reality, but as economical, illuminating, fruitful etc. Admittedly he obscures and underemphasizes this point.

A final analogy which illuminates Wittgenstein's doctrine of autonomy is with Berkeley's criticism of Locke's version of the causal theory of perception. Berkeley's criticism amounts to the claim that there is no independent point of view at which I can establish myself to see that my perceiving that p and the fact that p are causally related. My only 'access' to the fact that p is by means of my perceiving it. Hence the inference from 'I perceive that p' to 'p' cannot be inductive. Analogously there is no way of 'thinking' reality except by means of a form of representation. Yet it is the form of representation we employ which determines reality and what forms it has. One cannot conceptualize without concepts and hence one cannot in general justify a conceptual scheme by reference to reality as described in terms of that scheme. What I take to be reality is not independent of, but is logically related to, my conceptual scheme.

Is grammar then arbitrary? Wittgenstein replies that it is akin both to what is arbitrary and to what is non-arbitrary (Z, §358). Its arbitrariness is akin to that of an activity which is rule-governed but whose end is intelligible only by reference to the rules, which are, in this sense, constitutive. The rules of most games are thus constitutive; the goal of chess, i.e. bringing one's opponent to checkmate, is only intelligible by reference to its rules. One may of course change the rules, and change the end, e.g. Losing Chess. But if one does so, one is not playing the old game wrongly, but a new game (although there will naturally be border-line cases). The arbitrariness of this kind of rule-governed activity can be contrasted with rule-governed activities whose end is not determined by their rules. The instructions in a cookery book do not determine the concept of a good-tasting food which is the end of cooking. The acts which comply with the instructions stand in a causal relation rather than a conceptual one to the object of producing a tasty dish. Failure to follow the rules will frequently lead not to production of an alternative tasty dish, but of an inedible one. The rules of grammar are analogous to those of constitutive rules of a game, and are arbitrary in this way (Z, §320). If one changes the grammatical rules one creates an alternative form of representation; one moves from one language-game to another. A change of grammar is a shift of logical space, not of an occupant of logical space.

The quintessence of the autonomy thesis is expressed in a passage in the *Philosophische Grammatik*:

That which is so difficult to grasp can be expressed thus: that *as long* as one remains within the domain of the True-False-Game a change in grammar can only take us from one such game to another, but never from something true to something false. On the other hand, if we step outside the domain of these games, then we no longer call it 'language' and 'grammar', and so again we come into no contradiction with reality (*PG*, §68).

There are then two aspects to the autonomy of grammar. Firstly, there are alternative grammars. These are mutually autonomous. One is inclined to query here whether if we had not this grammar we could express *this* fact, thus indicating the fittingness of our grammar to things. This is misguided. For what does 'could' mean here (*PI*, §497)? What is logically possible is not determined extra-linguistically. In an alternative, relevantly different form of representation, what is actual in our grammar and thus logically possible is nonsense. It is not that Newtonian physics cannot express the relativity of time or the curvature of space. It is rather that it makes no sense in the Newtonian conceptual scheme to speak of such things. If a person is conceived of as a member of a uniquely determinable species, who by definition has an immortal soul, then the suggestion that a person is descended from an ape is as nonsensical as the idea that a chair is in pain. The second aspect of the autonomy of grammar is not relative to alternative grammars, but relative to reality. At no point does grammar come into *conflict* with reality.

Thus far, the case for the arbitrariness of grammar is sketched out by Wittgenstein. Yet it must be remembered that there is also a kinship to the non-arbitrary. In the course of exploring this, the harsh relativism of the two aspects of autonomy of grammar may be slightly softened and mitigated. Against the autonomy of grammar one is inclined to object:

Yes, but has nature nothing to say here? Indeed she has—but she makes herself audible in another way.
'You'll surely run up against existence and non-existence somewhere!' But that means against *facts*, not concepts (*Z*, §364).

This admission gives a ray of hope to the anti-relativist and provides a hint of a synthesis between the relativism of the doctrine of autonomy, and the confident rational absolutism of the alternative tradition within European philosophy. The way in which nature makes herself audible is one of the ways in which conceptual change is induced, and one form of representation relinquished in favour of another. Here there is a kinship with the non-arbitrary which we shall explore in the following section. There are other relations to the non-arbitrary. A rather obvious fact, but one which has often been disregarded by philosophers, is that by accepting a grammatical rule one commits oneself to a certain form of action, both linguistic and non-linguistic. A rule does not exist in language by fiat. Humpty-Dumpty can make words mean what he wants, but only in so far as he works hard at it, with a certain constancy and regularity. A single correlation between a noise and a fact does not create a rule; such a correlation must have normative consequences and has to involve commitment to the future use of the sign, and hence also to satisfy the conditions of the possibility of commitment (M, pp. 259, 277). These conditions are violated by the private linguist.[1] This kind of non-arbitrariness might be partially captured by saying that language is not a matter of whim. A further aspect of it is brought out by stressing not individual commitment but the social aspect of language. To take 'hate' as an intransitive verb would be arbitrary. For as a common word in *our* language it is transitive (M, p. 277). Grammar is laid down in our language before us. It is something we learn with language, a socially transmitted form of representation as deeply rooted within us as our nature qua social beings; it is indeed a dominant aspect of our social nature. A third and related aspect of the non-arbitrariness of grammar is emphasized in a rather dangerous analogy that Wittgenstein employs in the *Investigations*. Grammar is no more arbitrary than a style of painting. A style of painting may be arbitrary in so far as it is not dictated by external factors, but is non-arbitrary in so far as it constitutes a well-entrenched tradition guiding not only our standards of beauty and ugliness, correctness and incorrectness, but the very way in which we are able to represent things.[2] The most interesting aspect of the non-arbitrariness of grammar is the first. This can be clarified by examining Wittgenstein's views of the determinants of conceptual change.

4. *Determinants of Grammar and Concept-Formation*

Wittgenstein's thesis of the autonomy of grammar is bold and radical. It is firmly located in the voluntarist tradition of European

---

[1] See below ch. VIII.

[2] cf. E. Gombrich, *Art and Illusion* (Phaidon, London, 1962), ch. II. It is of course significant that when painting was conceived of as essentially representational, it was thought of as being on a par with the natural sciences and as a paradigm of an area of human activity in which progress is not only possible but actual. See e.g. Vasari's *Lives*.

metaphysics which, not surprisingly, gives it an historicist aspect. It is therefore correspondingly anti-rationalist. For its salient theme appears to be that no one thing stands firm in all conceptual schemes, or rather, if anything does stand firm, it need not. Its constancy is arbitrary and no reflection of the essence of the world. Nor, it seems, would any constant elements of all conceptual schemes with which we are acquainted be a reflection of 'the structure of the mind' in anything but a biological or sociological sense. The Kantian flavour which marked the *Tractatus* as a work of critical philosophy is preserved in Wittgenstein's later work. But it is deprived of its rationalist, ahistorical features. To be sure the mind forms nature, but the forms it imposes are not reflections of the necessary structure of the mind of any discursive intelligence. The grounds of our form of representation, in so far as one can speak of grounds here, involve no necessity; we are not necessitated by nature, nor are we given insight into what is 'great and important' (*PI*, §118).

The evaluation of Wittgenstein's claims here is particularly difficult. His remarks are obscure, often equivocal and always both unsystematic and incomplete. Sometimes it seems that he is claiming that grammar cannot be justified *tout court*, more often his claim takes the form of denying that grammar can be justified by reference to a description of what is represented (*PB*, §7). Similarly, the concept of grammar is sometimes used globally to designate the totality of linguistic rules, and sometimes more locally to designate the rules of a particular 'language-game'. The term 'language-game' is notoriously equivocal in Wittgenstein's later work.[1] It sometimes designates primitive simplified forms of language, whether natural or notional. Occasionally it designates the totality of language and the actions and activities into which it is interwoven. Frequently it is used to designate a fragment of language or linguistic activity. The latter use encompasses a highly heterogeneous class, varying from specific speech acts (both illocutionary and perlocutionary, or more fundamentally, simple semantic moods) to general speech activities on the one hand, and what might be called partial systems on the other. The latter kind of 'language-games' are exemplified by Wittgenstein's remarks on, e.g. the language-games with colour words, with sense impressions, with physical objects, with inductive reasoning, with cardinal numbers. A

[1] Specht, op. cit., ch. III, section 2.

concept ranging over so wide and disparate phenomena is not obviously perspicuous or useful. If it is limited to its latter use, it needs to be made substantially more precise. The importance of these considerations for the problem of autonomy should be obvious. For if we take the claim of autonomy in its standard form, and if we are permitted to take the concept of grammar locally rather than globally, then it is not at all clear that we cannot adduce rational criteria for choosing or preferring one local grammar to another. Like Neurath's sailor we cannot rebuild the whole ship simultaneously, but we can stand on one sound, leak-free plank and evaluate and reconstruct an adjacent one. Nature may make herself audible even if she cannot run us up against concepts, but only against facts, and our responses to her burblings need not be beyond reason and unreason.

Wittgenstein's main target here, as elsewhere in his later philosophy, is to free us of metaphysical prejudices. In this context in particular he is concerned with trying to shake us free from our conviction that our concepts are absolutely correct.

There is, of course, a certain correspondence between general facts of nature and our concepts. This correspondence, however, is not of a metaphysical kind, as was suggested by the *Tractatus*. By imagining changes in general facts of nature we can see how we might be induced to relinquish concepts, and we might see how alternative concepts are intelligible. Wittgenstein conducts his therapy by means of a host of examples. Almost all are highly specific, extremely sketchy and small-scale. They are also taken almost exclusively from familiar areas of mundane experience. Thus the concepts to which he invites us to consider alternatives are normally non-scientific and fundamental in that they are both familiar and woven into the texture of our life. We have already noted the claim that the similarity between the four primary colours is a product of our concept of primary colour, not a ground for it. We could 'create' a similarity between red, green and circular. The point is extended by further examples. One can imagine drawing distinctions where we see none, e.g. two concepts taking the place of our concept of pain—the one reserved for bodily injury and associated with pity, the other reserved for stomach-ache and associated with mockery. Do not such people notice the similarity? The important question is whether it is important to them; we do not have one concept wherever we see a similarity (*Z*, §380). One can imagine people not drawing distinctions where we do, e.g. not having the concepts of modesty and swaggering, even though there are modest men and swaggerers. Something must hang on a difference to make it worth picking out (*Z*, §378). Different conceptual structures may involve conceiving certain properties in distinct categorial terms. In one language the concept 'red circle' might be expressed by a conjunction of two distinct symbols, an activity-word and a noun (*Z*, §337), whereas in another language there would be no such grammatical distinction. If we described colours by means of adverbs instead of adjectives we would conceive of what we now call colour, not as a property, a state of an object, but as a process, an activity of an object.[1] Some concepts have roots that reach so deep into our life that imagining them to be different involves virtually imagining different kinds of creatures. Thus one can imagine a tribe educated never to express feelings. They would have no concept of shamming and would be able to see no point to having one. Their life would run on quite differently to ours. What interests us—what is significant and important to us—would be irrelevant to them. We could barely recognize them as human. Yet such forms of behaviour and such an array of concepts is conceivable (*Z*, §§383–90).

Like a legal system (*Z*, §120, §350) our concepts rest upon certain normality conditions, though they are not justified by reference to these. The sense in which they are so supported is not that of constituting a foundation, nor of necessitating us to adopt certain concepts. 'Experience does not direct us to derive anything from experience', Wittgenstein wrote in *On Certainty* (*OC*, §130), 'No, experience is not the ground for our game of judging. Nor is its outstanding success' (*OC*, §131). For experience could only be a ground for our system of judgement if we already had one, and the success of our system of judgement could not be a reason for adopting it, for its success is only determinable by reference to the standards set by the system itself. It is rather that in the absense of certain kinds of regularity and constancy of specific natural phenomena the applicability of concepts would be rendered either wholly impossible, or the point of kinds of concept-laden activities would be lost or else substantially changed. Our concepts of weights and measures only have application and point in a world with

---

[1] This example is F. Waismann's; see 'Verifiability', in *Logic and Language*, 1st series, ed. A. Flew (Blackwell, Oxford, 1951) pp. 137 ff.

relatively constant gravitational fields, and relatively stable rigid objects (NFL, p. 287n.; *RFM*, p. 98). Of course one could conceive of an activity similar to our measurement of length even though rulers were highly elastic (*RFM*, p. 4). But one could also imagine circumstances in which nature rendered measurement pointless. This need not stop me going through the 'motions' of weighing and measuring. There is a sense in which I can stay in the saddle however much the facts buck; but that does not mean that a horse will remain beneath the saddle. For whether we would still call the motions I go through 'weighing and measuring' is another matter (*OC*, §§615–20). It is, of course, not only the constancy of external nature which, in this sense, conditions our forms of representation, but also the constancy of human nature. Changes in our physiology and psychology would cause or prompt conceptual change. We have already seen that possession of a common colour vocabulary requires not only a constancy in the nature of things, but also an agreement and regularity in human responses to them. Our psychological concepts would have no application if human behavioural responses to internal and external states were not—as a brute fact of nature—shared, regular, and relatively uniform.

Although Wittgenstein wrote quite extensively, if unsystematically, about the kind of correspondence which exists between general facts of nature and our concepts,[1] he had relatively little to say about the nature of conceptual change. He did apparently think that choice between certain kinds of concepts can sometimes be guided, though not determined, by more or less pragmatic considerations. New facts may induce conceptual change for theoretical or pragmatic reasons, producing shifts from qualitative to quantitative differentiations, or a shift in importance attributed to a phenomenon (*Z*, §352). On the other hand some concepts, some principles, and some *factual beliefs* are too deeply rooted in our nature, in contingencies of experience, and in our current world-picture to be subject to guided choice at all. When two world-pictures confront each other, when predictions based on physical science confront predictions based on oracle-consultation, then proof of correctness is impossible (*OC*, §609). One imparts a world-picture by persuasion (*OC*, §262). Experiments cannot prove the correctness of a

---

[1] He stresses rightly the fact that measuring by pacing was for all its crudity, measuring. Yet, one may retort, it does not make quantitative astronomy possible. Foot and ell are *natural* units of measurement for mankind, but in order to do atomic physics one requires units such as angstrom or Bohr radii.

world-picture, although they may change our whole way of looking at things, inducing a conversion. For although reasons *can* be given, at the end of reasons comes persuasion (*OC*, §612).

Fragmentary remarks such as these give one hints of the general direction of Wittgenstein's thought, but little more. They raise as many problems as they solve. Out of the wide range of issues involved in the study of the relationships between different forms of representation and their concommitant world-pictures, the following seem to me, in this context, the most interesting and important. Firstly, what is the nature of the reasons which can be adduced to justify the adoption of one form of representation, or part of a form of representation, rather than another? How far can rational argument reach, in principle at any rate, and what is the nature of the persuasion to which we have to resort? Secondly, do distinct forms of representation have a core of common principles of inference and concepts? If not, how is any 'transcategorial' communication possible at all? If so, is the existence of such a nucleus a contingent result of constant features of human nature and of regularities in the world, or is it ascribable to some unifying categorial principles necessary to any conceptual scheme? A thorough answer to these two sets of questions is impossible in this context. All I shall attempt to do is to give a crude outline of possible answers and suggest a substantial criticism of Wittgenstein.

One obvious area where distinct grammars or parts of grammar are frequently in conflict is in the natural sciences. The nature of concept formation, theory construction and rejection in the history of natural science has been explored in detail by T. S. Kuhn.[1] His views bear a marked similarity to Wittgenstein's unsystematic remarks on grammar. Although, as pointed out above, conflicts between large-scale scientific paradigms are not resolvable by proof, the option is not an existential leap. There are regulative principles[2] at work providing grounds, although not proof, for adopting one or other scientific theory and framework of concepts. These can be roughly specified, they are the stock-in-trade of the philosopher of science. The dimensions by reference to which choice between conflicting theories should be guided are such considerations as relative simplicity, aesthetic value, high degree of predictive

---

[1] e.g. T. S. Kuhn, op. cit., and also 'Logic of Discovery or Psychology of Research', and 'Reflections on My Critics', in *Criticism and the Growth of Knowledge*, ed. I. Lakatos and A. Musgrave (C.U.P., Cambridge, 1970).

[2] The term is of course Kant's, but the specific use here is Waismann's, ibid., p. 142.

accuracy within the standards of the epoch, provision of a set margin of error consistently satisfied in a given field, scope, internal consistency, external compatibility with other currently accepted theories and fruitfulness in enabling formulation of puzzles which are susceptible to solution in terms of currently available techniques or techniques made available by the novel conceptual scheme in question. These dimensions of evaluation are not, of course, reducible to a unitary scale of a single value. Such considerations cannot prove one theory to be preferable to another, but they can make it reasonable to adopt one rather than another, and thus persuade one to do so.[1] The possibility of employing these diverse criteria depends upon the fact that normally the scientific community can produce at least a few concrete research results which are describable in mutually intelligible terms to proponents of competing theories, even though they may not explain them in the same way. This provides common ground upon which to stand. Kuhn is well aware of the narrowness of its scope in periods of scientific crisis. But in the last resort, natural scientists tend to share a common non-scientific natural language or languages from which translation, however cumbersome, may proceed, and hence a degree of mutual intelligibility be achieved.

Wittgenstein's interests, however, were not primarily in the forms of representation constituted by the superstructure erected by scientists on the ordinary linguistic substructure. His concern was with the grammar of ordinary language and its dual autonomy. If alternative grammars are possible here, and Wittgenstein laboured to show us that there is nothing unique about ours, then how is choice, comparison and translation possible? One can do no more in this context than sketch possible strategies and related difficulties. One move is to make a rigorous distinction between information and explanation, and assume that while explanation is dependent upon one's categorial framework there is some sense of 'information' for which this is not so.[2] The difficulty involved here lies in

---

[1] The importance of such considerations was somewhat obscured in the first edition of Kuhn's book, and the balance only set aright in the postscript to the second edition and 'Reflection on My Critics'. It is of course crucial to stress that such principles are only obviously operative at times of scientific revolution and crisis. For normal science the question of rejecting the framework does not arise.

[2] This is the line taken by S. Körner in *Categorial Frameworks*, p. 64. Körner suggests a pragmatist behaviouristic analysis of identity of the informative content of sentences from distinct categorial frameworks. His remarks are, however, too brief to

eliciting such a sense of 'framework-free' information. If one relaxes the notion of categorial framework to the point at which it merges with Wittgenstein's imprecise notion of a grammar, then the idea of preserving identity of sense throughout change of grammar is nonsensical (*PB*, §154; *OC*, §65, etc.). An alternative but equally radical move is to embrace an extreme Whorfian thesis. But this commits one not merely to anthropological relativism but to some form of socio-linguistic solipsism; all language will perforce be *our* language. For the grounds in terms of which we can identify an alternative conceptual scheme as a conceptual scheme will be whisked from under our feet. Not only will alternative grammars be incomparable, they won't even be identifiable.

The route to steer between the 'objectivist' Scylla and Whorfian Charybdis must commence by observing a range of truisms. We do occupy a common unified spatio-temporal objective world. Although there may be peripheral differences in perception conditioned by our mutual grammars, we cannot identify a creature as a concept-employing animal unless we assume some similarities of perception.[1] Consequently, we must assume a degree of common nature if we are to be able to identify perceptual responses for what they are. Linguistic concepts rest upon a broad range of recognitional capacities which manifest themselves in characteristic responses. Only by reference to such assumptions can we identify a *prima facie* case of a language-using creature. To claim this, of course, is not to claim that all language-using creatures must conform to conditions which will enable us to identify them as such. To confirm a *prima facie* case as an actual one requires us to identify assenting and dissenting behaviour, and to postulate that our creatures assent to what they take to be true and dissent from what they take to be false. We must also assume that most simple everyday beliefs of 'the cat is on the mat' type are true. These postulates and assumptions are neither arbitrary nor dispensible. Nor are they sufficient for our purposes. For the identity of the sense of a sentence depends upon the logical relations it bears to other sentences, and we must assume not only a common, if tacit conception of truth,

---

know whether the standard objections to pragmatist analyses of belief are inapplicable to this notion of informative content. Moreover, Körner's subsequent switch to speaking of *information* as framework-free is highly questionable.

[1] See M. Hollis, 'Reason and Ritual', in *Philosophy*, xliii (1968), 231–47, from whence the following argument is taken.

but a common if unarticulated conception of logic. The assumptions of the laws of non-contradiction, identity, modus ponens, etc. are not optional. There must be some such limiting assumptions determining what we may take to be a conceptual scheme.

Of course such limitations are limitations of what *we* take to be a conceptual scheme. It is *our* concept of thought, language, and representation which is thus moulded. Wittgenstein himself brings out this important feature in criticism of Frege's introduction to *The Basic Laws of Arithmetic*. Frege castigated the psychological logicians for confusing laws of truth with laws of people's taking-to-be-true. Laws of logic do not describe how human beings think, but prescribe how one ought to think. A law of people's taking-to-be-true would interpret the Principle of Identity thus: 'It is impossible for people . . . to acknowledge an object as being different from itself.' The corresponding law of logic is: 'Every object is identical with itself.' Laws of truth are not psychological laws,

they are boundary stones set in an eternal foundation, which our thought can overflow, but never displace. It is because of this that they have authority for our thought if it would attain to truth. They do not bear the relation to thought that the laws of grammar bear to language; they do not make explicit the nature of our human thinking and change as it changes.[1]

Why ought one to think as these eternal and immutable laws prescribe? Logic can only answer, Frege replies, in so far as it can reduce one law of logic to another. If it cannot do that, logic can give no answer. If one steps outside logic, however, it is clear that laws of taking-to-be-true must accord with laws of logic if truth is to be obtained. The suggestion that there might be people for whom different laws of logic are valid, as opposed to different laws of taking-to-be-true applying, is madness. It may indeed be constitutionally impossible for us to reject the law of identity. This however is a causal thesis rather than a logical one. It may be that we must acknowledge this law unless we wish to reduce our thought to confusion and finally renounce all judgement whatever. This is a pragmatic principle, giving a reason for our taking something to be true, not a reason for its being true.

This prescriptive interpretation of the laws of logic leads readily to a Platonistic descriptive conception.[2] For the step from the claim

---

[1] G. Frege, *The Basic Laws of Arithmetic*, Introduction, p. 13 (p. xvi in German edition).

[2] See G. H. von Wright, *Norm and Action*, p. 4.

that laws of logic prescribe how one ought to think if one wishes to think correctly (preserve truth throughout inferences) to the claim that they describe truths about relations between logical entities (propositions, truth-values, etc.) and *hence* have a prescriptive function, is a small one. Moreover it is supported by the normal form of logical laws, and by the fact that they are normally thought of as having a truth-value.

Wittgenstein, not surprisingly, criticizes this Platonistic view, not because he agrees with the psychological logicians, but because he finds both thesis and antithesis misguided. The idea of people thinking in accordance with the Law of Identity, and hence of there being a sociological law of people's taking-to-be-true, is unintelligible (*RFM*, p. 41). The impossibility of recognizing an object as different from itself is not, as Frege suggested, either causal or pragmatic. Like the impossibility of moving facts from one drawer to another, it is the impossibility of the nonsensical. The sentence 'This lamp is different from itself' is nonsense. The reason why there is no law of people's taking-to-be-true that an object is different from itself is not human wisdom, but the unintelligibility of the putative law. Laws of thought do not describe the immutable relations between eternal entities, nor are they laws of nature; they *determine* our concept of thought. The laws of logic show what we call 'thinking', they bring out 'the essence, the technique, of thinking' which they determine. To be sure, if we did not acknowledge the laws of logic, we would be reduced to confusion. But this is not a pragmatic, extra-logical consideration. The laws of thought are not 'anankastic sentences'[1] upon which technical norms of thought are constructed. They are rather constitutive or determinative of thought. They define the limits of the range of all possible 'True-False-Games', and so of what we call 'language' and 'grammar'.[2] In this respect indeed they do make explicit the nature of human thinking, as well as thinking in general. That much truth was perceived, somewhat obscurely, by the psychological logicians.

Wittgenstein's eagerness to combat Platonism led him to obscure if not to underestimate the universal features of thought and the common structural elements of conceptual schemes, and he correspondingly over-emphasized the arbitrary features of our conceptual scheme and the parochial implications of the fact that whatever

---

[1] See von Wright, op cit., pp. 10 f., for the concept of an 'anankastic sentence'.
[2] See the quotation from *PG*, §68, on pp. 164 f above.

limitations we place upon our concept of thought and language, it is *we* who place them upon *our* concept. But if this is to be parochial, the accusation loses its sting. We can do no other than locate the bounds of what *we* conceive to be thought and language. It is the fundamental task of the metaphysics of experience and the philosophy of language to uncover what these are.

If this conclusion is correct, then it will not be surprising to find that:

There is a massive central core of human thinking which has no history—or none recorded in histories of thought; there are categories and concepts which, in their most fundamental character, change not at all.[1]

It is by reference to such a common core of thought that argument and persuasion concerning novel and partial forms of representation may take place. There is no reason to think that the range of relevant regulative principles providing grounds for preferring a conceptual innovation to an engrained element of a conceptual scheme are not similar, although no doubt even more imprecise, than those mentioned above as bearing upon the justifiability of conceptual innovation in the natural sciences.

Two superficial responses must be warded off. Firstly, it might be suggested that such a common core of thought is itself contingent. It is nothing other than a reflection of the blessed regularities of nature and an element of constancy in mankind. These features could be different. Secondly, the roughly-sketched truisms which condition the possibility of our identifying creatures as concept-employing animals bear upon nothing other than our ability to identify such creatures. It provides no reason for thinking that there is a common core to all conceptual frameworks in which experience of a world and a world experienced can be described. There is a single riposte to both objections. It is true that we can conceive of microscopic or macroscopic creatures with wholly different perceptual faculties to ours such that we might not be able to identify them as language-users. But to think of the existence of such creatures as language-users requires us to think of them employing symbols according to rules which fall within the bounds set by our concept of language. The concept of language outlined by Wittgen-

[1] P. F. Strawson, *Individuals*, p. 10.

stein in his later philosophy does indeed lay down quite rigorous conditions delimiting the bounds of sense.[1] But not only are such formal logical requirements (of e.g. criterial relations as determinants of the sense of sentences) not dispensable; if we are to conceive of concept-exercising creatures capable of describing an objective world, a further range of concepts and principles becomes a necessary part of such a conception. Nature as we know it and human societies with which we are acquainted have numerous constant though arbitrary features. But these *can* be readily abstracted, still leaving a substantial framework of concepts which can only be dropped at the expense of rendering unintelligible the idea of a description of experience and its objects. The conceptions of possible knowledge of an objective world and of subjective experience alike carry with them a host of closely-interwoven conceptual commitments which cannot be relativized to forms of representation, but which must constitute a common element of any form of representation. To conceive of metaphysics in a thorough-going historical fashion[2] or to conceive of categorial frameworks as lacking any stable core of elements and principles is to claim that there are no restrictions upon the concept of a language, and no general necessary conditions of the possibility of conceptualized experience of an objective world. To be sure, it is a contingent fact of nature that the world contains sufficient regularity to be an object of empirical thought. But given that it is so, it by no means follows that the conceptualization of experience of such a world is limited by no bounds of sense. If, as I shall argue in subsequent chapters, Wittgenstein's refutation of solipsism and denial of the possibility of a private language are analogues of Kant's refutation of idealism and doctrine of the correlativity of knowledge of objects and knowledge of subjective experience, it is by no means obvious that the promptings of nature are not after all limited by the forms of thought. Similar considerations apply to the forms of language as suggested by the constructivist semantics implicit in Wittgenstein's doctrine of the criterial determination of the sense of sentences.

---

[1] Support for this contention will be forthcoming in subsequent chapters.

[2] e.g. R. G. Collingwood, *An Essay on Metaphysics* (Clarendon Press, Oxford, 1940), III B; S. Körner, *What is Philosophy?* Part 4; and *Kant* (Penguin, Harmondsworth, 1955), ch. 4.

5. *Grammar and Metaphysics*

It has already been remarked upon that the doctrine of the autonomy of grammar is heir to the doctrines in the *Tractatus* of the inexpressibility of logical form. The line of descent, however, is irregular, and in the process much is lost, much undergoes deep change, and the spirit which was imbued in the parent doctrine is wholly missing in its progeny. According to the *Tractatus*, logical form can only be shown, not said. Attempts to express logical form cannot but result in senseless propositions, or nonsensical propositions which violate the logical syntax of language. The world has an *a priori* structure and likewise language has an *a priori* structure. These structures are identical, although this isomorphism can only be shown, not said. Ordinary language is in perfect logical order, for despite the different and variable superficial forms of representation, the unnoticed conventions and the intentional elements contributed by language-users, there is and must be one unique pictorial form which mirrors the form of the world. Thus the essence of the world is mirrored in the logical syntax of language. All necessity, according to the official doctrine of the *Tractatus*, is logical necessity. Although any language must in principle, once it is properly analysed, be able to show every essential feature of the form of the world, logical necessity is neither conventional nor relativized to particular languages. The nature of necessary truth is explained in terms of the metaphysics of objects, facts and possible worlds, and the semantics of logically proper names, elementary propositions and truth-functional composition. Necessary truths are a revelation of reason, not a creation of the will. Although any future metaphysics wishing to present itself as a science is impossible, the impossibility is not due to the illusoriness of its object, but to the inherent limits of language.

The collapse of the *Tractatus* system traced out schematically in chapter IV led, among other things, to the doctrine of the autonomy of grammar. Without the metaphysical underpinning, the doctrine of the autonomy of grammar, heir to the doctrine of the inexpressibility of logical form, became the expression not of the ineffability of insight into the *a priori* structure of reality, but of a warning against illusions generated by the shadows cast by arbitrary linguistic conventions upon a formless world. The connection between the two doctrines of autonomy in Wittgenstein's later

philosophy is that in the absence of metaphysical simples, correlated with linguistic simples by means of some mechanism constituting a connection between language and reality, the theory of
the limits of thought and the logical structure of the world becomes
radically conventionalist, and metaphysical truths become not
simply inexpressible, but illusory reflections of grammatical conventions.

'Like everything metaphysical', Wittgenstein wrote in the
Grammatik (*PG*, §112), 'the harmony between thought and reality
is to be found in the grammar of the language.' The enigmatic
remark probably appealed to him since it was deposited in his
'*Zettel*' box, and appears in the book his literary executors have
wrought out of these snippets (*Z*, §55). The irony underlying the
enigma is that this remark is equally applicable to the philosophy of
the *Tractatus* and to that of the *Investigations*, but its significance
changes dramatically from one context to another. The deceptive
continuity of deep doctrines is further reinforced by remarks such
as '*Essence* is expressed by grammar' (*PI*, §371), and 'Grammar tells
us what kind of object a thing is' (*PI*, §373). The veil of deception
begins to lift, however, when the conventionalism of the later
philosophy is revealed. It is put in strikingly Fregean terms in the
Foundations of Mathematics: 'it is not the property of an object
that is ever "essential", but rather the mark of a concept' (*RFM*,
p. 23). A few pages later the Fregean terminology reappears, again
in the context of a Fregean heresy: 'For what is the characteristic
mark of "internal properties"?'; Wittgenstein's response begins
from common Platonist grounds: 'That they persist always,
unalterably, in the whole they constitute; as it were independently
of any outside happenings.' And then in two powerful metaphors
his new conception is revealed: 'As the construction of a machine
on paper does not break when the machine itself succumbs to
external forces—Or again, I should like to say that they are not
subject to wind and weather like physical things; rather are they unassailable, like shadows' (*RFM*, p. 30). For the Platonist, a geometrical proof consists in revealing the essential properties of shapes.
The author of the *Tractatus*, like Plato, conceived of properties as
ingredients of a thing (*RFM*, p. 22).[1] Thus a geometrical proof that
'this shape consists of these shapes' is thought of as showing that

[1] See above ch. IV, p. 97, and in more detail in Wittgenstein's criticism of the
Tractatus doctrines concerning objects *PG*, *Teil* I *Anhang*, esp. 1–4.

a given shape has been constructed once and for all, by whoever put the essential properties into things. It is as if God had constructed shapes thus. 'For if the shape is to be a thing consisting of parts, then the pattern-maker who made the shape is he who also made light and dark, colour and hardness' (*RFM*, p. 22). The substance of the world, objects that are unalterable, and subsistent independently of what is the case (*TLP*, 2.024–2.027) had seemed to be, not shadows, but the bricks of reality. The scaffolding of logic had appeared to be both as pure as crystal and as hard or harder than concrete (*PI*, §97). Under the spell of such a vision Lukasiewicz wrote:

Whenever I am occupied even with the tiniest logistical problem, e.g. trying to find the shortest axiom of the implicational calculus, I have the impression that I am confronted with a mighty construction, of indescribable complexity and immeasurable rigidity. This construction has the effect on me of a concrete tangible object, fashioned from the hardest of materials, a hundred times stronger than concrete and steel. I cannot change anything in it; by intense labour I merely find in it ever new details, and attain unshakable and eternal truths. Where and what is this ideal construction? A Catholic philosopher would say: it is in God, it is God's thought.[1]

It is against such conceptions that Wittgenstein struggles in his later philosophy. The simile of God the creator is misleading. For were it the case that 'in the beginning was the word' it would not be the word of God, but of human convention. Yet this is not the case, for underlying human convention are human actions. Thus, '... write with confidence "In the beginning was the deed."'[2] Connections which are not causal, but stricter, harder, more rigid, are always connections in grammar (*RFM*, p. 40). For the unshakeable certainty that seems attached to such connections is simply a reflection of our determination to employ them as part of our form of representation (*RFM*, p. 81). The 'hardness of the "logical must"' indicates our inability, or our refusal, to depart from a concept (*RFM*, p. 121); it designates an element of our grammar (*RFM*, p. 37). The inexorability of the laws of logic is *our* inexorability in applying them (*RFM*, p. 36). Of course, our commitment to a form of expression, especially when it is couched in

---

[1] J. Lukasiewicz, quoted and trans. by P. Geach in *A Wittgenstein Workbook*, by C. Coope, P. Geach, T. Potts, and R. White (Blackwell, Oxford, 1970), p. 22.

[2] Quoted in *OC*, §402 from Goethe, *Faust*, Pt. I.

the material mode rather than in the formal mode will not only look metaphysically necessary, since it seems to be about objects rather than signs, it will also seem *a priori* true. For our very avowal of adherence to this form of representation excludes its opposite as impermissible, as nonsense (*Z*, §442). The notion of the logically possible—detached, as it has become, from the meta-physics and semantics of the *Tractatus*—is now bound to a grammar. What is logically possible or impossible is wholly dependent upon what our grammar permits, what makes sense in a given language system (*PI*, §520). All logical possibility is relative to a language. What makes sense in a given grammar is dependent upon the con-ventions that constitute that grammar. They are, as already noted, the only correlate in language to intrinsic necessities (*PI*, §372). Essences are reflections of forms of representation, marks of con-cepts, and thus made rather than found. We create our forms of representation, prompted by our biological and psychological character, prodded by Nature, restrained by society and urged by our drive to master the world. Essences are a product of will, not a discovery of reason. All talk of essence is talk of conventions, and what seems to us to be the 'depth' of the essences is in fact the depth of our need for the conventions (*RFM*, p. 23).

Wittgenstein's respect for the natural disposition of mankind to metaphysics is as great as Kant's. Like Kant he saw dogmatic metaphysics as the illusions generated by the mind's self-explora-tion; while worthy of respect, it requires exposure. The essential thing about metaphysics is that it obscures the dividing line between empirical and conceptual problems (*Z*, §458). In metaphysics we characteristically express our puzzlement concerning our forms of representation by factual questions about objects in the world instead of grammatical questions about language (*BB*, p. 35). The way in which grammatical rules are concealed in metaphysical sentences has already been examined. In them a linguistic con-vention is represented in the form of a barrier of a supra-physical kind. 'I can't feel your toothache' appears superficially similar to the contingent assertion 'I can't feel pain in your tooth'. The metaphysical formulation of our conventions concerning the grammar of colour expressions makes it appear as if one colour gets in the way of another and hence two colours cannot be in the same place simultaneously (*BB*, p. 56).[1] We sense our conventions as

[1] As Wittgenstein himself had thought (RLF, p. 169); see above chapter IV, p. 89.

limits, and so indeed they are—they are limits of sense. But that is not how they are taken by the metaphysician. For he projects our grammatical conventions on to the world and then views them as *de re* necessities. The claim that either you win a bet or you lose it is a misguided projection of the Law of the Excluded Middle which is manifestly incorrect for bets upon material implications (*Z*, §677). The claim that states of affairs must be completely determinate, if not in kind then in degree, is no more than an avowal of adherence to a form of expression which makes use of the form of an ideal of accuracy (*Z*, §441). Fregean logic and the *Tractatus* were erected on the foundations of adherence to determinacy of sense and thus ultimately to the Excluded Middle. Indeed the *Tractatus* became for Wittgenstein a paradigm of philosophy in the grip of metaphysical illusion. This can be shown in many ways, and in subsequent chapters Wittgenstein's refutation of idealism and solipsism will be related to the *Tractatus* doctrines and fallacies against which it is in part directed. Here the truth of this contention will be exemplified by a brief account of Wittgenstein's exposure of the metaphysics of subsistent simples which underpinned the *Tractatus* semantics as a projection of the grammar of expressions which include rules introducing samples into language.

Russell's terms[1] (units, individuals, entities) were conceived as immutable and indestructible; though they may come into existence and pass away, they never cease to be. For if they lacked being they could not be spoken of or conceived. Wholes are composites of which terms are parts. Likewise Wittgenstein's objects are simple indecomposable elements of reality. They too are beyond existence and inexistence: they subsist eternally, constituting the unchanging substance of the world. Some of the distortions which give rise to such misguided doctrines are analysed in the *Investigations*. If one conceives of reality as composed of complexes constructed out of elements, then it may indeed seem that one can attribute neither existence nor non-existence to the ultimate elements. For, in the first place, coming into existence and passing away will be explained in terms of composition and decomposition of complexes. The elements which thus come together and separate cannot intelligibly be said to exist or not to exist. Secondly, if an element did not have

---

[1] Russell, *The Principles of Mathematics*, §47, pp. 43 ff., and §427, pp. 449 ff.

being or subsist, one could not name it, and so there would be nothing of which one could say that it was not. Finally, putting the first two points together, what simple names signify must be indestructible, for it must be possible to describe the state of affairs in which everything destructible is destroyed. It is no coincidence that when asked for examples of such elements one standardly thinks of 'concrete universals', of situations in which one is confronted by an instance of a simple perceptual quality. Although colours were not thought of as ultimate simples in the *Tractatus* because of the colour exclusion problem, shades of colours were. In the *Foundations of Mathematics* Wittgenstein points out that the word 'being' has been used 'for a sublimed ethereal kind of existence' (*RFM*, p. 23). 'One is tempted to pronounce a sentence like "Red *is*"', Wittgenstein continues, 'when one is looking attentively at the colour; that is, in the same situation as that in which one observes the existence of a thing (of a leaflike insect, for example).' Staring thus at a colour, or simply thinking of 'the nature of colour' one is inclined to claim that although something red can be destroyed, torn up or pounded to bits, the colour red is indestructible. One cannot say, so one might be led to think, that red exists. For if there were no red, the utterance 'Red does not exist' would be without any meaning. And if red is, then the utterance contradicts itself just because red exists, in some sense, 'in its own right'. A necessary condition of an expression being a name is that it cannot be substituted for the variable in '*X* exists'. Thus the word 'red' appears to be a genuine name; names so conceived signify elements of reality which *must* exist.

Thus far the metaphysical illusion which beset the author of the *Tractatus*. The therapy which will return the metaphysician from the pure pellucid heights, at which he attempts to fly without friction,[1] to the hard ground of reality is grammatical. Whatever it is that gives words their meaning cannot be destroyed without the words losing their meaning. For ordinary names, however, such as 'Mr. N. N.', the bearer of the name is not what gives it its meaning, even though the man is what corresponds in reality to the name. For the death of Mr. N. N. does not deprive the name of its meaning. What then of *real* names, like 'red'? Certainly it makes no sense to speak of pounding the colour red to pieces, or tearing it to shreds. What

---

[1] For an interesting comparison of metaphor see Kant, *Critique of Pure Reason*, A 5, B 9, and Wittgenstein, *PI*, §107.

corresponds to the name 'red' without which it would have no meaning is a paradigm in language used in a certain way by a linguistic community. 'Red is, has being, exists in its own right' are tortuous metaphysical insights into a simple grammatical truth: 'Red' has meaning. For what appears in metaphysics to be an assertion about colour and its essence is in fact as assertion about the use of the word 'red' and the function of colour paradigms in language. The metaphysician's use of language here, as so often in metaphysics, is aberrant. 'Red is' is only a sentence on sufferance. To speak of a colour existing is a misleading way of speaking of a coloured object's existing. Although it is senseless to speak of 'destroying red', it is possible to lose a paradigm which is a part of our language. This could happen in various ways, e.g. by our forgetting which colour 'red' is the name of, by an impoverishment of our discriminatory abilities with respect to colour, by the destruction of all red things in the universe. The word 'red' would then have lost its use, and our colour grammar would change. What seems to be an indestructible element in a language-game is a means of representation, it is part of our method of representation, not an object represented thereby. 'What looks as if it *had* to exist, is part of language. It is a paradigm in our language-game; something with which comparison is made' (*PI*, §50).

The task of philosophy is to clear the ground of language from such houses of cards (*Luftgebäude*). Metaphysics leads us to the limits of language and beyond. Critical Philosophy, conceived of as a philosophical study of grammar, brings us to see the limits of language and to understand their nature. Perhaps Wittgenstein would not have frowned overmuch upon Kant's comment:

Metaphysics, in the dialectical essays of pure reason (which we do not undertake arbitrarily or wantonly, but are driven to them by the nature of reason itself), leads us to boundaries; . . . that is the end and utility of this natural disposition of our reason which has borne metaphysics as its favorite child whose generation, like every other in the world, is not to be attributed to unforeseen accident but to an original germ which is wisely organised for great ends.[1]

---

[1] Kant, *Prolegomena to Any Future Metaphysics*, p. 120.

VII

THE REFUTATION OF SOLIPSISM

1. *Introduction*

Wittgenstein's claims that a philosophical problem has the form—
'I don't know my way about' (*PI*, §123) and that his own purpose
in philosophy was 'to show the fly the way out of the flybottle'
(*PI*, §309) are notorious. What is less well known is that the archetypal fly in the original flybottle was the solipsist. In the 'Notes for
Lectures on "Private Experience" and "Sense Data"', written
between late 1934 and early 1936, Wittgenstein wrote:

The solipsist flutters and flutters in the flyglass, strikes against the walls,
flutters further. How can he be brought to rest? (NFL, p. 300).

The puzzles surrounding solipsism thus became for Wittgenstein a
paradigm of the diseases of the intellect to which philosophers are so
prone[1] and through which they must, it seems, pass before they can
acquire a proper grasp of a sound human understanding. The
solipsist, like the idealist, is caught in the net of grammar, and by
disentangling the knots tied by his futile struggles one can better
understand Wittgenstein's conception of philosophy and its
methods. It will also highlight the extent to which epistemological
matters are, in Wittgenstein's later philosophy, closely interwoven
with semantic issues. His refutation of solipsism comes in three
phases. The first stage is to be found in the writings and reports
of the transitional period from 1929 to the academic year 1932/3.
The *Bemerkungen* is particularly important here, but the sets of
notes from Waismann and Moore are also significant. The second
and most revealing phase of his concern with uncovering the errors
of solipsism (in particular) and idealism (in general) is between
1933 and 1936. The *Blue Book* and 'Notes for Lectures' contain
Wittgenstein's most important arguments in refutation of solipsism.

---

[1] And not only philosophers, e.g. Tolstoy, *Childhood, Boyhood and Youth*, trans. by
R. Edmonds (Penguin Books, Harmondsworth, 1964), p. 159.

The third and final phase finds its full expression in the *Investigations*, with some additional material in *Zettel*. Here the direct and overt interest in solipsism is diminished, and its place taken by the fully-developed argument against the possibility of a private language, a brief sketch of which had already appeared in the 'Notes for Lectures'. Although solipsism is only indirectly alluded to, most of the arguments developed in the second phase reappear in highly condensed form in the *Investigations* and *Zettel*. The task of the present chapter is to trace the process whereby Wittgenstein gradually freed himself from metaphysical illusion. I shall first examine the intermediate period between the *Tractatus* and the *Blue Book*, and then show how the elegant and comprehensive refutation of solipsism and idealism emerged in the second, mature phase. The argument against the possibility of a private language will be examined in detail in the following chapter.

Solipsism is the doctrine according to which nothing exists save myself and mental states of myself. Moreover nothing else *could* exist, for we can make no sense of existential claims concerning any other objects unless we construe them as a *façon de parler*. While idealism denies the existence of objective material particulars, but allows for the existence of objective spiritual substances, solipsism presses on rigorously and relentlessly to the logical conclusion that other minds can enjoy no more privileged a position than bodies. Indeed, taken to its ultimate conclusion the doctrine culminates in what Russell called 'solipsism of the moment'. On this view only the present experiences of myself exist. Neither the past nor the future can be said to be real. Only my immediate present experience 'has reality'. The doctrine has been relatively little discussed in recent years, although both idealism and scepticism concerning the existence of other minds have separately and individually been extensively debated. But in the inter-war years the topic of solipsism engaged much attention. This may well have been a partial consequence of the enigmatic remarks of the *Tractatus* on the subject.[1]

---

[1] C. I. Lewis in 'Experience and Meaning' (repr. in *Readings in Philosophical Analysis*, ed. H. Feigl and W. Sellars, Appleton-Century-Crofts Inc., New York, 1949, pp. 128–45) p. 131, implies that *TLP*, 5.6's are a source of the positivist's methodological solipsism, but Carnap, in his discussion of his choice of the auto-psychological basis for construction and of his system of methodological solipsism, does not mention the *Tractatus* at all; see R. Carnap, *The Logical Structure of the World*, trans. by R. A. George (Routledge and Kegan Paul, London, 1967), §§64–6. There were of course numerous other sources of the doctrine.

Russell, in an article entitled 'Vagueness'[1] written in 1923 when he was still very obviously under the spell of the book, proclaimed that whereas all illegitimate philosophical problems derive from misunderstood symbolism, and all genuine philosophical problems, barring one, are answerable by means of physics, solipsism constitutes the ineradicable exception. 'If you are willing to believe that nothing exists except what you directly experience,' Russell wrote,[2] 'no other person can prove you wrong, and probably no valid arguments against your view exist.' What is the intractable problem Russell saw? He expressed it thus: 'Is there any valid inference ever from an entity experienced to one inferred?' On this position, Russell declared, he could see no refutation of the sceptical solipsist viewpoint.

Russell's position was nevertheless very different in this respect from the Viennese logical positivists. They took Wittgenstein's opaque remarks on solipsism in the *Tractatus* to point in the diametrically opposite direction from scepticism or genuine solipsism. Carnap, in *The Logical Structure of the World*, adopted a thoroughgoing logical empiricism consisting of a marriage of Mach's ontology with Russellian logic under the slogan of 'wherever possible, logical constructions are to be substituted for inferred entities'. His programme was to show that all meaningful statements (*Aussage*) could be reduced to primary statements. He chose as his base what he called 'the autopsychological', and endeavoured to show how statements about physical objects, 'the heteropsychological' or other minds, and cultural objects are reducible to statements about bare unowned experiences. Accordingly he named the constructional programme 'methodological solipsism'. Other members of the Vienna Circle, e.g. Schlick and Feigl, though they disagreed with Carnap on some matters of detail, adopted a similar position. The 'egocentric predicament', as they called the puzzles of solipsism, was, so they thought, a piece of metaphysics, relying as it did upon an illegitimate conception of ownership of experience. But it contained within it grains of truth which they put to good use. For, according to their view, statements about the experiences of others as well as statements about other bodies are constructed out of statements describing possible experiences or 'data' which verify them. From 1927 onwards the members of the circle, especially

[1] B. Russell, 'Vagueness', *Australasian Journal of Philosophy*, i (1923), 84–92.
[2] Russell, ibid., p. 92.

Waismann and Schlick, had Wittgenstein's authority and insight to sustain them in their endeavour. How much each influenced the other is a matter for debate. Whether the members of the Circle ever appreciated the Schopenhauerian transcendentalism of the *Tractatus*, 5.6's which is so evident in the *Notebooks* is very doubtful. Both Schlick and Carnap had developed their views on solipsism and the other minds problem prior to their actually meeting Wittgenstein. On the other hand Schlick's paper 'Meaning and Verification'[1] is Wittgensteinian through and through and acknowledged as such by Schlick. What is clear is that by 1929 the transcendental solipsism of the early period had been replaced in Wittgenstein's mind by a positivist methodological solipsism which, as has been suggested above, was already implicit in the *Tractatus*. The transcendentalism dropped away leaving a radical positivist programme. Until about 1933 this represented Wittgenstein's position.

2. *From Transcendental Solipsism to Methodological Solipsism*

Just as the transition from the realist semantics of the *Tractatus* to the criterial theory of the *Investigations* passed through an intermediate phase of extreme verificationism, so too Wittgenstein's metaphysics of experience passed through an intermediate phase. In the 1929 discussions with Waismann and Schlick, in the *Bemerkungen*, and in the Cambridge lectures of 1930–3 Wittgenstein adopted a classical logical positivist position on the problem of other minds and on the diagnosis of the dialectical illusions of solipsism. In most essential matters his position differed from that of the main members of the Vienna Circle only in its obscurity of expression, calculated ambivalence, and irony.

It will be remembered, from the discussion in chapter IV above, that Wittgenstein's point of departure in his work in the early 1930s is that of an attempt to construct a general and unified theory of meaning which would apply both to empirical propositions and to mathematical ones. Relinquishing part of the *Tractatus* model, he tried to create a novel semantic theory, relying on a principle of verification to account for the meaning of mathematical propositions in terms of the availability of a proof or method of proof which will justify asserting it, and for the meaning of empirical propositions in terms of empirical verification as justification conditions. Meaning

---

[1] See Feigl and Sellars, op. cit., pp. 146–70.

was equated with use, and use—with respect to experiential propositions—equated with the method of comparison with reality for truth or falsehood. His verificationism was extreme. A proposition has a sense only if it is completely and conclusively verifiable. Accordingly, he distinguished between genuine propositions describing immediate experience which are so verifiable, and hypotheses which are constructions out of genuine propositions and rules for derivation of genuine propositions. Thus first person, present tense, experiential propositions fulfil part of the original role of the now obsolete elementary proposition, and completeness of verification fulfils part of the role of the original determinacy of sense.

The general form of genuine, conclusively verifiable propositions is 'I have . . .' or 'I feel . . .'. Wittgenstein's primary example was 'toothache' or more generally 'pain'. Propositions such as 'I have pain' or 'I have no pain' are compared with what is actually the case to establish their truth or falsity. 'I have no pain' means, Wittgenstein declared (*PB*, §62), that if I compare the proposition 'I have pain' with reality it is shown to be false. Having pain or having toothache are primary or direct experiences. In these cases, unlike e.g. 'I have a bad tooth', 'I' does not denote a possessor. No physical eye need be involved in seeing, Wittgenstein remarked (*M*, p. 306) in a turn of phrase reminiscent of the *Tractatus*, 5.633, and similarly no Ego is involved in thinking or having toothache. The Cartesian *res cogitans* is an illusion; as Lichtenberg had pointed out, we should say 'it thinks', like 'it rains', rather than 'I think'. 'I' in the context of primary experience is an eliminable expression (*WWK*, p. 49). Its elimination would of course not be more correct, but would enable one to grasp the logical essentials of the form of representation of facts of personal experience (*PB*, §57). The experience of pain, as Hume had noticed, is not that a person—namely I—has something. I can distinguish in a pain an intensity, a location and other phenomenal characteristics, but no owner (*PB*, §65). Or rather, more perspicuously, it makes no sense to speak of an owner, because it makes no sense to speak of an unowned pain. A matchbox can have an owner, because it can lack one. It makes sense to speak of ownership only where it makes sense to speak of none. Here ownership is transferable. If we thought of pains thus, i.e. as objective particulars, it would be the perception of the pain that would be unpleasant rather than the pain. And this in turn would involve no owner. In short, ownership here is logical ownership, not contingent transferable ownership.

While 'I have . . .' in 'I have toothache' has no signifying function because it does not delimit a place within a logical space but merely indicates primary experience, the relation between primary experience and a particular physical body is contingent. That that pain which I call mine occurs in this body is a fact learnt by experience. As things are, seeing is universally correlated with physical eyes, but this is a contingent fact, and could be otherwise. Equally pains are uniformly correlated with a specific body in the sense that I do not feel pains in another person's body but only in the body I call 'mine'. But it is readily conceivable that this should be otherwise, that I should suffer toothache which I locate in someone else's mouth, flinch when his tooth is touched, and recover when his abscess is healed (*PB*, §60).

This distinction between the illegitimate sense of logical ownership of experience by an illusory Ego and the causal dependency of experience upon a particular body is no more than an expansion of what remains of the implicit *Tractatus* doctrines once the transcendentalism is removed. The distinction can now be brought to bear upon the solipsist's predicament. The solipsist contends that only his experience is real. 'I can experience only my own experiences' and 'I cannot have the pains of others' seem to him to be irrefutable claims illuminating the essence of the world. Upon them he builds his metaphysics. If they are true, it seems, then the concept of experience in general is only intelligible with reference to that which I have. If 'pain' means that which I have when I say truly 'I am in pain', then the supposition that there can be pain which I do not have is unintelligible. The assumption that other persons exist, have experiences, own perceptions, possess affections must be one which transcends all possible experience. It is not that I can know only of my own experiences but can achieve no higher standard than belief with respect to the experiences of others. It is rather that the belief that another ego has, e.g. pain, is unintelligible. If such a belief is unintelligible, so *a fortiori* is any conjecture, for one can conjecture only that which is in principle knowable, for the limits of knowledge coincide with the bounds of sense. The problem is initially set by the sceptic. All words describing personal experience, Wittgenstein later stressed, involve an asymmetry that urges one to say 'I know when I see something just by seeing it, without hearing what I say, or observing the rest of my behaviour, whereas I know *that* he sees, and *what* he sees only by observing his behaviour, i.e. indirectly' (NFL, p. 278). But if indirectly, then not at all. The solipsist is more rigorous and consistent than a weak-kneed sceptic. For how can something be established as good inductive evidence for an inner state if the inner state is not an object of possible experience? And 'how can I ever come by the idea of another's experience if there is no possibility of any evidence for it?' (*BB*, p. 46).

Wittgenstein's analysis in the first phase of his treatment of the predicament took the first few steps in the right direction, and then took the wrong turn leading to a position as wrong headed as the previous transcendentalism. The solipsist's error, he pointed out, is to confuse a fact of grammar with a metaphysical necessity. In the mouth of the solipsist 'I cannot feel your toothache' is a grammatical sentence not a description of a feature of the world, but an explanation of a linguistic convention. 'I cannot feel your toothache' simply means '"I feel your toothache" is nonsense'. But if so, then:

In the sense of the word 'sense datum' in which it is inconceivable that another should have it, one cannot on the same grounds say that another does not have it. And on exactly these grounds it is senseless to say that *I*, in contrast to others, *have* it (*PB*, §61).

How is this 'no-ownership' theory[1] established?

Wittgenstein proceeds by way of a comparison of 'I have toothache' and 'He has toothache'. If the term 'toothache' in the two sentences is univocal, then it must be possible both to distinguish his toothache from mine, and to establish whether he has the same toothache as I. The solipsist contends that another person could not have the same toothache as he. What is the force of 'could not' here? My toothache and his toothache will be identical, Wittgenstein suggests, if all the properties of my toothache, e.g. intensity, location, and other phenomenal characteristics, are also properties of his. If this can be established, then he and I have the same toothache. It will not help the solipsist to say, 'But for all that, his is his and mine is mine, and surely that is a difference!' For this move transforms the owner of an experience into a property of the experience. But in that case 'I have toothache' says nothing at all,

---

[1] P. F. Strawson, *Individuals*, pp. 95 ff.

for it is analytic. For 'toothache' here means no more than this cluster of phenomenal features, one of which is 'being had by me'. So if it is possible to establish identity, he and I can have the same pain. But is it possible? What is meant by 'He has the same tooth-ache as I'? The temptation is to try to explain 'He has . . .' by reference to my knowledge of what is involved in 'I have . . .'. I know what it means for me to have toothache, so when I claim that he has toothache I mean that he has what I previously had. But this only makes sense, Wittgenstein contends, if 'having toothache' involves only contingent ownership, and 'toothache', like 'match-box' names an objective particular. If so, then it would make sense to think of him having now what I had before, i.e. of toothache, standing first in a relation to me, and then to him. If that were so, then it would make sense for me to be conscious of his toothache, just as I can perceive the purse in his hand which was previously in mine. But these suppositions do not make sense.

Similarly, if it made sense for me to have toothache which I do not feel, then it would make sense for him to have toothache which I do not feel (*PB*, §62). But these are not genuine possibilities; our grammar does not permit locutions such as 'I have toothache which I do not feel'. 'He' and 'I' are not both values of the same senten-tial-function 'X has toothache'. 'He' and 'I' are not variously substitutable in 'X has toothache which X does not feel'. Where we are concerned with primary experience such as toothache, 'I have . . .' and 'I feel . . .' do not differ. The primary is compared directly with reality, it is not possible to 'have it' and not be 'conscious of it'.

If we take 'toothache' to mean a sensory datum, a primary experience, then toothache could occur in the mouth of another person only in the sense in which it is logically possible to feel toothache in another person's mouth. In our grammar we would not represent this fact by 'I feel his toothache', but by 'I feel toothache in his mouth'. In short, 'toothache' in 'I have toothache', and 'toothache' in 'He has toothache' have different meanings. I verify 'I have toothache' by a direct comparison of the concept of toothache as a datum with reality. The verification does not require the identification of an owner. The 'my' in the solipsist's assertion 'I feel my pains' is a free-running cog, for nothing in the experience of pain justifies the 'my'; the requisite logical multiplicity is missing in the feeling of pain. But when I say 'A has toothache' the verification is completely different, the identification of A enters into the justification of the utterance, and the representation (*Vorstellung*) of pain sensation as a datum is used only in the same way as the concept of flowing is used when one speaks of an electric current flowing (*PB*, §64). But the concept of the flowing of an electric current is not used in the way in which the concept of the flowing of a river is used. The one is verified e.g. by an ammeter, the other by watching the motions of the water upon the river-bed. Analogously, in verifying 'A has toothache' the concept 'toothache' as a sensory datum is not used.

But if 'toothache' in 'I have toothache' and 'He has toothache' do not mean the same, then do others really have toothache at all? Has the analysis not committed us to claiming that other people never really have what I have, that they do not have real toothache (M, p. 308)? This is to slip back into the solipsist's fallacy. For the investigation has shown such sentences to be nonsensical. If 'not-p' has sense then 'p' must have sense. Hence to say that others have no toothache presupposes that it is meaningful to say that they have toothache (*PB*, §65). But it has been shown that it is nonsense to say that 'another has what I have'. Hence it is nonsense to say that another does not have what I have. What then is meant by the claim that another person has toothache? The claim is, Wittgenstein suggested, not a proposition *stricto sensu*, but an hypothesis. Hence it is confirmed by the verification of its symptoms. We are under the illusion that the two hypotheses (1) that other people have toothache, and (2) that other people behave as I do when I have toothache, but have no toothache, are distinct. But they can be identical in sense if we conceive of them as involving two different *forms* of expression. The first form of expression is our normal one. We do say of others that they have toothache, and we pity a person whom we judge, on the grounds of his behaviour and physical condition, to have toothache. But our philosophical investigation has shown us that 'toothache' is ambiguous. An alternative form of representation would involve using 'toothache' univocally to mean only a datum. In this second form of expression we shall assert the hypothesis that others behave as I do when I have toothache, but of course they (analytically) have no toothache. If we employed this form of expression we would of course talk in tones of pity of people who, as we would say, have no toothache but who behave as we do when we have toothache. For to be sure, the two apparently distinct hypotheses, that others have pains, and that they have none but merely behave as I do when I have them, must be identical in sense if all possible experience which confirms one, confirms the other too. For the meaning of an hypothesis is given by the range of possible experience which confirms it. Since the two hypotheses do have identical confirmatory ranges, they are identical in their meanings.

Wittgenstein's position is indeed that of a 'no-ownership' theorist. He argued that 'I' has two uses, in one of which it is on a level with 'he', as in 'I have a matchbox' or 'I have a bad tooth', and in the second of which it is not on a level with proper names or other personal pronouns, e.g. 'I have toothache', but is eliminable in favour of the form 'there is toothache' (M, pp. 308 ff.). Nevertheless his doctrine, though it suffers from grievous defects, is not open to the criticism which Strawson brings against his reconstructed version of the no-ownership theory. In Strawson's version of the theory, the protagonist contends that while 'All my experiences are had_1 (i.e. causally dependent upon) body B' is contingently true, the apparently necessary truth 'All my experiences are had_2 (i.e. owned) by an Ego E' is the product of illusion. For both E and $having_2$ are pseudo-concepts. Strawson correctly points out that this contention is incoherent, for the no-ownership theorist utilizes the allegedly illegitimate sense of ownership ($having_2$) in presenting his case for its illegitimacy. In explaining that the ego is illusory he has to state what he takes to be the contingent truth that is the source of the illusion, namely—'All *my* experiences are had_1 by B'. But any attempt to eliminate '*my*' from the statement would result in something that is not contingently true: 'The proposition that *all* experiences are causally dependent on the state of a single body B, for example, is just false.'[1] But in Wittgenstein's positivist version of the no-ownership theory, as in Schlick's, the proposition that all primary experiences are had by a single body B, in the mouth of B, is not 'just false' at all. It is just true, although as the emphasis laid upon the possibility of pain occurring in some other body shows, only contingently true. 'Experience teaches us', Schlick wrote, 'that all immediate data depend in some way or other upon those data that constitute what I call "my body".'[2] The primitive experience thus dependent upon B is, Schlick emphasizes, absolutely neutral, or, he says, quoting

---

[1] Strawson, op. cit., p. 97.
[2] M. Schlick, 'Meaning and Verification', in Feigl and Sellars, op. cit., p. 162.

Wittgenstein, 'immediate data have no owner'. Thus far, as the above discussion shows, Schlick and Wittgenstein are in accord, and immune to the criticism to which Strawson's reconstruction is susceptible. Primary experience is contingently had_1 by me, i.e. B, and 'had_2' is a pseudo-concept.

The price paid for this positivist ploy is high. How is communication possible? How can I understand what you mean when you say 'I have pain'? Schlick, in 'Meaning and Verification', did not even touch upon the issue. But Wittgenstein faced it squarely. Both in the Waismann notes (*WWK*, pp. 49 f.) and in the *Bemerkungen* (*PB*, §58), Wittgenstein explains his position thus: one can, he suggests, construct many different languages in each of which a particular person is the centre. The centre would, in his language, say 'There is pain', instead of 'I am in pain'. When others are in pain this is expressed by saying 'They behave as Centre behaves when there is pain'. One could indeed imagine an oriental despot forcing everyone to speak the language of which he alone is centre. In such a case someone A other than the despot would express his pain by saying 'A behaves as the centre when there is pain'. Clearly, Wittgenstein argues, such a mono-centred language is intelligible and univocal; moreover such a language can have anyone as centre. Finally, any two such languages are inter-translatable. The proposition in L_1 that there is pain is equivalent to the proposition in L_2 that C_1 behaves as C_2 behaves when there is pain. Our language is in fact composed of as many isomorphic, inter-translatable, mono-centred languages as there are speakers. Wittgenstein adds one further point in which the shadow of his previous transcendental solipsism is still evident:

Of all the languages which have different people as centre and all of which I understand, that language of which I am the centre has a special status. It is especially adequate. How can I express this? i.e. how can I give a correct verbal expression of its advantage? This is not possible. For if I do so in the very language which has me as a centre, the special status of the description of this language in its own terms is no surprise, and in the form of expression of a different language my language has no special status. The special status lies in the application, and if I describe this application then the special status again fails to be expressed, for the description of the language depends upon the language in which it is given. And which description means that which I have in mind, again depends upon its application (*PB*, §58).

The application of language is the way in which it is laid alongside reality. The special position of every mono-centred language *vis-à-vis* its centre lies in its being compared directly with primary experience for verification. Since primary experience in any given language *L* is unique and incomparable, and since different languages differ only in their application, then all that can be expressed about them is their equivalence, and their uniqueness is inexpressible.

There is a great deal wrong with this philosophical account. Wittgenstein's elaborate dialectic, especially in the *Philosophical Investigations*, unravels the knots in the thread of argument with consummate skill. Hence the detailed criticism of this position will be deferred until we come to examine his later critical views on solipsism and private languages, where explicitly or by implication methodological solipsism is shown to be incoherent. But it is worth while making explicit some of the salient commitments of the theory. Firstly, it is clear that despite appearances to the contrary there is no such thing as a shared public language. Each speaker possesses his own private language, although to be sure, they are conceived of as inter-translatable. Secondly, the assumption of inter-translatability requires psycho-physical parallelism. For if the proposition in L_1 'There is pain' is to be extensionally equivalent to 'C_1 behaves as C_2 when there is pain' in L_2, there must in general be a uniform correlation between behaviour and primary experience. Thirdly, in ordinary language one never legitimately ascribes a univocal experiential predicate both to oneself and to others. All experiential predicates in normal parlance are ambiguous. Finally, when *A* says 'I am in pain' (in ordinary language) I cannot, strictly speaking, understand his meaning. Rather I must take his utterance as a sign rather than a symbol, a symptom of '*A* is in pain'.

From Moore's notes of Wittgenstein's lectures in 1930–3 it seems that Wittgenstein's initial reason for abandoning his position concerned the nature of what he had called 'genuine propositions'. Descriptions of 'the primary' were conceived as paradigms of propositions in being conclusively and directly verifiable by collation with reality. But in his lectures of 1932–3 he pointed out that phenomenological propositions are not verifiable at all. It makes no sense to ask how 'I have toothache' is verified. 'How do you know that you have toothache?' is a nonsense question. The two standard ploys of those who take the pseudo-question to be a genuine question with a trivial answer are misguided. 'I know I have pain because I feel it' is vacuous because 'I feel pain' and 'I have pain' have the same meaning. 'I know by inspection' is wrong because it erroneously suggests a perceptual model of inner sense. I cannot look and see whether I have a pain. From this first insight much of the later grasp of the errors of solipsism and idealism is, it seems, derived. For in the *Blue Book*, written in 1933–4 Wittgenstein has already substantially consolidated his position. The verificationist constructivism has been replaced by the novel criterial constructivism, and the methodological solipsism completely abandoned. Wittgenstein's reformulation of the solipsist's predicament is comprehensive and assured. It is to this that we shall turn first, prior to examining his detailed refutation of solipsism in the post-1933 writings.

3. *The Solipsist's Predicament: A Restatement and Second Diagnosis*

Solipsism, Idealism, and Realism, Wittgenstein claimed, are all metaphysical theories. Solipsism and Idealism, striving futilely to illuminate the essence of the world, to throw light upon the nature of reality and our experience of it, run violently counter to common sense. Realism conceives of itself as the philosophy of common sense, purporting to defend the beliefs of common sense against the idealist and solipsist onslaught by means of philosophical argument. This common-sense philosopher is, however, as far removed from the common-sense understanding as is the solipsist and idealist (*BB*, p. 48). The solipsist and idealist sense a problem. To be sure, they misunderstand it, and the solution they offer is an outgrowth of their misunderstanding. The realist (or 'naïve-realist' as this stock character is better known) does not solve the problems over which the solipsist and idealist stumble. Not understanding them properly, he disregards them. The solipsist does not understand how another can possibly have experience. The realist's naïve response is to claim that there is no difficulty at all here, since for another to have experience is for him to have what I have when I have experience. This he conceives to be a 'common-sense answer' to the predicament. But common sense is not philosophy, and common-sense philosophy is bad philosophy. The naïve-realist does not even see the point which the solipsist sees, namely that inner sense does not provide us with a criterion of identity which would make it intelligible to ascribe experiences to others. That explanation by means of identity which the realist naïvely suggests cannot work in this way. Genuine common sense, however, cannot resolve philosophical difficulties. Common sense would respond to the solipsist with questions like 'Why do you tell us this if you do not believe that we really hear it?' (*BB*, p. 58) or, like Dr. Johnson, would kick a stone to refute idealism (*M*, p. 311). Common sense is out of its depths when it turns to philosophy. The philosopher's bafflement cannot be resolved by any information which common sense can produce. The restatement of commonsensical views of the world will not relieve the philosopher of his difficulty in uncovering the conceptual articulations which make that view possible.

Neither the solipsist nor the idealist maintains that his claims are empirical (*M*, p. 311). There is no suggestion that they have found out by reference to the common criteria of inner experience that everyone who has said 'I am in pain' was cheating (*BB*, p. 57). The solipsist does not disagree with us about any *practical* matter of fact. He does not say that we are simulating when we complain of pains, and he pities us as much as anyone else (*BB*, p. 59). Nevertheless the solipsist is under the impression that his claims penetrate to the very essence of things in a way in which ours do not. When he claims that a person cannot have someone else's pains he understandably has the impression that his claim, though not causal, and hence not a matter of psychology or physiology, is nevertheless about the nature of pain:

It seems as though it would be not false but nonsensical to say 'I feel his pains', and as though this were because of the nature of pain, of the person etc. So that the assertion would after all be an assertion about the nature of things.

So we speak perhaps of an asymmetry in our mode of expression and we look on this as a mirror image of the nature of things (*NFL*, p. 277).

Once the web of intellectual deception is spun, the solipsist can even find a kind of experiential basis for his metaphysical views. Wittgenstein, harking back to his own younger days, again and again connects the perplexities of solipsism with the phenomenon of staring, e.g.:

Thus we may be tempted to say 'Only this is really seen' when we stare at unchanging surroundings, whereas we may not at all be tempted to say this when we look about us while walking (*BB*, p. 66).

In the appropriate frame of mind this confused metaphysician will be driven to say 'This is what is really seen', gesturing not at the material objects of his vision, but at his visual field. Sometimes, Wittgenstein suggests, the most satisfying expression of his point of view seems to be 'when anything is seen (really *seen*), it is always I who see it' (*BB*, p. 61). Not only does staring give one the feeling that reality is, as it were, diaphanous, that the *only* reality is, as Wittgenstein expressed it in the *Bemerkungen* (*PB*, §54), the experience of the present moment, it also lies at the root of the feeling that what one means by an experiential predicate, e.g. 'toothache', 'pain', or 'seeing' (NFL, p. 276; *PI*, §293; NFL, pp. 287 f. respectively), is essentially private. The solipsist drives himself into the position of having to say that what gives these words their meaning is something which only he has, and which no one else could conceivably have, hence it is unintelligible to him that others should have experiences. He:

tries to bring out *the* relation between name and thing named by staring at an object in front of him and repeating a name or even the word 'this' innumerable times (*PI*, §38).

Staring rigidly, he impresses upon himself that 'at any rate only I have got THIS' (*PI*, §398), 'I *am* in a favoured position. I am the centre of the world' (NFL, p. 299), or 'I am the vessel of life' (*BB*, p. 65), although if these expressions of his doctrine are to satisfy him it is essential not merely that others do not understand him but that it be logically impossible—meaningless—to say that they understand him.

What is amiss here? If the disagreement between our metaphysicians is not indeed about the facts, then the disagreement is about the notation or grammar by means of which the facts are represented. The solipsist is in effect demanding a different form of representation, and objecting that our current notation is inadequate. His claim that only his own present toothache is real toothache amounts to recommending that instead of saying 'So-and-so (the solipsist) has real toothache' we should say 'There is real toothache'. Of course, we could do this, though if we did, we should have to find a new way of marking the distinction between real and simulated pain (*BB*, p. 59). The solipsist fails to appreciate two crucial points. Firstly, that nothing can be changed by the new notation (*BB*, p. 57). Secondly, that he is under an illusion if he thinks that the new notation that he is suggesting has a special metaphysical justification lying in the essence of things. Grammar has no justification in the nature of what it describes, and the essence of that which is described by grammar is itself but a reflection of grammar. Wittgenstein makes the first point by means of a Fregean metaphor.[1] He compares the solipsist to someone who wishes to redraw the county boundaries of a country. But this pseudo-geographer, instead of saying 'Isn't it absurd to make *this* a county, to draw the boundaries *here*?', and giving us pragmatic reasons, makes his point quite differently. He declares passionately that the *real* county of, e.g. Devonshire, is not where the conventional boundaries are drawn, but elsewhere, where he is inclined to draw them. He thinks he can justify his convention by reference to its truth in the reality of things. But grammar is autonomous. We could reply to the pseudo-geographer that one does not change geographical facts by a new notation, although one may change administrative ones. In the *Investigations* Wittgenstein clarifies his point further:

> You have a new conception and interpret it as seeing a new object. You interpret a grammatical movement made by yourself as a quasi-physical phenomenon which you are observing. (Think for example of the question: 'Are sense-data the material of which the universe is made?')

> But there is an objection to my saying that you have made a 'grammatical' movement. What you have primarily discovered is a new way of looking at things. As if you had invented a new way of painting: or, again, a new metre, or a new kind of song (*PI*, §401).

What the solipsist is in effect suggesting is a new form of representation. His fault is twofold. In the first place he believes that grammar is justified by reference to what it depicts. In the second place his suggestion is not self-conscious. Hence he thinks that he has made a discovery about the nature of the world which in some sense contradicts what we take to be the case. Dissatisfied with our form of representation of experience and its objects the solipsist and idealist suggest fragments of an alternative one. But in their confusion they treat the sentences of their novel grammar, e.g. 'There is real toothache', which can only justifiably be said when the solipsist has toothache, as if they belonged to our conventionally accepted grammar. But in our grammar the solipsist's thought is expressed

---

[1] See Frege, *The Basic Laws of Arithmetic*, p. 11 (p. xiii in German edition).

by '*S* (the solipsist) has toothache'. The solipsist (in particular the methodological solipsist) may point to (the representation of) the man's cheek who says he has toothache, and say 'There is no toothache there'. In our grammar this is expressed by his saying 'I have no toothache there' (NFL, p. 308). Nothing changes through change of notation but the style of looking at the world.

The sound and fury of the metaphysical controversies throughout the ages derive largely from chasing shadows:

> *this* is what disputes between Idealists, Solipsists and Realists look like. The one party attack the normal form of expression as if they were attacking a statement; the others defend it as if they were stating facts recognised by every reasonable human being (*PI*, §402).

4. *The Refutation*

Wittgenstein's most important argument against solipsism in particular and idealism in general is his argument against the possibility of a private language. This undermines both solipsism proper, and methodological solipsism, just as it refutes idealism as well as linguistic phenomenalism. However, in the course of his numerous struggles with the problems involved in the metaphysics of experience, Wittgenstein elaborated a variety of arguments. The detailed discussion of the private language argument will be deferred for a while, and I shall attempt to collate Wittgenstein's arguments in refutation of solipsism. Since these arguments come from different periods of his thought a certain, but I hope not undue, amount of artificiality is involved in this collation.

Wittgenstein, as we have already seen, gave various striking formulations of solipsism. Three of these, given in order of increasing atomicity, are as follows. (1) Whenever anything is really seen, it is always I who see it (*BB*, p. 61). (2) The only reality is *my* present experience (M, p. 311). (3) Whenever anything is seen it is *this* which is seen (*BB*, p. 64). Wittgenstein's strategy is to probe each individual element of these formulae to discover weaknesses, and ultimately to prove that the employment of that element presupposes for its intelligibility the existence of a set of conditions which the solipsist repudiates. So his use of the element in question is illegitimate. The order in which I shall present his analysis is as follows: firstly, with what right does the solipsist use the term 'present' in declaring that only his experience of the present moment is real? Secondly, given the solipsist's framework of thought, is he entitled to use the personal pronoun 'I' as he does? Thirdly, when the solipsist says that at any rate he *has this*, what is the nature of the 'having'? Fourthly, and related to the first three points, is his claim that it is *always* he who sees whatever is seen intelligible? Fifthly, when the solipsist speaks of *experience*, be it seeing, toothache or pain, is this, given his fundamental presuppositions, a meaningful term? Sixthly, when the solipsist gestures ostensively towards his sensory field to indicate 'reality', what is he really doing?

(1) *The Temporality Condition*: Wittgenstein's first point is made emphatically in the Waismann notes (*WWK*, p. 107) and in the *Bemerkungen*, §54. It is made briefly and with little argument. The proposition 'Only the experience of the present moment is real', Wittgenstein remarks, seems to contain the final consequences of solipsism. Why so? The chain of argument here must be from naïve realism to idealism, from idealism to solipsism, from ordinary solipsism to a no-ownership solipsism of the present moment. But in this formulation of the ultimate conclusion of solipsism, what contrast is being drawn by the solipsist in his use of 'present'? Not that I did not get up this morning, Wittgenstein retorts; nor that what I cannot remember at this moment is unreal. The word 'present' as employed by the solipsist is redundant; it does not stand in contrast to past and future. Wittgenstein tries to express his thought by means of two of his favourite metaphors. 'Present' in the mouth of the solipsist is not something within a space, as it would be if it made room for past and future, but is itself a space. 'Present' for the solipsist does not designate a point within a system of temporally related events. Indeed the very contention of the solipsist excludes any other possible points within 'temporal space' from being potentially real. Hence the term is redundant, it means nothing.

The second metaphor Wittgenstein uses is that of the film projector or magic lantern. He expressed this as follows:

The present about which we are talking here is not the picture upon the filmstrip which is just now in the objective of the lantern in contrast with the pictures before and after it which have either already been, or not yet been there; but the picture on the screen—which is incorrectly called present, for 'present' here is not used in contrast with past or future. So it is a meaningless term (*PB*, §54).

This metaphor first appears, as far as one can tell from his published work, in his conversations with Waismann in 1929 (*WWK*, p. 50). He used it frequently in the early and mid-thirties to illuminate the confusions of idealism.[1] It makes sense to refer to the film-frame which is in the objective at the moment as 'the present one'. For it has 'neighbours'. There are prior and subsequent frames. But the picture upon the screen can only be thought of as 'the present projected picture' by reference to the serially related frames upon the film-strip on the spool. Independently of the film on the spool, the film on the screen—to mix two metaphors—is not within a space.

Metaphors are not a substitute for sustained argument, but it is interesting how close these metaphors stand to one of the masterly rejections of idealism which is an almost equally compressed discussion. This is of course Kant's 'Refutation of Idealism'. The magic lantern analogy in particular seems apt to illustrate Kant's point:

All grounds of determination of my existence which are to be met within me are representations; and as representations themselves require a permanent distinct from them, in relation to which their change, and so my existence in time wherein they change, may be determined.[2]

It is puzzling that Wittgenstein appears to have dropped his attack upon the temporality condition as part of his refutation of solipsism in his later work.

(2) *The Personal Identity Conditions:* Whenever anything is really seen, the solipsist claims, it is always I who see it. But *who* is the solipsist referring to when he says 'always *I*'? Wittgenstein replies for the solipsist, and he provides a retort:

I am tempted to say: 'It seems at least a fact of experience that at the source of *the visual field* there is mostly a small man with grey flannel trousers, in fact L.W.'—Someone might answer to this: It is true you almost always wear grey flannel trousers and often look at them (NFL, p. 298).[3]

Of course the solipsist's 'I' is not intended as a reference to his empirical self. He might, in reply to this rebuttal, say 'Although

---

[1] See M, p. 310; NFL, p. 297, and *BB*, pp. 71 f. where he uses the phrase 'having neighbours' but without the original film metaphor.

[2] Kant, *Critique of Pure Reason*, B xl note a.

[3] Compare Frege, 'The Thought', in *Philosophical Logic*, ed. P. F. Strawson (O.U.P., Oxford, 1967), p. 32.

by the word "I" I don't mean L.W., it will do if the others understand "I" to mean L.W., if just now I am in fact L.W.' (*BB*, p. 64).
What then does he mean? He struggles vainly to express what
seems to him to be so crucial: 'Surely . . . if I'm to be frank I must
say that I have something which nobody has. But who's I?' (NFL,
p. 283). The solipsist's difficulty is that nothing within his sensory
field provides him with a connection between what is seen (or
heard, or felt) and a person. If *this* is what he sees, it is also what is
seen *simpliciter*. How can he bring out the connection between the
unique self and that which is seen when 'the idea of a person does
not enter into what's seen' (M, p. 309). There is no way for the
solipsist to express himself except by more and more picturesque
and striking (Schopenhauerian) descriptions of his sense of uniqueness: 'But I *am* in a favoured position. I am the centre of the world'
(NFL, p. 299). But this favour belongs to the geometrical eye, not
the physical eye. The apparent uniqueness is formal; it belongs, as
Kant might have put it, to 'consciousness in general'.

The difficulties which give rise to the particular knot into which
the solipsist has tied himself with regard to 'I', are one and the
same set of difficulties which incline him and sceptics concerning
the existence of other minds to say 'We can never know what
someone else sees when he looks at something', or 'We can never
know whether what someone else calls "blue" is the same as what
we call "blue"' (*BB*, p. 60). To the sceptic this appears to be the
limit of the knowable; human cognition can reach thus far and no
farther. But what appears to mark out the limits of knowledge in
fact, as we have seen, demarcates the bounds of sense. For 'knowing
what he sees' in the mouth of the solipsist means 'seeing what he
sees',[1] and 'seeing what he sees' means 'doing his seeing for him',
i.e. having his visual experiences. This is impossible. But its
impossibility is not because of the frailty of the human intellect,
but because of the unintelligibility of 'having another's experience'.
Even God, in *this* sense, cannot see what I see.

One of the roots of the confusion, Wittgenstein argued in the
Blue Book, lies in the grammar of the word 'I' (*BB*, p. 66). He
distinguished between the use of 'I' as object (e.g. I have broken
my arm, I have grown six inches, I have a bump on my forehead)
and the use of 'I' as subject (e.g. I see so and so, I hear so and so,

---

[1] e.g. Hume, 'Suppose we could see clearly into the breast of another, and observe
that succession of perceptions which constitutes his mind...', *Treatise of Human
Nature*, I.iv.6.

I try to lift my arm, I think it will rain, I have toothache).[1] The salient feature of the use of 'I' as subject is that it is immune to error through misidentification of the subject. When I say sincerely that I see or hear, think or have toothache, it is not possible that I should have correctly identified (or have a title to predicate) the seeing, hearing, thinking, or toothache, but be mistaken in thinking that it is I who see, hear, think, or have toothache (i.e. be unjustified in predicating it of myself). The solipsist is deceived by the fact that we feel that

in the cases in which 'I' is used as subject, we don't use it because we recognise a particular person by his bodily characteristics; and this creates the illusion that we use this word to refer to something bodiless, which, however, has its seat in our body. In fact *this* seems to be the real ego, the one of which it was said, 'Cogito, ergo sum' (*BB*, p. 69).

He is of course right that self-ascription of current experience involves no recognition of a person, but he is wrong to jump to the conclusion that the 'I' in 'I sense X-ly' refers to a *res cogitans*.

A comparison with Kant on this matter is illuminating. Kant too noticed the above-mentioned feature, and grasped its significance. He stresses again and again that transcendental self-consciousness is original, underived, that the personality of the soul cannot be regarded as inferred, that it precedes *a priori* all one's determinate thought. It is these features (as is the 'use of "I" as subject') that lead to the Cartesian confusion, which Kant exposes with such skill in the Paralogisms:

The dialectical illusion in rational psychology arises from the confusion of an idea of reason—the idea of a pure intelligence—with the completely undetermined concept of a thinking being in general. I think myself on behalf of a possible experience, at the same time abstracting from all actual experience, and I conclude therefrom that I can be conscious of my existence even apart from experience and its empirical conditions. In so doing I am confusing the possible *abstraction* from my empirically determined existence with the supposed consciousness of a possible *separate* existence of my thinking self,[2] and I thus come to believe that I have *knowledge* that what is substantial in me is the transcendental subject.

---

[1] See S. Shoemaker, 'Self-Reference and Self-Awareness', *Journal of Philosophy*, lxv (1968), 555–67.

[2] The confusion of what is an abstraction from the empirically determined self with the supposed consciousness of the existence of a *res cogitans* finds its slightly less abstract, but still precise, parallel in Descartes' confusion of the self with the self-*qua*-known-for-certain. See A. J. P. Kenny, *Descartes, A Study of his Philosophy* (Random House, New York, 1968), chap. 4.

But all that I really have in thought is simply the unity of consciousness, on which, as the mere form of knowledge, all determination is based.[1]

The rationalist claim that self-consciousness assures us of our numerical identity through time and hence of our relative permanence (our complete permanence, i.e. immortality, being assured para-logistically through the putative simplicity of self-consciousness) must be combatted. Kant's line of attack in the third paralogism is to show that the evidence upon which the rational psychologist's proof rests, namely the unity of apperception, is perfectly compatible with a multiplicity of numerically distinct but qualitatively identical selves:

The identity of consciousness of myself at different times is therefore only a formal condition of my thoughts and their coherence, and in no way proves the numerical identity of my subject. Despite the logical identity of the 'I', such a change may have occurred in it as does not allow of the retention of its identity, and yet we may ascribe to it the same sounding 'I', which in every different state, even in one involving change of the thinking subject, might still retain the thought of the preceding subject and so hand it over to the subsequent subject.[2]

That Wittgenstein had the same target in mind can be seen from a passage in the 'Notes for Lectures':

It seems that I can *trace* my identity, quite independent of the identity of my body. And the idea is suggested that I trace the identity of something dwelling in my body, the identity of my mind (NFL, p. 308).

It is interesting to see that Wittgenstein dispels the illusion by much the same means as Kant's '*coup de grâce* to Cartesianism'.[3] For the mirror image of Kant's above-quoted argument is produced in the 'Notes for Lectures' in reply to the question—How am *I* defined?

may I lift my hand to indicate who it is?—Supposing I constantly change and my surrounding does; is there still some continuity, namely, by it being *me* and *my surrounding* that change? (Isn't this similar to thinking that when things in space have changed entirely there's still one thing that remains the same, namely space.) (NFL, p. 300).[4]

---

[1] Kant, *Critique of Pure Reason*, B 427.   [2] Kant, op. cit., A 363.
[3] P. F. Strawson, *The Bounds of Sense* (Methuen, London, 1966), p. 168.
[4] The argument is further elaborated at NFL, p. 308, with the supposition that I change my body every day.

The failure of the idealist to meet the personal identity conditions stems, according to Kant, from the confusion of the unity of apperception with the perception of a pure unity. The purity and simplicity of the 'I think' that must be capable of accompanying all my representations is being fallaciously conceived of as the purity and simplicity of a substance which is the object of intuition. Much the same insight can be found in Wittgenstein, although his constructive analysis of first person, present tense, psychological sentences is wholly different from Kant's. He tried, he said, in 'Notes for Lectures', to bring the whole problem of idealism and solipsism down to our not understanding the function of the word 'I' (NFL, p. 307). Wittgenstein recognized, as we shall see in a moment, that there is a great variety of criteria of personal identity. But none of them determine (i.e. constitute justificatory grounds for) my saying that *I* am in pain (*PI*, §404). The utterance of first person, present tense, psychological sentences such as this lacks criterial evidence, i.e. it makes no sense to justify what I say by reference to further grounds. But although I say what I say without a justification, it does not follow that I say it without right (*PI*, §289). I shall refer to sentences of the kind in question as involving *criterionless self-ascription of experience*, but for the time being this must not be taken as committing one to anything other than the negative thesis. The complexities of Wittgenstein's non-cognitive thesis of avowals will be examined and evaluated in chapter IX below.

It is not, I think, a contingent feature of experience as we conceive it that it is criterionlessly self-ascribed. But for criterionless self-ascription to be possible, certain general conditions must be satisfied. These general conditions are whatever conditions provide criteria for the employment of our concept of a person, for our use of personal pronouns (other than 'I'), and for our use of proper names. They include physical appearance, but also characteristic habits, behaviour, and memory. Were this complex array of facts different in certain conceivable ways, our concept of a person and, as a result, the identity of a person and our notion of personality would undergo fundamental change. Our present concepts would have no grip. Wittgenstein invites us to consider three thought experiments (*BB*, pp. 61 f.).[1] The first experiment is this: imagine

[1] For elaboration of the thought experiments, see F. Waismann, *The Principles of Linguistic Philosophy*, pp. 213–16.

that all human bodies looked identical but different sets of characteristics, always clustered together, were instantiated now in one body, now in another. Under these circumstances it would be possible to assign proper names to bodies, but there would be no more need to do so than there is now need to christen furniture. One might however name the groups of character-traits and say that they change their habitation among the various bodies. The use of these names would correspond *roughly* with our use of proper names. The second experiment is a generalisation of the Jekyll and Hyde tale. Imagine that each man's body and character alternate thus regularly. We could christen each man with two names and talk of a pair of persons in his body. We could also construct our form of representation differently. We are not forced in any one direction. The third experiment is equally bizarre. Conceive of a man's memory on even days including only events that have happened to him on even days, and on odd days his memory, with no sense of discontinuity, comprising only events that occurred on odd days. A further variant of the experiment is to conjoin it with the second so that alternating memories combine with alternating appearance and characteristics. In none of these cases does our present concept of a person dictate an answer to questions such as— Are Jekyll and Hyde one person or two? Are two persons inhabiting the body on alternate days, or only one person with two 'memory systems'? In Wittgenstein's opinion our ordinary concept of a person is not tailored for normality conditions fundamentally different from our familiar ones. What is certainly made clear by the examples is that our concept of a person, and whatever 'legitimate heirs' it might have under different normality conditions, are dependent for their intelligible use upon there being conventionally determined grounds in experience for the use of person-referring terms upon which experiential predicates are predicated. Only if there are such grounds is groundless self-reference and self-ascription intelligible.

Returning now to the solipsist we must press him to reveal what underlying conditions legitimize his use of 'I'. Certainly not his bodily appearance. When he claims that when anything is seen it is always he who sees, it is not necessary that part of his body should be seen. It is not necessary that if his body is seen it should always look the same. The truth of what he says does not seem to be affected even if he has no body, no behavioural characteristics, no memories.

But now his use of 'I' is totally free-floating, tied to no empirical conditions and referring to no empirical phenomenon. He can still express his solipsism by saying 'I am the vessel of life', but it is logically impossible for others to know what 'I' means in this utterance. For it is logically impossible for the solipsist to know what he means by 'I', because the conditions under which the use of 'I' is meaningful and under which it has referential force are disregarded or denied to pertain by the solipsist.

(3) *The Ownership Condition*: The failure of the solipsist to meet the necessary conditions for the employment of 'I' carries in its wake his failure to meet the requisite conditions of the intelligibility of ownership of experience. In response to the objection that Wittgenstein is neglecting experience—the *world* behind the mere words—Wittgenstein replies:

here solipsism teaches us a lesson: It is that thought which is *on the way* to destroy this error. For if the *world* is idea it isn't any person's idea. (Solipsism stops short of this and says that it is my idea.) But then how could I say what the world is if the realm of ideas has no neighbour? What I do comes to defining the word 'world' (NFL, p. 297).

The argument of the *Blue Book* (*BB*, pp. 53 ff.), repeated in a more condensed form in the *Investigations* (*PI*, §246 ff.), consists of a redevelopment of the arguments of the *Bemerkungen*. The diagnosis of the solipsist's error remains much the same. He confuses grammatical sentences with empirical ones, and conceives of features of our form of representation as metaphysical truths about the world. But whereas in the *Bemerkungen* Wittgenstein had argued that toothache is ambiguous, and that 'having' in 'I have toothache' and 'He has toothache' is a different symbol, he now suggests a quite different analysis. When the solipsist claims that he cannot have the same pain as another, and builds his metaphysics upon this base, we must distinguish, with respect to experiences, qualitative from numerical identity. To claim that two persons cannot have the numerically identical pain is a commitment to a certain form of representation. Accordingly the numerical identity of experiences is dependent upon their owners, and 'He has my pain' and 'I have his pain' are ruled out of language as ill-formed. Thereby, of course, one also rules out (because analytically true) 'I have *my* pain'. And this indeed is all the solipsist's insight amounts to. For it does not imply that two people cannot have (qualitatively) identical pains in the same sense in which we say that two books have the same colour. To object to the claim that in so far as it *makes sense* for two people to have the same pain, then indeed they *can* have the same pain is analogous to objecting to the claim that two books can have the same colour. To try to differentiate his pain and my pain by reference to the 'fact' that 'He has his, and I have mine, and that is a crucial difference' is like claiming that since this book has its own colour, and the other book has its own colour, therefore they cannot both have the same colour.

The unique ownership which the solipsist purports to find is no more than the convention that an essential criterion of numerical identity for experiences is provided by the owner of experience. But since the solipsist failed to give an adequate account of the subject of experience, he cannot explain what he means by 'owning' experience. One of the primary sources of the solipsist's confusion, as of so many of the salient problems of the metaphysics of experience, lies, I believe, in the nature of self-ascription of experience. Our perception of what we call 'the world' involves perceiving substances, our descriptions of what we perceive involve ascribing properties to particulars. In inner sense, however, we seem to be aware of the instantiation of experiential properties independently of the 'substance in which they inhere'. There is therefore a temptation, enshrined in our grammar,[1] to reify our experiences. This is nowhere more evident than in Hume: 'we have no perfect idea of a substance; but taking it for *something that can exist by itself*, it is evident every perception is a substance . . .'[2] As long as we adhere to the perceptual model of introspection, we cannot help treating our experiences as private objects. We consequently generate a multitude of illusions which we enshrine in a metaphysics, including the illusion of unique and inalienable ownership.

(4) *The Continuity Condition*: The solipsist's use of 'I' was intended to refer to a substance. This spiritual substance was subsequently thought of as the only conceivable existing substance. It was the vessel of life, the sole owner of all conceivable experience. Barring solipsism of the present moment, it was thought to possess a traceable identity through time. Hence a corollary of the solipsist's disregard of the conditions which legitimize the use of the personal

---

[1] See NFL, p. 302: 'In "I have toothache" the expression of pain is brought to the same form as a description "I have five shillings".'

[2] Hume, *Treatise of Human Nature*, I.iv.5.

pronoun and his inability to understand the meaning of 'ownership of experience', is his failure to satisfy the requisite conditions of continuity. The use of 'I' seemed to indicate a continuous substance throughout the duration of experience to which the experience could be ascribed. As he realizes that his use of 'I' is wholly independent of any empirical features of himself as a person, he may now find himself attempting to express his solipsism without using 'I'. Instead of saying 'whenever anything is seen, it is always I who see it', he will now say 'whenever anything is seen, always *something is seen*'. What is unique is experience; the world is idea.

(5) *The Experiential Condition*: The solipsist has given a lot of ground. Indeed his position can barely be intelligibly articulated. It is a no-ownership solipsism of the present moment, moreover his position is now identical with the constructional base chosen by the methodological solipsist. All that exists is the experience of the present moment, and this experience is unique, without being owned. Wittgenstein pursues the issue relentlessly. His answer to this part of the solipsist's claim is embodied in his argument against the possibility of a private language. Although with the benefit of hindsight we can see that there are faint seeds of this argument in the *Blue Book*, it first emerges in the 'Notes for Lectures', and is clearly formulated in the *Investigations*. For the moment all I wish to do is to anticipate the discussion of the next chapter. I shall present the salient conclusions of the argument in so far as it bears upon the solipsist's case in order to show that if it is valid then the solipsist must retreat from this point too.

A condition of the possibility of criterionless self-ascription of experience is, tautologically, possession of the concept self-ascribed. The sense of an expression is determined by the criteria which justify its use. The sense of sentences ascribing psychological properties to a person is determined by those sentences which describe the behaviour that is necessarily good evidence for the truth of the psychological sentences. A condition of the possession of a psychological concept which one can intelligibly ascribe to oneself without justificatory grounds is that one knows which justificatory grounds do, in general, justify the ascription of that concept, for only then does one know what the sense of the concept-word is. Hence for one's self-ascription of experience to be intelligible there must be a 'grammatical', non-contingent link between inner state and outward manifestation, between the concept of experience and the concept of evidence for experience. The solipsist (and his idealist ancestors) denies the existence of any such link. Consequently his contention (and that of his methodological solipsist heir) is that a given experiential predicate can be meaningful even though its ascription to others is inconceivable. Hence his belief is that such terms can be given meaning and explained (subjectively) exclusively by reference to the actual experiences to which they refer. Wittgenstein's contention is that this is not possible. In the absence of a criterial link with behavioural manifestations the solipsist is left with nothing but a vacuous mental gesture. The experience itself cannot serve as a paradigm by reference to which the name of the experience is given sense (NFL, p. 314). If this is correct, then the solipsist has no right to pick out the experience which he is currently experiencing as unique. For if his claims are correct, he can have no concept with which to pick it out.

(6) *The Ostensive Gesture Conditions*: The solipsist's last stand is to attempt a final reinterpretation of his position. Instead of the variously chosen formulae which we have examined and rejected he now reformulates his claims thus:

'whenever anything is seen, it is *this* which is seen', accompanying the word 'this' by a gesture embracing my visual field (but not meaning by 'this' the particular objects which I happen to see at the moment). One might say, 'I am pointing to my visual field as such, not at anything in it' (*BB*, p. 64).

It is essential to this formulation, Wittgenstein adds, that the pointing should be 'visual' (*BB*, p. 71), that I point to things which I see, not to things which I do not. Better still, I should point only 'mentally'. Any other pointing would be irrelevant, indeed meaningless, from the solipsist's point of view. Wittgenstein begins his reply to this with two metaphors. The solipsist's gesture is like that of a man travelling in a car who is in a hurry, and to speed things up pushes against the dashboard. The solipsist's pointing does not serve to pick one thing out in contrast with another; consequently it picks out nothing. When it makes sense to say 'I see this' while pointing at what I see, it also makes *sense* to say 'I see this' while pointing behind me at what I do not see. Wittgenstein connects this with his second metaphor. The solipsist robs his pointing gesture of any possible significance 'by inseparably connecting that which points and that to which it points'. It is as if he had constructed a clock, connected the hands to the dial, and expected the clock to tell the time.

The solipsist's pointing gesture, like his 'present moment', his 'I', his 'ownership', has no neighbour. It is not within a space, it is not the actualization of one possibility among others. Wittgenstein compares the error of the solipsist's gesture to that of a man who thinks that saying 'I am here' will make sense under any conditions whatever, and moreover will always be true. But this is to forget that the referential force of 'here' depends upon the existence of a public space in which objects are locatable and reidentifiable by reference to their spatial path through time. For 'I am here' to make sense, it must be intended to be—and be capable of—drawing attention to a point in *common space*. If 'here', however, is intended to point to a spot in subjective space, as the solipsist's gesture and 'this' points to his visual field, then 'I am here', Wittgenstein suggests (*BB*, p. 72), amounts to 'Here is here'. The solipsist's gesture is only a pseudo-gesture. If the solipsist however points, not to his 'visual space' but to common space, and says 'This is really seen', we can reply—'We could adopt a notation in which whatever L.W. sees at a given moment is called "Things really seen". But there is no reason to do so.'

Wittgenstein's refutation of solipsism has now been traced through all its stages. I have concentrated upon the two main relevant works of the intermediate phase. But there is no doubt that much the same target is under continual fire in the *Investigations*. There are very many passages which might confirm this, but the most striking is the following, which encapsulates much of the six-stage argument in one paragraph:

'But when I imagine something, or even actually *see* objects, I have *got* something which my neighbour has not.'—I understand you. You want to look about you and say: 'At any rate only I have got THIS.'—What are these words for? They serve no purpose.—Can one not add: 'There is here no question of a "seeing"—and therefore none of a "having"—nor of a subject, nor therefore of "I" either.'? Might I not ask: In what sense have you *got* what you are talking about and saying that only you have got it? Do you possess it? You do not even *see* it. Must you not really say that no one has got it? And this too is clear: if as a matter of logic you exclude other people's having something, it loses its sense to say that you have it.

But what is the thing you are speaking of? It is true I said that I knew within myself what you meant. But that meant that I knew how one thinks to conceive this object, to see it, to make one's looking and pointing mean it. I know how one stares ahead and looks about one in this case—and the rest (*PI*, §398).

The solipsist claimed that the present moment is unique, that he is privileged, that it is always he who sees, that what he has when he sees is unique, that his seeing is exceptional, that 'this' is incomparable. Each move is illegitimate. The illegitimacy of each move damns not just solipsism, but phenomenalism and indeed any form of idealism. However, when the ostensive gesture and the utterance 'This is seen' *are* genuine, they point to the world. 'The self of solipsism shrinks to a point without extension and there remains the reality coordinated with it.' When Wittgenstein wrote this in 1916 he meant something very different from what he later thought about solipsism and idealism. But what this *says* is equally appropriate for his later views.

> We shall not cease from exploration
> And the end of all our exploring
> Will be to arrive where we started
> And know the place for the first time.[1]

[1] T. S. Eliot, 'Little Gidding', *Four Quartets*, IV, lines 239–43.

VIII

PRIVATE LINGUISTS AND PUBLIC SPEAKERS

---

1. *Introduction*

In Chapter I of the Transcendental Doctrine of Method in the first *Critique* Kant wrote:

... where the illusion that besets us is very deceptive and the harm that results from error is very considerable, there the *negative* instruction, which serves solely to guard us from errors, has even more importance than many a piece of positive information by which our knowledge is increased. The compulsion, by which the constant tendency to disobey certain rules is restrained and finally extirpated we entitle *discipline*.[1]

Wittgenstein's notorious argument against the possibility of a private language belongs to that part of philosophy which Kant entitled 'The Discipline of Pure Reason'. It is an argument which tries to show that a certain conception of language and thought which implies and is implied by the various forms of philosophical scepticism about the existence of other minds and the external world, as well as by solipsism, methodological solipsism, and the classical causal theory of perception, is incoherent. It is a 'negative instruction' in so far as it is, after a fashion, a *reductio ad absurdum*. It does, however, also have a positive side, a constructive theory which shows how to avoid the illusions, harm, and error which stem from the absurd private language which is either explicit or tacitly presupposed in a philosophical theory. This positive side is sketchy and incomplete.

Wittgenstein's argument has two main aspects. On the one hand it involves a detailed criticism of a theory of meaning. In the course of this criticism it explores, again in a largely negative way, what is involved in acquiring, possessing and exercising a concept. The picture which the theory under attack has of conceptualization is

[1] Kant, *Critique of Pure Reason*, A 709, B 737.

held to be radically mistaken. Equally, the nature of teaching language, of communication by means of language, and so too of meaning is, Wittgenstein argues, completely distorted. The other aspect of the argument concerns a range of related epistemological and metaphysical doctrines which form a syndrome of misunderstandings of the nature of possible experience and knowledge. The most complete, indeed classical, embodiment of this syndrome is the doctrine of solipsism, whether in its naïve form, or in the more sophisticated transcendentalist or methodological solipsist forms. Yet many apparently less invidious epistemological theories involve the same set of misconceptions. Idealism in most of its forms, and so too phenomenalism, are, Wittgenstein implies, no less incoherent, and are indeed incoherent in essentially the same way, and for essentially the same reasons, as solipsism. The idealist and phenomenalist have merely failed to think their position through to its ultimate conclusions with the consistency and relentlessness of the solipsist. Equally, epistemological realism, in the form in which it was espoused by philosophers such as Frege,[1] errs in the same way. The demonstration of the incoherence of these diverse metaphysical theories is undertaken by means of obtaining a general surview over our form of representation of experience and its objects. The private language argument[2] is essentially one stage in Wittgenstein's broader strategy of displaying the articulations of our conceptual framework in order to dispel illusion and remove confusion.

One can, without undue caricature, conceive of Wittgenstein's purpose in the private language argument as being an endeavour to extend and elaborate the Kantian dictum that intuitions without concepts are blind. Kant stresses again and again the necessity of the co-operation of the two faculties of the mind, the understanding and sensibility. Only thus are objectively valid judgements possible. But there are, he says, two great philosophers, representatives of two incompatible views of philosophy, who fail to appreciate this:

Leibniz *intellectualised* appearances, just as Locke, according to his system of *noogeny* (if I may be allowed the use of such expressions) *sensualised* all concepts of the understanding.[3]

Kant was more interested in taking Leibniz and his Wolffian followers to task than in criticising Locke. But the suggestion that

---

[1] Frege, 'The Thought', in Strawson (ed.), op. cit.

[2] The argument *against* the possibility of a private language has come to be known as 'the private language argument'. I shall abide by this convention for the sake of brevity.

[3] Kant, *Critique of Pure Reason*, A 271, B 327.

Locke 'sensualised' concepts was a perceptive one. The task of exploring the ramifications of this criticism fell to Wittgenstein.

Characteristically, Wittgenstein does not indicate explicitly the personal targets of his attack in his discussion of the impossibility of a private language. It is, however, clear that his own logical positivism of 1929–31 is beyond dispute committed to the incoherent doctrines of the private linguist, and it is reasonable to see in the *Tractatus* a tacit commitment to such a position. Apart from an implicit reference to Frege,[1] the discussion is ahistorical and egocentric. Nevertheless, it is obvious that Wittgenstein's adversary in the debate represents the presuppositions of most empiricist and some rationalist epistemology and metaphysics from Descartes[2] to logical positivism. Locke's[3] theories, however, are an exceptionally good example of the kind of conception of language and thought that Wittgenstein was criticizing. None of the great classical empiricists was so self-consciously concerned with a philosophical theory of meaning and language as Locke. None of them so explicitly advocated a theory of the relation between language and the world which so exactly fits Wittgenstein's conception of a private language. Hence in the following exposition of Wittgenstein's argument it is Locke rather than the younger Wittgenstein who will be presented as a possible adversary. This has two advantages. On the one hand it makes it clear that Wittgenstein was not simply and solely arguing against himself. It shows that the explicit viewpoints which Wittgenstein foists upon his adversary are not wholly fanciful and extravagant. On the other hand it brings out the unity of the views of Wittgenstein's adversary. For although they are not always consistent, often presenting two or three alternative and incompatible answers to one and the same question, they do constitute variations upon one and the same theme. Locke's semantics and epistemology serve to show this. I am not, of course, suggesting that Wittgenstein had Locke in mind, indeed there is no evidence in

---

[1] The phrase '*uns Allen Gegenüberstehendes*' in scare quotes at *PI*, §273, is a quotation from Frege's *Grundgesetze der Arithmetik*, p. xviii, '*etwas Allen gleicherweise Gegenüberstehendes*'. It is clear from much of the argument that Wittgenstein has Frege in mind at a number of points in the dialectical debate. For a detailed comparison of Frege's epistemology with Wittgenstein's, see P. M. S. Hacker, 'Frege and the Private Language Argument', *Idealistic Studies*, ii (1972).

[2] For the application of Wittgenstein's argument to Descartes see A. J. P. Kenny, 'Cartesian Privacy', in *Wittgenstein, The Philosophical Investigations, A Collection of Critical Essays*, ed. G. Pitcher (Doubleday, New York, 1966), pp. 352–70.

[3] For a brief application of Wittgenstein's argument to Locke see A. Flew, *Hume's Philosophy of Belief* (Routledge and Kegan Paul, London, 1961), pp. 39–42.

hitherto published memoirs or in Wittgenstein's writings that he had ever read Locke. To be sure, while Locke was explicit in his pre-suppositions about meaning, language, and thought, philosophers such as Descartes, Berkeley or Hume[1] were no less guilty of the confusions which Wittgenstein seeks to lay bare, and indeed the sceptical consequences of the theories of meaning they presuppose are no less evident in their work than in Locke's and are often more striking. They, no less than Locke or the young Wittgenstein, stand in need of a Discipline of Pure Reason.

2. *Philosophical Investigations, §243*

Wittgenstein's discussion of a private language begins at §243 of the *Philosophical Investigations*:

A human being can encourage himself, give orders, obey, blame and punish himself; he can ask himself a question and answer it. We could even imagine human beings who spoke only in a monologue; who ac-companied their activities by talking to themselves.—An explorer who watched them and listened to their talk might succeed in translating their language into ours. (This would enable him to predict these people's actions correctly, for he also hears them making resolutions and decisions.)

But could we also imagine a language in which a person could write down or give vocal expression to his inner experiences—his feelings, moods and the rest—for his private use?—Well, can't we do so in our ordinary language?—But that is not what I mean. The individual words of this language are to refer to what can only be known to the person speaking; to his immediate private sensations. So another person cannot understand the language.

Each of these two paragraphs presents problems of its own which must be clarified before embarking upon the private language argument proper.

The first paragraph represents the last stage in a deliberately paradoxical discussion in §§ 240–2. It also links the subsequent discussion of the private language with the prior argument about learning, teaching, and possessing concepts. The apparent paradoxes

---

[1] Wittgenstein seems to have despised Hume. He commented that he knew far too much about the subject of Hume's writings to find reading Hume anything but a torture. (See K. Britton, 'Portrait of a Philosopher', in *Ludwig Wittgenstein, The Man and his Philosophy*, ed. K. T. Fann, p. 61.) Certainly Hume made almost every epistemological and metaphysical mistake Wittgenstein could think of.

are resolved in the course of the private language argument. The second paragraph is linked with the first by means of the contrast between the imagined soliloquists and the private language speaker. The soliloquists give vocal expression to their inner experience for their own private use, and their comments can be understood by others—for the explorer translates them. The private language is characterized by its being unintelligible to others. I shall start by examining the problems involved in the first paragraph of the passage quoted above.

§§ 142–240 of the *Investigations* are concerned largely with the acquisition, possession, and exercise of concepts. Having a concept, Wittgenstein stresses, involves mastery of a technique. Knowing what a word means, possessing a concept expressed by a word in the language, understanding the meaning of an utterance— these may all be accompanied by mental processes such as imaging, feelings of familiarity or appropriateness. But they are not them- selves mental processes. They are capacities; a person knows what a word means when he is able to use the word in a regular, rule- governed way. Language, in Wittgenstein's view, consists (among other things) of rules for the use of words. Possessing a concept involves being able to use a word in accordance with a standard of correctness, and hence in being able to use it in application to the same kinds of cases, where these cases do not necessarily form a closed class. These rules or standards linking expressions with the circumstances justifying their use are embodied in the behaviour and practices of a linguistic community. In §206 Wittgenstein had already raised the case of an explorer visiting a foreign land, trying to discover the language of the inhabitants. 'The common behaviour of mankind', he said, 'is the system of reference by means of which we interpret an unknown language.' If there is no regular connection between the sounds they make (which the explorer is trying to interpret) and their actions, then we cannot judge them to have a language. The scaffolding of a common language is constituted by the rules or standards determining the use of the words of the language and so ensuring the possession of common concepts. In §240 Wittgenstein writes:

Disputes do not break out (among mathematicians, say) over the question whether a rule has been obeyed or not. People don't come to blows over it, for example. That is part of the framework on which the working of our language is based (for example, in giving descriptions).

The terms 'rule', 'agreement', and 'same' are, as Wittgenstein has already argued, internally related.[1] But does this not imply that 'human agreement decides what is true and what is false'? It is what people *say*, the judgements they make, and the opinions they express that are true or false. They *agree* in the language they use. Agreement in language, possession of common concepts is what Wittgenstein here calls 'a form of life', a common way of conceptualizing experience together with the accompanying kinds of behaviour. This 'agreement', it seems, is a presupposition of agreement or disagreement of judgements. But this is, after all, misleading. It suggests erroneously that agreement in concepts and agreement in judgements are wholly independent one of the other. In §242 Wittgenstein moves from the thesis to the antithesis of the argument:

If language is to be a means of communication, there must be agreement not only in definitions but also (queer as this may sound) in judgments. This seems to abolish logic, but does not do so.

It is not enough that there should be agreement in language, in definitions, in concepts. For this in itself already involves agreement in judgements, and so, in a qualified sense, human agreement does appear to decide what is true and what is false.

The indignation of Wittgenstein's interrogator lies in the fact that this monstrous suggestion seems to abolish logic by collapsing truth into meaning. It seems to imply that whether a sentence has sense depends upon the truth of another sentence.[2] But this is not so. Wittgenstein reconciles the apparent conflict in the following passage:

It is one thing to describe methods of measurement and another to obtain and state results of measurement. But what we call 'measuring' is partly determined by a certain constancy in results of measurement.

As long as the method of measurement is separable from the results of measurement, measuring is possible. But the separability of the two is consistent with their being closely related. The metaphor of a 'method of measurement' is one which, as we have seen, already appears in Wittgenstein's earliest writings. Agreement over a method of measurement means agreement over the sense of a sentence, and thus over the judgement which it is used to make.

---

[1] See *PI*, §§224–5 and §136.　　　[2] Compare *TLP*, 2.0211.

Hence it implies agreement over the language and the concepts expressed by the words of a given sentence. A proposition (*Satz*) is compared to a method of measurement in so far as it is conceived of as a description of a possible state of affairs which the world either satisfies or does not. If it does, the method of measurement yields the result—true. If it does not, it yields the result—false. Agreement determines the method of measurement, and the world determines its result. Thus far the original thesis of separability is correct. The antithesis, however, which seemed to abolish logic, is also correct in a qualified sense. Something which looked like measurement but yielded nothing that resembled constant and consistent results of measurement could not be conceived of as measurement at all, just as something could look like a language but be too irregular to be one (*PI*, §207). Our agreement in definition is not independent of our agreement in judgements for we identify our agreement in definitions in part at least by reference to our agreement in judgements (and ultimately by reference to 'the common behaviour of mankind'). The idea that we could share a common language, possess common concepts, but disagree radically in our judgements is as empty as the suggestion that we might *not* possess common concepts and nevertheless *agree* in our judgements.[1] So far then the thesis of non-independence is correct. However, thus explained, it is not the case that 'logic is abolished'. Our agreement in 'methods of measurement' does not make our sentences determine the world, but only the possibilities which the world must satisfy.

The first paragraph of §243, however, presents a new puzzle to replace the one just resolved. §§240-3 were concerned with a shared language, but we are now introduced to the conceivability of a soliloquist's language which is designed not for communication, but for 'private use'. Does this not conflict with the previous suggestions? I think not. The soliloquist has a language which is as 'rule-governed' as ours. Even if the soliloquist is quite solitary, his language, though not shared, is sharable. Although there may be no one to agree with him in his judgements, if there were someone, he could

---

[1] This is exemplified in the inverted spectrum problem—in which it is supposed that the 'private meaning' of colour words, i.e. the private experience of a particular colour or some mental surrogate of it which serves as an exemplar, differs from person to person in a perfectly symmetrical fashion. Nevertheless, it is suggested, they might always appear to 'agree in judgements'. Their behaviour would satisfy all the criteria of agreement, but in fact their colour concepts, it is supposed, differ radically.

agree. The necessity of agreement adumbrated in §§240–2 concerns only what must be possible, not what must be actual. Just as the requisite agreement in language determines only truth-possibilities, so too the necessary conditions involved in the existence of language (and hence of thought) imply only possible sociality, only the possibility of inter-personal discourse, not its actuality. What is ruled out in the following private language argument is not the imaginary soliloquist (solitary or in groups) but one whose concepts, rules, and opinions are essentially unsharable rather than contingently unshared.[1] The importance of the soliloquists is both to stand in contrast with the speaker of a putative private language, and to clarify Wittgenstein's intentions. These are *not* to make trite points about the social nature and genesis of language.

The second paragraph of §243 clarifies what Wittgenstein means by a private language. The imaginary soliloquists employ their language for their own private use. In our ordinary language we can write down our feelings, moods and inner experiences. Neither of these constitutes a private language. Wittgenstein characterizes a private language by reference to three features: (a) the words of the language are to refer to what can only be known to the speaker, (b) the words of the language are to refer to the speaker's immediate private sensations, (c) another person cannot understand the language. (c) is presented as a conclusion from (a) and (b), and should therefore not be taken as a primary characterization of a private language.

The discussion from §244 to §256 consists largely of a preliminary clarification of (a) and (b) as conceived by the private linguist. (a) specifies the epistemic privacy of the objects to which the words of the private language refer. The objects are private in so far as only the speaker of the language knows what they are and when they occur. (b) specifies the privacy of ownership. The objects of the language are owned by the speaker, and could not be owned by any

---

[1] For this reason A. Manser's claim ('Pain and Private Language', in *Studies in the Philosophy of Wittgenstein*, ed. P. Winch (Routledge and Kegan Paul, London, 1969), p. 168) that a language of a socially isolated individual is inconceivable, because language is always a social activity involving rules that only a social institution can provide, involves a fundamental misunderstanding of Wittgenstein's point. Wittgenstein's argument would not lose its point even if we possessed innate concepts (see e.g. *BB*, p. 12). So too the debate concerning the possibility of Crusoe inventing a language (A. J. Ayer and R. Rhees, 'Can There be a Private Language?', *Proceedings of the Aristotelian Society*, supp. vol. xxviii (1954), 63–94) is beside the point.

one else. Sensations (*Empfindungen*) are said to be private in both ways—only the person who has the sensations can really know for certain that he has them, and what he has are unsharable and non-transferable. No one else can have my pain and I cannot have their sympathy.[1]

Wittgenstein does not clarify explicitly what he means by sensation; his main example in the ensuing discussion is pain (§§244–6, 250, 253, 257, 271, 281–4, 286–8, 293, 295–6, 300, 302–4, 310–15). This is misleading, and has misled commentators. Could there be a language in which referential and denotative expressions consisted exclusively of a Rylean array of aches, twinges, tickles and itches? and if there could, what philosophical interest would this have? Yet Wittgenstein intimates that *all* the words in the language are to refer to a person's immediate private sensations. Certainly 'pain' is the name of a sensation, but the distinction between perception and sensation is not significant for Wittgenstein's purposes in the private language argument. It is noteworthy that he refers to objects in the visual field, *conceived in a particular way*, as sensations in a broad sense of the term. He speaks of a 'private sensation of red' (§273), of 'colour impressions' (§276), 'visual impressions' (§277), 'visual sensations' (§312), of the private visual image before the mind's eye in acts of imagination (§280), and in general, of states of mind, mental and inner processes (§§290, 305–6). All these then can be taken to fall under the category of 'immediate private sensation'. Indeed it is noteworthy that in the first occurrence of the notorious diary example (*PI*, §258), the inner object whose occurrence the private linguist is trying to record is the visual experience of red (see NFL, p. 291). Thus while pain is his paradigm, it is experience in general and its 'phenomenal contents', conceived of under the spell of a misguided metaphysics, that are his target. This is partially clarified in §§274–79, but it is quite explicit in works which precede the *Investigations*, in particular the *Blue Book* and the 'Notes for Lectures'. When we think about the relation of objects to our experiences of objects, Wittgenstein points out in the *Blue Book* (p. 45), we are immediately beset by a host of philosophical temptations. We are tempted to conceive of two distinct kinds of world, the mental and the physical. The former seems peculiarly gaseous and aethereal. Later we are inclined to

---

[1] Frege, 'The Thought', in Strawson (ed.), op. cit., p. 28.

view the mental as the only real, knowable world. While we are thinking thus, our grasp of reality begins to slip. We are left with nothing but personal experiences, which seem elusive and indescribable. Ordinary language seems imprecise and vague, and we begin to hanker after an ideally precise language. It is against such temptations that the private language argument is directed. The argument is one among the many critical tools Wittgenstein employs to dispel these philosophical illusions. Again, in the 'Notes for Lectures', Wittgenstein's explicit targets are sense-datum theories in epistemology, although the prominent example is, as in the *Investigations*, a sensation (not pain in general, but toothache). One should thus beware of letting the specific (and often misleading) example of pain distort one's vision of the point of the argument.

3. *The Private Language*

In the *Investigations* Wittgenstein constructs his target and then knocks it down stage by stage. At no point does he produce a perspicuous representation of his adversary's position as a whole. Moreover, the epistemological and semantic aspects of the private language are, in Wittgenstein's exposition, closely interwoven. I shall separate the description of the private language from its criticism, the theory of meaning from its fallacious but validly inferred sceptical consequences, and Wittgenstein's description of the private linguist's epistemological theories from his critical analysis of their flaws.

The almost perfect example of a private language of the kind Wittgenstein had in mind is that described by Locke in his exposition of the elements of our thought and language in Books II and III of *An Essay Concerning Human Understanding*.[1] Therefore I shall use Locke's theory of language as an 'ideal type' to which Wittgenstein's imaginary private language approximates very closely indeed. 'Words', Locke proclaims, 'in their primary or immediate signification, stand for nothing but *the ideas in the mind of him that uses them* . . . nor can anyone apply them as marks, immediately, to anything else but the ideas that he himself hath' (III.ii.2). Similarly, the words of Wittgenstein's imaginary private

---

[1] Locke, *An Essay Concerning Human Understanding*, ed. A. C. Fraser (1894, republished by Dover Publications Inc., New York, 1959). For some qualifications of this view of Locke's semantics see N. Kretzman, 'The Main Thesis of Locke's Semantic Theory', *The Philosophical Review*, lxxvii (1968), 175–96.

language refer to the speaker's immediate private sensations. 'I know what the word "toothache" means,' remarks Wittgenstein's adversary (NFL, p. 315), 'it produces one particular image in my mind.' The words of the private language *refer* to elements of one's experience: pain, or the red patch in one's visual field when one looks at a red object. But if that is their reference, what is their sense? Sometimes Wittgenstein's private linguist conceives of the experience itself, the sensible intuition, as providing the concept. '"The experience which I have seems, in a certain sense, to take the place of a description of this experience."—"It is its own description."' (NFL, p. 277.) On other occasions he suggests that a meaningful term is associated with a replica of an element of one's experience, an exemplar which serves as a paradigm for the meaning of the term (NFL, p. 314; *PI*, §272). Apropos the recognition of an object as falling under a given concept, seeing an object as a so-and-so, Wittgenstein, in setting out his adversary's position, employs a typically Lockean metaphor:

This shape that I see—I want to say—is not simply *a* shape; it is one of the shapes I know, it is a shape marked out in advance. It is one of those shapes of which I already had a pattern in me; and only because it corresponds to such a pattern is it this familiar shape. (I as it were carry a catalogue of such shapes around with me, and the objects portrayed in it *are* the familiar ones.) (*Z*, §209).

The private experience, whether it is the actual experience *S*, or a recollected image of *S* reproduced by the mind, serves as a paradigm to provide the word '*S*' with its meaning:

It is as if when I uttered the word I cast a sidelong glance at the private sensation, as it were in order to say to myself: I know alright what I mean by it (*PI*, §274).

How is language learnt, and how is the connection between a word and what it names set up? Locke suggests an elaborate process. The first stage is to stock our memory, the storehouse of ideas (II.x.2) with objects. This is done by means of attention and repetition (II.x.3) which fix a private exemplar of each experience type within our minds. It is then the business of memory to 'furnish to the mind those dormant ideas which it has present occasion for' (II.x.8). Once the store of exemplars is established, children:

... begin by degrees to learn the use of signs. And when they have got the skill to apply the organs of speech to the framing of articulate sounds, they begin to make use of words . . . These verbal signs they sometimes borrow from others, and sometimes make themselves, as one may observe among the new and unusual names children often give to things in the first use of language (II.xi.8).

The use of words is to be the 'sensible marks of ideas, and the ideas they stand for are their proper and immediate signification' (III.ii.1). Wittgenstein's private linguist draws a very similar although slightly different picture of the process. The private linguist *associates* names with sensations and uses the names as descriptions. How is this process of association established? One suggestion might be that one pronounces the name while one has the sensation and concentrates upon the sensation (NFL, p. 290). One gives oneself a private ostensive definition of the private object by *attending* to the object, as it were, mentally pointing at it, while saying the word to oneself or writing it down—one *impresses* upon oneself the connection between sign and sensation (*PI*, §258) in order to remember the connection correctly in the future. Another suggestion would be that one *undertakes* to use the sign in the future to refer to the exemplar (*PI*, §262). The function of memory for Locke is to provide the filing cabinet for the speaker's exemplars, and to produce the correct exemplar for each word as the speaker has need of it. Thus memory ensures that one uses the same sign for the same idea. Wittgenstein's private linguist envisages a similar procedure. He conceives of a table or dictionary consisting of exemplars and words associated with them. Only unlike ordinary dictionaries, this one exists in the imagination alone, and provides the subjective justification that the word '*S*' means the (private) object *S* (*PI*, §265). It is a representation or quasi-concretization of memory and association (*PI*, §53 and §73).

In Locke's model of language, words which stand for simple ideas and which are the foundation of language in so far as they provide the basic links between language and its objects are lexically indefinable (II.xx.1). The only way of knowing what they mean is to have the simple ideas they stand for. Consequently, two strange possibilities are conceivable. Firstly, it is possible that:

by the different structure of our organs it were so ordered, that *the same object should produce in several men's minds different ideas at the same time*; v.g. if the idea that a violet produced in one man's mind by his eyes were the same that a marigold produced in another man's, and *vice versa* . . .

this could never be known, because one man's mind could not pass into another man's body, to perceive what appearances were produced by those organs (II.xxxii.15).

Secondly, grammatical and semantic propriety in speech is no guarantee that the noises that are uttered are really words. For unless they are 'backed up' by ideas, the noises lack meaning:

He that hath words of any language, without distinct ideas in his mind to which he applies them, does, so far as he uses them in discourse, only make a noise without any sense or signification ... For all such words, however put into discourse, according to the right construction of grammatical rules, or the harmony of well-turned periods, do yet amount to nothing but bare sounds and nothing else (III.x.26).

Precisely these possibilities occur to Wittgenstein's private linguist. At *PI*, §258, Wittgenstein remarks to his adversary that a definition of the sign '*S*', which the private linguist claims to associate with his sensation *S*, cannot be formulated. The inverted spectrum problem, which did not greatly bother Locke,[1] is presented by Wittgenstein as one of the unacceptable consequences of the private linguist's thesis (*PI*, §272). The second possibility was likewise envisaged by Wittgenstein:

Imagine a person whose memory could not retain *what* the word 'pain' meant—so that he constantly called different things by that name—but nevertheless used the word in a way fitting in with the usual symptoms and presuppositions of pain (*PI*, §271).

For Locke, language has two uses, 'the recording of our own thoughts' and 'the communicating of our thoughts to others'. Regarding the first use, it matters little, when we discourse with ourselves, which signs we use to stand for which ideas, as long as our use of the signs is consistent, and our memory reliable. But the matter is different in the case of the second use:

The chief end of language in communication being to be understood, words serve not well for that end, neither in civil nor philosophical discourse, when any word does not excite in the hearer the same idea which it stands for in the mind of the speaker (III.ix.4).

[1] He comments thus: 'I am nevertheless very apt to think that the sensible ideas produced by any object in different men's minds, are most commonly very near and undiscernibly alike. For which opinion, I think there might be many reasons offered: but that being besides my present business I shall not trouble my reader with;' (II.xxxii.15).

So if words are to serve their end successfully, the same associative mechanisms between word and exemplar that exist in the speaker's mind must exist in the hearer's mind. But words which stand for simple ideas are, as we have seen, indefinable. Words which stand for complex ideas are definable only in terms of words that stand for simple ones. So the meaning of words that stand for simple ideas must be shared if successful communication is to ensue:

the only sure way of making known the signification of the name of any simple idea, is *by presenting to his senses that subject which may produce it in his mind*, and make him actually have the idea that word stands for (III.xi.14).

Once this is secured, men can converse with each other. Locke sums up his picture of the public use of language thus:

[words are] immediately the signs of men's ideas and by that means the instruments whereby men communicate their conceptions, and express to one another those thoughts and imaginations they have within their own breasts; there comes, by constant use, to be such a connection between certain sounds and the ideas they stand for, that the names heard, almost as readily excite certain ideas as if the objects themselves, which are apt to produce them, did actually affect the senses (III.ii.6).

We have then a view about the teaching of a language, about the purpose of language and linguistic acts, and about the mechanism of communication. Identical views are to be found in the mouth of Wittgenstein's private linguist or in Wittgenstein's critical comments upon his adversary's position. The idea that the point of inter-personal uses of language is always to let the hearer know what is going on in the mind of the speaker is emphasized by Wittgenstein as being part of the private linguist's model:

we are so much accustomed to communication through language, in conversation, that it looks to us as if the whole point of communication lay in this: someone else grasps the sense of my words—which is some-thing mental: he as it were takes it into his own mind. If he then does something further with it as well, that is no part of the immediate purpose of language (*PI*, §363).

More emphatic is his earlier remark:

As if the purpose of the proposition were to convey to one person how it is with another: only, so to speak, in his thinking part and not in his stomach (*PI*, §317).

In the discussion of the possibility of a private language, Wittgenstein does not explore what must be involved in teaching another person the meaning of the terms of one's private language. He makes it clear from the start that such a language is neither teachable, nor intelligible to others. This is unfortunate, for this is a conclusion towards which he should, I think, have argued explicitly. It has also misled commentators into thinking that a premise in Wittgenstein's critical argument is that an unteachable language is logically impossible. This is quite mistaken. The fact that we must learn language is a contingent fact about our constitution. It would be perfectly conceivable that a child genius should invent names for his sensations (*PI*, §257) like Locke's children (II.xi.8) or that we be born with innate knowledge of language (*BB*, p. 12). But it is true that if the private linguist's model of language were correct, and if we did have to teach it, the way in which it would have to be taught would be the way which Locke describes. Wittgenstein did explore this in detail in 'Notes for Lectures'.[1] The issue arises in the context of a discussion of how a private linguist conceives of our teaching a blind man to say of himself that he is blind. Blindness, of course, is not behaviour, for a man can behave like a blind man and not be blind. But it is his overt behaviour which is common knowledge to himself and to us. On the basis of his behaviour we say that he sees nothing. He correlates a certain experience (one might 'think of the picture of blindness as a darkness in the soul or in the head of a blind man' (*PI*, §424)) with his behaviour and concludes that 'being blind' means this experience. The underlying notion of the private linguist is that expressions which refer to personal (or private) experience (and the private linguist claims that all descriptive words do so) are taught *indirectly*. Wittgenstein constructs an analogy. Imagine teaching a child colour words, not by exhibiting colour samples, but by using a white sheet of paper, and various differently shaped spectacles with different lenses which make me see the white paper in a different colour. When I look through the circular spectacles I see the white paper as red. When I put the elliptical ones on I see it as green. Wittgenstein now imagines that we teach the child colour concepts thus:

when I see him putting the circular ones on his nose I say the word 'red', when the elliptical ones 'green', and so forth. This one might call

---

[1] The same analogy crops up in *Zettel*, §421.

teaching the child the meanings of the colour names in an indirect way, because one could in this case say that I led the child to correlate the word 'red' with something that I didn't see but hoped the child would see if he looked through the circular glasses. And this way is indirect as opposed to the direct way of pointing to a red object etc. (NFL, p. 286).

The indirect way of teaching here, which is contrasted with the direct way, is the exact analogue of Locke's picture of teaching someone the meaning of a term. But in Locke's model there is no analogue of direct teaching: all teaching must be indirect 'because one man's mind could not pass into another man's body' (see also *BB*, p. 185). The notion that teaching someone the meaning of a word—and so bringing it about that he acquires the concept—involves presenting him with an object and ensuring that he associates the word one utters with the object (or representation) it refers to or some surrogate for it appears in a later section of the *Investigations*:

it seems to us as though in this case the instructor *imparted* the meaning to the pupil—without telling him it directly; but in the end the pupil is brought to the point of giving himself the correct ostensive definition. And this is where our illusion lies (*PI*, §362).

The same conception of teaching is outlined in *Zettel*:

When the child behaves in such-and-such a way on particular occasions, I think he's feeling what I feel in such cases; and if it is so then the child associates the word with his feeling and uses the word when the feeling reappears (*Z*, §545).

With this conception of teaching a common language goes a certain conception of the mechanism of communication. Wittgenstein portrays this strikingly in the course of constructing his imaginary language-games. The language-game in question is the one in which *B* learns to bring a building stone on hearing the word 'Column!' called out. One might imagine the mechanism thus, Wittgenstein suggests:

In *B*'s mind the word called out brought up an image of a column, say; the training had ... established this association ... this case is strictly comparable with that of a mechanism in which a button is pressed and an indicator plate appears. In fact this sort of mechanism can be used instead of that of association (*BB*, p. 89).

In the *Investigations* an even more felicitous analogy is used. The picture of communication in this language-game (No. 2) and in the classical empiricist's conception of language in general is one in which 'Uttering a word is like striking a note on the keyboard of the imagination' (*PI*, §6).

So much for the private linguist's and empiricist's conception of language and meaning. It involves a theory of concept-acquisition, and hence of teaching and learning language. It includes a theory of concept-possession and so of what is involved in knowing what a word means, and of meaning something by what one says. Finally, it encompasses a theory of the exercise of a concept and thus of the purposes of the use of language and the mechanisms of communication. Each of these aspects is criticized in exhaustive detail by Wittgenstein. Before elaborating his criticism, however, I shall turn to the epistemological theory which is upheld by the private linguist.

4. *The Epistemology of the Private Linguist*

The opening sections of the private language argument in the *Investigations*, as we have seen, explore two senses of 'private'—epistemic privacy and privacy of ownership. Something is epistemically private for a person if only he can know it; it is private in the second sense if, in principle, only he can have it. From these two notions of privacy and their relationship to the private linguist's view that the meaning of a word is given by acquaintance with an 'object' that constitutes the meaning, stem the salient epistemological doctrines of the private linguist. Three separate doctrines may be distinguished. The first doctrine might be called classical (non-sceptical) empiricist. I know of the occurrence of my own experiences with a certainty and incorrigibility which are unavailable to others who judge me to be having a certain experience. For while I know that I am having experience E because I am having it, because it is, as it were, before my mind's eye, and I cannot fail to identify it correctly, others know that I am experiencing E only from my behaviour. Since my behaviour is only inductively correlated with my experience and since the proposition that I am behaving in the way in which people normally behave when they experience E does not entail that I am experiencing E, the knowledge others have of my inner states lacks the certainty of my own knowledge. I am, as it were, acquainted with my experience from the 'inside', others can only know it from the 'outside' (NFL, p. 279). Of course the classical empiricist claims to be able to make perfect sense of the judgement that another person is experiencing E. One is simply judging that the other person has the same as one has oneself when one experiences E.

This epistemological doctrine leads readily to what might be called 'weak-kneed scepticism'. Since I have a 'privileged access' to my own experiences, and others must make do with my behaviour, it may seem appropriate to claim that 'only I can know whether I am really in pain; another person can only surmise it' (*PI*, §246), or 'I can only *believe* that someone else is in pain, but I *know* it if I am' (*PI*, §303). In my own case, I know 'directly' that I am experiencing E, just by experiencing E (NFL, p. 278). But in the case of others, it is only their behaviour that is available to me which gives only 'indirect' access to their inner experiences. I cannot know, the sceptic concludes, whether another person is really experiencing E, or merely behaving as I do when I experience E. Hence the most I can achieve with regard to the inner states of others is belief. It may be that 'So-and-so has excellent health, he never had to go to the dentist, never complained about toothache; but as toothache is a private experience, we can't know whether he hasn't had terrible toothache all his life' (NFL, pp. 289–90). It is worth noting that there is little if any disagreement between the supporter of the argument from analogy and the weak-kneed sceptic, except over terminology. They both agree about the conceptual relations involved, and differ only over the denomination of their currency. The sceptic refuses to debase the term 'knowledge' by employing it both for the case of his incorrigible cognitions of his own inner experience, and for his corrigible and apparently dubious conjectures about the inner states of others, even when these conjectures are correct.

The third position is more tough-minded. It is the doctrine of the solipsist. It results from the conjunction of the doctrine of epistemic privacy, the doctrine of privacy of ownership, and the private linguist's theory of meaning. The solipsist accepts the common premise of his two predecessors—namely that he knows of the occurrence of his own experiences. As they do, he too adheres to the doctrine of private ownership of experience. No two people can have the same pain, and the pain that I have could not possibly be owned by someone else. However, unlike them, he is self-conscious about the theory of meaning that is implicit in the two doctrines of privacy. In this he is also more consistent and relentless than they in pushing the theory to its ultimate conclusions. He admits (as Locke did):

The essential thing about private experience is really not that each person possesses his own exemplar, but that nobody knows whether other people also have *this* or something else. The assumption would thus be possible—though unverifiable—that one section of mankind had one sensation of red and another section another (*PI*, §272).

But this disturbing consequence is not the worst that is to come. For if ownership of experiences is private and non-transferable, and if the meaning of a word is the private exemplar of the object, then 'I know what I mean by "toothache", but the other person can't know it' (NFL, p. 276). For now it is obvious that the private language is unintelligible to others. When I see red, and say 'this is red', 'this is the only real case of communication of personal experience because only I know what I really mean by "red"' (NFL, pp. 276 f.). Another person cannot understand what I say, because in order to understand it he would have to have my experiences for which my words stand, or the surrogate exemplars of my experience which I possess. Nor does it help to say that others will after all understand me provided that they have the same as I have when I experience *E*, for *ex hypothesi* two people can't have the same experience. Ultimately the tough-minded solipsist will castigate the weak-kneed sceptic, for not only is the private language unintelligible to others, but it does not make sense to talk of *believing* as opposed to knowing that others have experiences. The very idea of experiences belonging to another, and *a fortiori* of believing them to belong to another, must, in all consistency, be nonsensical. For 'experience' means something which is uniquely mine. To suppose that there could be other subjects is nonsense, for I alone am the locus of all experience. To believe that others have experience is to make an hypothesis which transcends all possible experience (*BB*, p. 48). And such an hypothesis could not be backed by meaning (see also *PI*, §302).

5. *Wittgenstein's Criticism of the Private Language*
Wittgenstein's criticism of the private language can be divided into two main parts. The first is the claim that nothing in the private

linguist's theory provides room for the formation and possession of a concept. Hence the fact that the private language is unteachable and unintelligible to others is the least of evils. The really serious criticism is that it is unintelligible to its speaker. The second line of attack is the claim that the elements in the private linguist's theory are insufficient to provide the structure and articulations necessary for the formation of sentences. Moreover the underlying conception of language and communication is radically misconceived. I shall deal with each separately.

The first set of criticisms is prominent in the *Investigations*, §§257–70, and crops up repeatedly in later sections of the book. It is also strikingly supported in *Zettel*, §§332–3, 545–8. The first part of the criticism is concerned with concept formation. The private linguist's first move is to claim that he names his pain (*PI*, §257). We should not, however, let him go beyond this stage. For forming new concepts, bringing a particular object, or the instantiation of some general characteristic, under a general concept, expressed by means of a word, presupposes a variety of complex conditions, or—as Wittgenstein puts it—a great deal of stage-setting. How then does the private linguist form his concept, and are the background conditions he describes adequate for his purposes? As we have seen, the private linguist tries to construct a concept S of a sensation by means of associating a word 'S' with the occurrence of the sensation S. 'S' is lexically indefinable, he admits, but he gives it a stipulative definition by mental ostention. He impresses it upon himself that 'S' is to be associated with S. This however won't do. A definition gives a sign a meaning, it must determine for future occasions what kind of item to refer to by means of the sign.

Making sure that you know what 'seeing red' means, is good only if you can make use of this knowledge in a further case. Now what if I see a colour again, can I say I made sure I knew what 'red' was so now I shall know that I recognise it correctly? In what sense is having said the words 'this is red' before a guarantee that I now see the same colour when I say again I see red? (NFL, p. 289).

But concentrating on S while enunciating 'S' does not bring it about that I will remember that 'S' means S, unless concentrating on S will transform the sound 'S' into the expression of a concept. If it does not, then subsequent enunciations of 'S' will be empty noises, 'whatever is going to seem right to me is right' (*PI*, §258), for no standard has been established by reference to which the subsequent use of 'S' can be evaluated as correct or incorrect. Nor will it do for the private linguist to say—'well, of course I might forget that "S" is connected with S, but when I later use "S", I believe that it refers to the sensation S' (*PI*, §260). For in order to believe that reference is being made to S, one must possess the concept of S, but this is precisely what the private linguist so far lacks. Private ostensive definition gives the impression of being a possible procedure precisely because we do have the concepts of the 'objects' in question. More generally, ostensive definition as such is a possible procedure for conveying or establishing the meaning of a word only for people already in possession of a language. Pointing to the king in chess and saying 'This is the king' is only of use to someone already wholly conversant with the rules of the game up to this last point: the shape of the king (*PI*, §31). Those who, like Augustine, conceive of language learning as a process of understanding ostensive definitions are confusing the position of a person who comes to a foreign country already equipped with a language and intent upon learning another one, with the position of initial language-acquisition. 'Ostensive definition explains the use—the meaning—of the word when the overall role of the word in the language is clear' (*PI*, §30). The learner of a foreign language is acquainted with a range of syntactical categories in virtue of which his guesses of the meanings of ostensive definitions given him are possible. The learner of an initial language is not in such a position. Private ostensive definition, or subjective ostensive definition, seems possible to us because we do know what 'pain' means. Hence we are under the illusion that one could always 'pick out' the sensation pain from one's stream of consciousness and name it. But 'picking it out' already presupposes that we possess the concept and so cannot serve to explain our acquisition of it. Wittgenstein clarified this further in *Zettel*:

Do not believe that you have the concept of colour within you because you look at a coloured object—however you look. (Any more than you possess the concept of a negative number by having debts.)

'Red is something specific'—that would mean the same as: '*That* is something specific'—said while pointing to something red. But for that to be intelligible, one would have already to mean our *concept* 'red', to mean the use of that sample (*Z*, §§332-3).

Put paradoxically, for '*S*' to mean *S*, it must, tautologically, mean *S*, and the object cannot give the sign its meaning.

It is precisely this point which Wittgenstein proceeds to explore. Having dispensed with the unacceptable picture of concept-acquisition, he examines the notion of possession of a concept. For the private linguist, as we have seen, possessing a concept is akin to having a mental filing cabinet in which exemplars are correlated with labels. This functions as a mental dictionary, providing a subjective justification for the use of a word. Of course, one must bear in mind that one uses words more often in the absence of the objects or properties they refer to than in their presence. The mental dictionary justifies us in thinking the word we use means what we take it to mean, not in thinking that the object before us is rightly referred to as *S*. We must be able to refer to the pseudo-dictionary when we deny that an object is *S*, when we conjecture that *S* is going to appear any minute, when we claim that *S* was here yesterday, and so on. This fairytale account of having a concept is radically incoherent. If we need to appeal to something for justification, that which justifies cannot be identical with that which needs justifying. 'Justification consists in appealing to something independent' (*PI*, §265). Certainly one memory may support another. My uncertain memory that the train leaves at 9.40 may be supported by my vivid memory of the page in the time-table in which the third line says 'Oxford–London 9.40—10.55'. And the latter memory can be checked against the actual timetable. But if I have a hazy memory that '*S*' means *this* exemplar, there is no memory against which I can check this in order to know the meaning of '*S*'. For if the meaning of '*S*' is an exemplar stored in my memory then there is no way in which I can check whether the exemplar my memory produces is the one that belongs with '*S*', or the one that belongs with some other sign. The memory mechanism must produce the right memory correlation.[1] But not only is it impossible for the private linguist to distinguish a correct sign-exemplar correlation, but, given the privacy of the exemplar, it is impossible in principle to distinguish a correct from an incorrect correlation. So again, 'Whatever is going to seem right to me is right. And

[1] See J. Hintikka, 'Wittgenstein on Private Language: Some Sources of Misunderstanding', *Mind*, lxxviii (1969), 423–5, and A. J. P. Kenny, 'The Verification Principle and the Private Language Argument', in *The Private Language Argument*, ed. O. R. Jones, pp. 218 f.

that only means that here we can't talk about "right"' (*PI*, §258).

Wittgenstein's next move is to imagine the case which, as we have seen, Locke explicitly mentions. Could we not imagine a case in which a man could not remember what (i.e. what private exemplar) the word 'pain' means in his private language. Despite this, he uses the word in a way that fits in with the usual symptoms and pre-suppositions of pain. 'Here I should like to say', Wittgenstein retorts, 'a wheel that can be turned though nothing else moves with it, is not part of the mechanism' (*PI*, §271).[1] The piece of redundant mechanism here is the exemplar, the private object which the private linguist alleges gives meaning to his words. The redundancy of the private object for the meaningfulness of one's words is pursued further in the famous beetle-in-the-box example (*PI*, §293). The private linguist claims, as we have seen, that it is only from his own case, his own experiences, that he knows what the word 'pain' means. But if so, Wittgenstein replies, he must also say (as indeed Locke does) that others only know what 'pain' means from their own case.[2] The position of a group of people who *do* succeed in communicating with each other is, on the private linguist's model, analogous to the following: Suppose everyone had a box with some-thing in it. Each person calls the object in his box 'beetle'. No one has access to the contents of others' boxes and each knows what 'beetle' means by looking into his box. Now *if* we suppose that 'beetle' has a use in the language, then the object in the box and its nature are irrelevant. 'If we construe the grammar of the expression of sensation on the model of "object [*Gegenstand*] and name [*Bezeichnung*]"[3] the object drops out of consideration as irrelevant' (*PI*, §293); i.e. on the private linguist's conception of the relation between a name and the object it refers to, then, *if communication is*

---

[1] See also *PI*, p. 207: 'Always get rid of the idea of a private object in this way: assume that it constantly changes, but that you do not notice the change because your memory constantly deceives you.'

[2] Wittgenstein adds here the comment: 'And how can I generalise the *one* case so irresponsibly.' This is not, as some commentators have supposed (e.g. A. J. Ayer, 'The Concept of a Person', in *The Concept of a Person and Other Essays* (Macmillan, London, 1963), p. 87), an oblique reference to the argument from analogy. The generalization in question is of the pseudo-meaning nexus of word and exemplar.

[3] Anscombe translates '*Bezeichnung*' as 'designation'. But in paragraph 2 of §293 she translates '*So wäre er nicht der der Bezeichnung eines Dings*' as 'If so it would be used as the name of a thing.' Its recurrence in paragraph 3 '*Gegenstand und Bezeichnung*' should therefore be translated similarly.

possible, the private object allegedly referred to is a piece of idle machinery and plays no part in the mechanism of communication, and conversely *if the private object does play a part*, then communication is impossible. The naming relation as conceived by the private linguist has nothing to do with the explanation of what is involved in knowing the meaning of a word, or in meaning something by a word, or in understanding what someone else means by a word. In 'Notes for Lectures', Wittgenstein emphasizes that we are here torn between two contrary inclinations. On the one hand it seems that the private experience ought to serve as a paradigm to provide a term with meaning, and on the other hand it becomes increasingly obvious that it cannot do so.

The 'private experience' is a degenerate construction of our grammar (comparable in a sense to tautology and contradiction). And this grammatical monster now fools us; when we wish to do away with it, it seems as though we denied the existence of an experience, say, toothache (NFL, p. 314).

The private linguist endeavours to explain what he means by a word. He attempts to explain by a mental gesture at a private object. 'This' gives his words meaning. But nothing can be said about 'this'. And what started out by looking like an explanation turns out to be a delusion (NFL, p. 315).

It involves a fundamental misunderstanding, Wittgenstein remarks (*PI*, §314), to think that one can clarify the philosophical problems concerning sensations by studying one's own headache. For one's headache or one's thought are phenomena, and what we are studying in philosophy are concepts rather than objects, and hence the use of a word rather than the object to which the word refers (*PI*, §383). The mistake at the root of the private linguist's troubles is to think that a sensible intuition can do the work of a concept, that—to use Kant's faculty terminology—sensibility can yield knowledge without the co-operation of the understanding. But acquaintance with an object falling under the concept does not provide one with a concept. Wittgenstein compares the private linguist to a person who, when he doubts whether another person is in pain, pricks himself with a pin in order to be sure what 'pain' means (not being content with his imagination which only supplies him with a faint copy of the actual pain). When he has a genuine pain, then, he tells himself, it is the possession of *this* by someone else that he is to doubt. This, however, is absurdly wrong. 'It is as if I were told: "Here is a chair. Can you see it clearly?—Good—now translate it into French!"' (*Z*, §547.) In order to doubt whether another person is in pain, what we need is not a pain, but the *concept* pain (*Z*, §548). The private linguist may still feel baffled. If 'the object drops out of consideration as irrelevant' then does Wittgenstein not commit himself surreptitiously to behaviourism? But surely there is a difference between pain behaviour accompanied by pain and pain behaviour without pain? 'What greater difference could there be?' Wittgenstein concedes. But how can he agree?

. . . 'yet you again and again reach the conclusion that the sensation itself is a *nothing*'—Not at all. It is not a *something*, but not a *nothing* either! The conclusion was only that a nothing would serve just as well as a something about which nothing could be said (*PI*, §304).

This brief passage has caused commentators much trouble, and has often led to the wholly misguided view that Wittgenstein denied that we ever refer to, or say anything about, private sensations.[1] The point however is in part an elementary Kantian one: 'appearances might, indeed, constitute intuition without thought, but not knowledge; and consequently would be for us as good as nothing'.[2] So much for the first part of the criticism of the private language.

The second kind of criticisms is embodied in Wittgenstein's own constructive account of meaning and language. I shall not attempt to outline his positive views. In the course of his diverse discussions of learning, meaning and intending there are a number of critical remarks which have a direct bearing upon the conception of thought and language involved in the private linguist's viewpoint. I shall select a few of these in which Wittgenstein's emphasis is upon the formation of sentences and the requirement of syntactical and semantical conventions.

The private linguist (and Locke in particular) conceives of meanings as mental exemplars, ideas (in Locke's case) or images (*Vorstellungen*) (in the case of Wittgenstein's adversary). But the use of a word in the formation of a well-formed, meaningful sentence involves, among other things, certain syntactical principles. Pictures, mental or not, lack a syntax. The mental image of pain cannot

---

[1] e.g. G. Pitcher, *The Philosophy of Wittgenstein*, pp. 298 ff.
[2] Kant, *Critique of Pure Reason*, A 111.

do the work of 'pain'. An image of the absence of pain cannot stand in for the negation of 'pain'. Locke claimed that in 'recording our own thoughts for the help of our memories, whereby, as it were, we talk to ourselves, any words will serve the turn' (III.ix.2). In a trivial sense this is right, and in an important sense, quite wrong. Of course one may soliloquize in code; one language may be translated into another, and there is no reason in principle why one should not talk to oneself in a language unknown to others. On the other hand, a sign is not converted into a symbol by being associated with an image. What gives life to a sign is not any kind of object (*PI*, §432). 'Sounds', Locke says, 'are voluntary and indifferent signs of any ideas', so one may use them as one pleases to signify one's ideas, as long as one is consistent in one's use of the signs. But while it is arbitrary that a given word in a language means what it does in so far as another sound could replace it, the nature of the arbitrariness is strictly circumscribed. Wittgenstein intimates this in the following passage:

Can I say 'bububu' and mean 'If it doesn't rain I shall go for a walk?'—It is only in a language that I can mean something by something. This shews clearly that the grammar of 'to mean' is not like that of the expression 'to imagine' and the like (*PI*, p. 18e, n.).[1]

'Bububu' does not have the articulations which would make it possible for it to mean 'if it does not rain I shall go for a walk'. A word is part of a language, and has meaning only as part of a complex structure. The sound or sign may be arbitrary, but its location within the structure and hence its possible combinations and operations are not. To use Wittgenstein's favourite chess analogy, it is arbitrary that the king in chess is the tallest piece, but in deciding that the tallest piece shall function as the king in the game, one is committing oneself to many further consequences (M, pp. 257–61). Part of the point being made is not essentially different from the Fregean point, already adhered to in the *Tractatus*, that the sentence is the fundamental unit of communication and that the concept of the meaning of a word must be understood in terms of the contribution a word makes to the senses of the sentences in which it may legitimately appear. It is mistaken to suppose that the notion of a word is logically independent of the notion of its possible roles within different kinds of sentences. This requires both syntactical

---

[1] See also *Z*, §§6, 154, and *PI*, §508 ff., §665.

and semantical principles which a picture or image cannot supply by itself.

A related array of criticisms with multiple ramifications (which will not be examined here) concerns the private linguist's failure to appreciate the philosophical implications and importance of the fact that 'the *speaking* of language is part of an activity, or of a form of life' (*PI*, §23). The 'keyboard' model of communication is radically misguided. The point of communication does not consist in bringing about a mental event in the mind of the hearer (which is how the private linguist conceives of grasping the sense of the speaker's words) the relation of which event to the hearer's future behaviour is irrelevant to the communicative act (*PI*, §363). Nothing in the private linguist's fantasy makes room for semantic mood operators. But it is a deep misconception to think that one can account for the sense of a sentence independently of its point. This is like thinking that one can give an adequate description of chess without involving the notions of winning and losing. Moreover the private linguist's theory wholly obscures the indefinitely many kinds of use of sentences in speech, the huge diversity of language-games, in the activity of mankind. One cannot attain a proper grasp of, e.g., the meaning of 'pain' without appreciating the roles which sentences containing the word play in our life, in entreaties and pleas, requests for mercy, help or alleviation, threats or warnings, expressions of sympathy and pity, prayers and exclamations. Failure to understand this invites disaster in philosophical investigation. To neglect the extent to which speaking is an activity integral to human life is to shatter the unity of practical and theoretical reason. This cannot but produce distortion, misrepresentation and illusion.

The conception of thought underlying the private linguist's contentions is radically mistaken. Wittgenstein discusses the concepts of thinking, understanding and knowing at length. The general line of argument is to induce us to look at capacities and abilities, dispositions and potentialities and their criteria in behaviour, instead of seeking for mental states and inner processes as the essence of thought and understanding which justify the assertion that a person is thinking or has understood. Wittgenstein's point is not to deny the possibility of internal on-goings accompanying performance or achievement of understanding, it is rather to deny that such events are either necessary, sufficient, or criteria for understanding or thinking. For present purposes it suffices to point out two striking sections which illustrate rather than argue for Wittgenstein's objections to the private linguist's conception. Speech with and without thought is not, as Locke suggested, a matter of observable events accompanied by, and caused by, internal unobservable events in contrast with observable events unaccompanied by the appropriate mental events. It is rather comparable to playing a piece of music with and without thought (*PI*, §341). Although we often call the accompaniment of speech by a mental process 'thinking', the accompaniment is not what is meant by 'a thought'. Wittgenstein invites us (*PI*, §332) to say a sentence with understanding, and then not to say it at all, but merely do what we accompanied the saying with when we said it with understanding. Contrary to the conception of the private linguist or Lockean:

when I think in language, there aren't 'meanings' going through my mind in addition to the verbal expressions: the language is itself the vehicle of thought (*PI*, §329).

6. *Wittgenstein's Criticism of the Private Linguist's Epistemology*

The private linguist adheres to the doctrine of epistemic privacy of experience. Only I can know that I am in pain, others can only surmise it. To this Wittgenstein's reply is that this is partly false and partly nonsense. The claim that others cannot know that I am in pain, or that I cannot know what experiences, if any, others are having, is false, if taken in the ordinary sense of 'know'. There are innumerable occasions upon which we pass judgement upon the 'inner states' of others, upon the basis of good evidence, and in which our judgement is true. If the sceptically-minded retort that what is 'inner' is hidden from us, Wittgenstein's riposte is that the future too is hidden from us, but the astronomer calculating an eclipse of the sun does not say that he cannot in principle know when there will be an eclipse, but only surmise it (*PI*, p. 223). Similarly, 'if I see someone writhing in pain with evident cause I do not think: all the same, his feelings are hidden from me' (*PI*, p. 223). Thus far by way of reminders. The problematic idealist's next move is to query whether those cases where we ordinarily have no doubts whatever about the experiences of others might not be pretence. Is it not possible that the smile of the unweaned infant, the howl of the injured dog, are mere pretence? To this Wittgenstein's answer is, at one level, simple, at another, highly complex. At the simpler level his response is that not *any* behaviour will be allowed as falling under the concept of pretending. Of certain kinds of conduct one may justifiably say 'One *can't* pretend like that'. One's grounds for such a judgement may be empirical, or may be conceptual. The conceptual basis for such a judgement would be expressed not by the claim that the man writhing in a pool of blood will not suddenly get up and grin, but by the claim that *this* can no longer be called pretence. Wittgenstein invites us to compare such a judgement with analogous ones such as 'one cannot talk like that without thinking' and 'one cannot act like that involuntarily' (*Z*, §570). Pretence is an acquired skill which depends upon prior familiarity with forms of behaviour which characterize the pretended action, if not upon possession of the concept of the act which constitutes the object of pretence. 'A child has much to learn before it can pretend', Wittgenstein points out, and adds 'There might actually occur a case where we should say "This man *believes* he is pretending"' (*PI*, p. 229). At a much deeper level Wittgenstein's answer depends upon his theory of criteria the detailed examination of which must be deferred until later. The general direction of the argument is to claim that those psychological terms which we ascribe to ourselves, with every right but without any justificatory evidence, depend for their sense upon the existence of natural manifestations of inner states. These natural expressions of psychological states constitute part of the criterial evidence which justifies others ascribing the relevant psychological predicates to us. Our self-ascriptions are not made on the basis of criteria, but they only make sense because there are such criteria. Thus Wittgenstein emphasizes the significance of natural, pre-conceptual forms of behaviour: 'The language-games with expressions of feelings are based on games with expressions of which we don't say that they may lie . . . It is senseless to say: the expression may always lie' (NFL, p. 293). To suppose that all behaviour might always be pretence is to suppose that the concept of pretending might lack behavioural criteria, and that is not possible (*Z*, §571).

Not all doubts are yet quelled. Granted that I can know the inner states of others, can I know these with the certainty with which I know other things? Wittgenstein's reply is that I can indeed be as certain, e.g., that someone is depressed as I am certain that $25 \times 25 = 625$, or that I am of such and such an age. But this should not mislead us. There are important logical differences involved (*OC*, §447). The certainty is of different kinds. But the differences in kind are not, as the sceptically-minded may think, psychological differences. It is not that my certainty that $25 \times 25 = 625$ involves a stronger feeling of certainty than my certainty that someone is depressed. The *feeling* of certainty, the absence of doubt, may well be the same. The criteria for our feeling certain about a matter lie in our behaviour, and as far as that is concerned, we are no less certain, in general, about the states of mind of others than about mathematical judgements. Now the sceptic may retort: 'While you can have complete certainty about someone else's state of mind, still it is always merely subjective, not objective, certainty' (*PI*, p. 225). Wittgenstein's response is that these two words 'subjective' and 'objective' imply not a difference in degree of reputability, but a difference in language-games. These differences, he suggests, are logical: 'the kind of certainty is the kind of language-game' (*PI*, p. 224).

According to Wittgenstein the criterion of certainty is laid down in the grammar of sentences. The sense of a sentence is explained by explaining its grammar. The grammar of a sentence is constituted by the rules for its use. These consist *inter alia* of specifications of the grounds of a sentence. The grounds of a sentence are criterially related to it, constituting non-inductive evidence for the truth of the sentence in question (*PI*, §481; *Z*, §437). In the absence of countervailing evidence their truth is also a condition for justifiable certainty. We are justified in being certain that 'p' is true if we have criterial evidence justifying its assertion and no grounds, in these circumstances, for doubting whether 'p' is true. The criteria for the truth of 'p' are also, *ceteris paribus*, the criteria for certainty. In laying down the grammatical grounds for belief, one is also laying down grounds for certainty (*OC*, §373). The notion of doubt, Wittgenstein laboured to stress in his last writings, can only enter on the background of such rules of evidence which help to fix the meaning of sentences of a given kind. Doubt is parasitic upon certainty (*OC*, §§115, 370, 519, etc.; *Z*, §§410–16). It needs grounds which can only be specified relative to grounds for certainty. The sceptic confuses logical differences in kind of certainty (e.g. conditions justifying us in claiming to know a mathematical theorem, namely deductive proof, in contrast with conditions justifying us in claiming to know that another is in pain, namely pain behaviour) with different psychological degrees of certainty. Moreover he fails to realise that a grounded belief is innocent unless proved guilty.

This principle of Natural Epistemic Justice is not optional. In its absence doubt is unintelligible.

What then of my certainty that I am in pain? Do I not know that I am in pain in a way, and with a degree of certainty, that is unavailable to others? This, Wittgenstein suggests, is nonsense. 'I know I am in pain' either means the same as 'I am in pain' or else it is nonsense. One can, according to Wittgenstein, only use 'I know' as a sentence-forming operator upon sentences if one can also use 'I doubt' and 'I believe' or 'I suspect'. But it is nonsense to say 'I doubt whether I am in pain', or 'I believe it hurts me, but I may be wrong'. And if this is nonsense, then, in Wittgenstein's view, 'I know I am in pain' is also nonsense. The truth of the matter, according to him, is that it is not possible to doubt that one is in pain. But it does not follow that one is certain that one is in pain (when one is in pain). On the contrary, the exclusion of doubt also excludes certainty. First person psychological utterances in the present tense have the peculiarity that if the speaker is sincere he will tell us what his inner states are, but, by way of contrast, my sincerity won't guarantee the truth of my guess as to his inner states (*PI*, p. 224).[1] The sceptic, as always, misinterprets the reflection of grammar in the mirror of linguistic practice. He takes doubt to be excluded by certainty—the certainty residing in the immediacy of experience. But it is grammar which excludes doubt, not experience.

Is there any truth then in the doctrine of epistemic privacy? In the end only a mouse comes forth. The sceptic suggests that I cannot know the inner states of others. Wittgenstein's answer, for the various reasons adumbrated, is that not only can we sometimes know the inner states of other persons, but that we also sometimes say of a person that he or she is completely transparent to us. *But* it is also true that one human being can be a complete enigma to another (*PI*, p. 223). This will be brought strikingly to our attention when visiting a completely alien country with wholly different practices. Here the grounds for their actions, and (at least some of) the ends they pursue will be enigmatic. Similarly, although we can sometimes know the inner states of others, we may at other times fail to discover what they are. A thought is 'private'—is *de facto* unknown to others—if it is not revealed (or manifested). But it is

---

[1] For a detailed examination of the non-cognitive theory of avowals see below, ch. IX.

no longer 'private' if it is not kept secret (*PG*, §41; NFL, p. 314; *PI*, p. 222). In neither case is anything *a priori* opaque or private, nor is there any metaphysical boundary which sets the limits of possible human knowledge at the portals of other minds.

The second sort of privacy upon which the epistemological doctrines of the private linguist rest is the privacy of ownership. Another person, he claims, cannot have my pains. To this Wittgenstein's retort is brief. 'In so far as it makes *sense* to say that my pain is the same as his, it is also possible for us both to have the same pain' (*PI*, §253).

The brief argument Wittgenstein gives encapsulates the conclusions of his thought upon the subject of ownership of experience from 1929 onwards. His previous discussions of the subject have already been examined in some detail. Here the threads of the argument may be briefly drawn together. 'Which are *my* pains?' Wittgenstein queries. 'What counts as a criterion of identity here?' He does not reply directly, but invites us to consider, by way of contrast, what makes it possible in the case of physical objects to speak of two objects being exactly the same. Of a chair we may say, he points out, that it is not the one that was here yesterday, but it is exactly the same. Physical objects, to use Strawson's[1] technical term, possess identifiability-independence. One can identify a particular material or physical object without either explicit or implicit dependence upon a non-material or non-physical object. The physical world provides, in the form of material objects, a 'comprehensive and sufficiently complex type-homogeneous framework of reference'. The system of material objects provides the framework for spatial location within which any particular material object can be identifyingly referred to. Two chairs may be exactly the same (but numerically distinct) so long as despite the identity of all their non-spatial properties, they occupy distinct spatial locations at the same time. The criteria of numerical identity of a chair, or a material object in general, include the continuity of the spatial positions it occupies through time.

Pains, unlike chairs, suffer from identifiability-dependence. The principles of individuation of pains (and experiences in general) include of necessity explicit or tacit reference to the person whose pains they are.[2] The properties we distinguish in a pain are its

---

[1] P. F. Strawson, *Individuals*, pp. 40 ff.

[2] My own pains and my references to them in thought and speech may appear to offer a counter-example, but any such appearance is wholly illusory.

phenomenal characteristics, and its location. The spatial location of a material object provides in general, a principle of individuation for the object. Is it so with pains? Wittgenstein denies this. If Siamese twins have a pain at the point of juncture, there is one location but two pains. The phenomenal characteristics and location of a pain provide the criteria of its qualitative identity. The numerical identity of the pain, however, is dependent upon the owner of the pain. The criterion of ownership of pain is not therefore given by the location of the pain in the body (the owner of a phantom pain might locate his pain in the body of the person sitting beside him) but by the pain behaviour of the person who suffers. He who manifests pain is its owner (*PI*, §302).

The spatial matrix provides a means of securing unique reference to particular material objects. What space is for objects, persons are for pains. No two objects can be in the same place at the same time, and no single object can be at different places at one time. This however does not prevent two chairs being 'exactly the same'. Similarly, the fact that pains are identifiability-dependent upon owners does not prevent two people having exactly the same pain. If my pain tallies with your pain in phenomenal characteristics, then we both have the same pain, and perhaps the same disease. Of course the two chairs can exchange places and retain their numerical identity, but persons can't exchange pains. But this is merely a confusing way of saying that chairs are objective particulars which enjoy identifiability-independence, and pains owe their numerical identity to their owner. A person who strikes himself on the breast and says 'Surely another person can't have THIS pain!' (*PI*, §253) is confusing himself in precisely this way. He is like the person who says 'No other chair could stand where this chair is standing', and thinks that he has said something about the metaphysical immobility of chairs. 'One doesn't define a criterion of identity by emphatic stressing of the word "this",' Wittgenstein concludes, 'Rather, what the emphasis does is to suggest the case in which we are conversant with such a criterion of identity, but have to be reminded of it.' The blow on the chest and emphasis upon 'this' is merely a reminder that persons are the individuators, the identificatory matrix of pains (or experiences in general) which are identifiability-dependent upon them, just as the remark about the chair is a reminder that space is an individuator of material objects which are identifiability-independent. But the identifiability-dependence of experiences is by no means a unique feature of experiences. If you cannot have my pains, neither can you sneeze my sneezes, and nor for that matter can you catch my cold. Nevertheless this kind of privacy does not make the sceptic immune to infection. Nor does identifiability-dependence constitute a barrier to knowledge—the fact that you can't have my experiences does not mean that you cannot know that I have them. You cannot have the smile of the Sphinx, but it is not this which makes the smile enigmatic.

One puzzle remains. 'In so far as it makes *sense* to say that my pain is the same as his, it is also possible for us both to have the same pain.' It should by now be clear in what sense we can both have the same pain. But we have seen that in a trivial sense 'another person can't have my pains' is a truism. Wittgenstein, however, suggests that it is nonsense. Why?

7. 'One Plays Patience by Oneself.'
At §248 of the *Investigations*, Wittgenstein remarks oracularly:

The proposition 'Sensations are private' is comparable to: 'One plays patience by oneself'.

This may seem puzzling at first sight. After all, it is true that one plays patience by oneself. Yet the privacy of sensations is precisely what is being denied, at least in two senses of the expression. Wittgenstein's comment may be illuminated by applying the solipsist's style of thought to the remark about patience. The solipsist would say 'Only I can play patience' instead of 'One plays patience by oneself'.[1] A similar sleight of hand occurs in the way in which the solipsist construes the claim that sensations are private. Further light is thrown upon the matter by a remark in *Zettel*:

Do not say 'one cannot', but say instead: 'it doesn't exist in this game'. Not: 'one can't castle in draughts' but 'there is no castling in draughts'; and instead of 'I can't exhibit my sensation'—'in the use of the word 'sensation' there is no such thing as exhibiting what one has got' (*Z*, §134).

The claim that sensations are private is interpreted by the misguided metaphysician to mean that I can't know your experiences, and you

---

[1] In NFL, p. 283, Wittgenstein writes 'Does the solipsist also say that only he can play chess?'

can't have mine. Wittgenstein has endeavoured to show that this interpretation is wholly confused. But if the claim about epistemic privacy, which overtly looks as if it is delimiting human knowledge, is reinterpreted as a grammatical claim, then it is no longer as objectionable. If, in the course of explaining what 'intention' (or 'pain', or any psychological verb manifesting asymmetry between first and third person) means, one said 'Only you can know that you had that intention', and meant thereby that in one's own case it makes no sense to doubt or be uncertain, then one's comment, though misleading, is correct (*PI*, §247). It is misleading because although 'I know' may mean 'I do not doubt', it does not mean 'Doubt is logically excluded' (*PI*, p. 221). It is, however, correct as long as it is understood to be an *a priori* claim and not an empirical one. That one plays patience by oneself is not a fact about all hitherto discovered card-playing societies. It is rather about the 'essence' of patience. Similarly the contention that only I can know that I am in pain, if interpreted to mean that in my own case it makes no sense for me to doubt whether I am in pain, is taken by Wittgenstein to be a correct claim about the meaning of 'pain'. It is, in his semi-technical term, a 'grammatical' claim.

Analogous considerations apply to the second kind of privacy which the solipsist attributes to experiences. Experiences are private, he suggests, because you can't have my pains. But this, as we have seen, is misguided. In a perfectly ordinary sense of 'same' one person can have the same pain as another. In a trivial sense, which Wittgenstein says is 'nonsense', another person can't have my pains, or my smiles or sneezes. But the matter should not be represented thus. The truth is that only the pains I have are called 'my pains'. What is intimated by this tautology is the *a priori* truth that pains are identifiability-dependent. 'The great difficulty here', Wittgenstein remarked, 'is not to represent the matter as if there were something one *couldn't* do' (*PI*, §374). Thus 'sensations are private' can be interpreted as an expression of two 'grammatical' truths, and in this respect it is indeed comparable to 'one plays patience by oneself'.

The essential thing about metaphysics, in the pejorative sense of the term, is that it obliterates the distinction between factual and conceptual investigations. The fundamental controversies over scepticism and the metaphysics of experience have done precisely this. The sceptic wants his theses to specify genuine limits to human knowledge; he claims that there are specifiable kinds of fact which lie beyond possible cognition. Yet he also wants to say that things could not be otherwise. The clash of metaphysical doctrines about the nature of reality and our knowledge and experience of it is a story of shadow boxing in the dark, a bizarre tale of self-delusion.

Where . . . we come upon a whole system of illusions and fallacies, intimately bound together and united under common principles, a quite special negative legislation seems to be required, erecting a system of precautions and self-examination under the title of a *discipline*, . . . a system in face of which no pseudo-rational illusion will be able to stand, but will at once betray itself, no matter what claims it may advance for exceptional treatment.[1]

[1] Kant, *Critique of Pure Reason*, A 711, B 739.

IX

'A CLOUD OF PHILOSOPHY CONDENSED INTO A DROP OF GRAMMAR'

1. *Can One Know that One is in Pain?*

To try to outline the limits of the knowable is one of the traditional tasks of epistemology. Some epistemological doctrines concerning the possibility of knowledge are both intelligible and reasonable, such as Kant's demand that the employment of the categories be confined to the province of possible experience if knowledge is to be achieved. Other theories are intelligible without being reasonable: the various forms of scepticism confine our possible knowledge within unduly restrictive limits for reasons that are comprehensible, but not adequate. Yet other theories may appear neither reasonable, nor altogether intelligible. Normally one might wish to brush these aside. But when a philosopher of Wittgenstein's standing puts forward such an epistemological claim, we should do well to pay careful attention. As we have seen, Wittgenstein claimed that one cannot know that one is having a given experience. One cannot know this, not because one lacks information, nor because one only knows how one appears to oneself rather than how one is in oneself, but because sentences such as 'I know that I am in pain' are nonsense. This claim has little intuitive plausibility. Moreover it is somewhat bizarre. What is the point of delimiting possible knowledge in this particular way? Kant drew the boundaries of the knowable in the way he did in order to put an end to the pretensions of dogmatic metaphysics. The Cartesian sceptic misguidedly draws the boundaries at the limits of knowledge of subjective experience because the gap between knowledge of subjective experience and knowledge of objects does not seem to him to be bridgeable. In both these cases, and in many others, the general motivation—whether justifiable or not—is reasonably clear. But the Wittgensteinian limitation is puzzling, for there is no obvious rationale to it. When a philosopher is led to deny what appears intuitively obvious, it ill behoves us to be satisfied with a Johnsonian refutation. We should rather examine his argument with even greater care than normal to discover what drove him to take up an apparently indefensible position.

Wittgenstein's doctrine on this matter has been adopted by his most eminent followers. As is notorious, Malcolm defends the claim that psychological sentences in the first person and present tense (or a specifiable sub-class of such sentences often referred to as 'Avowals')[1] can be neither true nor false, but should be assimilated to behavioural manifestations of psychological states.[2] It is because 'I am in pain' is not used to make assertions, and does not bear truth-values that 'I know I am in pain' is nonsense. Geach quotes the doctrine with approval, though also with qualification.[3] Von Wright[4] applies the theory to axiology, and argues that first person, present tense hedonic judgements such as 'I like this' or 'I find this pleasing', and first person, present tense eudaimonic judgements such as 'I am happy' are not statements at all, and hence bear no truth-values. They express one's pleasure or happiness rather than state or describe that one is pleased or happy. The adoption of the doctrine by these philosophers should perhaps give us pause.

Nevertheless, the issue as to whether 'I am in pain' can be true or false and 'I know I am in pain' makes sense or not may seem minor and insignificant. It is not *obviously* linked with any major philosophical concern. It is *unobviously* linked, however, with some of the central problems in the metaphysics of experience on the one hand, and important considerations in philosophical logic and the theory of meaning on the other. As Wittgenstein himself stressed, the question at issue is fundamental to the differences between Realists, Idealists, and Solipsists. In his later work Wittgenstein

---

[1] I shall use 'avowal' to refer both to an act and to the sentence used to perform it. The context will make clear which is intended.

[2] N. Malcolm, 'Wittgenstein's *Philosophical Investigations*', in *Wittgenstein: The Philosophical Investigation, A Collection of Critical Essays*, ed. G. Pitcher, pp. 77–83.

[3] P. T. Geach, *Mental Acts* (Routledge and Kegan Paul, London, 1957) p. 121.

[4] G. H. von Wright, *The Varieties of Goodness* (Routledge and Kegan Paul, London, 1963), pp. 73 f., p. 98.

associated the doctrine with the private language argument, and it might be thought that the two doctrines stand or fall together. It is therefore important to explore their interrelationships. Furthermore, the doctrine of the non-cognitive status of avowals is intended to provide a way of avoiding the rational psychology of Cartesian dualism and its concomitant account of self-consciousness. At a deeper level still the doctrine is part of Wittgenstein's general onslaught upon the philosophical search for foundations. We have already noted his antagonism to the endeavour to establish the foundations of mathematics in anything beyond the activity of mathematical reasoning, and his trenchant opposition to his own earlier attempts to establish the foundations of language in metaphysics. One can see his doctrine of avowals as his third thrust against the search for foundations, directed against the endeavour to provide foundations for our empirical knowledge in our knowledge of how things subjectively appear to us to be. From the point of view of philosophical semantics the status of avowals raises equally profound and general issues. If the sense of a sentence is given by its criteria, how is it possible that there be some sentences which may be asserted without grounds? An account is needed both of the sense of avowals and of the possibility of criterionless self-ascription of experience. This must be compatible with the general approach of Wittgenstein's criterial semantics, and do justice to the nature of self-consciousness. The study of avowals is a logical exploration of these topics. It has multiple ramifications: the general relation between sense and the possibility of cognition, the nature of indexical expressions and the similarities and differences between 'I', 'He', and 'This', the logical form of egocentric sentences in general and the similarities and differences between self-ascription of psychological predicates and the self-ascription of non-psychological predicates, the similarities and differences between self-ascription and other-ascription of psychological predicates. These, and other related issues are preliminaries to the actual problem of Wittgenstein's non-cognitive thesis of avowals and the general debate as to whether self-knowledge and self-awareness are or are not rightly expressed by sentences such as 'I know that I am in pain'. The affirmation or denial of the non-cognitive thesis does indeed condense a cloud of philosophy into a drop of grammar (*PI*, p. 222).

2. The Non-Cognitive Thesis of Avowals

Wittgenstein's non-cognitive analysis of avowals emerged only gradually in the early 1930s. Bearing in mind his transitional verificationist phase it is obvious why this should have been so. In the *Philosophische Bemerkungen* he clearly thought that avowals could be used to make true or false assertions, and were knowable. He makes the first claim at §62:

'I have no pain' means: if I compare the proposition 'I have pain' with reality, it is shown to be false. It must be possible for me to compare it with what actually is the case. And this possibility of comparison—even though it does not fit—is what we mean by the expression: that which is the case must be in the same space as its negation; only it must *be different*.

The second claim is made at §66, where Wittgenstein refers to the phenomenon of pain sensation in his tooth, which phenomenon, he says, he knows. This is consonant with the general philosophical position adopted in this book. For Wittgenstein himself is in effect defending a positivist foundations theory of knowledge.

It is not surprising then that the doctrine of avowals does not emerge until after Wittgenstein's realization that what he had called 'genuine propositions' have no verification. It makes no sense to ask 'How do you know you have toothache?' nor to query 'Are you sure that you wish so-and-so?' It makes no sense to doubt whether one is having a given experience and if it makes no sense to doubt there can be no such thing as being certain. If it makes no sense to be certain, it makes no sense to speak of knowledge. The main lines of the doctrine stand out clearly in the *Blue Book* and 'Notes for Lectures'. The central contention is clearly stated. 'I know I have pain' either means nothing or the same as 'I have pain' (*BB*, p. 55; NFL, p. 309). The doctrine is prominent in most subsequent writings. In the *Philosophical Investigations* it is asserted many times in numerous different ways. The central statement of the doctrine occurs, as has been mentioned in the previous chapter, in the opening sections of the argument against the possibility of a private language:

It can't be said of me at all (except perhaps as a joke) that I *know* I am in pain. What is it supposed to mean, except that I *am* in pain (*PI*, §246).

In *Zettel* too, the doctrine is reiterated, and discussed at length.

If we are to read general philosophical significance into the non-cognitive thesis of avowals thus formulated then it should be generalized. There are at least three relevant directions of logically and epistemologically significant generalization of the formula—'"I know I am in pain" is either nonsense or else means the same as "I am in pain".' The first was made by Wittgenstein himself. His favoured examples are 'I have toothache' and 'I have pain'. Other examples which are mentioned are 'I have consciousness', 'I see red', 'I think', 'I am afraid', 'I want (wish, believe, feel) . . .'. The thesis is generalized in *Zettel*, §472 to all psychological verbs in the first person present tense. It would seem that Wittgenstein thought that 'pain' is merely a vivid example which represents the common features of present tense self-ascriptions of psychological verbs.[1] If one may use the predicate variable 'have ϕ' as a convenient variable for a psychological verb of the kind in question, then one may render the first generalization of the noncognitive thesis of avowals thus: 'I know I have ϕ' is either nonsense or means the same as 'I have ϕ'.

The second direction of generalization concerns introducing explicit temporal references to the formula. Wittgenstein's normal formulation is in the present tense throughout. But in the 'Notes for Lectures' he wrote:

I can tell you the fact that p because I know that p is the case. It has sense to say 'it rained and I knew it' but not 'I had toothache and knew that I had'. 'I know that I have toothache' means nothing or the same as 'I have toothache' (NFL, p. 309).

It would seem from this that it is not the present tense that is essential but that the time of the instantiation of the psychological verb be the same as the time at which knowledge is ascribed. The thesis rules out as senseless that I know at t that I have ϕ at t. It does not seem to rule out that I know at $t+1$ that I have ϕ at t, or that I know at t that I have ϕ at $t+1$. Knowledge of past and future pains is apparently perfectly possible.

---

[1] This generalized formulation is both imprecise and incorrect. It is imprecise because the term 'psychological' is not sharply delimited. It is incorrect because many predicates that are intuitively thought of as psychological do not share the features of avowals, e.g., 'intelligent', 'mentally defective', 'schizoid', 'neurotic', 'repressing', 'sublimating', etc. However, neither the imprecision nor incorrectness matter for present purposes.

The third direction of generalisation is slightly more difficult, for there is, as far as I know, no evidence in Wittgenstein's writing to license it. Is the non-cognitive thesis directed solely against the first person pronoun formulation, or is 'He knows at t that he has ϕ at t' equally senseless? If the generalized thesis applies not only to the first person pronoun but also to any other personal pronoun (or singular personal pronoun), we still want to know whether it can be further generalized. Is 'N.N. knows at t that N.N. has ϕ at t' ruled out? Should the completely generalized formula apply to any name or definite description of a person, or is it restricted to indexical expressions? Is the thesis that a person, under any description, who has a certain experience, cannot know (or fail to know) at the time at which he has the experience that he has it? Should the thesis say that in the formula 'X knows at t that X has ϕ at t', it is impermissible to substitute the same term (or more strongly a name or description referring to the same person) in the two variable places X? If so, the final form of the thesis is: 'X knows at t that X has ϕ at t' is either nonsense or means the same as 'X has ϕ at t'. In what follows I shall, for most purposes, use Wittgenstein's formulation. But it will be well to bear the generalized formulations in mind for at certain crucial points they bear upon important aspects of the theory.

The non-cognitive thesis is supported by a variety of arguments in Wittgenstein's writings. These can be distinguished by reference to the following: one set of arguments bears upon the question of whether an avowal can be true or false. The fundamental contention is that despite the assertoric form of the surface grammar of avowals they cannot be used to make assertions. Avowals are not assertions, nor are they descriptions. They bear no truth-values, and hence it makes no sense to speak of knowledge or ignorance, doubt or certainty. The second array of arguments do not rest the non-cognitive thesis upon the alleged truth-valueless status of an avowal, but presuppose that avowals do bear truth-values, which, for further reasons are not cognizable. The third kind of argument reverses the first kind, and bypasses the second. It claims that the non-cognitive thesis is true, not because avowals bear no truth-values and hence are not proper objects of cognition, but rather that they are not cognizable, and hence bear no truth-values. For a sentence has sense only in so far as grammar has laid down grounds for its assertion. Despite the obvious importance of this issue for

Wittgenstein's philosophy, many of his arguments are not only fragmentary but also equivocal.

The Expressive Thesis of Avowals runs ambiguously through all of Wittgenstein's later writings. In the *Blue Book* he wrote:

The difference between the propositions 'I have pain' and 'he has pain' is not that of 'L.W. has pain' and 'Smith has pain'. Rather it corresponds to the difference between moaning and saying that someone moans (*BB*, p. 68).

There are many differences between moaning and saying that someone moans. Moaning is a natural expression or manifestation of pain. It does not describe pain, it is not true or false, it is not learnt, and it cannot be operated upon with an epistemic operator to yield a sentence. It is a natural, primitive kind of pain behaviour, and that someone moans is a criterion for the truth of the assertion that he is in pain. Saying that someone moans differs on all these points. If the difference between 'I have pain' and 'He has pain' corresponds to these differences, then, it seems, 'I have pain', though not a natural pain expression, is not an object of possible knowledge, is not a description, is not true or false, is an acquired kind of pain behaviour, and is, qua utterance, a criterion for the truth of the assertion that he is in pain.

Just these points are explored by Wittgenstein in his subsequent work. In the 'Notes for Lectures', Wittgenstein wrote:

Roughly speaking: The expression 'I have toothache' stands for a moan but does not mean 'I moan' . . .

You couldn't call moaning a description! But this shows you how far the proposition 'I have toothache' is from a description, and how far teaching the word 'toothache' is from teaching the word 'tooth' (NFL, pp. 301–2).

The same argument is prominent in the *Investigations*. Avowals are conceived of as extensions of natural expressive behaviour:

words are connected with the primitive, the natural, expressions of the sensation and used in their place. A child has hurt himself and he cries; and then adults talk to him and teach him exclamations and, later, sentences. They teach the child new pain behaviour (*PI*, §244).

Again, in *Zettel* he stresses that whereas sentences in the third person, present tense of a psychological verb convey information, sentences in the first person are expressions (Z, §472). These passages, and many similar ones, have led to the most common interpretation of the doctrine of avowals.[1] This view rests the non-cognitive thesis upon the expressive thesis and interprets the latter as denying that avowals bear truth-values. An avowal does not say that the world is thus and so, it is a manifestation of its being so. Just as the emotive theory of ethics denied that sentences of the form '*A* is good' can bear truth-values, and interpreted them as expressions of emotion or as concealed imperatives, so the expressive thesis is taken to deny that 'I am in pain' can be either true or false and to interpret it as an expression of pain. Since only what is true or false is an object of possible knowledge or ignorance, avowals are excluded from the domain of the cognizable.

It is, however, significant that the argument may move along two different routes. It is customary to view the expressive thesis as establishing the truth-valueless thesis, and the latter as establishing the non-cognitive thesis. However it would be more consonant with Wittgenstein's criterial semantics to move directly from the expressive thesis to the non-cognitive thesis, for whether a sentence has sense or not is determined by its having grammatically fixed grounds justifying one in claiming it to be true.

However, the evidence is equivocal. It should be noted that the above quotation from the 'Notes for Lectures' is preceded by 'roughly speaking', and that *Zettel*, §472 is followed by the parenthetical remark 'Not quite right', and immediately thereafter 'The first-person of the present akin to an expression'. How close did Wittgenstein conceive the kinship? Is his view that avowals are manifestations of inner states and are not assertions, or that they are not assertions because they are manifestations of inner states, or that they are *also* manifestations of inner states and hence that though they are assertions they are peculiar? Are avowals descriptions or not? Wittgenstein's remark that 'I have toothache' is very far from a description (NFL, p. 302) has already been noted. Later on in the 'Notes' he repeats the point. To say that I have toothache I need not observe my behaviour in the mirror. But it does not follow that I *describe* an observation of inner sense. Moaning is not the description of an observation, and 'I have toothache'

[1] See e.g. P. F. Strawson, 'Review of *Philosophical Investigations*', repr. in *Wittgenstein: The Philosophical Investigations*, ed. G. Pitcher, pp. 45 ff., and N. Malcolm, 'Wittgenstein's *Philosophical Investigations*', ibid., p. 82.

is not *derived* from what I observe (NFL, p. 319). This implies reasonably clearly that an avowal is not a description. His position in the *Investigations*, however, is more wary. At §290 he emphasizes the point we have already encountered many times—I do not identify my sensation by criteria. The beginning of this 'language-game' is not an identification but the criterionless use of an expression. Is the beginning the sensation—which I describe? 'Perhaps this word "describe" tricks us here,' Wittgenstein replies, 'You need to call to mind the differences between the language-games.' 'I am in pain', or 'I am afraid' may sometimes be wrenched from us in agony or terror, and sometimes may be a quite cool response to a clinical question. I may tell the doctor 'Now I am hearing with this ear again' (*PI*, §416). It is noteworthy that Wittgenstein appears to shift between two different conceptions of a description, an epistemological one and an intentional, speech-act, one. It is unclear whether descriptions, in the latter sense, are cognizable. If they are, then if 'I am in pain' is sometimes a description then 'I know I am in pain' can make sense. In the second, unfinished part of the *Investigations*, Wittgenstein appears to have shifted ground considerably from the position of the 'Notes for Lectures'. In particular contexts, he writes, I do describe my state of mind. 'No, no! I am afraid' is a cry of fear, but 'I am still a bit afraid, but no longer as much as before' is a description of my state of mind. That the second utterance is a description is not a result of my observing my soul out of the corner of my eye as I said it (*PI*, p. 188). Both utterances are used without criteria (*PI*, p. 174), it is their having or lacking a purpose, and the nature of that purpose in the context of utterance that determines their status. Wittgenstein concludes with three remarks which highlight the contrast with the 'Notes for Lectures':

A cry is not a description. But there are transitions. And the words 'I am afraid' may approximate more, or less, to being a cry. They may come quite close to this, and also be *far* removed from it.

We surely do not always say someone is *complaining*, because he says he is in pain. So the words 'I am in pain' may be a cry of complaint, and may be something else.

But if 'I am afraid' is not always something like a cry of complaint and yet sometimes is, then why should it *always* be a description of a state of mind (*PI*, p. 189).

Putting aside the issue of the descriptive status of avowals, do avowals have truth-values? Again Wittgenstein's position is equivocal. In *Zettel*, §401 Wittgenstein suggests that the claim that 'I have consciousness' is a statement about which no doubt is possible says no more than '"I have consciousness" is not a proposition [*Satz*].' One should treat such words as whistling or humming. The impossibility of doubt, in Wittgenstein's view, implies the impossibility of knowledge. Here the denial that 'I have consciousness' is a genuine *Satz*, i.e. has sense and bears truth-values, seems to rest upon the non-cognitive thesis, rather than *vice versa*. Should the remark about consciousness be generalized to yield the claim that the impossibility of doubt, a general characteristic of avowals, implies that avowals cannot have a truth-value and cannot be used to make assertions? In *Zettel*, §549 Wittgenstein says that the expression of a sensation can only misleadingly be called a statement, but he uses the expression '*Behauptung*' rather that '*Satz*'. By contrast, however, he speaks of the importance, with respect to 'I have toothache', of the distinction between cheating and telling the truth (NFL, pp. 319 f.), and he talks of saying 'I have toothache' as an assertion (NFL, p. 315), as opposed to saying it as an example of a sentence. It might be thought that in so far as Wittgenstein denies that an avowal is a description, thus far he must deny that it can bear truth-values. However, in an important passage in the *Investigations*, Wittgenstein, applying the non-cognitive thesis to 'I am thinking', affirms that it can be true or false while denying both that it is a description and that it is cognizable.

The criteria for the truth of the *confession* that I thought such-and-such are not the criteria for a true *description* of a process. And the importance of a true confession does not reside in its being a correct and certain report of a process. It resides rather in the special consequences which can be drawn from a confession whose truth is guaranteed by the special criteria of truthfulness (*PI*, p. 222).

If one takes Wittgenstein to be claiming that avowals are, at least sometimes, true or false, and are, at least sometimes, descriptions, then the non-cognitive thesis must rest on other foundations than those so far scrutinized. Such an argument has been ingeniously constructed by A. J. P. Kenny, who first drew attention to the possibility of detaching the non-cognitive thesis from the truth-valueless thesis.[1]

'I am in pain' may be a lie, and hence may be meaningful but false. Hence it satisfies the bipolarity test for being a proposition. To be a description, however, it must be compared with something independent of itself in order to be assessed for truth or falsity, i.e. it must have independent criteria for its truth. The criteria for being in pain consist of behaviour that expresses pain. But the utterance of 'I am in pain' is itself an expression of pain. Consequently, Kenny concludes, 'if it is a description of my state, it is a description of a special kind: for it is a description which is to be compared with—*inter alia*—itself; and this is a unique type of comparison'.[2] Knowledge involves the possession of a true description of a state of affairs. Since 'I am in pain' is not a true description in the normal sense, Wittgenstein denies that it can intelligibly be said to be an object of knowledge.

To sum up the argument thus far: on the traditional interpretation the non-cognitive thesis rests upon the expressive thesis of avowals which denies that avowals can be used to make assertions, denies that avowals can bear truth-values, and hence denies their cognizability. Alternatively, the non-cognitive thesis is not derived from the truth-valueless, thesis, but implies it. It rests upon the senselessness of doubt (or, as I shall call it, 'the Argument from Epistemic Operators') and the related criterial argument, both of which will be scrutinized below. On the novel interpretation the non-cognitive thesis allows avowals truth-values (while stressing the peculiarity that truthfulness guarantees their truth), but denies that they are, in the 'normal sense', descriptions, because the utterance of an avowal is a criterion of its own truth.

A different, but equally ambivalent array of arguments is involved in the 'Use-of-"I"-as-Subject' thesis. In the 'Notes for Lectures' Wittgenstein states a version of the central non-cognitive thesis: 'I know that I have toothache' means either nothing or the same as 'I have toothache'. His following comment is startling: 'This', he says, '. . . is a remark about the use of the word "I", whoever uses it' (NFL, p. 309). The whole problem surrounding first person,

[1] A. J. P. Kenny, 'The Verification Principle and the Private Language Argument', in *The Private Language Argument*, ed. O. R. Jones, pp. 224–8.
[2] Kenny, ibid., p. 224.

present tense psychological sentences boils down, Wittgenstein now suggests, to our not understanding the function of 'I' (NFL, p. 307). The issue is explored in Wittgenstein's writings. It is the use of 'I' as subject[1] which is especially puzzling. For it is as a result of the peculiar features of sentences in which 'I' is used as subject—i.e. avowals—that we are led to think that there is a form of empirical knowledge that is non-evidential or immediate. What are the peculiar features of the personal pronoun 'I' in the context of psychological sentences such as 'I am in pain' or 'I see red'? The salient peculiarities that caught Wittgenstein's attention stem from the fact that no criteria determine my saying 'I am in pain'. The use of 'I' as subject involves no identification of one particular object among others to function as the subject of the psychological predicate.[2] When I say that I am in pain, I do not *recognize* a particular person to whom I then ascribe the pain. As there is neither identification nor recognition, there is no room for mis-identification or misrecognition. The use of 'I' as subject is immune to error of identification or recognition of the subject.

It is because of this feature that Wittgenstein makes two unusual claims about the personal pronoun 'I'. Firstly, 'I', when used as subject, does not denote a possessor. It is no more a name than 'here' is a name of a place, or 'now' a name of a time. Nor does it, so used, refer to a particular person. 'I', for me, is not 'a signal calling attention to a place or person' (NFL, p. 307), for in using 'I' I do not pick out one person from among a group of people (*BB*, p. 68). There is no possibility of my misidentifying who is in pain. It is true that others identify who is in pain by reference to what I do or say. The owner of the pain is he who manifests or avows it, but 'I do not choose the mouth which says "I am in pain" or groans'. Secondly, 'I' is not a demonstrative pronoun (*BB*, p. 68). Demonstrative pronouns such as 'This' depend for their reference upon the speaker's intention, are subject to referential failure (e.g. when an after-image is taken for a coloured patch upon the wall, and 'This is red' is uttered), and are replaced by a description in subsequent references to the same item (or else involve an identi-fication and hence the possibility of misidentification). 'I', on

---

[1] See above ch. VII, pp. 204 f.

[2] The use of 'I' as subject is discussed in detail in S. Shoemaker, 'Self-Reference and Self-Awareness', in *Journal of Philosophy*, lxv (1968), 555-67. Many of the following points are drawn from this illuminating paper.

recurrent occasions of its use as subject by the same person, is not susceptible to referential failure, it does not refer to a different object according to the intention of the speaker, and the past tense equivalent of, e.g., 'I am in pain' expressed on the basis of memory is 'I was in pain', and here too 'I' is used as subject.

Consequently Wittgenstein goes on to claim '"I have pain" is no more a statement *about* a particular person than moaning is' (*BB*, p. 67). Hence 'I know I am in pain' is illegitimate. For 'When I say "I am in pain", I don't point to a person who is in pain, since in a certain sense I have no idea *who* is' (*PI*, §404). Similarly, Wittgenstein argues, 'it has no sense to ask "how do you know that it is *you* who sees it?" for I don't *know* that it's this person and not another one which sees before I point [at what is seen]' (NFL, p. 310). The thread of argument, however, is tangled. Is Wittgenstein's claim that 'I', in its use as subject, is not a referring expression at all? Is his claim that 'I have pain' is not an assertion about a particular person, or that it is not an assertion? And so again, is the non-cognitive thesis supported by the contention that an avowal cannot be used to make a genuine assertion, or merely that it is peculiar?

The third argument in support of the non-cognitive thesis may be called the Criterial Argument. It is nowhere explicitly stated by Wittgenstein, but it is clearly near the surface of the discussion, and although I can see no satisfactory way of resolving the difficulties it raises, it is worth bringing to light. Boldly stated it appears straightforward, but its ramifications reach to the heart of Wittgenstein's criterial semantics. The sense of a sentence is determined by its criteria. The criteria for a sentence consist of the non-inductive grounds for its application or use, i.e. the grounds that justify one in asserting the sentence. How then is one to account for the sense of a sentence which, as Wittgenstein puts it, one uses with a right, but without justification. Avowals do not rest upon criteria. When I say truly that I am in pain it is my being in pain that makes what I say true, but it is not my justification or ground for saying what I say. I have no justification or ground. Should one then claim that an avowal has no sense? Or should one claim, more plausibly it might be thought, that the sense of an avowal is a function of the sense of its constituents? The sense of the constituent psychological predicate which is criterionlessly self-ascribed, is given by the grounds which justify its other-ascription. So the fact that an avowal has no grounds does not imply that it lacks sense and truth-value.

The absence of grounds for an avowal provide, in Wittgenstein's conception of knowledge, justification for affirming the non-cognitive thesis. For he suggests, admittedly in a different context, that 'I know' is correctly used only when one is ready to give compelling grounds (*OC*, §243). One is justified in making a cognitive claim only in relation to the possibility of demonstrating the truth of what is claimed. This point is embodied in a characteristically equivocal remark in *Zettel*: 'To call the expression [*Äusserung*] of a sensation a *statement* [*Behauptung*] is misleading because "testing", "justification", "confirmation", "reinforcement" of the statement are connected with the word "statement" in the language-game' (*Z*, §549). Presumably then only statements or *Behauptungen* are cognizable, and an *Äusserung* is not. An *Äusserung* cannot be known and hence, presumably, is not a *Satz*.

The final prominent array of arguments Wittgenstein offers is indeed connected with the previous claim. They have already been encountered and referred to as 'Arguments from Epistemic Operators'. The first argument claims that knowledge is possible only where doubt makes sense and error is conceivable. The expression of doubt with respect to others' pains makes sense, and hence too the expression of knowledge. But 'I doubt whether *I* am in pain' and 'I doubt whether *this* that I have is pain' are nonsensical utterances. The employment of an epistemic term in the first person and present tense such as 'I believe that', 'I am not sure whether', 'I do not know whether', operating upon an avowal does not indicate, as it normally would, uncertainty or doubt, but lack of mastery of the psychological concept in question (*PI*, §288). But 'I know that p' does not mean '"I doubt that p" is senseless', although it may mean 'I do not doubt that p' (*PI*, p. 221). Hence when 'p' is an avowal it is illegitimate to operate upon it with 'I know that'. Equally 'I know that' is only legitimately employable where one can also say 'I believe...', 'I suspect...' (ibid). Thirdly, only that which I can come to know can I be said to know or be ignorant of. Only what one can find out can one know (ibid.). Hence there is no such thing as knowledge of one's sensations or experiences, because one does not come to know them or learn of them, one has them (*PI*, §246). Fourthly, one may stand the argument from doubt upon its head to bring it into line with the previous discussion of certainty. Knowledge implies absence of doubt not the senselessness of it. Absence of doubt is certainty. But the criteria for the objective certainty of an assertion are identical with the criteria justifying the assertion. Yet if 'p' is an avowal, asserted criterionlessly, then there is no room for certainty and hence no room for knowledge.

It should be noted that the arguments concerning the use of epistemic operators have been taken in different ways. One can interpret them as supporting the non-cognitive thesis independently of the question of whether avowals can be true or false. Kenny's interpretation takes them in that way. Alternatively one can take them together with the criterial argument to show that avowals have no sense, for sense is not detachable from the conditions of the possibility of knowledge.

A final brief point in support of the thesis is the argument from the Identity of Speaker's Meaning. The suggestion is that there is no *point* in uttering 'I know I am in pain' that is not equally satisfied by uttering 'I am in pain' (*BB*, p. 55; *PI*, §246). 'I know that' adds nothing to 'I am in pain'. What is the cash-value of 'I know I see red' as opposed to 'I see red' (NFL, p. 284). The speaker cannot mean something by the epistemic utterance which he would not mean by the bare avowal. So the two are either identical in meaning, or one is nonsense.

In the following two sections I shall evaluate the non-cognitive thesis of avowals, first by scrutinizing the arguments which deny avowals truth-value, and then by examining the independent arguments which are compatible with avowals being true or false.

3. Rejection of the Truth-Valueless Thesis

The main points supporting the contention that 'I am in pain' cannot be used to make an assertion, can bear no truth-values, and hence cannot be known to be true or false, are derived from the first three groups of arguments examined above. I shall investigate these first, for if it can be shown that 'I am in pain' and other relevantly similar psychological sentences can be used to make true or false assertions, then the non-cognitive thesis must rest on grounds other than the claim that 'I am in pain' cannot be said to be true or false and hence can no more be known than 'Ouch' or 'Shut the door!'.[1] The argument from the use of epistemic operators which, on one interpretation, implies the truth-valueless

[1] See Kenny, op. cit., p. 213.

thesis, but at any rate need not rest upon it, will be examined in the next section.

The first contention to be examined is the traditional interpretation of the expressive thesis. Its central claim is that 'my sentences about my present sensations have the same logical status as my outcries and facial expressions'.[1] The apparent incorrigibility of such utterances is no more than the 'incorrigibility' of a groan. One may accept that there is a kinship between groaning and a sincere avowal of pain. That A groans in the appropriate circumstances, and that A says 'I am in pain', are both criteria for the truth of the assertion that A is in pain. Similarly a groan has no grounds, it does not rest on evidence, and likewise an avowal of pain has no criteria. Moreover to learn to express one's pain in first person psychological utterances is to acquire a new form of pain behaviour. It involves acquiring a set disposition to respond to a situation in a verbal way over and above, and often instead of, the natural primitive responses. Finally, such verbal responses, like the corresponding natural responses, are frequently emitted without any communicative intention; they may, as already mentioned, be wrenched from one like a cry. None of these facts, however, should incline us to view the logical status of such sentences as identical with that of the primitive behaviour, if any, which they may replace.

The fundamental features around which the counter-argument must revolve concern the fact that 'I am in pain' has, after all, a structure. As such it is complex or articulated. My use of this sentence is only intelligible in so far as I know what 'pain' means, i.e. know how to apply the predicate on the basis of those criteria which constitute its meaning. For this, as we have seen, is a precondition for my ascribing it to myself without criteria. Equally I must know how to use the personal pronoun 'I'. And this involves possession of the concept of a person and a grasp of the relations between 'I' and 'You' and 'He'. The following array of arguments against the truth-valueless thesis involves exploring the consequences of these elementary features of the sentence 'I am in pain'. Firstly, 'I am in pain' is a base for sentence-forming operations upon sentences. Thus, for example: 'He thinks (knows, believes, hopes, fears, etc.) that I am in pain.' Such complex sentences are thought of as true or false; no such operations can be carried out

---

[1] N. Malcolm, 'Wittgenstein's *Philosophical Investigations*', in G. Pitcher (ed.), op. cit., p. 82.

upon ejaculations. Secondly, the traditional interpretation has never extended to denying truth-values to 'I was in pain' or 'I will be in pain'. But these are the past and future tense transformations of the sentence in question. Moreover if it is now the case that I was in pain, then it was the case that I am in pain, and if it is the case that I will be in pain then it will be the case that I am in pain, none of which can be the case if 'I am in pain' has the logical status of an outcry or facial expression. Thirdly, 'I have been in pain for hours' is not plausibly analysable into a past tense sentence conjoined with an assertoric expression of pain, but it does imply 'I am in pain'. Fourthly, the expressive thesis appears to make assertions of identity such as 'The pain I have now is the same throbbing pain I had yesterday' unintelligible. Fifthly, 'I am in pain' seems to contradict 'No one is in pain' and to imply 'Someone is in pain'. Sixthly, 'I am in pain' can appear in molecular sentences, e.g. 'I am in pain and the doctor has not come', without the molecular sentence lacking a truth-value or being non-truth-functional. Seventhly, 'I have a pain' can appear as a premise in a valid argument, e.g. 'All persons with a pain of such and such a kind suffer from disease D, I have a pain of such and such a kind, therefore I suffer from disease D.' Eighthly, one is not only able to give a criterionless avowal of pain and its location,[1] but also a criterionless description of its phenomenological features, e.g. that it is dull or sharp, throbbing or nagging, searing or stinging, etc. Indeed we have a rich, if under-employed, vocabulary for the phenomenology of sensation. These descriptions, even though not descriptions of an *observation*, are informative and supply important

[1] There is a noteworthy inconsistency in Wittgenstein's remarks on the cognizability of pain location. In Z, §481 and §483, Wittgenstein claims that one has criterionless knowledge of the location of one's own pain. In OC, §41 he denies that it makes sense to say 'I know where I am feeling pain'. It would appear that the cognizability of the location of one's pain is inconsistent with the non-cognitive thesis. Can one find a compromise? Descartes suggested that the judgement that I have a pain may be clear and distinct, while the judgement that I have a pain in my foot, though clear, is not distinct. One may err either in assuming that something exists in the part affected similar to the sensation of pain of which one is conscious, or in assuming there to be an affected organ where there is none—as in the case of phantom limbs. Since in general anything Descartes conceived of as clear and distinct and so a proper object of knowledge Wittgenstein ruled out of the domain of possible cognition, his position could be expressed thus: In so far as 'I have a pain in my foot' leaves room for possible error, as in the case of phantom limbs (i.e. is not clear and distinct) it is cognizable. In so far as judgements of pain location cannot be mistaken, they are not objects of possible knowledge.

diagnostic data. They are ordinarily conceived of as true or false. Moreover there is, by and large, no natural expressive behaviour which manifests those phenomenological features, and our descriptions of them do not replace any primitive behaviour. Ninthly, 'I am not in pain' is the negation of 'I am in pain'. It is, like the sentence it negates, asserted without evidence, and similarly truthfulness guarantees its truth. But it is normally informative rather than expressive, and it cannot, I think, be said to be a learnt substitute for a natural form of 'absence-of-pain behaviour'. These nine points suggest that 'I am in pain' said by A can be used to make assertions, bears truth-values, indeed has truth conditions identical with 'He is in pain' said of A. When the traditional interpretation is extended to other first person psychological sentences such as 'I see red', 'I remember my third birthday', 'I am thinking of Gödel's theorem', or 'I believe that it is Tuesday today', its weaknesses are still more evident. For the assertion of such sentences (and of their negations) does not, in any sense, replace a primitive natural form of behaviour, and cannot, by any stretch of the imagination, be thought of as having the logical status of outcries and facial expressions. Yet such sentences do share the central perplexing features of 'I am in pain'. They are asserted without criteria, they involve no identification of a subject, truthfulness guarantees their truth, their assertion is a criterion for the truth of the corresponding third person sentence, and it makes no sense to doubt the applicability of the psychological predicate to oneself.

Does the 'Use-of-"I"-as-Subject' Argument provide any grounds for denying truth-values to sentences in which 'I' is used as subject and which are immune to misidentification relative to the subject? I think not. The features stressed by the argument are important and illuminating. They indicate the logical possibility of a different form of representation analogous to that which Wittgenstein contemplated in the *Bemerkungen* in which each speaker is the 'centre' of the language he speaks.[1] In such a language instead of 'I am in pain' one would say 'There is pain'. One must not, of course, claim that 'pain' in 'There is pain' has a different meaning

[1] See A. N. Prior, 'Egocentric Logic', *Noûs*, ii (1968), 191–207, for a much more radical suggestion of an egocentric logic in which not only is the personal pronoun 'I' eliminated, but all reference to persons is reduced to statements about the speaker who, being the subject of all that can be said, goes unmentioned. Here indeed 'the world is my world', and the limits of my language are the limits of the world.

from that which it has in sentences such as 'He is in pain'. But this possibility of change in form of representation in no way suggests that 'I am in pain' is not capable of being true or false. It merely highlights the logical peculiarities of criterionless self-ascription of experience, and points to strong disanalogies between 'I am in pain' and 'He is in pain'. Moreover, while the features Wittgenstein ascribes to the use of 'I' as subject are correctly ascribed, his conclusions obscure more than they reveal.

Even if 'I', when used as subject, is not a demonstrative pronoun, and is not a name, even if it lacks genuine referential force, nevertheless my use of 'I' requires that I know what a person is, and know that I am one, and so know (tacitly) the criteria of identity of persons. It is true that in saying that I have pain (remember so and so, am thinking of such and such, etc.) I do not exercise my ability to identify a person. But though I do not exercise this ability, my ability to ascribe an experience to myself presupposes that I possess it. Moreover, I must know that if I sincerely say 'I am in pain', then bystanders are in a position to assert of me 'He is in pain', and if they do so, will assert truly. Equally I must recognize other people's sincere utterances of tokens of this sentence as grounds for saying of them that they are in pain.

Furthermore, the use of 'I' as subject is neither arbitrarily nor contingently related to its use as object. 'I' is used as object, according to Wittgenstein, in sentences such as 'I have broken my arm', 'I have grown six inches', 'I have a bump on my forehead'. He characterizes the use of 'I' as object by reference to the fact that such cases involve the recognition of a particular person, and that the possibility of error has been provided for (*BB*, p. 67). This elides two importantly different kinds of case, uses of 'I' which involve an identification or recognition, and those which do not. 'I' is used as object when grounds for the instantiation of the relevant predicate are available, but it is possible that one errs in ascribing it to oneself. Such sentences need not, and often do not, involve an identification or recognition. 'I am being looked at by him' ('He is looking at me') involves no self-identification or recognition, but is not immune to error relative to the subject. I may be right in judging that he is looking at a person, but wrong in thinking that person to be myself because he is actually looking at the person behind me. By contrast *A*'s assertion 'I have just been appointed Captain-General' said on the basis of having received a letter addressed to A does involve a self-identification. It involves knowing that the person appointed Captain-General is A, and knowing independently that he himself is A. Two significant points emerge. The first is that 'I' is used without identification or recognition of a person in a very much wider range of cases than avowals, and hence cannot be a sufficient ground for the non-cognitive thesis without the thesis being stretched absurdly to cover an even wider class than the already embarrassingly large class of sentences allegedly beyond possible cognition. Secondly, the possibility of the use of 'I' as object presupposes the possibility of its use as subject.[1] For the justificatory grounds of both kinds of uses of 'I' as object consist of assertions in which 'I' is used as subject.

The issues at stake have even deeper ramifications. For it is not merely that any self-ascription presupposes the (potential) possibility of that criterionless self-ascription of psychological predicates involved in avowals, it is rather that any conceptualized experience presupposes the (potential) possibility of self-consciousness. The grounds of the possibility of consciousness of objects are identical with the grounds of the possibility of self-consciousness. This Kantian dictum reaches deeper into the puzzling features of avowals than do Wittgenstein's remarks upon the use of 'I'. 'Intuitions are nothing to us', Kant remarks,

and do not in the least concern us if they cannot be taken up into consciousness, in which they may participate either directly or indirectly. In this way alone is any knowledge possible. We are conscious *a priori* of the complete identity of the self in respect of all representations which can ever belong to our knowledge, as being a necessary condition of the possibility of all representation.

. . . All representations have a necessary relation to a *possible* empirical consciousness. For if they did not have this, and if it were altogether impossible to become conscious of them, this would practically amount to the admission of their non-existence. But all empirical consciousness has a necessary relation to a transcendental consciousness which precedes

---

[1] S. Shoemaker, op. cit., p. 561: 'Identifying something as oneself would have to involve either a) finding something to be true of it that one independently knows to be true of oneself, i.e. something that identifies it as oneself, or b) finding that it stands to oneself in some relationship (e.g. *being in the same place as*) in which only oneself could stand to one. In either case it would involve possessing self-knowledge . . . which could not itself be grounded on the identification in question.'

all special experience, namely, the consciousness of myself as original apperception.[1]

The Kantian point can perhaps be taken in a Wittgensteinian key thus: We learn to ascribe concepts to objects by learning to recognize the appropriate circumstances in which we are justified in saying that things are thus or so. The most elementary and fundamental utterances, of the form 'The so-and-so has such-and-such perceptual property', are justified by the circumstance of perceiving the relevant material object complex. Knowing the meaning of the relevant sentences involves the ability to recognize the circumstances which would justify asserting the sentence as so justifying its assertion. The circumstances in which one is justified in making the objective assertion are precisely the circumstances in which one is entitled to make the subjective assertion, given that one is in possession of the requisite concepts of a person and the relevant perceptual modes. The implications of this contention will be examined below. To conclude, it is inadvisable to emphasize the peculiarities of the use of 'I' as subject to the point of denying that it is a referring expression or that it denotes an owner. Rather one should correlate these important peculiarities with the use of 'I' in general, with the relationship between criterionless self-ascription and self-ascription in general, and with the relationship between self-consciousness and knowledge of objects. There is no reason for thinking that the use of 'I' as subject deprives one of the possibility of true assertion. Nor, on the whole, is it obvious that Wittgenstein suggests as much.

In view of the foregoing arguments one should, I think, take the criterial argument as pointing to a general difficulty in the criterial account of meaning rather than as constituting grounds for denying truth-values to first person, present tense psychological sentences. The move from accounting for the sense of a sentence in terms of its truth conditions to accounting for its sense in terms of the criteria which constitute its non-inductive justification opens a wide gap with respect to sentences which lack criteria. It seems quite clear that the psychological predicate criterionlessly self-ascribed is univocal. It is also clear that its intelligent criterionless use requires knowledge of the criteria which would justify its use in a third person ascription. For the sense of a concept word is, it seems,

[1] Kant, *Critique of Pure Reason*, A 117 and 117a.

given by the criteria justifying its use in third person ascriptions. Although a blind man does not infer that he is blind from his behaviour, nor does he justify his claim that he is blind by reference to his behaviour, nevertheless, Wittgenstein points out, 'if the person behaves in that particular way, we not only call him blind but teach him to call himself blind. And in *this* sense his behaviour also determines the meaning of blindness for *him*' (NFL, p. 285). On the other hand, it is clear that there are no criteria justifying the use of 'pain' in 'I am in pain', nor are there criteria justifying my saying 'I am in pain'. It is, of course, true that 'I am in pain' has the same truth conditions as 'He is in pain' said of the same person. But the criteria for the truth of 'He is in pain' are not the criteria for 'I am in pain'. I do not know how to resolve or dissolve the difficulties involved here. It is perhaps worth bearing in mind that the problems which arise for a constructivist account of the sense of avowals and the relation between 'I am in pain' and 'He is in pain' are partly parallel to the constructivist difficulty over accounting for the sense of sentences about the past and the relation between, e.g., 'He is ill' and 'He was ill'.[1] This is no coincidence.

4. Rejection of the Non-Cognitive Thesis

The non-cognitive thesis of avowals cannot rest upon the truth-valueless thesis. Can it stand upon its own feet? I shall examine the arguments in turn and after evaluating them give some further independent counter-arguments. I shall begin with Kenny's interpretation. The non-cognitive argument thus interpreted turns upon the contention that 'I am in pain' is a special kind of description (if it is one at all) which is to be compared with itself for its own truth. Hence it is not an object of possible knowledge, for knowledge requires possession of a true description of a state of affairs which is independent of what it describes. This is not a conclusive argument. In the first place, it is false that 'I am in pain' has to be compared with itself, i.e. is a criterion for its own truth. It is rather that the *utterance* of the sentence 'I am in pain' is the criterion for the speaker's being in pain. It is not obvious that the unexpressed judgement 'I am in pain' is a criterion for his being in pain. Secondly, saying 'I am in pain' is not a criterion for the truth of 'I am in pain'. 'I am in pain' has no criteria; the avowal

[1] See M. Dummett, 'The Reality of the Past', *Proceedings of the Aristotelian Society*, lxix (1968–9), 239–58.

is a criterion for the truth of 'He is in pain'. Thirdly, there are many sentences the assertion of which provides grounds for their truth which are not obviously psychological sentences, e.g. 'I speak English', 'I exist', 'I am alive', 'I am awake', 'I can articulate multi-syllabic words', etc. According to the Kenny interpretation, Wittgenstein should deny that it makes sense to know that one is alive or awake, that one can speak English or articulate multi-syllabic words. This is not intuitively an appealing position to adopt. Finally, it is worth stressing that no reason has been given why a description like 'I am in pain', which is not independent of what it describes in the sense that the assertion of the description is a ground for the truth of the description, is unknowable.

The second argument concerns the use of 'I'. It is true that in an avowal 'I' is used as subject, and so in a certain sense when I say 'I am in pain' I have no idea who is in pain. The point might be expressed thus: the conditions under which I have a title to say 'I am in pain' do not *require* that I be in possession of an identifying description of myself. But for another to say of me 'He is in pain', he must be able to identify me by ostension or by description. But this point is a quite general feature of the first person pronoun.[1] If I know that I (N.N.) am ill, it does not follow that I know that N.N. is ill. This carries over to the corresponding third person sentence. If N.N. knows that he is ill it does not follow that he knows that he himself, N.N., is ill. Thus if A knows that N.N. is ill, and N.N. knows that he is ill, it need not be the case that they know the same thing. So there may be grounds for claiming that if it is true that he knows that I am in pain he knows something different from that which I know if I know that I am in pain. But this is no ground for denying that it makes sense to speak of someone knowing that he is in pain. He may, in the relevant sense, not know who is in pain. But he knows that some person is in pain, and that he is that person. Moreover this argument in no way rules out sentences of the form 'N.N. knows that he, N.N., is in pain'.

The argument from justification is right to deny the intelligibility of my claiming that I am in pain, and then going on to verify my contention. It is also true that 'How do you know that you have pain?' is out of place. But it does not follow that the expression of a sensation is not a statement unless it is true that only that which I

[1] See H. N. Castañeda, 'On the Logic of Self-Knowledge', *Noûs*, i (1967), 9–21.

can test, confirm, verify, etc. is a statement (*Behauptung*). But this is a premise which needs independent support. Of course the criterial argument previously discussed provides such support. But, as has been seen, it is by no means obvious that the noncognitive thesis provides the most satisfactory answer for a criterial semantics to the problems of the logic of egocentric sentences. Detached from the criterial argument, the claim that I know is correctly used only when one is ready to give compelling grounds is, in itself, mere assertion. It is at least as plausible to claim that I can acquire and justify knowledge by testing and confirmation only if I can possess knowledge independently of testing and confirmation. For the alternative seems to imply either an infinite regress, or the possibility of giving compelling grounds which are themselves unknowable. 'How do you know that you are in pain?' is out of place because I do not know this *any* how. There are no means whereby I acquire such knowledge. Introspection, like perception, can be deemed to be, in the traditional terminology, a source of knowledge. But unlike perception, it involves no sensory modes; I do not know that I am in pain by looking with my mind's eye. Wittgenstein was right to force us to abandon the perceptual model of introspection, but wrong to think that the price to be paid for this is the denial of the possibility of self-knowledge.

The battery of arguments from the use of epistemic operators carry considerable conviction. But though persuasive, they do not constitute a proof. The premises of the arguments can be accepted without accepting their conclusion and the countervailing arguments are, I think, more powerful. It is true that doubt and uncertainty with respect to, e.g., one's being in pain are nonsensical. It is at least plausible to think that the negation of a nonsense is a nonsense and if so, absence of doubt and certainty are equally nonsensical. It is true that 'I know that p' does not mean '"I doubt that p" is senseless'. But it does not follow that I cannot know the truth of a sentence which it is senseless for me to doubt. To be sure knowledge excludes doubt. It is as senseless to doubt that I exist or that $2 + 2 = 4$ as it is to doubt that I am in pain. Here too expression of doubt is a ground for thinking that the speaker does not understand what he says. Of course Wittgenstein would deny the possibility of such knowledge too. But consistency is not tantamount to truth. Equally, it is inappropriate to say 'I believe that I am in pain'. But one may explain this by reference to the fact that believing that I am in pain is a sufficient condition for knowing, and that saying that I believe conversationally implies that I do *not* know, and hence would, in these cases violate a fundamental convention of communication. Similarly, it is true that I do not learn, or come to know, that I am in pain, *if* 'learn' or 'come to know' means 'to acquire knowledge by observation, hearsay, inductive, or deductive inference'. But then it may well be argued that coming to know things presupposes the possibility of knowing some things without coming to know them. Does it then, after all, follow that to speak of knowledge of one's current experiences is nonsensical? Only, it seems, if to speak of ignorance is nonsensical. To be sure, someone else may be ignorant of my pains, my wishes, my beliefs or my thoughts. Moreover, *I may know* that he does not know that I am in pain, that I wish I were not, that I believe that it will pass within the hour and that I think it is caused by an ulcer. But does it make sense to be ignorant of one's own pain? The exclusion of doubt and certainty exclude the possible *expression* of ignorance of pain. 'I do not know whether I am in pain' is nonsense. But it is less clear that unstatable ignorance is impossible. For if I lacked the requisite concepts I could neither say nor think that I am in pain, and in this (perhaps tenuous) sense, would not know that I am in pain. Knowledge of subjective experience is a peculiarity of concept-exercising creatures. All sentient creatures can suffer pain, want or enjoy things. Only self-conscious creatures, capable of ascribing experiences to themselves, know that they are in pain, that they want such-and-such, that they are enjoying this or that.

The argument from the identity of speaker's meaning fares no better. It may be true that in normal contexts my uttering 'I am in pain' fulfils every purpose that 'I know I am in pain' can fulfil. Yet in as much as my utterance demonstrates mastery of the concept of pain, and if it is true that mastery of the concept precludes erroneous self-ascription, then my sincere utterance of 'I am in pain' can equally be thought to imply that I know that I am, rather than to show that the supposition of self-knowledge is nonsensical. Moreover, it is precisely because mastery of a concept manifests itself in the correct use of the relevant word, and because mastery of the concept 'pain' precludes erroneous self-ascription, that it is the assertion of 'I am in pain' that shows everything that 'I know I am in pain' says. But it does not follow that what the former shows, the latter cannot say. 'I know I am in pain' says that I possess the entitlement to assert that I am in pain. Finally, averting one's eyes a moment from the somewhat misleading and obsessional concern with pain, one should bear in mind such sentences as 'I know what I want, but I am not going to tell you', or 'I know where it itches but I won't show it'. Epistemic privacy, as we have seen, amounts to little more than the possibility of concealment. But I may confess that I intend to conceal that which I could, if I wished, reveal.

So much for the additional arguments in support of the non-cognitive thesis. There are, however, further points which may dissuade one from opting for it. Firstly, the theory of inference is normally construed as saying that one is entitled to claim to know the conclusion of an argument only if one knows the truth of the premises and knows the argument to be valid. Avowals, as we have seen, can appear in such arguments. So either the non-cognitive thesis is false, or one can know the truth of the conclusion of some sorts of valid arguments without knowing the premises. Secondly, 'He is in pain' is knowable, and 'I know he is in pain' is undoubtedly a legitimate sentence. But what of 'He knows that I am in pain'? Can it be that I know that he knows that I am in pain without it being possible for me to know that I am in pain? Thirdly, sentences such as 'My pain will stop shortly', 'I have been in pain since 3.00 p.m.', 'The pain I have now is the same as the pain I had before the operation', all imply that I have pain now. Either they too are unknowable, or else, e.g., I can know that my current pain is qualitatively identical with a past pain without knowing that I have a pain. Neither alternative is very palatable. Fourthly, lying is normally conceived of as asserting something one knows to be false, with the intention of deceiving. Obviously the doctrine of avowals must find an alternative analysis. For it claims that when I say 'I am not in pain' when I am, it is not the case that I know I am; but, presumably, I do know that I am lying. It is difficult to see how I can know that I am lying unless I know that the negation of what I say is true. Similar considerations apply to my knowing that he is lying when he says that I am not in pain. Finally, in the standard analysis, 'I remember that p' implies that I previously knew that p. So 'I remember that I was in pain' implies that it was the case that I knew that I was in pain, or else the standard analysis of 'remember' must be modified.

The non-cognitive thesis of avowals, whether it is taken to rest upon the truth-valueless thesis, or whether it is taken to be independent of it, should be rejected.

5. The Private Language Argument, Self-Consciousness and the Foundations of Knowledge

The non-cognitive thesis of avowals appears prominently, in the *Investigations*, in the course of the exposition of the argument against the possibility of a private language. It might be thought that the two doctrines are so intimately related that the denial of the non-cognitive thesis cannot but damage the private language argument. I shall try to show two things. Firstly, that the two arguments are independent one of the other, so that the falsity of the doctrine of avowals does not imply the falsity of the argument against a private language. This is the weaker thesis. The stronger thesis is that the truth of the argument against private languages requires the falsity of the doctrine of avowals in the traditional interpretation.

Part of the argument Wittgenstein conducts involves a contrast between our public language and the pseudo-language presupposed by Cartesians and traditional empiricists. Wittgenstein begins the discussion at §243 by asking whether we could imagine a language in which a person could write down or give vocal expression to his inner experience for his own private use. He replies rhetorically: 'Can't we do so in our ordinary language?' But this is not what is meant by a 'private language'. That is a language in which the words refer to what can only be known to the speaker. This contrast suggests that in ordinary language I can write a record—perhaps for medical purposes—of my experiences, including my pains. Later on in the discussion at §258 this suspicion is confirmed. For the force of the diary example depends upon the contrast with a public language in which one could keep such a diary. We can record our pains, fears, thoughts, and beliefs in a diary because in a genuine language the 'inner processes' do have 'outward criteria'. It is intuitively plausible to regard such a record as consisting of true or false descriptions of one's suffering. In so far as this intuition is correct the truth-valueless interpretation of the non-cognitive thesis conflicts with this part of the private language argument. For if we deny that first person, present tense psychological sentences bear truth-values and claim that they have the logical status of facial expressions and groans, then it is unclear in what way we are, in respect of keeping a record of true descriptions of our experiences, any better off than the private linguist. The point of contrast in Wittgenstein's diary example is lost. The private linguist's attempt to register the recurrence of sensation S fails, for 'S' lacks sense, the putative assertion lacks truth-value, and there is no room for possible knowledge. But on the traditional interpretation of the thesis of avowals the public speaker's utterance (or inscription) 'I have pain' likewise lacks truth-value, and it too is not an object of possible knowledge.

So much for the stronger thesis. It is, however, important to notice that if the doctrine of avowals is dropped, the force of the argument against a private language is in no way diminished. Affirming the intelligibility of knowledge of subjective experience does not commit one to affirming the possibility of a private language. On the contrary, one may claim that a condition of the possibility of knowledge of subjective experience is the (at least tacit) acknowledgement of the criterial grounds for the ascription of experience to others. It is then open to one to draw a powerful contrast between the speaker of a public language and the private linguist. For the former can both know that he experiences S and that others experience S. And he can know the one only if he can know the other.[1] The private linguist, however, claims to know that he experiences S, but bewails the metaphysical barriers which prevent him knowing that others do. The thrust of Wittgenstein's argument thus construed is that the price of scepticism about other minds, implicit in Cartesianism and classical empiricism is inarticulateness (*PI*, §261). One can deny the possibility of knowing facts about other minds only if one acknowledges the impossibility of knowing anything about one's own. The classical attempt to establish truths about other minds on the basis of the argument from analogy can work only if one can know truths about one's own mind. But Wittgenstein's argument, even stripped of its connections with the doctrine of avowals, shows that if one can know or assert truths about one's own mind, one does not need the argument from analogy to establish and justify cognitive claims about other minds. The famous argument from analogy is useless,

---

[1] See P. F. Strawson, *Individuals*, ch. 3.

for if it is required it cannot be employed, and if it can be employed it is redundant.[1]

We have already noted[2] Wittgenstein's objections to the Cartesian doctrine of the soul. Like Kant he located the source of the Cartesian fallacies in the phenomenon of underived self-ascription of experience. One may view his doctrine of avowals as constituting part of his onslaught upon Cartesianism. The doctrine of avowals succeeds in restraining the inclination to see underived self-ascription of experience as irrefutable evidence for the reality and substantiality of the *res cogitans*. The rejection of this Cartesian theory was, as we have seen, one of Wittgenstein's earliest concerns. Secondly, the Cartesian ascription of cognitive status to avowals seems to lead to scepticism about other minds, a scepticism which is parasitic upon a paradigm of knowledge provided by self-knowledge. By denying the intelligibility of this kind of self-knowledge the natural path to this sort of scepticism is blocked. Thirdly, by denying avowals cognitive status, the way of the classical empiricist is rendered impassable, for a foundations theory of knowledge cannot be constructed if sentences about subjective experience do not bear truth-values.

It has been argued thus far that the doctrine of avowals is, in every one of its forms, unacceptable. This, however, does not resuscitate the Cartesian doctrine of the soul. The logical possibility of self-knowledge does not imply the possibility that self-knowledge involves acquaintance with or reference to a pure ego. Equally, scepticism about other minds is not revived. For, as has been seen, the conditions of the possibility of self-knowledge are dependent upon the conditions of the possibility of knowledge of other minds. But if the possibility of self-knowledge is reinstated, is the empiricist's foundations theory of knowledge not simultaneously reinstated? If it does make sense to talk of knowing that I see such-and-such, or knowing that I hear thus and so, then is it not also arguable that my knowledge of how things objectively are rests ultimately upon my knowledge of how things subjectively

---

[1] I have elaborated this point in greater detail in 'Other Minds and Professor Ayer's Concept of a Person', in *Philosophy and Phenomenological Research*, xxxii (1971–2).

[2] See above ch. VII, pp. 205 ff.

appear to me to be? Does empirical knowledge then not have foundations?

Wittgenstein's answer to this problem is to be found in a brief but illuminating discussion of colours and the subjective appearance of colours in *Zettel*. It makes no sense, Wittgenstein argues, to begin to teach someone colour concepts by teaching him when to say 'That looks red'. For that must be said *spontaneously* when he has learnt what 'red' means (Z, §418). Learning what 'red' means is learning, e.g. to call out 'red' on seeing something red, to bring a red thing on demand, to arrange objects according to colour. Only then can the distinction between being red and appearing red be taught, not because it is a subtle distinction, like that between scarlet and crimson, but because the concept of seeming thus and so is parasitic upon the concept of being thus and so. The red visual impression, Wittgenstein emphasizes, is *a new concept* (Z, §423). In 'the first language-game', i.e. in discourse of the objective, a person does not occur as perceiving subject. Introducing the concept of subjective appearance involves giving language a *new joint*. Now a person does appear as perceiving subject, and, we may note, 'I' is used as subject. In the following passage Wittgenstein makes a remark which is at odds with the more extreme versions of the doctrine of avowals, and which is much nearer the truth. The new articulation, he says, enables us 'to turn our attention on to things, and on to sensations. We learn to observe and to describe observations' (Z, §426). That the novel move is available does not of course mean that it is always made. The availability of the concept of how things subjectively seem to me does not imply that it is now the constant basis of actual inferences, or the tacit object of all descriptions. Moreover, the description of how things subjectively seem to me to be is not the description *of an object* at all (Z, §435). The description is of course akin to the description of an object, just as marrying money is akin to marrying a spouse, or transferring pride in possessions is akin to transferring possessions. Just for that reason, Wittgenstein emphasizes, it does not function as the description of an object. It is logically parasitic upon the description of an object. For the concepts of the perceptions criterionlessly self-ascribed are dependent upon the concepts of the objects of which they are taken to be perceptions.

Nor is the description of what is subjectively seen derived from an inward glance at a sensation (Z, §426). That truth at any rate is captured by the doctrine of avowals. For such a derivation would involve the possibility of error. One does not *recognize* the inner experience, for there is no room for misrecognition as opposed to misunderstanding. The assertion 'This is red' involves recognition and so the possibility of misrecognition and error. Hence the question 'How do you know?' has *some* application here. For the 'new joint' of the concept of subjective appearance provides a way of giving an answer to it other than by asserting 'I speak English', namely by a spontaneous description of the relevant perceptual observation. Learning what 'This is red' means involves learning to recognize the conditions under which one is justified in asserting 'This is red'. 'This looks red to me' describes my recognition of these conditions. But there is no recognition of the recognition of the appropriate conditions. The latter kind of assertion is groundless; it has no justification. It makes no sense to ask of it 'How do you know?' for it is derived from nothing. It is a manifestation of our mastery of the relevant perceptual concept, thus presupposing our knowledge of its criteria, and simultaneously a manifestation of our mastery of the component concepts of the objective (in this case 'red') contained within the description.

We could—and in some uses of perceptual verbs do—interpose an additional stage in the structure of justification. Perceptual verbs are sometimes used as achievement verbs such that they are truly applicable only if their object exists; i.e. 'I hear a noise' is true only if there exists a public sound. But then it makes sense to claim that the speaker is mistaken, to say that it only seemed to him that he heard a noise, and that it was the truth of the latter sentence which justified him in asserting the former which was not true. But now seeming to hear is not subject to error. It is self-ascribed without criteria. We have no use for a further stage of seeming to seem to hear.

How then does the foundations theorist fare? Not as badly as the sceptic, but not as well as he might hope. If his claim that knowledge has foundations means that it makes sense to challenge every cognitive claim to the point of a claim about how things subjectively seem to one to be, then this much may be granted. Justification comes to an end with descriptions of how things appear to one to be. If his claim that assertions about subjective experience provide the foundations for assertions about objects means that the former are conceptually linked with the latter, then this too is true. But if he goes on to claim that the sense of a sentence about an objective particular such as 'This is red' is given by sentences about subjective experience such as 'This looks red to me', then he is deeply misguided. For the argument in *Zettel* makes it quite clear that the sense of 'This is red' is logically prior to the sense of 'It looks red to me', as it is to the sense of 'It looks red to him' or 'It looks red to N.N.'. But in so far as the arguments against the non-cognitive thesis carry conviction, then it seems equally clear that 'It looks red to me' provides a non-inductive justification for 'It is red'. And here a serious problem for the criterial account of sense is presented. For it seems that the direction of epistemic dependence runs in a diametrically opposite direction to that of the logical or semantic dependence. For although one does not normally infer that an object is red from the fact that it looks red to one, but rather one asserts non-inferentially that something is red just in those cases in which it looks red, nevertheless its looking red is a justificatory ground for the assertion. It is not a contingent truth that red things normally look red. Foundations theories of knowledge, such as those of the logical positivists, or of Wittgenstein himself in 1929–31, have traditionally been reductionist. The view propounded in *Zettel* is strongly anti-reductionist. The argument against a private language leaves no other alternative.

So the point at which the spade hits bedrock is not the point to which the sense of sentences about the objective is reducible. The ramifications of this contention will be further explored in the next chapter. The foundations theorist is thus left high and dry. For while the letter of his theory may, in a sense, have been saved by rejecting the non-cognitive doctrine of avowals, especially in its traditional form, the general spirit has been quite discarded. This perhaps is not too far removed from Wittgenstein's intention.

X

THE PROBLEM OF CRITERIA

1. *Introduction*

Wittgenstein's conception of philosophy and his metaphysics of experience constitute the two main themes of this book. The development of his ideas upon these two subjects has been traced from his earliest writings through his intermediate period to his masterpiece, the *Philosophical Investigations*, and to his last notes, published as *On Certainty*. The discussion of these two themes is almost concluded. The back-cloth upon which they were displayed was the development of Wittgenstein's semantics. This, as initially announced, has only been sketched in. But one unredeemed pledge is a survey of Wittgenstein's use of the term 'criterion'[1] which plays so large a part in his later conception of meaning. This final chapter is an attempt to fulfil this task.

The term 'criterion' has been extensively used thus far. It has been suggested that the concept of a criterion is best understood in the context of Wittgenstein's attempt to produce a constructivist semantics. The determination of sense by truth conditions which dominates the realist *Tractatus* is replaced by a constructivist account of sense in terms of use or application. The notion of use or application must be understood as conditions which justify using a term or sentence, in the first instance, assertively. Criteria, then, can be seen as those conditions which non-inductively justify the assertion of a sentence and in terms of which the sense of the sentence is to be accounted for. This novel logical relation has been mentioned frequently in the account of Wittgenstein's resolution of the problem of our knowledge of other minds and of his treatment

---

[1] A detailed bibliography of writings on criteria, as well as an index to Wittgenstein's use of the term, can be found in W. Gregory Lycan, 'Non-Inductive Evidence: Recent Work on Wittgenstein's "Criteria"', *American Philosophical Quarterly*, 8 (1971), 109–25. The most comprehensive treatment of the subject from a constructivist angle is in G. P. Baker's 'The Logic of Vagueness', to which the following discussion is indebted.

of self-consciousness or self-ascription of experience. It has also
been used in the incomplete discussion of Wittgenstein's treatment
of our knowledge of objects. My intention in adopting this expository
strategy was to put the tool to work first and to survey its mechanism
later. One might hope that its performance is sufficiently impressive
to suggest that it is worth developing. To be sure it is not 'a shining
new tool to crack the crib of reality'. It needs clarification, explication, and much refinement. But to reject the notion as inadequate,
as so many of Wittgenstein's critics[1] have done, because it has not
been adequately refined and explicated, may well be to reject 'one
of the greatest and most valuable discoveries that has been made of
late years in the republic of letters'.

The following discussion is not an attempt to satisfy the need
for such refinement and explication. It is rather the much more
modest task of providing a preliminary survey of Wittgenstein's
use of the term 'criterion'. This is done with a number of purposes in
mind. Firstly, it is desirable to draw together the scattered threads
of the discussion of criteria in the preceding chapters. This will
involve a certain amount of recapitulation. Secondly, a survey of
Wittgenstein's use of 'criteria' will, I hope, be of some exegetical
value. It will provide the material from which to extract a variety
of general claims about the logical features of the criterial relation.
Furthermore it will serve to correct errors in current claims about
Wittgenstein's conception of a criterion. Thirdly, a brief summary
of Wittgenstein's philosophical application of the criterial relation
will serve both to highlight its merits, and to bring out some of the
difficulties surrounding this notion.

Before turning to the exegetical task one further warning is in
order. Like all terms, 'criterion' has a history. In particular, as a
term of art in Wittgenstein's later philosophy it undergoes considerable change and development. The term '*Kriterium*' is occasionally
used, in a non-technical sense, in the *Philosophische Bemerkungen*.
The notion is present in the *Grammatik*,[2] but it only emerges in a
developed form in the *Blue Book*. Thenceforth it is used extensively
but still undergoes important changes. The emergence of the notion

---

[1] e.g. H. Putnam, 'Dreaming and Depth Grammar', in *Analytical Philosophy*, ed.
R. J. Butler (Blackwell, Oxford, 1962) and 'Brains and Behaviour', in *Analytical Philosophy*, 2nd Series, ed. R. J. Butler (Blackwell, Oxford, 1965), or C. S. Chihara and J. A.
Fodor, 'Operationalism and Ordinary Language', in *American Philosophical Quarterly*,
2 (1965), 281–95.

[2] e.g. *PG*, §10; compare *PI*, §182.

of a criterion thus coincides with Wittgenstein's abandonment of his version of logical positivism of the early thirties. One must therefore beware of some obvious pitfalls. In the first place the concept of a symptom plays an important role in both phases of Wittgenstein's development: as part of the crucial symptom-hypothesis relation in the *Bemerkungen* and the 1930–2 lectures, and as a contrast to the criterial relation in the *Blue Book* and thenceforth. Although there are important relations between the two uses of the concept one must not assemble Wittgenstein's various remarks about symptoms on the assumption that one concept is in view. Thus his claim that 'if we say "The fact that the pavement is wet is a *symptom* that it has been raining" this statement is "a matter of grammar"' (M, pp. 266 f.) cannot be taken to apply to his later notion of a symptom. Secondly, although the *Blue Book* introduces the notion of a criterion as a term of art there are apparent inconsistencies in the *Blue Book*'s use of the term. Thus exegesis of the *Blue Book*'s account of criteria must be particularly wary, and any comparison of later uses of 'criteria' with those of the *Blue Book* must specify which section of the *Blue Book* is in question. Thirdly, one must bear in mind that there are important changes between the conception of the criterial relation and its philosophical application in the *Blue Book* and in the later writings. These must be brought to light and explained.

2. *Some Logical Features of the Criterial Relation*

Wittgenstein speaks of such-and-such a thing being a criterion for another thing. He speaks of a thing having criteria. A criterion is a relation between kinds of things. What kinds of items does it relate? What sorts of entities are criteria? In the *Blue Book* we find various kinds of item so referred to. He speaks of 'a phenomenon' as being 'the defining criterion' of a thing (*BB*, p. 25). This is repeated in the *Brown Book* (*BB*, p. 135): 'all sorts of phenomena are used as criteria for "his seeing that . . ."', and in *Zettel* 'a phenomenon [is] regarded . . . as a criterion . . .' (*Z*, §438). He also speaks of 'behaviour' as being criteria (*BB*, p. 24), a turn of phrase repeated in 'Notes for Lectures': 'what is our criterion for blindness? A certain kind of behaviour' (NFL, p. 285), and in the *Investigations* 'there are certain criteria in a man's behaviour for the fact that he does not understand a word' (*PI*, §269). Subsequently he speaks of facts as being criteria—'one must examine what sort of facts we call criteria for a pain' (*BB*, p. 49), a phrase not repeated elsewhere. On pages 51–2 of the *Blue Book* he speaks of propositions and of 'evidences' as being criteria. The latter is also implied in *Zettel*, §554. Finally, on page 61 he refers to the 'many characteristics which we use as the criteria for identity'. In later writings one finds even more diversity. The remark in *Zettel*: 'The causes of our belief in a proposition are indeed irrelevant to the question what we believe. Not so the grounds, which are grammatically related to the proposition, and tell us what proposition it is' (*Z*, §437) is particularly noteworthy.

If we turn now to look at the second term of the relation, at the kinds of entities which are said to *have criteria*, we find equal diversity. Starting from the *Blue Book* we find that he speaks of phrases as having criteria (pp. 24, 55), although in one of these cases he gives a sentence or sentential function as his example: 'so-and-so has toothache' (p. 24). He also speaks of words as having criteria, e.g. 'It may be practical to define a word by taking one phenomenon as the defining criterion' (p. 25; cf. p. 57). In subsequent works he continues to speak of words as having criteria (e.g. NFL, p. 285) and gives numerous examples. It should be stressed that in the *Investigations* he shows a marked preference for the material mode rather than the formal mode. However the range of syntactical or formal entities spoken of as having criteria is not exhausted. Expressions have criteria (*BB*, p. 57; *Z*, §438), so do concepts (*Z*, §§438–9, §571). In the *Blue Book* facts, states of affairs, and propositions are all said to have criteria (pp. 51–2). Facts are again said to have criteria in the *Investigations* (*PI*, §269). States of affairs are referred to as having criteria in *Zettel* (*Z*, §438) as are propositions (*Z*, §437, quoted above). All are exemplified in the many examples given in the *Investigations* and *Zettel* (e.g. *PI*, §182, §269, §354, p. 222, etc.; *Z*, §§472 ff.).

What then are we to make of these heterogeneous items allegedly connected by the criterial relation? The simplest way of introducing order into the medley would seem to be by treating entities specified in the material mode as criteria as derivatively so specified. Since the criterial relation is, as we shall see, a grammatical or logical relation, a matter of linguistic convention rather than natural law or extralogical necessity, it is to be thought of as holding between linguistic entities. Thus one may of course speak of states, processes, and events as having criteria, and of phenomena, kinds of behaviour, characteristics, as being criteria. But this is the equivalent, in the material mode, of speaking, in the formal mode, of words, phrases and expressions as having criteria, and of sentences (or 'propositions', bearing in mind Wittgenstein's usage here), 'evidences' or grounds as being criteria. Facts and states of affairs are of course spoken of as being and having criteria, and there is no harm in so doing as long as it is taken that facts and states of affairs are logical constructions. To claim that the fact that p is a criterion for the fact that q is tantamount to claiming that p is a criterion for q which in the formal mode may be restated in terms of a criterial relation between 'p' and 'q', i.e. a sentential relation. One important reason for taking the terms of the criterial relation to be sentences and not, e.g., propositions concerns the doctrine of avowals explored in the previous chapter. I shall thus take the criterial relation to hold between sentences, and suggest that other uses of 'criteria' can be reduced to this.

This decision must be made consistent with the recurrent talk of criteria for phrases, expressions, words and concepts. What is the relation between criteria for a sentence and criteria for a word? The problems of the doctrine of avowals and of criterionless self-ascription of experience might tempt one to argue that it is primarily words or concepts that have criteria, and that criterionless self-ascription of experience involves ascribing to oneself a predicate, which has criteria, without *using* these criteria. This however is too short a route to a solution. The criteria for a word or concept are the criteria for the assertion of a sentence in which the relevant word is appropriately employed. Thus in the *Blue Book*'s explanation of the concept of a criterion, Wittgenstein explains that the criterion for 'angina' is given by giving the criterion for saying 'This man has got angina', i.e. 'He has such-and-such bacillus in his blood' (*BB*, p. 25). In the later parts of the *Blue Book* he explains that we could give the phrase 'unconscious pain' sense by fixing experiential criteria for the case in which a man has pain and does not know it (*BB*, p. 55). In the 'Notes for Lectures' he argues that the meaning of blindness is given by specifying the criteria for blindness which are constituted by the grounds for calling someone blind (NFL, p. 285), i.e. the criteria for 'He is blind'. In *Zettel*, Wittgenstein suggests that one learns a word, i.e. its use, under certain circumstances, which one does not learn to describe. Learning the use of a word involves learning to assert or deny it of those kinds of items of which, according to the applications of our language, it may be intelligibly asserted or denied (*Z*, §117). So here again the notion of the meaning of a word cannot be prior to the notion of the meaning of an assertion in which it is applied.

The criterial relation is clearly an evidential one. In the *Blue Book* introduction of the notion, Wittgenstein says that criteria are specified by giving one kind of answer to the question 'How do you know that so-and-so is the case?', by giving a justification for saying that so-and-so is the case (*BB*, pp. 24 f.). In the later, very different, discussion of criteria in the *Blue Book* Wittgenstein continually refers to criteria as 'evidences'. He speaks of criteria for my finger touching my eye, or for 'my finger moves from my tooth to my eye'. These are 'evidence' for the 'propositions' in question which characterize 'the grammar of the proposition' (*BB*, p. 51). In *Zettel* he speaks of criteria as grounds or evidence for a sentence (*Z*, §§437–9 and §§554–6). In the *Investigations* he suggests that criteria for '*p*' are the circumstances which would justify one in saying that *p* (e.g. *PI*, §182). His numerous investigations into specific psychological and dispositional terms employ the concept of a criterion extensively in precisely this sense.

A criterion must, however, be distinguished from a sufficient, or necessary and sufficient, condition. The differences are crucially important. Wittgenstein's writings on the subject initially caused considerable confusion among commentators, for the passage in the *Blue Book* in which the concept of a criterion is first introduced suggests that a criterion logically implies that for which it is a criterion:

If medical science calls angina an inflammation caused by a particular bacillus, and we ask in a particular case 'why do you say this man has got angina?' then the answer 'I have found the bacillus so-and-so in his blood' gives us the criterion, or what we may call the defining criterion of angina . . . to say 'A man has angina if this bacillus is found in him' is a tautology or it is a loose way of stating the definition of "angina" (*BB*, p. 25).

This notorious passage, although it introduces the concept of a criterion as a technical term, and is indeed the only passage in Wittgenstein's writings in which the term is explicitly examined, is misleading. It clearly suggests that a criterion is a sufficient condition or even a necessary and sufficient condition. It is quickly noted that this concept of a defining, decisive criterion is at odds with the notion of a criterion at work in the *Investigations*. However it is equally obvious that Wittgenstein's extensive employment of 'criterion' in the second half of the *Blue Book* no more coincides with this first explanation than does his usage in his later works. For his treatment of the problem of the relation between judgements about subjective experience, e.g. 'I see my hand move', 'I feel my finger touch my eye', etc., and judgements about material objects, e.g. 'My hand moves', 'My finger touches my eye', makes it quite clear that although the truth of the former kind of sentences is criterial evidence for the truth of the latter, it is perfectly possible for the former to be true yet the latter to be false. Thus he writes:

Now if I say 'I see my hand move', this at first sight seems to presuppose that I agree with the proposition 'my hand moves'. But if I regard the proposition 'I see my hand move' as one of the evidences for the proposition 'my hand moves', the truth of the latter is, of course, not presupposed in the truth of the former. One might therefore suggest the expression 'It looks as though my hand were moving' instead of 'I see my hand moving'. But this expression, although it indicates that my hand may appear to be moving without really moving, might still suggest that after all there must be a hand in order that it should appear to be moving, whereas we could easily imagine cases in which the proposition describing the visual evidence is true and at the same time other evidences make us say that I have no hand (*BB*, p. 51–2).

This clearly implies that though 'p' may be a criterion for 'q', 'p' may be true and 'q' may be false. This implies that the criterial relation is distinct from entailment. It is also inconsistent with the previously cited passage (*BB*, p. 25). It does however conform in this respect with Wittgenstein's later usage. In his discussion of the criteria for 'to see something' in the 'Notes for Lectures', p. 286, Wittgenstein stresses that although we would have no use for this expression if its application were severed from its behavioural criteria, it is perfectly possible for someone to see red and not show it, i.e. for 'He sees red' to be true but for the criteria for it not to be satisfied. This possibility of concealment is an essential feature of our concepts of 'inner states'. Conversely it is equally essential that the criteria for 'p' may be satisfied yet 'p' be false. What a person says is a criterion for what image he has (*PI*, §377), but he may be lying; pain behaviour is a criterion of pain, but one may be pretending (*PI*, §244, §§249–50); certain sensations of wet and cold, such-and-such visual impressions are criteria that it is raining, but sense impressions can deceive us (*PI*, §354). The criterial relation, barring Wittgenstein's introductory passage in the *Blue Book*, is conceived as distinct from and weaker than entailment and, *a fortiori*, than mutual entailment.

To the classical logician this of course would suggest that the criterial relation is merely some kind of inductive evidence. Wittgenstein laboured to rule this out by his frequent and emphatic distinction between criteria and symptoms. In the *Blue Book*'s introduction of the concept of a criterion, Wittgenstein presents it by contrasting it with the concept of a symptom. To the question 'How do you know that so-and-so is the case?' one can answer by specifying criteria or symptoms. To justify one's cognitive claim by reference to symptoms is to adduce inductive evidence which has been discovered in experience to correlate well with so-and-so's being the case. 'I call "symptom" a phenomenon of which experience has taught us that it coincided, in some way or other, with the phenomenon which is our defining criterion' (*BB*, p. 25). Although the concept of a criterion as elaborated in this section is later modified, the contrast with 'symptom' thus understood remains. There is, as we shall see, a fluctuation between criteria and symptoms, especially marked in the area of scientific concepts. This fluctuation makes it appear as if there were nothing but symptoms, i.e. inductive correlations taught by experience, e.g., falling barometric pressure and rain. The appearance however is deceptive (*PI*, §354; see *BB*, p. 113). The distinction and its importance is again stressed in *Zettel* (*Z*, §438, §466).

Symptoms are discovered in experience, but criteria are fixed by convention. In the first discussion of 'criterion' in the *Blue Book*, Wittgenstein contrasts the two. One justifies one's citation of a symptom in support of one's assertion by reference to the established empirical correlations. But when called upon to justify the citation of a criterion we 'find that here we strike rock bottom, that is we have come down to conventions' (*BB*, p. 24). In the later discussion of 'criteria' in the *Blue Book* the point is made again: if we wished we could 'give the phrase "unconscious pain" sense by fixing experiential criteria' (*BB*, p. 55). Similarly, in criticism of the solipsist who objects to the way 'pain' is commonly used, Wittgenstein remarks that 'he is not aware that he is objecting to a convention' (*BB*, p. 57). The point recurs in the later writings. In the *Investigations* he speaks of 'fixing criteria of identity' (*PI*, §322), of an evidential (criterial) relation between appearance and reality being 'founded on a definition' (*PI*, §354). In *Zettel* he talks of 'setting it up as a criterion of so-and-so that . . .' (*Z*, §245), and of its being usual in science 'to make phenomena that allow of exact measurement into the defining criteria for an expression' (*Z*, §438). Finally, in *On Certainty* he speaks of 'what I make count as determinants for [a] proposition' (*OC*, §5).

The symptoms for the truth of '*p*' are not part of the sense of the sentence. Its conventionally fixed criteria are. The sense of a sentence or expression is given by specifying the rules for its use. These are given by specifying the criteria which justify applying or asserting the sentence or expression. If '*q*' is a criterion for '*p*' then it is part of the sense of '*p*' that '*q*' is *a priori*, non-inductive, conventionally fixed evidence for the truth of '*p*'. The evidence for these contentions can be readily deployed. The general equation of meaning with use is a commonplace of the *Investigations*.[1] Equally obvious is the explanation of use in terms of rules, highlighted by the continual employment of the analogy between language in general and games, and between words and chess pieces.[2] To specify the rules for the use of a sentence is to specify the criteria justifying the application or assertion of the sentence in question. That the criteria for the truth of a sentence are part of its 'grammar'—that the meaning of a word is determined by the criteria for its application—is a thread, originating in the *Blue Book*, which runs through all Wittgenstein's later writing. Thus he wrote:

The grammar of propositions . . . about physical objects admits of a variety of evidences for every such proposition. It characterizes the grammar of the proposition "my finger moves, etc." that I regard the propositions "I see it move", "I feel it move", "He sees it move", "He tells me that it moves" etc. as evidences for it (*BB*, p. 51).

Of course it is not claimed that if '*p*' is a criterion of '*q*' then '*p*' is equivalent to '*q*', nor is it claimed that '*p*' entails '*q*', nor that '*q*' entails '*p*' as one of an indefinite series of disjunctive 'symptoms' for the hypothesis that *q*. Rather it is claimed that the sense of '*q*' is partially specified by the fact that the truth of '*p*' is non-inductive evidence justifying the application of '*q*'. Some pages later in the

---

[1] e.g. *PI*, §§30, 41, 43, 120, 138, 197, 421, 532, 556, 559; pp. 175-6.
[2] e.g. *PI*, §§53-4, 83-8, 108, 125, 196 ff, 492, 559 ff.

Blue Book Wittgenstein, while discussing 'pain' speaks of 'the criteria ... which give our words their common meanings' (*BB*, p. 57). The criteria for 'pain' are given by specifying what would justify one in saying 'He is in pain'. If a person manifests pain behaviour in appropriate circumstances one is justified in asserting that he is in pain. But of course 'pain' does not mean 'pain behaviour'. Rather it is part of the sense of 'He is in pain' that the truth of 'He screamed when he touched the red-hot poker' is non-inductive evidence for it (*PI*, §244). The explanation of the sense of an expression or sentence by reference to the criteria for its use is a theme which reappears in the 'Notes for Lectures' in a passage which we have previously dwelt upon:

Now whom shall we call blind? What is our criterion for blindness? A certain kind of behaviour. And if the person behaves in that particular way, we not only call him blind but teach him to call himself blind. And in *this* sense his behaviour also determines the meaning of blindness for *him* (NFL, p. 285).

In the *Investigations* Wittgenstein explains the grammar of certain words, the 'game' with them—'their employment in the linguistic intercourse', by examining their criteria (*PI*, §182). Criteria, he claims, justify us in using a word (*PI*, §§288-9). The same thread of argument runs through *Zettel*. The important passage in which Wittgenstein asserts that the grounds for a sentence are grammatically related to it (*Z*, §437) has already been cited, as has the passage in which use is equated with circumstances justifying assertion (*Z*, §§114-20). Learning language involves learning to recognize (but not necessarily to describe) the circumstances justifying the use of an expression. Thereby one acquires a tacit intuitive knowledge of the criterial rules justifying the employment of the expression. Thus one test for whether 'p' is a criterion for 'q' is whether one could come to understand 'q' without grasping that the truth of 'p' justifies one in asserting 'q'.

A corollary of the contention that the sense of an expression is given by specification of its criteria is of course that an expression without criteria lacks sense. It is unnecessary to elaborate this point at length for it constitutes the crux of the argument against the possibility of a private language which has already been examined in detail. The point is made concisely a number of times. In 'Notes for Lectures' Wittgenstein's antagonist claims that since one can conceal one's toothache, it follows that 'the word "toothache" has a meaning entirely independent of a behaviour connected with toothache'. Wittgenstein's reply is dogmatic: 'The game we play with the word "toothache" entirely depends upon there being a behaviour which we call the expression of toothache' (NFL, p. 290). The dogmatism receives its scintillating defence in the argument against the possibility of a private language. A similar point is made in *Zettel*. A concept which lacked criteria in behaviour would be unusable (*Z*, §571), for criteria define an expression (*BB*, p. 104, *Z*, §438).

To sum up the results thus far: the criterial relation holds between sentences and derivatively between other entities. It is a fundamental semantic relation unrecognized by classical logic. It is weaker than entailment but stronger than inductive evidence. It is a relation of *a priori*, non-inductive, or necessarily good evidence.[1] It replaces the notion of truth conditions which occupied so funda- mental a position in the realist account of sense. It thereby brings about a major reorientation of epistemology and the metaphysics of experience, some aspects of which have been explored.

3. *Further Ramifications*

Further clarification of Wittgenstein's conception of a criterion can be achieved by examining some of its complex ramifications in his work. This provides greater insight into the novelty and structure of the relation, although admittedly it brings in its wake as many problems as it solves. The first point to examine grows out of a distinction already discussed. It has been noted that the concept of a criterion is introduced in the *Blue Book* to stand in contrast with that of a symptom. Wittgenstein immediately adds (*BB*, p. 25) that in practice one may find it difficult if not impossible to distin- guish a symptom from a criterion except by an arbitrary *ad hoc* decision. Moreover one may easily be persuaded to change one's definition of a term, e.g. 'angina'. We may decide to take what was hitherto considered a symptom to be the defining criterion. These remarks, it should be noted, occur in the context of Wittgenstein's first conception of a criterion, which is subsequently modified. They apply, in this context, to a criterion for a scientific concept. However

[1] The first correct explanation of Wittgenstein's conception of a criterion along these lines was suggested by S. Shoemaker in *Self-Knowledge and Self-Identity* (Cornell University Press, New York, 1963).

the general theme of a criteria/symptoms fluctuation recurs in Wittgenstein's later work, and he often stresses that this fluctuation is particularly obvious in our employment of scientific terms (*PI*, §79). In *Zettel*, §438 he remarks that 'Nothing is commoner than for the meaning of an expression to oscillate, for a phenomenon to be regarded sometimes as a symptom, sometimes as a criterion, of a state of affairs.' A consequence of this claim is that terms which are susceptible to such fluctuation have no fixed sense, or, alternatively, that they are continually undergoing a shift of sense. Wittgenstein, in the passage in question, suggests that what is involved in the criteria/symptoms fluctuation characteristic of science is a continual shift of sense. In science it is common to make phenomena that allow of precise measurement into the defining criteria of an expression. A term that was previously determined by qualitative criteria is often changed when quantitatively measurable correlations are discovered. This shift of meaning is usually not noticed. If it is, one is inclined to interpret the change as involving the *discovery* of the *proper* meaning of the expression. This is, of course, an illusion. Perhaps a measurable quantity has been discovered, e.g. temperature; maybe a new technique of measurement has been invented, e.g. thermometric readings, but meanings are not found. Such advances in science often lead to conceptual changes, explications, introductions of wholly novel concepts. The measurable phenomenon replaces the non-measurable one as a criterion for the application of the relevant term, and the non-measurable phenomenon may become a symptom. The term in question consequently changes its sense.

A further point to emerge from Wittgenstein's discussion of the criteria/symptoms fluctuation is therefore the contention that a change of criteria is a change of sense. This is quite clear in the above passage from *Zettel*. Both the addition of a novel criterion for '*p*' and the elimination of a hitherto accepted criterion for '*p*' constitute a change in the sense of '*p*'.[1] The point is confirmed by reference to other remarks in Wittgenstein's writings. Any change of rules for the use of a term constitutes a change of meaning (*PI*, p. 147 n.). When a concept presents serious philosophical puzzles, as does the concept of the dawning of an aspect, this cannot be resolved by introducing a new, e.g. physiological, criterion for

---

[1] For a different view see A. J. P. Kenny, 'Criterion', in *The Encyclopedia of Philosophy*, ed. P. Edwards, vol. 2.260.

seeing. For this changes the concept in question, screening the old problem from view rather than solving it (*PI*, p. 212).

One should, however, stress that in practice the criteria/symptoms fluctuation characteristic of science, the difficulty, or impossibility, with regard to many scientific terms, of establishing what is symptom and what is criterion, the continual change in the sense of many scientific terms under the pressure of scientific discoveries, may matter very little. For given that the range of phenomena associated with the truth of '*p*' does not change, i.e. the general correlations of evidence '*a*' . . . '*f*' hold, it may matter little whether '*d*', which refers to a phenomenon that has been found to be accurately measurable by some novel instrument, be included in the list of criteria '*a*' . . . '*c*' for '*p*', or whether it be treated as good inductive evidence, or whether it be left wholly indeterminate whether '*d*' is criterial or inductive evidence for the truth of '*p*'. One may say that one uses a particular scientific term without a fixed meaning, but the term is no worse for that (just as a table that stands on four legs instead of three and hence sometimes wobbles is no worse for it). Should one say that one is then using a word without knowing its meaning? 'Say what you choose', Wittgenstein replies, 'so long as it does not prevent you from seeing the facts' (*PI*, §79).

The criteria/symptoms indeterminacy is one of the many grounds of Wittgenstein's continual anti-Fregean and anti-*Tractatus* insistence upon the *natural* indeterminacy of sense of language. There are however many other routes to this conclusion. One learns the use of a word under certain circumstances. An ability to describe such circumstances is not itself a criterion of knowing what the word means. 'I cannot enumerate the conditions under which the word "to think" is to be used', Wittgenstein writes, '—but if a circumstance makes the use doubtful, I can say so, and also say *how* the situation is deviant from the usual ones' (*Z*, §118). The criterial grounds are themselves indeterminate in the sense that there may be many thinkable cases which neither clearly justify the application of the term in question nor clearly justify withholding its application. The criterial rules embodied in the linguistic practice of a human community are tailored for normal conditions. Wittgenstein draws an analogy with law here. A law, he stresses, is given for human beings, and a legal official may apply it successfully to ordinary cases. So the law has its use, it makes sense. But it presupposes a wide range of unthought normality conditions. If these break down, if the being to whom the law is to be applied is quite deviant from ordinary human beings, then, e.g., the decision whether he acted with evil intent will be not just difficult but quite impossible (*Z*, §350). The law was not given with such cases in view (*Z*, §120), but that does not mean that it is senseless. So too with criterial rules determining sense. An inexact concept is a concept for all its inexactness. A vague border line delimits an area as much as a precise one (*PI*, §§71, 88). To be sure we can make concepts more precise, refine them for certain technical purposes (just as judicial legislation is involved in meeting 'hard cases'). But there is no single ideal of exactness or precision. These standards are relative, and the imprecision of a concept may render it defective for one purpose while in no way impairing it for others. There is in general no *complete* list of criteria. 'We must be on guard', Wittgenstein warns, 'against thinking that there is some totality of conditions corresponding to the nature of each case (e.g. for a person's walking) so that, as it were, he *could not but* walk if they were all fulfilled' (*PI*, §183). For not only is the range of criteria indeterminate, but criteria for '*p*' are dependent upon an indeterminate range of circumstances and are essentially defeasible. The behavioural criteria, for, e.g., the occurrence of a given mental state, are criteria only in certain circumstances. One and the same type of behaviour may, in one circumstance, be e.g. a criterion for the application of one psychological predicate and, in a different circumstance, be a criterion for the application of a totally unrelated psychological term. The point is made explicitly in *Zettel*:

Pain-behaviour and the behaviour of sorrow—these can only be described along with their external occasions. (If a child's mother leaves it alone it may cry because it is sad; if it falls down, from pain.) Behaviour and kind of occasion belong together (*Z*, §492).

But though some kinds of circumstance dependence can be satisfactorily enumerated (e.g. 'He cried after falling down' is a criterion for his being in pain), one must still heed the warning that there is no final totality of conditions corresponding to his being in pain. Crying after falling down on stage as part of the play is not a criterion of being in pain but of acting the role of an injured man. But of course crying after falling down on stage as part of the play and limping off stage calling for a doctor to tend one's wounded leg is again a criterion for being in pain. And so on indefinitely. This highlights the fact that a criterion does not entail that for which it is a ground. A criterion is not decisive evidence, it can always be rebutted by citing additional evidence which will defeat the criterial support, though in the absence of defeating evidence the criterial evidence justifies a cognitive claim. It is defeasible, but being defeasible does not imply being defeated. Grounds for rebuttal must be available, for a grounded belief is innocent until proved guilty.

Wittgenstein repeatedly emphasizes the importance of normality conditions for understanding the nature of our form of representation. The circumstances under which the use of a word is learnt are the normal, standard, circumstances for its application. Certain kinds of question are not (normally) raised. '"Do fishes think?"' Wittgenstein says, 'does not exist among our applications of language' (*Z*, §117). What could be more natural, he continues, than such a state of affairs? One does not teach the meanings of words by beginning with border line cases to which they questionably apply. One begins with paradigmatic, undisputed cases, and teaches border line cases by reference to their deviance from the norm. Equally one would not teach the meanings of words in contexts of fundamental aberrations and abnormalities 'just as in writing we learn a particular basic form of letters and then vary it later, so we learn first the stability of things as the norm, which is then subject to alterations' (*OC*, §473). In Wittgenstein's repeated insistence upon this point, in his emphasis upon the importance of unnoticed, because utterly pervasive, general facts of nature, one can find a thin analogue of Kant's elaborate argument to establish the necessity of universal causal law as a general and fundamental condition of the possibility of conceptualized experience. For our concepts of objects to have any grip, for them to have a use, three pervasive kinds of interwoven regularities are necessary. Nature must display a high degree of regularity, our perceptual experiences must display a high degree of rule-governed connectedness, and human responses must manifest a broad agreement. 'It is only in normal circumstances that the use of a word is clearly prescribed' (*PI*, §142), Wittgenstein stresses. These normal circumstances involve regularities of succession and regularities of coexistence. Psychological terms such as 'pain', 'fear', 'joy' depend for their use upon regular, characteristic behaviour of animate creatures in standard circumstances. Our notions of an object and of measurable magnitudes, of weights, and spatial dimensions have application only in a world pervaded by causal law. The point of the game, Wittgenstein remarks apropos weighing, depends upon what usually happens (NFL, p. 287). Measuring would entirely lose its ordinary character if the world were so irregular that twelve one-inch lengths put end to end did not ordinarily yield a twelve-inch length. Our concepts of measurement and their *a priori* links are *grounded* in the physical and psychological facts that make techniques of measurement possible (*RFM*, p. 159). Equally, our sense experiences cohere in a regular way. When it looks as if it is raining it normally feels wet, when something appears spherical it normally feels round, when something looks as if it is at a distance it normally takes some paces to reach it. Upon such regular coincidences our concepts of objects and our correlative concepts of our subjective experiences of objects are built (cf. *BB*, p. 51). Such facts are not *justifications* of our conceptual structures, they do not make our concepts uniquely correct. Language is autonomous. But radical changes in the normal flow of events would render large segments of our form of representation useless. The necessary agreement in response to external stimuli has already been extensively discussed. Colour predicates, *pace* idealists, both dogmatic and representational, are neither subjective nor relational. But they are essentially anthropocentric, and the existence of a colour language depends upon agreement in response to paradigms. 'The game depends upon the agreement of these reactions;' Wittgenstein writes, 'i.e. they must *call* the same things "red"' (NFL, p. 287). Such agreement, because it enters into the determination of whether a person understands a given colour predicate, is 'part of the framework on which the working of our language is based' (*PI*, §240). The 'language-game' only works when agreement in response to coloured objects prevails, although to be sure agreement does not enter into the game, it is not part of the concept of a particular colour (*Z*, §430). 'Red' does not mean 'what most people call "red"'. It is rather that if most people did not call the same things 'red', this particular segment of language, the colour vocabulary, would lose its use.

It is easy to imagine and elaborate the kinds of radical breakdowns of normality conditions which would 'throw us out in all our judgments' (*Z*, §393). If every time I looked from the window of my room quite different surroundings were to be seen, if Magritte's quietly nightmarish paintings were records of common experience, if animals spoke while men barked and mewed, one would be inclined to think that one had lost one's sanity, and this would express one's inability to judge. The more abnormal things become, the more doubtful it becomes what we are to say. 'If rule became exception and exception rule; or if both became phenomena of roughly equal frequency—this would make our normal language-games lose their point' (*PI*, §142). Weighing things would be pointless in a world in which lumps of matter on a scale suddenly shrink or grow for no obvious reason (ibid.) or where, though they retained their size and shape, they weighed different weights at different times for no detectable reason (NFL, p. 287 n.). We employ colour predicates under certain normality conditions. Objects by and large retain their colour for a length of time, most people's colour judgements coincide. If this were not so, if objects continually changed colour, if people disagreed in their colour judgements in wholly irregular fashion, then one could not, Wittgenstein submits, retain 'one's meaning' of 'red', 'blue', etc. Of course we are under the illusion that once the word is 'fastened to a particular personal experience' it will retain its (subjective) meaning come what may. But saying '"seeing red" means a particular experience' is useless unless one can back it up by saying 'namely this', while pointing to a public object. A mental sample cannot do service for a real one (NFL, pp. 287 ff.).

The important thing to note about such fantasies or 'artificial natural histories' is that there is no sharp border line between such radical breakdowns and the normal conditions in which we use language. Up to a point, no doubt, apparent irregularities are swept under the carpet. If a body changes weight, we look for the cause of the change. Even if we cannot account for it, we do not say that weighing has lost its point. The pervasiveness of causal law still guides our search, for our concepts of objects are grounded therein. Our concept of weight is such that change of weight requires some further correlated change. However given an excessive degree of unruliness, then our concept of weight becomes useless. We would give up the 'game of weighing' (NFL, p. 287). There is thus a gentle gradation from exceptions disregarded on trust, to hesitation over the applicability or non-applicability of an expression, to the relinquishing of a term as pointless. This lack of a sharp border line does not betoken an inadequacy in our concepts. If what looked like a chair suddenly disappeared as we approached it, reappeared a minute later enabling us to sit down, disappeared when we got up, etc., we should not know what to say.[1] But it is no defect in a term to be unequipped with provisions to cope with circumstances which never arise. The absence of a ruling on whether to assert or deny that the object in question was a chair does not mean that 'chair' lacks sense. Terms whose sense is determined by multiple criteria are used as they are, and have the point they have, because these various criteria normally coincide. But one can readily imagine divergence between the various criteria. We have already examined Wittgenstein's discussion of the different 'geometries' which might be heirs to our concept of a person if the multiple criteria of personal identity were to cease to coincide in all normal cases.[2] But our current use of 'same person' is not defective as a result of not providing a ruling on what to say if memory, appearance, idiosyncratic behavioural characteristics, character etc., fell apart.

At first sight, examination of such imaginary examples of breakdowns of normality conditions appears to invite one to invoke the Law of the Excluded Middle. Do fishes think? We intuitively respond—either they do or they do not, there is no other alternative; how we establish it is irrelevant. We may not be able to measure a given rod, or weigh a given lump of cheese, but it either has such-and-such length or weight or it does not. 'One is inclined to say', Wittgenstein remarks, '"Either it is raining, or it isn't—how I know, how the information has reached me, is another matter"' (*PI*, §356). So we are inclined, and it is from these inclinations that Wittgenstein endeavours to emancipate us. The Law of the Excluded Middle provides us with a *picture*, Wittgenstein repeatedly stresses (*PI*, §352; *RFM*, p. 139). The picture or model appears superficially attractive and perspicuous. In the expansion of π either four consecutive sevens appear or they do not. God sees even if we do not. We use the picture of a visible series disappearing into the distance. We cannot see what it is like beyond the range of our vision, but, we think, it can be seen. Another person either has such-and-such an experience or he does not (*PI*, §352). We may not know, but surely *he* must. It seems as though this picture provides a solution.

---

[1] *PI*, §80; compare with J. L. Austin's famous bullfinch example in 'Other Minds', *Philosophical Papers*, ed. J. O. Urmson and G. J. Warnock (Clarendon Press, Oxford, 1961), pp. 51 ff.

[2] See above ch. VII, pp. 207 f.

But it lacks an application (cf. NFL, p. 285 n.). The negation of a criterion for '*p*' is not a criterion for the negation of '*p*', and the perceptual model of introspection is fallacious. The concepts of infinite decimals in mathematical sentences are not concepts of series but of the limitless technique of expanding series (*RFM*, p. 144). It is both surprising and unfortunate that Wittgenstein gave so little explicit attention in his general philosophical writings of the later period (as opposed to his notes on the philosophy of mathematics) to the ramifications which the adoption of a criterial semantics has in respect of the abandonment of the realist adherence to the Law of the Excluded Middle. Given that there are multiple criteria for the application of an expression, that criteria rather than truth conditions determine sense, that the criterial relation is that of necessarily good evidence and so weaker than entailment, that the list of criteria and of their defeasibility conditions is indeterminate, the Law of the Excluded Middle must, it seems, be relinquished.

Wittgenstein's introduction of the concept of a criterion with the angina example did, of course, suggest that there is one definitive and decisive criterion for the application of 'So-and-so has angina'. But on the same page he talks of different criteria for a person's having toothache, an example which recurs in later sections of the book (*BB*, pp. 49–53). Similarly in his investigations into the relation of sense experience and knowledge of objects the diversity and multiplicity of criteria is stressed (*BB*, p. 51). In the discussion of personal identity (*BB*, p. 61), Wittgenstein emphasizes that 'many characteristics are used as criteria for "the same person"'. The *Brown Book* is unequivocal in its emphasis on this point (e.g. pp. 104, 135, 144), as is the *Investigations* (e.g. *PI*, §§141, 164, 182, 404, etc.) and *Zettel* (§§438, 472 ff.). It remains unclear, however, whether all expressions have multiple criteria. In a rule-governed orderly world the various criteria for expressions which have multiple criteria normally coincide. We use our expressions as we do as a result of this (*BB*, pp. 52, 61, 63). Of course the various criteria we accept as justifying the application of a term are not always co-instantiated. Nor need they be to justify the use of the expression for which they are criteria. Screaming in appropriate circumstances is a criterion of pain, but grimacing, clenching one's teeth, etc. are equally satisfactory. The satisfaction of the latter criteria in the absence of the former is not a case of conflicting criteria. Surprisingly, Wittgenstein has no sustained discussion of conflicts of criteria. In the *Blue Book* he suggests that some kinds of conflicts occur, and are settleable. Its looking thus and so may conflict with its feeling otherwise (*BB*, p. 52), and the latter evidence may make us withdraw our judgement about the objective. In the *Investigations* he points out that although memory of things being thus and so is a criterion, it is not necessarily 'the highest court of appeal' (*PI*, §56). It seems then that while acute conflicts leave us indecisive and may threaten to render our concepts useless, certain kinds of conflict are budgeted for by the rules of evidence and defeasibility conditions implicit in our linguistic practice. Clearly this is an area which requires further investigation.

The contrast between Wittgenstein's criterial semantics and the realist semantics of the *Tractatus* runs deep.[1] The main lines of disagreement can be sketched out on the basis of the preceding investigations. Where the realist explains sense in terms of truth conditions, Wittgenstein now suggests that sense be explained in terms of criteria. Where the realist adheres to determinacy of sense as a *sine qua non* of concepts, Wittgenstein repudiates this as an illusion. Consequently the realist's adoption of the Law of the Excluded Middle as a fundamental 'law of thought' is dismissed as a misleading (because not always applicable) picture or model. So, too, Frege's Platonism in mathematics is replaced by Wittgenstein's radical constructivism, and the search for foundations for mathematics is dismissed on the grounds of the autonomy of mathematics. Where the realist explains what is involved in knowing or understanding the sense of a sentence in terms of knowing what has to be the case for it to be true, Wittgenstein explains our possession of concepts in terms of our ability to apply expressions, our knowledge of the criteria which non-inductively justify asserting them. While for the realist the truth or falsity of a sentence is wholly independent of our cognition or the possibility of our cognition, Wittgenstein now claims that while truth or falsity 'belong' to our concept of a sentence they do not 'fit' it (*PI*, §136). Since sense is determined by the conditions of possible cognition, truth and falsity cannot be conceived of as independent of our capacity for knowledge.

From the point of view of the epistemological and metaphysical topics which have been the primary subject of investigation in this

---

[1] See M. Dummett, 'The Reality of the Past', for a contrast between realism and anti-realism. Surprisingly Dummett makes nothing of the concept of a criterion.

study, the most significant contrasts emerge from the substitution of criterial links to replace the inductive/deductive dichotomy with which classical epistemology had to work. This, together with the Principle of Natural Epistemic Justice, constitutes the source of Wittgenstein's main contribution to the theory of knowledge and metaphysics of experience.

4. *Applications: a recapitulation*

The central concern of the *Tractatus* had been to establish the bounds of sense. Epistemology is relegated, as it were, to applied philosophy. Certainly important epistemological doctrines emerge from the results of the central endeavour, for Wittgenstein concludes that there can be no ethical, aesthetic, or religious knowledge. But in general he is satisfied to establish the limits of intelligibility, thereby setting an outer limit to possible knowledge, and not to investigate the general question of whether the limits of knowledge are narrower than the bounds of sense, or coextensive with them. In his later philosophy Wittgenstein is still concerned to establish the bounds of sense, to teach philosophy and metaphysics not to overreach themselves in their inordinate ambition. But now the establishing of the limits of knowledge is no longer an incidental by-product of the investigation. On the contrary, according to the criterial semantics the limits of possible knowledge determine the bounds of sense. For the sense of an expression is determined by the conditions which justify asserting it and which legitimate a cognitive claim. A criterion, which determines meaning, gives one kind of answer to the question 'How do you know?' Thus epistemology is brought back into the heart of philosophical logic, without however making any undue concessions to psychological logicians.

The most striking general reorientation which Wittgenstein's criterial semantics brings about in epistemology is the establishment of the Principle of Natural Epistemic Justice. For the sceptic, the traditional *bête noire* of post-Cartesian philosophy, a belief is guilty until proved innocent. For Wittgenstein, as we have seen, a criterially-grounded belief is innocent unless proved guilty. The burden of proof is shifted to the sceptical challenger. Wittgenstein makes the point concisely in *On Certainty*:

The idealist's question would be something like: 'What right have I not to doubt the existence of my hands?' (And to that the answer can't be:

I *know* that they exist.) But someone who asks such a question is over-looking the fact that a doubt about existence only works in a language-game. Hence, that we should first have to ask: What would such a doubt be like? and don't understand this straight off (*OC*, §24).

Doubting, as the sceptic refuses to recognize, is a parasitic activity. The justification for Wittgenstein's reorientation of epistemology lies in the principle that doubt presupposes the possibility of certainty. The grounds for this principle are to be found in the fact that doubting is directed at the truth of a sentence, and this requires, if the doubt is to be intelligible, that what is doubted have sense. This in turn requires an account of sense. As long as epistemology took a realist conception of meaning for granted, as long as it was supposed that an adequate account of the sense of a sentence is given by its truth conditions, the sceptic could not be dislodged. For, on a realist view, sense is independent of the conditions of possible cognition. But once the criterial conception of sense replaces the truth-conditional one the sceptic is forced to give ground. For the sceptic can only make the notion of doubting whether '*p*' is true intelligible by rendering an account of the sense of '*p*'. And such an account can no longer be offered in terms of the truth conditions of '*p*' but must be given by specifying the criteria which would justify the assertion of '*p*' and which, in the absence of specific grounds for doubting, would justify one in asserting '*p*' with certainty.

Wittgenstein puts the novel tool of analysis to work in different areas, although the amount of attention given to each varies greatly. The lion's share is given to his account of the logical nature of psychological concepts. The investigation of the concepts of ability, capacity, potentiality, etc. is likewise carried through in some detail with the help of the notion of a criterial link. Here Wittgenstein's attention is concentrated upon mental abilities and capacities, but his inquiry extends to physical abilities too and to the powers of inanimate objects. A third area of great philosophical interest which he touches upon relatively extensively in the *Blue Book*, but only very rarely in later writings, is the relationship between sense data and objects, or, differently phrased, between subjective experience and objective particulars. Finally, as suggested by the recurrent reference to concepts in the natural sciences to exemplify the criteria/symptoms fluctuation, it seems that he thought that the notion of a criterion might be fruitfully applied in this area too. Wittgenstein, however, does not appear to have attempted this.

Although Wittgenstein's investigations of powers and abilities are of considerable importance, constituting the first major onslaught upon this difficult subject since Locke, they fall outside the main concern of this study, and will not be explored at all. Nor shall I attempt to survey his extensive treatment of psychological concepts in general. Rather I shall recapitulate his application of the concept of a criterion in the domain of the metaphysics of experience in order to exemplify in part his investigations into psychological concepts, and attempt to raise some general difficulties which a proper explication of the criterial relation must answer.

Negatively, the new semantic account enables Wittgenstein to refute behaviourism on the one hand, and idealism, phenomenalism, and solipsism on the other. The behaviourist is right to realize that psychological concepts are not logically independent of behavioural concepts. He is wrong to think that psychological concepts are, in some way or other, *reducible* to behavioural ones. The term 'toothache' would have no sense if it were wholly severed from behavioural criteria. We acquired the concept by learning, *inter alia*, what behaviour is called 'expression of toothache'. But of course one did not learn that 'toothache' means 'expression of toothache' (NFL, p. 293). The idealist, phenomenalist and solipsist are right to emphasize the immediacy of self-ascription of experience. I neither avow that I have a given experience, nor justify my avowal, on the grounds that I am behaving in a given way. But nor do I avow or justify my avowal on the basis of criteria of inner sense conceived along the perceptual model of introspection. If the argument against the possibility of a private language is correct, the idealist's account of immediate self-ascription of experience cannot be right. By the same token the idealist reduction of the material to the mental must be misguided.

Put to constructive use, the notion of a criterial nexus enables Wittgenstein to provide his account of the conditions of the possibility of self-ascription of experience, an account which, if the arguments of the previous chapter are at all correct, is not wholly satisfactory. It plays the major role in his solution to the problem of knowledge of other minds. Finally, it fulfils a somewhat uncertain role in Wittgenstein's fragmentary answer to the problem of our knowledge of objects and the relation between sentences about perceptual experience and sentences about objective particulars.

No doubt there are very many problems and difficulties which a proper logic of criteria must solve and overcome. In those areas of philosophy with which we have been concerned, and in which Wittgenstein applied his new conception of meaning to some of the classical problems of the metaphysics of experience, a more limited range of difficulties appear. It is worthwhile elaborating them briefly as a specification of part of the debt any adherent to Wittgenstein's criterial semantics and any supporter of his suggestions in the metaphysics of experience necessarily incurs and must, sooner or later, discharge.

The main problems which have been encountered in our previous explorations of Wittgenstein's contribution to the metaphysics of experience emerge in the course of the attempt to unravel the interwoven strands of the problems of self-consciousness, knowledge of other minds and knowledge of objects. Self-ascription of experience is criterionless. Yet it is far from obvious, especially if the doctrine of avowals should indeed be rejected, that first person, present tense psychological sentences lack sense. So an account must be given of the sense of such sentences. But it is clear that these are not the only kind of sentence asserted without grounds. For it seems that Wittgenstein thought that use of determinates of perceptual determinables involves no criteria but rather the criterionless exercise of a recognitional *cum* linguistic capacity. One cannot justify one's assertion 'This is red' by reference to criterial evidence. One can only reply 'I speak English' and proceed to show, not how one knows that this item is red, but that one knows what 'red' means; and this is done by pointing to a sample. Pointing to a sample to show this is not a criterion for an object's being red, but for a person understanding the meaning of 'red'. One might be inclined to argue that since criteria are, roughly speaking, the circumstances in which we learn to apply an expression, then the criterion for an object's being red is its looking red. For we learn to call an object 'red' when it looks red in normal conditions. But although 'looking red' is non-contingently related to 'being red', it appears that Wittgenstein will account for the sense of 'it looks red to him' in terms of criteria for visual experience in conjunction with being confronted by a red object in normal conditions.

One of the most striking divergences between the discussion of criteria in the *Blue Book* and subsequent discussions hinges on precisely this point. In the *Blue Book* Wittgenstein argues explicitly that it is part of the grammar of sentences about physical objects that they admit of a multiplicity of criterial evidence. It seems that he still thought that the sense of a physical object sentence could be given by specification of sense data sentences[1] the truth of which justifies its assertion. The general contention was that my assertions about my subjective experience are criteria for the truth of corresponding physical object sentences. This line of argument virtually disappears in the subsequent works, and the subject is never tackled head on. The only significant explicitly relevant remark upon the subject in the *Investigations* occurs at §354:

The fluctuation in grammar between criteria and symptoms makes it look as if there were nothing at all but symptoms. We say, for example: 'Experience teaches that there is rain when the barometer falls, but it also teaches that there is rain when we have certain sensations of wet and cold, or such-and-such visual impressions.' In defence of this one says that these sense-impressions can deceive us. But here one fails to reflect that the fact that the false appearance is precisely one of rain is founded on a definition.

It appears here that Wittgenstein is adopting much the same stance on the problem of the evidential relation of sense data sentences to physical object sentences as in the *Blue Book*. It is clear that he is denying that we have a symptom relation, and equally clear that the sentence about the sense impression may be true while the sentence about the objective is false. This does suggest a criterial relation. But perhaps the story is more complicated. We should be warned by an enigmatic remark in the unfinished second part of the *Investigations*:

It is like the relation: physical object—sense-impressions. Here we have two different language games and a complicated relation between them.— If you try to reduce their relations to a *simple* formula you go wrong (*PI*, p. 180).

If we bear in mind the passage in *Zettel* previously examined,[2] it is clear that the remark 'here one fails to reflect that the fact that the false appearance is precisely one of rain is founded on a definition' is consistent with denying that 'it visually appears to me to be raining' is a *criterion* of 'it is raining'. For one may well argue, as Wittgenstein does in *Zettel*, that the sense of the latter sentence is

---

[1] It is surprising that he mentions 'He sees it move', 'He tells me that it moves', as criteria for 'My finger moves' as well as 'I see it move', 'I feel it move' (*BB*, p. 51).
[2] See above ch. IX, pp. 280 ff.

logically prior to that of the former, that a sense impression can be identified as one of rain only in so far as the concept of rain is already available, and that the criteria for 'It seems to him to be raining' include 'It is raining' rather than vice versa. The problem posed, therefore, is the one already encountered. Is it consistent with the new semantic theory to argue that 'It looks to me as if thus and so' is *a priori* evidence for 'Things are thus and so', as Wittgenstein here appears to suggest, without arguing, but rather denying, that it is part of the *sense* of the latter sentence that the assertion of the former is evidence for it?

This line of argument seems to approximate much more closely to Wittgenstein's later thought than the initial interpretation. It is also consonant with his continual insistence that knowledge has no foundations, that grounds come to an end in action not in intuition. For if the sense of sentences about sense data or subjective perceptual experience is given by specification of criteria which include behaviour manifesting recognition of the appropriate perceptual object, thus including specification of the given perceptual object, then justification in one sense comes to an end in action—in our linguistic behaviour. For although to be sure we learn to call 'red' just those things that look red to us, the game rests on our behaviour, on our calling such things 'red', on calling 'red' what everyone else calls 'red', not on intuitive knowledge such as 'It looks red to me'. For the latter sentence presupposes that 'red' has a sense, and cannot therefore be, via the criterial nexus, part of the sense of 'It is red'. Thus although justification may in a sense regress as far as the assertion of sentences about subjective appearances, we do not find here a firm pillar upon which the superstructure of both knowledge and language may securely rest. We find the illusion of such a foundation, which upon closer examination reveals, as it were, a dangling loop, supporting nothing, but hanging from the bedrock of human linguistic behaviour.

Giving grounds, however, justifying the evidence, comes to an end;— but the end is not certain propositions striking us immediately as true, i.e. it is not a kind of *seeing* on our part; it is our *acting* which lies at the bottom of the language-game (*OC*, §204).

Sentences describing subjective appearances provide no foundations, for their sense is parasitic upon the sense of sentences about the objective. Though an avowal of a perceptual experience may terminate a chain of justification, its sense does not contribute to the *sense* of that which it supports. On the contrary, it has what sense it has because the sentence about the objective has an established sense. The use of language in application to the objective is primary, and logically prior to its use in specifying experiences of the objective, whether those of oneself or of others. Common recognitional abilities, innate imitative propensities, shared primitive responses and training in established conventions underpin our 'language-games'. These are taught and learnt in their application to the objective. The 'new joints' are added later.

We do not learn the practice of making empirical judgments by learning rules: we are taught *judgments* and their connection with other judgments. A *totality* of judgments is made plausible to us.

When we first begin to *believe* anything, what we believe is not a single proposition, it is a whole system of propositions. (Light dawns gradually over the whole) (*OC*, §§140–1).

If Wittgenstein's suggestions, interpreted along the lines suggested in this book, appear plausible, then the further development of a criterial theory of meaning is imperative. For the solutions which Wittgenstein offers to the central problems in the metaphysics of experience can only stand firm if they are supported by a comprehensive and systematic account of a criterial semantics which he delineated unsystematically and obscurely. The task of the logical theorist is to provide a general and consistent account of the complex relationships between the three kinds of sentences which have been tentatively discussed here.

BIBLIOGRAPHY

1. Wittgenstein's works cited in the text (given in order of composition).

'Notes on Logic, September 1913', repr. in *Notebooks 1914–16*, pp. 93–106.

'Notes Dictated to G. E. Moore in Norway, April 1914', repr. in *Notebooks 1914–16*, pp. 107–18.

Notebooks 1914–16, ed. G. H. von Wright and G. E. M. Anscombe, trans. by G. E. M. Anscombe (Blackwell, Oxford, 1961).

ProtoTractatus—An Early Version of Tractatus Logico-Philosophicus, ed. B. F. McGuinness, T. Nyberg and G. H. von Wright, trans. by D. F. Pears and B. F. McGuinness (Routledge and Kegan Paul, London, 1971).

Tractatus Logico-Philosophicus, trans. by D. F. Pears and B. F. McGuinness (Routledge and Kegan Paul, London, 1961).

'Some Remarks on Logical Form', *Proceedings of the Aristotelian Society*, supp. vol. ix (1929), 162–71.

'A Lecture on Ethics', *The Philosophical Review*, lxxiv (1965), 3–12.

Ludwig Wittgenstein und der Weiner Kreis, shorthand notes recorded by F. Waismann, ed. B. F. McGuinness (Blackwell, Oxford, 1967).

Philosophische Bemerkungen, ed. R. Rhees (Blackwell, Oxford, 1964).

'Wittgenstein's Lectures in 1930–33', repr. in G. E. Moore, *Philosophical Papers*, pp. 252–324 (Allen and Unwin, London, 1959).

Philosophische Grammatik, ed. R. Rhees (Blackwell, Oxford, 1969).

'Letter to the Editor', *Mind*, xlii (1933), 415–16.

The Blue and Brown Books (Blackwell, Oxford, 1958).

'Notes for Lectures on "Private Experience" and "Sense Data"', ed. R. Rhees, *The Philosophical Review*, lxxvii (1968), 275–320.

Remarks on the Foundations of Mathematics, ed. G. H. von Wright, R. Rhees and G. E. M. Anscombe, trans. by G. E. M. Anscombe (Blackwell, Oxford, 1964).

Philosophical Investigations, ed. G. E. M. Anscombe and R. Rhees, trans. by G. E. M. Anscombe (Blackwell, Oxford, 1953).

Zettel, ed. G. E. M. Anscombe and G. H. von Wright, trans. by G. E. M. Anscombe (Blackwell, Oxford, 1967).

On Certainty, ed. G. E. M. Anscombe and G. H. von Wright, trans. by D. Paul and G. E. M. Anscombe (Blackwell, Oxford, 1969).

2. A comprehensive bibliography of writings on Wittgenstein can be found in K. T. Fann, *Wittgenstein's Conception of Philosophy*, pp. 113–78 (Blackwell, Oxford, 1969). A further supplement by K. T. Fann is in *Wittgenstein et le problème d'une philosophie de la science*, pp. 217–24 (Paris, 1970). The following bibliography contains only items cited in my text.

ALLAIRE, E. B. 'The "Tractatus": Nominalistic or Realistic?', repr. in *Essays on Wittgenstein's Tractatus*, ed. I. M. Copi and R. W. Beard, pp. 325–41 (Routledge and Kegan Paul, London, 1966).

—— '"Tractatus" 6.3751', repr. in *Essays on Wittgenstein's Tractatus*, ed. I. M. Copi and R. W. Beard, pp. 189–93 (Routledge and Kegan Paul, London, 1966).

AMBROSE, A. 'Wittgenstein on Universals', repr. in *Ludwig Wittgenstein: The Man and his Philosophy*, ed. K. T. Fann, pp. 336–52 (Dell, New York, 1967).

ANSCOMBE, G. E. M. *An Introduction to Wittgenstein's Tractatus*, 2nd ed. (Hutchinson, London, 1963).

AUSTIN, J. L. 'Other Minds', in *Philosophical Papers*, ed. J. O. Urmson and G. J. Warnock, pp. 44–84 (Clarendon Press, Oxford, 1961).

AYER, A. J. 'Can There be a Private Language?', *Proceedings of the Aristotelian Society*, supp. vol. xxviii (1954), 63–76.

—— 'The Concept of a Person', in *The Concept of a Person and Other Essays*, pp. 82–128 (Macmillan, London, 1963).

BAKER, G. P. 'The Logic of Vagueness', unpublished D.Phil. thesis (Oxford University, 1970).

BENTHAM 'Essays on Logic', *The Works of J. Bentham*, ed. J. Bowring, vol. viii (Tait, Edinburgh, 1843).

BLACK, M. *A Companion to Wittgenstein's Tractatus* (C.U.P., Cambridge, 1964).

BOLTZMANN, L. 'Theories as Representations', from *Die Grundprinzipien und Grundgleichungen der Mechanik I*, trans. by R. Weingartner, repr. in *Philosophy of Science*, ed. A. Danto and S. Morgenbesser, pp. 245–52 (World Publishing Co., Ohio, 1960).

BRAITHWAITE, R. B. 'Solipsism and the "Common Sense View of the World"', *Analysis*, i (1933–4), 13–15.

—— 'Philosophy', in *University Studies, Cambridge 1933*, ed. H. Wright, pp. 1–32 (Ivor Nicholson and Watson, London, 1933).

BRITTON, K. 'Portrait of a Philosopher', repr. in *Ludwig Wittgenstein: The Man and his Philosophy*, ed. K. T. Fann, pp. 56–63 (Dell, New York, 1967).

BROUWER, L. E. J. 'Mathematik, Wissenschaft und Sprache', *Monatshefte für Mathematik und Physik*, xxxvi (1929), 153–64.

CARNAP, R. 'Intellectual Autobiography', in *The Philosophy of Rudolf Carnap*, ed. P. Schilpp (Open Court, Illinois, 1963).
—— *The Logical Syntax of Language*, trans. A. Smeaton (Routledge and Kegan Paul, London, 1937).
—— *The Logical Structure of the World*, trans. by R. A. George (Routledge and Kegan Paul, London, 1967).
CASTAÑEDA, H. N. 'On the Logic of Self Knowledge', *Noûs*, i (1967), 9–21.
CHIHARA, C. S. and FODOR, J. A. 'Operationalism and Ordinary Language: A Critique of Wittgenstein', *American Philosophical Quarterly*, 2 (1965), 281–95.
CHISHOLM, R. *Theory of Knowledge* (Prentice Hall, New Jersey, 1966).
COLLINGWOOD, R. G. *An Essay in Metaphysics* (Clarendon Press, Oxford, 1940).
COPI, I. M. 'Objects, Properties and Relations in the "Tractatus"', repr. in *Essays on Wittgenstein's Tractatus*, ed. I. M. Copi and R. W. Beard, pp. 167–86 (Routledge and Kegan Paul, London, 1966).
CORNFORTH, M. 'Is Solipsism Compatible with Common Sense', *Analysis*, i (1933–4), 21–6.
DESCARTES *Philosophical Works of Descartes*, trans. by E. S. Haldane and G. R. T. Ross, Dover edn. (2 vols., Dover publications, Constable, London, 1955).
DUMMETT, M. 'Frege, Gottlob', article in *The Encyclopedia of Philosophy*, ed. P. Edwards, vol. 3.225–37 (Macmillan, New York, 1967).
—— 'Nominalism', *The Philosophical Review*, lxv (1956), 491–505.
—— 'The Philosophical Significance of Gödel's Theorem', *Ratio*, 5 (1963), 140–55.
—— 'The Reality of the Past', *Proceedings of the Aristotelian Society*, lxix (1968–9), 239–58.
—— 'Truth', *Proceedings of the Aristotelian Society*, lix (1958–9), 141–62.
——'Wittgenstein's Philosophy of Mathematics', *The Philosophical Review*, lxviii (1959), 324–48.
ENGELMANN, P. *Letters from Ludwig Wittgenstein with a Memoir*, ed. B. F. McGuinness, trans. by L. Furtmüller (Blackwell, Oxford, 1967).
FANN, K. T. *Wittgenstein's Conception of Philosophy* (Blackwell, Oxford, 1969).
FLEW, A. G. N. *Hume's Philosophy of Belief* (Routledge and Kegan Paul, London, 1961).
FODOR, J. A. See Chihara, C. S. and Fodor, J. A.
FREGE, G. *Begriffsschrift, eine der Arithmetischen nachgebildete Formelsprache des reinen Denkens*, (Halle AS, 1879, Louis Nebert).

FREGE, G. *The Basic Laws of Arithmetic : Exposition of the System*, trans. and ed., with an Introduction by Montgomery Furth (Univ. of California Press, Berkeley, 1964).

—— *The Foundations of Arithmetic*, trans. by J. L. Austin, 2nd ed. (Blackwell, Oxford, 1953).

—— *Translations from the Philosophical Writings of Gottlob Frege*, ed. P. Geach and M. Black, 2nd ed. (Blackwell, Oxford, 1960).

—— 'The Thought: A Logical Inquiry', trans. by A. M. and Marcelle Quinton, repr. in *Philosophical Logic*, ed. P. F. Strawson, pp. 17–38 (O.U.P., Oxford, 1967).

GARDINER, P. *Schopenhauer* (Penguin, Harmondsworth, 1963).

GASKING, D. A. T. and JACKSON, A. C. 'Wittgenstein as Teacher', repr. in *Ludwig Wittgenstein: The Man and his Philosophy*, ed. K. T. Fann, pp. 49–55 (Dell, New York, 1967).

GEACH, P. T. 'Frege', in *Three Philosophers*, by G. E. M. Anscombe and P. T. Geach (Blackwell, Oxford, 1961).

—— *Mental Acts* (Routledge and Kegan Paul, London, 1957).

GOMBRICH, E. *Art and Illusion*, 2nd ed. (Phaidon, London, 1962).

GRIFFIN, J. *Wittgenstein's Logical Atomism* (O.U.P., Oxford, 1964).

HACKER, P. M. S. 'Wittgenstein's Doctrines of the Soul in the Tractatus', *Kantstudien*, 62 (1971), 162–71.

—— 'Other Minds and Professor Ayer's Concept of a Person', *Philosophy and Phenomenological Research*, xxxii (1971–2).

—— 'Frege and the Private Language Argument', *Idealistic Studies*, ii (1972).

HAHN, H. 'Logic, Mathematics and Knowledge of Nature', trans. A. Pap, repr. in *Logical Positivism*, ed. A. J. Ayer, pp. 147–61 (Allen and Unwin, London, 1959).

HEMPEL, C. G. 'Some Remarks on "Facts" and Propositions', *Analysis*, ii (1934–5), 93–6.

HERTZ, H. *Electric Waves*, trans. by D. E. Jones (Macmillan, London, 1893).

—— *The Principles of Mechanics*, trans. by D. E. Jones and J. T. Walley (Macmillan, London, 1899).

HESSE, M. B. *Forces and Fields* (Nelson, London, 1961).

HINTIKKA, J. 'Wittgenstein on Private Language: Some Sources of Misunderstanding', *Mind*, lxxviii (1969), 423–5.

HOLLIS, M. 'Reason and Ritual', *Philosophy*, xliii (1968), 231–47.

HUME *A Treatise of Human Nature*, Everyman's Library (Dent and Sons, London, 1911).

ISHIGURO, H. 'Use and Reference of Names', in *Studies in the Philosophy of Wittgenstein*, ed. P. Winch, pp. 20–50 (Routledge and Kegan Paul, London, 1969).

JACKSON, A. C. See Gasking, D. A. T. and Jackson, A. C.

JOHNSON, W. E. *Logic*, 3 vols, (C.U.P., Cambridge, 1921).

KANT *Critique of Pure Reason*, trans. N. Kemp Smith (Macmillan, London, 1933).

—— *Critique of Practical Reason*, trans. T. K. Abbott in *Kant's Critique of Practical Reason and Other Works*, 6th ed. (Longmans, London, 1909).

—— *Prolegomena to Any Future Metaphysics*, trans. P. G. Lucas (Manchester Univ. Press, Manchester, 1953).

KENNY, A. J. P. *Action, Emotion, and the Will* (Routledge and Kegan Paul, London, 1963).

—— 'Cartesian Privacy', in *Wittgenstein, The Philosophical Investigations, A Collection of Critical Essays*, ed. G. Pitcher, pp. 352–70 (Doubleday, New York, 1966).

—— 'Criterion', in *The Encyclopedia of Philosophy*, ed. P. Edwards, vol. 2.258–61 (Macmillan, New York, 1967).

—— *Descartes, A Study of His Philosophy* (Random House, New York, 1968).

—— 'The Verification Principle and the Private Language Argument', in *The Private Language Argument*, ed. O. R. Jones, pp. 204–28 (Macmillan, London, 1971).

KNEALE, M. and KNEALE, W. *The Development of Logic* (Clarendon Press, Oxford, 1962).

KÖRNER, S. *Categorial Frameworks* (Blackwell, Oxford, 1970).

—— *Kant* (Penguin, Harmondsworth, 1955).

—— *What is Philosophy* (Allen Lane, London, 1969).

KRETZMAN, N. 'The Main Thesis of Locke's Semantic Theory', *The Philosophical Review*, lxxvii (1968), 175–96.

KUHN, T. S. 'Logic of Discovery or Psychology of Research?', in *Criticism and the Growth of Knowledge*, ed. I. Lakatos and A. Musgrave, pp. 1–23 (C.U.P., Cambridge, 1970).

—— 'Reflections on my Critics', in *Criticism and the Growth of Knowledge*, ed. I. Lakatos and A. Musgrave, pp. 231–78 (C.U.P., Cambridge, 1970).

—— *The Structure of Scientific Revolutions*, 2nd ed., International Encyclopedia of Unified Science, vol. ii.2, (University of Chicago Press, Chicago, 1970).

LEWIS, C. I. 'Experience and Meaning', repr. in *Readings in Philosophical Analysis*, ed. H. Feigl and W. Sellars, pp. 128–145 (Appleton-Century-Crofts, New York, 1949).

LEWY, C. 'A Note on the Text of the *Tractatus*', *Mind*, lxxvi (1967), 416–23.

LOCKE *An Essay Concerning Human Understanding*, ed. A. C. Fraser (1894; republ. Dover, New York, 1959).

LYCAN, W. G. 'Non-Inductive Evidence: Recent Work on Wittgenstein's "Criteria"', *American Philosophical Quarterly*, 8 (1971), 109–25.

LYONS, J. *Introduction to Theoretical Linguistics* (C.U.P., Cambridge, 1968).

McGUINNESS, B. F. '*Philosophy of Science in the Tractatus*' in *Wittgenstein et le problème d'une philosophie de la science*, pp. 9–18, Colloques Internationaux du Centre National de la Recherche Scientifique (Paris, 1970).

—— 'The Mysticism of the Tractatus', *The Philosophical Review*, lxxv (1966), 305–28.

MALCOLM, N. '*Wittgenstein's Philosophical Investigations*', repr. in *Wittgenstein, The Philosophical Investigations, A Collection of Critical Essays*, ed. G. Pitcher, pp. 65–103 (Doubleday, New York, 1966).

—— 'Wittgenstein on the Nature of Mind', *American Philosophical Quarterly Monograph*, No. 4: *Studies in the Theory of Knowledge* (1970), pp. 9–29.

MANSER, A. 'Pain and Private Language', in *The Philosophy of Wittgenstein*, ed. P. Winch, pp. 166–83 (Routledge and Kegan Paul, London, 1969).

MASLOW, A. *A Study in Wittgenstein's Tractatus* (Univ. of California Press, Berkeley, 1961).

MOORE, G. E. 'A Defense of Common Sense', repr. in *Philosophical Papers*, pp. 32–59 (Allen and Unwin, London, 1959).

—— 'The Nature of Judgment', *Mind*, viii (1899), 176–93.

—— 'Proof of an External World', repr. in *Philosophical Papers*, pp. 127–50 (Allen and Unwin, London, 1959).

PASSMORE, J. *A Hundred Years of Philosophy*, 2nd ed. (Penguin, Harmondsworth, 1968).

PEARS, D. F. *Bertrand Russell and the British Tradition in Philosophy* (Fontana, London and Glasgow, 1967).

PITCHER, G. *The Philosophy of Wittgenstein* (Prentice Hall, New Jersey, 1964).

PRIOR, A. N. 'Egocentric Logic', *Noûs*, ii (1968), 191–207.

PUTNAM, H. 'Brains and Behaviour', in *Analytical Philosophy*, 2nd series, ed. R. J. Butler, pp. 1–19 (Blackwell, Oxford, 1965).

—— 'Dreaming and "Depth Grammar"', in *Analytical Philosophy*, ed. R. J. Butler, pp. 211–35 (Blackwell, Oxford, 1962).

QUINE, W. O. 'Two Dogmas of Empiricism', repr. in *From a Logical Point of View*, pp. 20–46 (Harper and Row, New York, 1963).

RAMSEY, F. P. *The Foundations of Mathematics and other Logical Essays* (Routledge and Kegan Paul, London, 1931).

RAZ, J. *The Concept of a Legal System* (O.U.P., Oxford, 1970).

RHEES, R. 'Can There be a Private Language?', *Proceedings of the Aristotelian Society*, supp. vol. xxviii (1954), 77–94.

—— *Discussions of Wittgenstein* (Routledge and Kegan Paul, London, 1970).

RUSSELL 'On Propositions: what they are and how they mean', repr. in

Logic and Knowledge Essays, 1901–1950, ed. R. C. Marsh, pp. 285–302 (Allen and Unwin, London, 1956).

RUSSELL 'On Scientific Method in Philosophy', repr. in *Mysticism and Logic*, pp. 95–119 (Penguin, Harmondsworth, 1953).

—— 'On the Nature of Truth and Falsehood', repr. in *Philosophical Essays*, pp. 170–85 (Longmans, London, 1910).

—— *Our Knowledge of the External World as a Field for Scientific Method in Philosophy* (Open Court, Chicago, 1914).

—— *The Autobiography of Bertrand Russell* (3 vols., Allen and Unwin, London, 1967–9).

—— 'The Philosophy of Logical Atomism', repr. in *Logic and Knowledge, Essays 1901–1950*, ed. R. C. Marsh, pp. 175–281 (Allen and Unwin, London, 1956).

—— *The Principles of Mathematics*, 2nd ed. (Allen and Unwin, London, 1937).

—— 'Vagueness', *Australasian Journal of Philosophy*, i (1923), 84–92.

SCHLICK, M. 'Facts and Propositions', *Analysis*, ii (1934–5), 65–70.

—— 'Meaning and Verification', repr. in *Readings in Philosophical Analysis*, ed. H. Feigl and W. Sellars, pp. 146–70 (Appleton-Century-Crofts, New York, 1949).

SCHOPENHAUER *The World as Will and Representation*, trans. by E. F. J. Payne (2 vols., Dover, New York, 1966).

SHOEMAKER, S. *Self-Knowledge and Self-Identity* (Cornell Univ., New York, 1963).

—— 'Self-Reference and Self-Awareness', *The Journal of Philosophy*, lxv (1968), 555–67.

SPECHT, E. K. *The Foundations of Wittgenstein's Late Philosophy*, trans. by D. E. Walford (Manchester Univ. Press, Manchester, 1969).

STEBBING, L. S. 'Concerning Solipsism: Reply to R. B. Braithwaite', *Analysis*, i (1933–4), 26–8.

—— 'Logical Positivism and Analysis', *Proceedings of the British Academy*, xix (1933), 53–88.

STENIUS, E. *Wittgenstein's Tractatus, A Critical Exposition of Its Main Lines of Thought* (Blackwell, Oxford, 1960).

STERN, J. P. *Lichtenberg, A Doctrine of Scattered Occasions* (Thames and Hudson, London, 1963).

STRAWSON, P. F. *Individuals, An Essay in Descriptive Metaphysics* (Methuen, London, 1959).

—— 'Meaning and Truth', *Inaugural Lecture* (Clarendon Press, Oxford, 1970).

—— 'Review of Wittgenstein's *Philosophical Investigations*', repr. in *Wittgenstein, the Philosophical Investigations, A Collection of Critical Essays*, ed. G. Pitcher, pp. 22–64 (Doubleday, New York, 1966).

STRAWSON, P. F. *The Bounds of Sense, An Essay on Kant's Critique of Pure Reason* (Methuen, London, 1966).

THOMSON, J. J. 'Private Languages', *American Philosophical Quarterly*, 1 (1964), 20–31.

TOULMIN, S. E. 'From Logical Analysis to Conceptual History', in *The Legacy of Logical Positivism*, ed. P. Achinstein and S. F. Barker, pp. 25–53 (Johns Hopkins, Baltimore, 1969).

—— 'Ludwig Wittgenstein', *Encounter*, January 1969, pp. 58–71.

URMSON, J. O. *Philosophical Analysis, Its Development between the Two World Wars* (Clarendon Press, Oxford, 1956).

WAISMANN, F. *The Principles of Linguistic Philosophy*, ed. R. Harré (Macmillan, London, 1965).

—— 'Verifiability', in *Logic and Language*, 1st series, ed. A. G. N. Flew, pp. 117–44 (Blackwell, Oxford, 1951).

WIGGINS, D. 'Freedom, Knowledge, Belief and Causality', in *Knowledge and Necessity, Royal Institute of Philosophy Lectures*, vol. 3 (1968–9), ed. G. N. A. Vesey, pp. 132–54 (Macmillan, London, 1970).

WISDOM, J. O. 'Solipsism', *Analysis*, i (1933–4), 17–21.

VON WRIGHT, G. H. 'A Biographical Sketch', repr. in N. Malcolm, *Ludwig Wittgenstein, A Memoir*, pp. 1–22 (O.U.P., London, 1966).

—— *Norm and Action* (Routledge and Kegan Paul, London, 1963).

—— *The Varieties of Goodness* (Routledge and Kegan Paul, London, 1963).

ZEMACH, E. 'Wittgenstein's Philosophy of the Mystical', repr. in *Essays on Wittgenstein's Tractatus*, ed. I. M. Copi and R. W. Beard, pp. 359–75 (Routledge and Kegan Paul, London, 1966).

INDEX

Ability, 133, 241, 304
Aesthetics, 25, 73ff.
Augustine, 235
Avowals, 110, 207, 245, 251ff., 306

Bacon, F., 34
Baker, G. P., 104, 141n., 283n.
Bedeutung, see Meaning of Simple Signs
Behaviourism, 239, 305
Belief, 37, 60ff., 120
Bentham, J., 131
Berkeley, G., 138, 139, 163-4, 218
Black, M., 28-9, 49n., 56n., 64, 146n.
Boltzmann, L., 2, 4-5
Brouwer, L., 98, 99ff., 125, 136, 139, 147, 149

Carnap, R., 29n., 99, 102n., 186n., 187-8
Certainty, 150, 231, 243ff., 264-5, 304
Colour, 20-1, 90, 93, 96, 126-7, 153ff., 160ff., 168-9, 181, 183-4, 221n., 229, 234, 235, 280ff., 298-9, 306
    exclusion problem, 86ff., 153ff., 181
Common Structure, theory of, *see* Picture Theory of Meaning
Concepts, 15, 21, 34-5, 101, 119-20, 127, 129, 134, 135, 148-9, 160, 163, 168ff., 176-7, 215, 216, 219ff., 225, 230-1, 234ff., 238-9, 287, 296ff.
    formal, 19, 21ff., 29, 83, 90-1, 93
Constructivism, 102ff., 109, 148-9, 197, 272, 302
Criteria, 55, 105, 111, 152-3, 154, 160-1, 162, 207, 211-12, 243, 244, 253, 263, 271-2, 283ff., 300ff.

Darwin, C., 11
Death, 71ff.
Descartes, R., 34, 42n., 64, 66n., 136-7, 138, 205n., 217, 218, 267n.
Doubt, 244-5, 249, 260, 264, 274-5, 304
Dummett, M., 14n., 33n., 104, 272n., 302n.

Eliot, T. S., 214

Elucidations, 48ff., 95, 157ff.
Engelmann, P., 48n.
Epistemic Privacy, 54, 222, 231-2, 242, 245-6, 249, 276
Epistemology, 33-4, 36ff., 44, 45, 52, 55ff., 58, 162, 231ff., 242ff., 251, 302ff.
Essence, 19, 23-4, 26, 27, 39, 40, 128, 138, 140, 154, 179, 181, 200
Ethics, 25, 66, 73, 82ff.
Excluded Middle, Law of, 44, 101, 102, 103, 132, 143, 182, 300-1, 302

Family-Resemblance, 125, 134
Fann, K. T., 28n.
Feigl, H., 99, 187
Ficker, L. von, 82, 83
Form of Representation, 70, 98, 102-3, 114, 116, 118, 121-2, 124-5, 127, 137-8, 146, 147ff., 160, 164, 166, 167ff., 199-200, 209, 297-8
Foundations of Knowledge, *see* Knowledge, Foundations of,
Foundations of Language, *see* Language, Foundations of,
Frege, G., 1, 5, 6, 10, 11, 14, 15, 19, 25, 34ff., 42, 44, 98, 102, 112, 126, 134, 136, 139, 152, 174-5, 179, 200, 216, 217

Galileo, G., 11, 113
Geach, P., 252
God, 25-6, 68, 180, 204
Grammar, 4, 10, 11ff., 36, 93, 114-5, 127, 128ff., 150ff., 191, 199ff., 209, 210, 244, 245, 249, 291-2

Hahn, H., 109
Hempel, C., 53
Hertz, H., 2ff., 8, 9, 12, 14, 15, 48n., 139, 145
Hume, D., 37, 59-60, 189, 204n., 210, 218
Hypotheses, 107-8, 110, 189, 193-4

'I', 189, 203ff., 210–11, 261ff., 268ff., 273

Idealism, 2, 35, 126–7, 197–8, 200, 201, 203, 216, 305

Identity, criterion of, 56, 127, 197, 246ff.

James, W., 125, 127

Johnson, W. E., 4, 49

Judgement, 37, 38, 60ff., 135, 169, 220–1

Kant, I., 25–6, 30ff., 64, 65, 72, 76, 85, 125, 128, 134, 135n., 139, 140, 167, 177, 181, 183n., 184, 203, 204, 205ff., 215, 216, 238–9, 250, 251, 270–1, 279, 297

Kenny, A. J. P., 205n., 260–1, 265, 272–3, 294n.

Kneale, W., 94n.

Knowledge, 52ff., 56–7, 231–2, 242ff., 264–5, 274–5
 foundations of, 253, 254, 279ff., 308
 limits of, 25–6, 204, 246, 249–50, 251, 303

Körner, S., 172n.

Kuhn, T. S., 98n., 147, 171

Language, 5–6, 11ff., 17, 25–6, 40, 44, 47, 55, 76–7, 98, 100ff., 105–6, 114–15, 122ff., 129ff., 145, 151, 156, 166, 175ff., 178, 195–6, 217, 219ff., 225ff., 234ff., 309
 Foundations of, 42, 96, 124, 156ff., 253, 308–9
 Game, 94, 148, 167–8
 Ideal, 5–6, 13ff., 23ff., 44, 97–8, 122–3, 127
 Limits of, 25–6, 79–80, 82, 85, 176, 184

Leibniz, G., 14n., 216

Lichtenberg, G., 17, 189

Locke, J., 34, 163, 216ff., 224ff., 233, 237, 239–40, 242, 305

Logical Analysis, 5–6, 16, 26–7, 40, 80–1, 87ff., 117, 120, 123

Logical Positivism, 49, 54, 105–6, 108–9, 187–8, 217, 282

Lukasiewicz, J., 180

Mach, E., 2, 4, 187

Malcolm, N., 140n., 252

Manser, A., 222n.

Mathematics, 1, 100ff., 108–9, 115, 118, 148–9, 153

McGuinness, B. F., 76n., 146n.

Meaning (sense), 14ff., 39ff., 87, 95ff., 105ff., 111, 120–1, 130–1, 152–3, 161–2, 173, 183–4, 188–9, 211–12, 215ff., 224ff., 234ff., 241, 244, 263, 271–2, 283ff.
 of simple signs (*Bedeutung*), 21, 40ff., 45ff., 56, 77, 95–6, 107, 182ff.
 picture theory of (*see* Picture Theory of Meaning)
 realist theories of (*see* Realist Theories of Meaning)

Meinong, A., 6, 123

Memory, 225ff., 236–7

Metaphysics, 10, 30–1, 126, 130, 134, 177, 179ff., 199ff., 249
 of *TLP*, 15, 20ff., 41ff., 90–1, 182ff.

Mill, J. S., 34

Moore, G. E., 42, 60, 74n., 120, 150

Mystical, 2, 73ff., 76n., 78

Names in *TLP*, 21, 40ff., 45–6, 48ff., 56, 95, 107, 156ff., 183–4

Naming, 45, 49ff., 199, 226, 229, 237–8

Necessity, 44–5, 83, 89ff., 94–5, 156, 174ff., 178ff.

Nonsense, 17ff., 28ff., 154–5

No-ownership theory, 191–2, 194, 211

Objects in *TLP*, 20–1, 23ff., 41ff., 45ff., 51, 54, 61–2, 78, 90, 95ff., 157ff., 182ff.

Ostention, 16, 45–6, 49ff., 95–6, 135, 152, 156ff., 212ff., 226, 234–5

Other Minds, problem of, 54, 132–3, 186, 190ff., 204, 215, 231ff., 242ff., 278–9

Ownership of experience, 63, 79–80, 187, 189ff., 194, 199, 209ff., 222–3, 231, 232–3, 246ff.

Pain, 168, 189–90, 192ff., 195, 196–7, 198–9, 209–10, 223, 238–9, 241–2, 246ff., 257, 266, 292

Person, 61–2, 203ff., 246–7, 269, 300

Personal Identity, *see* Person

Philosophy, 8ff., 17ff., 25ff., 30ff., 93, 112ff., 145, 147, 184, 185
 contrasted with sciences, 8ff., 117ff., 140–1
 descriptive status of, 8ff., 117ff., 121, 136
 therapeutic nature of, 30, 116, 137ff., 145

Pictures, 131ff., 138, 300

Picture Theory of Meaning, 3–4, 14–15, 16, 17–8, 23, 39ff., 45, 48, 52ff., 92–3, 95–6, 107, 146–7

Plato, 84n., 138, 139, 179
Poincaré, H., 2, 109
Prior, A. N., 268n.
Private Language, 127, 152, 162, 166, 186, 196, 201, 211, 215ff., 253, 277–8
Private Knowledge of Experience, *see* Epistemic Privacy
Private Ownership of Experience, *see* Ownership of Experience
Properties, formal (internal), 19ff., 24, 179–80
Propositions (atomic, elementary), 7, 10, 26, 39ff., 52ff., 78, 87ff., 94ff., 157, 159, 189
Psychologism in Logic, 6, 11, 34–5, 174–5, 303
Psychology (Philosophy's independence of), 35–6, 37n., 38, 47–8, 55–6, 60, 62, 118, 120, 125

Quine, W. V., 149

Ramsey, F. P., 13n., 17n., 29–30, 43n., 79n., 99
Realism (epistemological), 58, 80–1, 197–8, 216
Realism (in semantics), 6, 42ff., 103, 293, 301–2, 304
res cogitans, 59, 64, 189, 205
Rules, 93, 105–6, 115, 121, 124, 135, 151ff., 164, 166, 219–20, 291
Russell, B., 1, 2, 5ff., 9ff., 19–20, 24–5, 28, 38, 42, 43n., 48, 60–1, 62n., 98, 99, 113, 116, 120, 123, 126, 133, 139, 182, 186–7

Samples, 51, 96, 127, 152, 154, 156, 158–9, 161, 182ff., 225ff., 235ff., 299, 306
Saying, 8, 18ff., 27–8
Sceptic (scepticism), 190–1, 204, 215, 232, 244–5, 249–50, 251, 278–9, 303–4
Schlick, M., 53, 96, 99, 112, 187–8, 194–5
Schopenhauer, A., 2, 58–9, 64ff., 70ff., 78, 82, 84n., 100, 102, 139, 204

Science, 2ff., 8ff., 118–19, 124, 133–4, 145ff., 171ff., 294–5
Self, 58–9, 60ff., 69, 70, 77, 80–1, 214
Sensations, 222ff., 229, 234, 238–9, 248
Sense, *see* Meaning
Senseless (*sinnlos*), 17–18, 28
Shoemaker, S., 262n., 270n., 293n.
Showing, 8, 18ff., 27–8, 76
Simples, *see* Objects
Solipsism, 58–9, 64, 67ff., 105, 126, 185ff., 215, 216, 232–3, 248, 249, 305
  Methodological, 186n., 187–8, 193ff., 211, 215, 216
  Transcendental, 76, 79ff., 188, 195, 216
Spinoza, B., 74
Stenius, E., 93
Strawson, P. F., 176, 194–5, 246
Surview (*übersicht*), 113ff., 119, 121, 124, 127, 132, 136–7, 141, 142
Symptom, 108, 193, 196, 285, 290–1

Theory, 3–4, 8, 98, 119, 145ff., 171–2
Time, 20, 72–3, 75, 76n., 202–3
Toulmin, S., 4n.
Transcendental Idealism, 67, 72, 76
Transcendental Solipsism (*see* Solipsism, Transcendental)

Übersicht, *see* Surview
Understanding, 51, 55, 106, 241–2
Unity of apperception, 64, 76, 205–6
Use, 106, 111, 124, 219, 283, 287, 291

Vagueness, 13ff., 295–6, 299–300
Verificationism, 44n., 99, 105ff., 161–2, 188–9

Waismann, F., 5n., 99, 141, 169n. 171n., 188, 207n.
Weyl, H., 105
Wiggins, D., 77
Will, 45, 47, 66, 100ff.
von Wright, G. H., 252